INTERNATIONAL HUMANITARIAN LAW

For my father,
Dr Arthur McCoubrey (1916–1997)

INTERNATIONAL HUMANITARIAN LAW

MODERN DEVELOPMENTS IN THE LIMITATION OF WARFARE

SECOND EDITION

HILAIRE MCCOUBREY
Professor and Director of Postgraduate Affairs in Law
University of Hull Law School

Routledge
Taylor & Francis Group
LONDON AND NEW YORK

First published 1998 by Ashgate Publishing

Reissued 2019 by Routledge
2 Park Square, Milton Park, Abingdon, Oxon, OX14 4RN
52 Vanderbilt Avenue, New York, NY 10017

Routledge is an imprint of the Taylor & Francis Group, an informa business

A Library of Congress record exists under LC control number:

Typeset by Manton Typesetters, 5–7 Eastfield Road, Louth, Lincolnshire

ISBN 13: 978-0-367-19463-5 (hbk)
ISBN 13: 978-0-367-19465-9 (pbk)
ISBN 13: 978-0-429-20256-8 (ebk)

Contents

Preface

The first edition of *International Humanitarian Law* was published in 1990. One might hope that the law of armed conflict would be a discipline in which there would be *no* new developments, as its continued development implies the continued existence of war. The same might be said of many other disciplines, both within and beyond the study of law. However, while armed conflict continues to afflict international relations, it is a basic function of public international law to seek to reduce its incidence and mitigate its practice. Over the seven years since the publication of the first edition, much has happened, both in the occurrence of conflict and in relation to its control and conduct. As a result, this 'second edition' is not so much an updating of the first edition as the presentation of a new book with a great deal of new material, both in relation to developments in substantive law and in the application of law to the all too many conflicts which have marked the closing decade of the 20th century.

In modern usage, 'international humanitarian law' has come to embrace the whole of the *jus in bello* (the law governing and seeking to mitigate the conduct of hostilities and to protect the victims of armed conflict). It covers both the 'Hague' and 'Geneva' sub divisions of the *jus in bello* – the former concerned with methods and means of warfare, and the latter with the protection of its victims – and in so doing emphasises the essential humanitarian basis of both. This book seeks to emphasise that international humanitarian law is no Utopian aspiration – there is nothing 'Utopian' about any aspect of war – but a severely practical prescription which is entirely workable in the harsh exigencies of warfare. Obedience to it does not impede legitimate military efficacy, nor does violation gain any real advantage, but merely gains the perpetrator a deserved reputation for barbarism, to the detriment of its relations with other states.

This book commences with a historical review of theory and practice in the limitation of warfare, before proceeding to chapters on the institutions and modes of implementation of the law. The four primary categories of victims of armed conflict – the wounded and sick on land; the wounded, sick and shipwrecked at sea; prisoners of war, and civilians – are considered next, including some of the many questions which have arisen, *inter alia*, in the 1990–91 Gulf Conflict, in former Yugoslavia and in Rwanda. The many important developments in controls on methods and means of warfare, including the restriction of blinding laser weapons and landmines and the International Court of Justice advisory opinion on nuclear weapons are considered. There have also been significant developments in the law relating to non-international armed conflicts, as well as an alarming number of actual and potential conflicts of this type. Finally, the potentially very significant proceedings of the International Criminal Tribunals for former Yugoslavia and Rwanda have raised, or renewed, a number of important questions about the modes and purpose of enforcement of international humanitarian law. These issues well merit our consideration at the turn of a new century.

H. McCoubrey
University of Hull Law School
November 1997

1 Humanitarianism in the Laws of Armed Conflict

International Humanitarian Law and the Laws of Armed Conflict

International humanitarian law is, broadly, that branch of public international law which seeks to moderate the conduct of armed conflict and to mitigate the suffering which it causes. It is founded upon ideas which, in their present forms, trace their origins to the mid-19th century: that methods and means of warfare are subject to clear legal and ethical limitation, and that the victims of armed conflict – meaning non-combatant civilians and all personnel who have been rendered *hors de combat* by injury, sickness, shipwreck (including ditching from aircraft) or capture – are entitled to humanitarian care and protection. This is one of two principal divisions of the international laws of armed conflict, and is correctly termed the *jus in bello* ('the law *in* war'). The other principal division is the *jus ad bellum* ('the law *to* war') or, as some now more accurately prefer, the *jus contra bellum* ('the law *against* war').[1]

The aim of the *jus ad bellum* is to avert and restrain resort to armed force in the conduct of international relations. This law assumed its modern shape in the years following the First World War, to some extent with articles 12, 13, 15 and 16 of the Covenant of the former League of Nations, but more significantly with the 1928 Pact of Paris, by which armed force was banned as a lawful means of international dispute-resolution. This position is now affirmed by article 2(3)(4) and Chapter VII, articles 39–51, of the United Nations Charter. It follows from these provisions that armed conflict is no longer a lawful condition of international relations, because, other than in the most bizarrely unlikely circumstances of mutual error, it can only result from unlawful action by at least one of the parties. Legitimate use of armed force in international relations is now limited to the exercise of the 'inherent' right of individual and collective self-defence by states in the event of armed attack, which is preserved by article 51 of the UN Charter, and action for the maintenance or restoration of international peace and security authorised by the UN Security Council.[2] The *jus ad bellum* is thus vested with the primary function of averting or terminating armed conflict and threats to the peace. Where that primary endeavour fails, the *jus in bello* is vested with the secondary, but vital, office of mitigating the impact and consequences of those armed conflicts which occur despite the *jus ad bellum*.

The *jus ad bellum* and *jus in bello* are to be considered quite distinct prescriptions. Certainly, the lawfulness or otherwise of a given party's original involvement in a conflict cannot negate the application of *jus in bello* norms: if that were the case, it would represent a renaissance of the very worst features of medieval 'just war' theory.[3] It is possible for *jus ad bellum* constraints to impose restrictions upon the scope of military action in addition to those inherent in *jus in bello* norms in a particular case, but this is an occasional and tangential effect.

The *jus in bello* itself has two principal subdivisions, which have conventionally been categorised as 'Geneva' and 'Hague' law, in recognition of the principal treaty series upon which each is founded. 'Geneva' law now rests primarily upon the four 1949 Geneva Conventions and the two 1977 Additional Protocols thereto. It is specifically concerned with the protection of the victims of armed conflict. 'Hague' law, so named in reference to the 1899 and 1907 Hague Conventions, is concerned with methods and means of warfare, including controls on weapons types and usage, and on tactics and the general conduct of hostilities.

The division between the 'Geneva' and 'Hague' sectors of the *jus in bello* has long been highly artificial from a number of points of view. Fundamentally, both sectors are based upon a humanitarian concern for the moderation and mitigation of warfare and its consequences, and for this reason there is a very large degree of overlap between the two: provisions of treaties arising in the one deal with matters which *prima facie* pertain to the other. Historically, the term 'international humanitarian law' was used to refer specifically to the 'Geneva' sector of the *jus in bello*, but this is now seen as an outdated and unhelpful usage. In modern usage, therefore, 'international humanitarian law' is taken to comprise the whole *jus in bello* in both its 'Geneva' and 'Hague' dimensions, and the term is used in this way in this book.

The Paradox of Humanitarianism in Armed Conflict

Beyond the questions of categorisation in the laws of armed conflict, there is a seeming paradox which must be considered in the very existence of laws, and certainly 'humanitarian' laws, of armed conflict. Sir Hersch Lauterpacht remarked pointedly:

> if international law is ... the vanishing point of law, the law of war is even more conspicuously the vanishing point of international law.[4]

Armed conflict is indeed the ultimate challenge to international legal order: not only is legal regulation stretched to the limits of its capacity, but the very existence of armed conflict is a defiance of that regulation. It might therefore seem odd to find a structure of legal norms designed to regulate the conduct of states in a condition of international relations which is essentially a descent into extra-legal violence. There is no direct equivalent in municipal law regulating, for example, the 'proper' conduct of an inter-personal assault, although there are admittedly norms addressing the level and forms of permissible self-defensive response at given levels of attack. There is a related argument that armed conflict, as an act of violence, is inherently not open to moderating regulation, and that efforts to establish such norms actually 'encourage' war by making it more 'acceptable'. Both of these superficially strong arguments against humanitarian laws of armed conflict may readily be countered.

The basic paradox was well stated by the great 19th-century Prussian military theorist Carl von Clausewitz in *Vom Kriege* ('On War') in remarking:

> If wars between civilized nations are far less cruel and destructive than wars between savages, the reason lies in the social conditions of the states themselves and in their relationships to one another. These are the forces that give rise to war; the same forces circumscribe and moderate it. They themselves however are not part of war; they already exist before fighting starts. To introduce the principle of moderation into the theory of war itself would always lead to logical absurdity.[5]

The anthropological assumptions made by von Clausewitz must, in the light of the 20th-century experience of 'total war', be considered more than questionable, but the basic paradox remains genuine enough. Their resolution is set out clearly in Clausewitz's statement, however. Even though the violence of armed conflict may not in itself be logically capable of regulation to moderate it, in reality such conflicts occur in cultural and political contexts which set limits, both immediately and prospectively, to what may be tolerated even in the extreme exigencies of combat. Such influences are, as von Clausewitz remarked, 'given conditions', but they do set parameters within which limits to the permissible modes of use of armed force will be set.

The second criticism, that humanitarian rules actually encourage wars, is implicit in the views of the novelist Leo Tolstoy, for example, who was a committed pacifist. In *War and Peace*, referring to the guerrilla resistance warfare which followed Napoleon's occupation of Moscow in 1812, Tolstoy wrote:

> From the time [Napoleon] ... took up the correct fencing attitude in Moscow and instead of his opponent's rapier saw a cudgel raised above his head, he did not cease to complain to Kutuzov and to the Emperor Alexander that the war was being carried on contrary to all the rules, as if there were any rules for killing people.[6]

This view – which is advanced in rather different forms by strategic 'realists' and by pacifists – again has a superficial force, but has a major flaw: unlimited brutality does not win wars; nor does the inherent cruelty of war serve as a means by which it will necessarily be ended. If the latter argument were correct – if war is not moderated, its very cruelty will rapidly bring it to an end – it is difficult to imagine how war could have been contemplated after the Somme campaign in the First World War, for example. The sad answer to this is that wars are rarely, if ever, started by those who have to fight in them or otherwise become their victims. To deny humanitarian mitigation to those who do find themselves caught up in armed conflict upon such a basis would be a cruel logic indeed. In the real world, it may be agreed that, as Schwarzenberger states:

> It is the function of the rules of warfare to impose some limits, however ineffective, to a complete reversion to anarchy by the establishment of minimum standards on the conduct of war.[7]

The avoidance of war is, as has been indicated above, the business of the *jus ad bellum*; the mitigation of its consequences where armed conflict non the less occurs does not impede that objective, and is, in its own sphere, a vital function.

Beyond this, there are obvious questions to be asked about the pragmatic effectiveness of legal limitations on the conduct of warfare, not least because the logic of violence does appear to suggest an inevitable escalation of extremities in the conduct of hostile operations. Such simple reasoning is misleading, however, and, in practice, principles of moderation have considerable moral and pragmatic force. The moral claim of moderation in armed conflict should be obvious, and rests ultimately upon the nature of human beings as social creatures, in the sense understood by Aristotle,[8] to whom a relationship of violent confrontation is not 'natural', but a divergence from a more co-operative norm of existence. The pragmatic considerations are, if anything, even more powerful. In the medium to long term, armed conflicts are, if only by reason of exhaustion, essentially temporary phenomena, after which some semblance of normal relations must be resumed by the parties.

Even during the armed conflict itself, there is a strong element of pragmatic benefit to be found in the implementation of humanitarian norms. A party to armed conflict who casts off significant legal constraints runs the risk of acquiring a 'pariah' status in the view of nations, which may compromise neutral political support even from states which might otherwise be disposed to be friendly. The record of Iraq in the 1980–88 Gulf War, including the use of chemical weapons, and in the subsequent 1990–91 Gulf Conflict inflicted much damage upon Iraqi international relations, and played a role in the near-unanimous opposition to Iraq in the latter conflict. Quite apart from this, an enemy who anticipates barbarous treatment upon capture or surrender may be driven into desperate resistance even when the conflict is clearly lost, whereas expectation of correct treatment might have counselled against this.

After the conflict, the greater the degree of cruelty shown in the conduct of operations, the more difficult the inevitably problematic processes of normalisation of relations will be. Even in such a 'textbook' armed conflict as the 1982 Falklands Conflict, in which both the British and Argentine forces generally conducted themselves correctly,[9] there was no lack of pain and suffering, and it was a decade or so before anything like normal Anglo-Argentine relations were able to be resumed. After more bitter conflicts, such as the 1980–88 Gulf War, the process is all the slower and more drawn out.

On these various bases, it may be contended that the seeming paradox of humanitarian regulation in armed conflict is really an illusion. Peace with justice is, properly, a central aim of public international law, but until that goal is achieved, the palliative measures represented by public international law are neither paradoxical nor an obstacle to progress; they are, on the contrary, a human necessity.

International Humanitarian Law and Human Rights

There is manifestly a significant degree of convergence between the concerns of international humanitarian law and those of the international law of human rights. However, the precise nature of the interface between these two sectors is a more controversial question. The idea of fundamental entitlements inherent in the human social condition is of ancient provenance, with long roots in the tradition of naturalist jurisprudence, and it has played a prominent role in the constitutional development of some states since the late 18th century. As a distinct sector of public international law, however, the law of human rights has taken shape largely since 1945, in response to the excesses of 20th-century totalitarianism, including especially, but by no means only, the experience of the Third Reich between 1933 and 1945.[10]

Since 1945, the law of human rights has greatly expanded and developed, and has, in particular, strongly introduced into the law of nations concepts of individual entitlement in relation to states, rather than norms governing relations between states. Ideas of humanitarian conduct in warfare represent at least as old a tradition, with many common jurisprudential roots.[11] The process of their statement as norms of modern public international law pre-dates the modern development of human rights law by nearly a century, and the earliest major expressions date from the 1860s.[12] Since the Second World War, the conceptual framework and modes of discourse of human rights have had a major influence on the shaping of public international law across a wide spectrum of issues. Not surprisingly, international humanitarian law has been no exception to this pattern.

The influence of the concepts and modes of discourse of modern human rights thinking can clearly be seen, for example, in the preliminary debates and ultimate phrasing of the 1977 Additional Protocols to the four 1949 Geneva Conventions. In this context, the late Professor-Colonel G.I.A.D. Draper wrote:

> The undeniable humanitarian texture of the post-1945 law of war drew to it, with magnetic force, the inexorable progress of the regimes of human rights. ... In the period between 1968 and 1971 we witness in the organs of the UN a mounting endeavour to effect a fusion of the humanitarian law of war with human rights, which is not the outcome of accident. This movement towards the fusion of the two legal regimes reflects the political currents flowing through the UN in those years.[13]

He was critical of this trend for a variety of reasons, but the practical influence of the law of human rights on the post-war development of international humanitarian law is undeniable. It is inevitably at its strongest in the development of provision for non-international armed conflicts, including in particular 1977 Additional Protocol II to the 1949 Geneva Conventions.[14] In such conflicts the essential issue of the treatment by a state of its own dissident citizens, as well as the treatment by the dissidents of government supporters, is one which converges closely with the core concerns of the international law of human rights. Beyond the readily acceptable ideas of influence and functional convergence, however, there arises the much more difficult question of whether international humanitarian law may properly be considered essentially a part of the international law of human rights.

On the one hand, it may be contended, as it is, for example, by Geza Herczeg,[15] that although there is clearly a link between international humanitarian law and the international law of human rights, the two cannot ultimately be identified with each other because the former presupposes the possibility of armed conflict, which is itself a violation of human rights. Whether there is indeed a 'human right to peace' is a question which merits discussion. The provisions of the United Nations Charter emphasise both the normativity and the inherent normalcy of peace in the conduct of international relations. The proposition is made overt especially in the Preamble to the Charter and in the provision of article 2(3)(4). To this extent, as has been suggested above,[16] armed conflict can, in all but the most unlikely situations, only result from unlawful action by at least one of the states involved. It may therefore reasonably be said that modern public international law enshrines at the very least a right of states to the peaceful conduct of international relations.[17] At the same time, the UN Charter recognises the possibility of armed conflict in practice by the provisions of Chapter VII of the Charter for the maintenance of international peace and security, including the preservation by article 51 of states' 'inherent' rights of individual and collective self-defence in the event of armed attack.[18] This is, of course, evidence of the imperfection of the existing condition of international relations, but in the context of a human right to peace, the question of the quality of that peace must inevitably be raised. The *defensive* use of force, which is permitted by the modern *jus ad bellum*, embodies a right to resist aggression and the consequent imposition of alien domination. In this context, the prospect must be faced that although war is unequivocally a great evil, armed resistance to aggression is not the only danger to human rights to be found in the modern world.

But this is not necessarily the definitive element in the determination of the relationship between international humanitarian law and human rights. In presenting his 'rights thesis', Ronald Dworkin remarked that:

> Individual rights are political trumps held by individuals. Individuals have rights when, for some reason, a collective goal is not a sufficient justification for denying them what they wish, as individuals, to have or to do, or not a sufficient justification for imposing some loss or injury upon them.[19]

It is implicit in this that rights become especially significant where an entitlement is, or is perceived to be, threatened. One does not commonly speak of a 'right' to do something or not to do something where, respectively, no constraint or compulsion is anticipated. As a general contention in the jurisprudence of rights, this might be challenged, but in the present context it is a compelling hypothesis. Armed conflict is manifestly a situation in which basic human expectations and entitlements are gravely imperilled, and therefore one in which a discourse of 'rights' might reasonably be expected to arise. It thus seems reasonable to conclude that humanitarian provision in the laws of armed conflict may best be regarded as an application of certain human rights principles in very particular and extreme circumstances. This view, which contrasts with that of Geza Herczeg,[20] may be found in the work of another writer from the former Eastern bloc, Igor P. Blishchenko, who stated that:

> ... the laws and customs of war ... are directed, in particular, towards the protection of human rights and freedoms. ... [T]he essential problem in all situations of armed conflict is the international protection of human rights; in other words, the fundamental objective of ... the laws of war is the protection of human rights. ... [21]

This, it may be suggested, is the preferable view. However, it must be added that the circumstances of armed conflict are so distinct and extreme in character that the applicable international humanitarian norms will inevitably and properly be treated as a distinct sector of international legal provision.

The Development of Humanitarian Norms in Armed Conflict

Ideas of humanitarian conduct in armed conflict have, contrary to popular opinion, a long if decidedly uneven history across a broad spectrum of societies and cultures. In ancient warfare, humanitarianism was rare, although not unknown. The common experience of captured enemies was death or enslavement, and mass forced population movements – 'ethnic cleansing' to borrow an offensive term from the armed conflicts in former Yugoslavia in the 1990s – were a frequent consequence of national defeat. Carved reliefs from ancient Egypt[22] and Assyria, as well as the later records of Imperial Rome, serve to emphasise these impressions, although the propagandistic elements of these records must not be forgotten. Contrary indicators may also be found. In the Jewish scriptures, known to Christians as the Old Testament, a stark contrast may be found between early and later texts dealing with the treatment of prisoners of war. In the Book of Numbers there is an account of the an Israeli victory over the Midianities, which includes the following:

> They warred against Midian ... and slew every male ... and took captive the women ... and their little ones. ... And Moses was angry

> with the officers of the army [saying] ... to them, 'Have you let all the women live? Behold these caused the people of Israel ... to act treacherously against the Lord ... Now therefore, kill every male among the little ones and ... every women who has known man ... but all the young woman who have not ... keep alive for yourselves ...'[23]

This stark savagery, coming from an early stage in the spiritual and cultural history of the people of Israel, may be contrasted with the much later treatment of a captured Syrian army recorded in the Second Book of Kings:

> ... the King of Israel ... said to Elisha, 'My Father shall I slay them?' ... He answered, 'You shall not slay them. Would you slay those whom you have taken captive with your sword and bow? Set bread and water before them, that they may eat and drink and go to their master.'[24]

Evidence of developing humanitarian norms may also be seen in ancient Indian warfare. A very remarkable instance may be seen in the outright rejection of militarism by the Emperor Asoka Maurya, who in *circa* 256BC achieved a sanguinary conquest of the three Kalinga Kingdoms, and thereafter converted to Buddhism and foreswore policies of conquest.[25] In a series of edicts promulgated shortly after the Kalinga war, he proclaimed that:

> the conquest of a country previously unconquered invokes the slaughter, death and carrying away captive of the people. This is a matter of profound sorrow and regret to His Sacred Majesty.[26]

This early anti-war policy of the Emperor Asoka did not long survive him, but distinctly humanitarian *'jus in bello'* norms may be found in other early Indian texts. A number of significant limitations on the conduct of warfare can be found in the Laws of Manu. Thus it is written:

> Fighting in a battle, [a King] ... should not kill his enemies with weapons which are concealed, barbed or smeared with poison or whose points blaze with fire. He should not kill anyone ... who folds his hands in supplication ... or who says 'I am yours' ... nor anyone who is in pain, badly wounded, terrified or fleeing ...[27]

These rules are strikingly similar to those of the basic rules and principles of modern international humanitarian law. A number of rather similar rules imposing humanitarian restrictions on the conduct of warfare are also described in the ancient epic poem the *Mahabharata*.[28]

Ancient Chinese ethical theory also included significant restrictions on warfare and its conduct, at least after the overthrow of the first Imperial Dynasty, the Chin, which glorified coercion and the arts of war as instruments of state. The 4th-century BC Confucian sage Mencius (Meng-tzu), who later did much to shape the Confucian doctrine which became the official orthodoxy under the Han and later dynasties, wrote:

> Confucius rejected those who enriched rules not given to the practice of benevolent government. How much more would he reject those who do their best to wage war on their behalf. In wars to gain land, the dead fill the plains; in wars to gain cities, the dead fill the cities. This is known as showing the land the way to devour human flesh.[29]

This basic disapprobation of war and the military arts ran deep in the political culture of Imperial China, but punitive wars – in a manner not dissimilar from the model of 'just war' advanced by St Augustine of Hippo – were considered necessary on occasion.[30] The lack in the orthodox Confucian canon of humanitarian provision for the *conduct* of hostilities, coupled with a punitive model which covertly preserved much of the harshness of formally abandoned Chin 'legalist' philosophy, often meant that when war did arise, it could be conducted harshly. However, this is not to say that humanitarian norms were absent or ignored. The more esoteric doctrines of Taoism contained a more substantive humanitarian doctrine, especially in emphasising the importance of compassion. Upon this, Da Diu remarks illuminatingly in a modern commentary that:

> [A military commander] ... must be compassionate in dealing with the civilian population living in areas affected by his army's activities. If he is kind towards them and able to prevent his troops from looting or destroying their homes, they will support him, and their aid may be invaluable. Finally, he must be compassionate toward the enemy. This does not mean that he should be reluctant to damage them when conditions are right. Rather it is a matter of maintaining a certain attitude which keeps fighting in its proper perspective.[31]

The principle here again has some significant modern resonances. However, the tendency of Taoists to avoid public life and office, in marked contrast with the Confucian scholar officials who were the classical Chinese ruling class prior to the Ch'ing (Manchu) invasion in 1644 and in practice largely remained so, reduced its impact on the practical conduct of military affairs. In fact, there *were* moderating '*jus in bello*' norms in classical China. As far as norms of military conduct *stricto sensu* are concerned, Zhu Li-Sun remarks that:

> [C]ustomary rules in Ancient China on the protection of war victims ... attach great importance to the protection of civilians, as the aim of war is to defeat those persons responsible for the war, not the innocent civilians. ... [F]or example ... rules ... in the 'Si Ma Code' ... [In battle] special attention is paid to killing as few and causing as little damage as possible. ... Thirdly, strict army discipline and the policy of not harassing enemy civilians are associated with the idea of being 'civilised'.[32]

Such principles again illustrate the common strands of the tradition of humanitarian norms in warfare in human social culture, and illustrate the falsity of the opinion sometimes asserted that humanitarian rules of warfare are an invention of mid-19th-century Europe.

Classical Greek and Roman tradition contained little coherent normative humanitarian tradition, although some principles, including a ban on poison weapons, in the modern *jus in bello* derive from this era. Interestingly, however, Roman Law made early, formal *jus ad bellum* provision in the *Jus Fetiale* dating from the ancient Roman Republic in the 6th century BC. This law required a certification of 'just cause' from the Fetial Priesthood before the Roman state could lawfully go to war.[33] The *Jus Fetiale* had little impact on Roman military aggression especially in the Imperial era, nor did it tend to mitigate the cruelty of the Roman practice of warfare, but it was a factor which was to play a part in later developments.

The medieval European laws of armed conflict derived from a fusion of the Hellenistic and Judaeo-Christian traditions which followed the official Christianisation of the Roman Empire after the promulgation of the Edict of Milan by Constantine the Great in 313 AD. The emphasis of late Roman and medieval scholastic analyses of war was upon the *jus ad bellum* rather than the *jus in bello*, and involved primarily the development of 'just war' theory.[34] The theory reached an early developed stage in the work of St Augustine of Hippo in the 5th century, and a mature form in the writings of 12- and 13th-century scholastic theorists such as Gratian, Laurentius Hispanus, Johannes Teutonicus, St Raymond of Penaforte and St Thomas Aquinas.[35]

The purpose behind 'just war' theory was to limit resort to armed force to the gravest possible cases of actual or threatened injury to the state. Sadly, although the doctrine lingered in diverse forms until the end of the early modern era of public international law in 1914, it suffered rapid debasement, and swiftly became little more than a pretext for aggression. 'Just war' theory also had an unintended negative impact on the development of the *jus in bello*, as the general presumption that if one party to a conflict was 'just', the other must be 'unjust'[36] led to a facile justification for gross cruelties in the conduct of warfare. Thus Jean Pictet has remarked that:

> ... the well known and malignant doctrine of the 'just war' ... did nothing less than provide believers with a justification for war and all its infamy ... [and] inevitably hampered humanitarian progress for centuries. Wishing at all costs to prove they are 'right' and searching for pretexts in faith, morality, justice or honour, both belligerents will fight until their forces are totally exhausted. ... [M]en on all sides have made use of it, to justify the cruelties ... which they had the effrontery to call the punishment of God.[37]

This was not by any means the intention of those who formulated the doctrine, indeed both St Augustine of Hippo and St Thomas Aquinas expressly stated that an originally 'just' cause might be rendered unjust by excessive or cruel pursuit,[38] but this appalling consequence nevertheless followed the implementation of the doctrine in practice.

There were certain ethical limitations on the practice of medieval warfare. Philippe Contamine remarks that:

> '[The medieval] *Jus in bello* ... was in very large measure the simple codification of the chivalric ideal which prohibited conduct contrary to 'all lordship and chivalry'. We may, however, note that this ideal was expressed simultaneously by moral imperatives governing the behaviour of soldiers, by rules of military discipline, and by a series of usages, customs and rites proper to the world of soldiers (the law of arms or *jus armorum*).'[39]

These norms were less than certain in content and by no means consistent in their application, but there was none the less clearly a concept of culpable wrongdoing in the medieval understanding of warfare. Early examples can be seen in the Penitential Decrees issued by the Western Church in response to the brutal conduct of the Burgundian army at the battle of Soissons in 923 and of the Norman army at the Battle of Hastings in 1066, including in the latter case the ensuing 'harrying of the north', which bordered upon the genocidal in modern terms.[40] From the end of the medieval period in Europe, striking evidence may be seen in the unease felt over the massacre of prisoners ordered by King Henry V at the Battle of Agincourt in 1415.[41] An even more pointed reference may be seen in the remarkable trial of Peter von Hagenbach in 1474, following the atrocious Burgundian occupation of Breisach.[42] Such promise as these admittedly limited constraints may have held out was lost in the European political and religious turmoil of the 16th century, in which the medieval European political and ethical order collapsed, leading ultimately to the horror of the Thirty Years War in the first half of the following century. Even in this cruel age, however, attempts to mitigate warfare did appear. Kenneth Ogren has drawn attention to articles 88–100 of the Articles of War promulgated to the Swedish army by King Gustavus II Adolphus in 1621, which in large part sought to protect the civilian population, including, by article 88, provision of the death penalty for rape.[43] Such attempts were unusual in the 17th century, and they were not, on the whole, very successful in the bitter and sanguinary conflicts of that era. From this, after the 1648 Peace of Westphalia, emerged the early modern era of public international law.

Humanitarian thought may also be seen in basic Islamic teaching on the conduct of warfare. Muhammad Hamidullah lists no less than 19 combat practices which are expressly forbidden by Islamic law.[44] He also remarks that:

> According to Muslim law, a prisoner *qua* prisoner cannot be killed. Ibn Rushd even records a consensus of the Companions of the Prophet to the same effect. This does not preclude the trial and punishment of prisoners for crimes beyond rights of belligerency. ... [But] Muslim jurists clearly recognise that a prisoner cannot be held responsible for mere acts of belligerency.[45]

These principles are echoed in modern international humanitarian law by articles 82 and 90 of 1949 Geneva Convention III.[46] Famous Islamic commanders known for their humane conduct of warfare include Caliph Abu Bakr and Salah al-Din (known in the West as Saladin). The practical history of Islamic warfare should no more be idealised than its equivalents in Christian and other cultures, but the quality of the humanitarian provision found in many aspects of the Islamic law relating to armed conflict counters the misconception that international humanitarian law is only 'Western' in derivation.

The early modern era of public international law is associated with the post-Westphalian phase of European history commencing in 1648. The 18th century saw a significant pragmatic development of humanitarian principles in norms of armed conflict. There were a number of practical factors which may have contributed to this. The feudal levies and ill-disciplined mercenary forces of earlier times were replaced in the later 17th century and the 18th century by disciplined armies under the command of such figures as Frederick II (the Great), the Duc de Conde and the Duke of Marlborough. In such an era of relatively small-scale 'professional' warfare, regulatory norms were *ex hypothesi* easier both to develop and to apply. The warfare of the 18th century was also primarily the product of territorial conflict between essentially similar dynastic states in which the opponent could be seen simply as such, and not as inherently 'evil' or an enemy of God. There were a number of instances of opposing commanders entering into local agreements on such matters as the collection and care of the wounded, and even the protection of civilians. Jean Pictet refers to a statement made by King Louis XV before the Battle of Fontenoy, remarking that:

> On the eve of the battle of Fontenoy in 1747, Louis XV was asked how the enemy wounded should be treated. He replied, 'Exactly like our own men, because when they are wounded they are no longer our enemies.'[47]

The ultimate death rate amongst the wounded in the field hospitals after Fontenoy was just over 9 per cent, a figure which compares very well with the Napoleonic or Crimean Wars.[48] A similar spirit can be seen in the statement by Jean-Jacques Rousseau in *Du Contrat Social*:

> La fin de la guerre étant la destruction de l'Etat ennemi, on a droit d'en tuer les défenseurs tant qu'ils ont les armes à la main; mais sitôt qu'ils les posent et se rendent, cesant d'être ennemis ... ils redeviennement simplement hommes et l'on n'a plus de droit sur leur vie. ... La guerre ne donne aucun droit qui ne soit nécessaire à sa fin. Ces principes ne sont pas ceaux de Grotius ... ils dérivent de la nature des choses, et sont fondés sur la raison.[49]

This means, in summary, that the end in war is to defeat the enemy, and in so doing there is a right to kill opponents while they remain armed and hostile, but this right ceases after they have laid down their arms and surrendered. War confers no rights beyond what is needful to achieve this end, and this principle derives not simply from the doctrines of Hugo Grotius, but is a law of nature founded upon reason.

Despite the expression of such ideas, the rather sporadic humanitarianism of the 18th-century 'Enlightenment' did not give rise to settled and uniform legal norms, even though Pictet does argue that at this time there may have been a developing customary international humanitarian law.[50]

Be that as it may, the spur to the modern development of international humanitarian law lay in the catastrophic decline in humanitarian standards witnessed in the first half of the 19th century, from the French Revolutionary and Napoleonic Wars at the turn of the century to the Franco–Austrian War in 1859. This phenomenon may be explained in various ways. In the Napoleonic Wars, the much increased scale of conflict and the development of new and much faster means of warfare tended simply to overwhelm the rudimentary military medical services which then existed. In varying degrees, these wars also took on the ideological colouring which tended to embitter them to a greater degree than had been the case for the dynastic conflicts of the 18th century. However, this is only a partial explanation: the later wars of the half-century were not on such a scale, and whilst revolutionary nationalism undoubtedly played a part in some of them, it was by no means a dominant factor. The simple truth may be that the early 19th century was an age of callous greed, in which humanitarianism found little place in official consciousness in either war or peace.

A nadir was perhaps reached with the Crimean War in 1854–55. The incompetence displayed at every level of the military led to major reforms of military organisation in Britain under Lord Cardwell as Secretary of State for War, and in Russia under D.A. Miliutin. The war also inspired important initiatives in relation to the military medical services. The state of the British military medical services at this time is shown clearly in the correspondence and other writings of Edward Mason Wrench, a military surgeon who served with the 34th Regiment of Foot at the siege of Sevastopol.[51] He wrote of the base hospital at Balaclava:

> I had charge of from 20 to 30 patients, wounded from Inkerman, mixed with cases of cholera, dysentery, and fever. There were no beds ... or proper bedding. The patients lay in their clothes on the floor, which from rain blown in through open [that is, broken and unrepaired] windows, and the traffic to and from the open-air latrines, was as muddy as a country road.[52]

He found no less terrible conditions in the field hospitals nearer to the front line. In a letter to his family written from the lines before Sevastopol in June 1855, he wrote:

> Things are in an awful state up here now and the patients, poor fellows, suffer terribly. ... [T]hey are literally dying from exhaustion and we have nothing to give them ... we have not got a drop of wine to give them although there is lots at Balaclava we have no means of getting it up. I managed to get some tea ... but I am sorry to say it is nearly all gone and I can get no more till I go down to Balaclava again, but which I hope to do on the first fine day.[53]

The lack of basic supplies, even though these were in fact available, and the reliance for their appearance upon the charitable endeavour of individual medical staff speaks eloquently of the condition of the medical services in the Crimea.

Men like E.M. Wrench understood all too well the deficiencies of the military medical service in which they worked, and these were replicated in the other armed forces of the time, but they were not able to press forward the fundamental reforms which were urgently necessary. The appalling conditions which were disclosed also inspired significant external initiatives, however. The work of Florence Nightingale at the British base hospital in Scutari was notable both for its radical innovations in nursing care and for the determination with which she overcame the impediments placed in her way by obscurantist officialdom. Today, her work is considered one of the founding steps in the development of modern nursing practice. Initiatives by committed outsiders also took place in other armies in the Crimean War. In the French army, notable work was done by the religious order of the Daughters of Charity of St Vincent de Paul. In the Russian garrison at Sevastopol, nursing and medical assistance was provided by the nursing order of the Exaltation of the Holy Cross, established by the Grand Duchess Helena Pavlovna, an aunt of the Tsar, with the medical guidance of Dr Pirogev. In Russia too, D.A. Miliutin's post-Crimean reforms included the establishment of the Imperial Military Medical Academy, which had brought about a major improvement in the medical provision available in the Russian army by the time of the 1877 Russo-Turkish War.[54]

The turning point in the development of international humanitarian law occurred some three years after the Crimean War, however, at the Battle of Solferino on 20 June 1859, during the Franco-Austrian War, fought as a dimension of the Italian struggle for liberation and unification. The French army of Louis Napoleon III defeated an Austro-Hungarian army at Solferino on the borders of Switzerland, and after the battle the sheer numbers of wounded so overwhelmed the still very inadequate military medical services that large numbers were left to die on the battlefield from simple neglect. Pierre Boissier remarks of the French medical services which, as those of the victorious army, were the ones on the spot:

> Right from the start it was evident that the medical services were insufficient, both in terms of men and material. ... In the aftermath of every battle the physicians remained behind with their wounded, and those still available for future campaigns became fewer and fewer. ... There was just no way [either] of producing the elementary dressings indispensable for the treatment of the wounded. Inertia and chaos had won the day. The battle of Solferino placed before the resourceless skeleton medical services a task which was manifestly far beyond their means.[55]

Upon this dreadful scene appeared a Swiss businessman named Henry Dunant, on his way to an audience with the Emperor Louis Napoleon in pursuit of his business interests. Dunant was so appalled by what he saw that he arranged *ad hoc* volunteer medical rescue and relief, as a result of which many soldiers' lives were saved. It was also noteworthy that, although Dunant's own political sympathies were very much with the French side, the medical assistance which he organised was directed impartially to the relief of both French and Austro-Hungarian wounded, establishing from the outset one of the fundamental principles of modern international humanitarian law. Humanitarian initiatives were not new: they had been seen in the Crimean War, and, even before that, in 1848 Dr Palasciano, another notable pioneer, had actually been imprisoned by the Neapolitan authorities for rendering impartial medical aid at the siege of Messina. (Dr Palasciano was later to be recognised in the naming of one of the principal Italian hospital ships in the First World War, originally the German liner *König Albert*, as *Ferdinando Palasciano*.[56]

Henry Dunant went beyond the immediate organisation of emergency relief to campaign for systematic international reform of the treatment of the battlefield wounded. He wrote a pamphlet entitled *Un Souvenir de Solferino*. ('A Memory of Solferino'),[57] in which he made two proposals to the community of nations:

> Would it not be possible ... to form relief societies for the purpose of having care given to the wounded in wartime?[58] ... Would it not be desirable ... [to convene an international] congress to formulate some international principle sanctioned by a convention inviolate in character, which ... might constitute the basis for societies for the relief of the wounded?[59]

The mid-19th century was a harsh age, but also one becoming aware of its gross humanitarian deficiencies, and in this climate of international opinion both of Dunant's proposals were positively received. They bore fruit, respectively, in due course, in the establishment of the international Red Cross movement and the conclusion of the first humanitarian Geneva Convention of 1864. In thus giving direction and substance to the perceived need for humanitarian reform, Henry Dunant's initiative may be considered to have marked the beginning of modern development in this area, and to have earned him the title of 'father of international humanitarian law'.

The Chronology of International Humanitarian Law

The proposals made by Henry Dunant in *Un Souvenir de Solferino* were initially taken up by an influential body of citizens in Geneva who had formed a Public Welfare Society. The society appointed a Committee of Five to study the proposals and to devise a campaign for their implementation. The committee comprised Dunant himself, Gustave Moynier (the President of the Public Welfare Society), General Dufour (the notably humane victor in the Swiss *Sonderbund* civil war of 1847), Dr Appia and Dr Maunoir – a group which embraced the military, medical and concerned civilian personnel, and voiced concerns which have shaped modern international law to the present day. In October 1863, an international conference at Geneva involving 16 states agreed to support the establishment of an organisation for the relief and assistance of the war wounded. The Committee of Five itself became the organising body, and in 1880 the title International Committee of the Red Cross (ICRC) was formally adopted.

The origin and consequent nature of the ICRC was thus in many ways a fortunate product of historical accident, in that Dunant happened to be Swiss, and the organising initiative originated in Geneva. In the early days of the organisation, the location of the committee in Geneva was challenged by some of the great powers, with suggestions that it should be relocated in Paris or London. The consequences of such a move for an international humanitarian organisation during, for example, the First and Second World Wars may readily be imagined. In practice, the Swiss identity and base of the ICRC has well served and protected its essential neutrality as an impartial humanitarian agency operating in the suspicious and delicate exigencies of armed conflict.[60]

Dunant's second proposal came to fruition when in August 1864 an international conference convened in Geneva by the Swiss Federal Council concluded the 1864 Geneva Convention for the Amelioration of the Condition of the Wounded in Armies in the Field. This convention, the precursor of the present 1949 Geneva Convention I, finally established the claim of the wounded in land warfare to impartial medical assistance, and the right of the wounded, and those charged with their care, to respect and protection.[61]

The 1860s also saw other highly significant steps in the development of the humanitarian *jus in bello*. In 1864, the United States Government concluded that the American Civil War had reached a stage at which some provision for the application of 'international' laws of armed conflict was essential. In response to this need, US Army General Order No. 100 was issued on 24 April 1864, known as the 'Lieber Code' after its principal author, Francis Lieber, who had fought in the Prussian army under Marshal Blücher at the Battle of Waterloo in 1815. The code set out a comprehensive summary of the then existing principles of battlefield conduct, and was widely accepted as what might now be termed a 'restatement' of this area of law. Geoffrey Best remarks of the Lieber Code that:

> It was so good and comprehensive that it became the prototype and model for Europe's emulation in the succeeding decades.[62]

A European codification of the *jus in bello* was attempted by the 1874 Brussels Conference on Proposed Rules for Military Warfare, and whilst the resulting draft never came into force as a multilateral treaty, it had a similar formative effect to the Lieber Code, and contributed significantly to the great Hague codifications of 1899 and 1907.

Development from the starting point of the modern *jus in bello* in the 1860s has broadly followed a pattern of expansion of protective coverage, increasing specification of prescription, and an endeavour to keep continuing military technological development within the regulation of humanitarian norms. Without seeking to revive the former artificial division between the 'Hague' and 'Geneva' limbs of the *jus in bello*, it is convenient at this stage to consider the parallel development of norms for the humanitarian protection of victims, controls upon tactical battlefield conduct, and arms control as if they were distinct processes. However, the degree of practical convergence and overlap may be illustrated from the outset by reference to an early, and still operative, arms control treaty, the 1868 Declaration of St Petersburg. This treaty resulted from the development by the Russian army in 1863 of an explosive projectile designed primarily for use against armoured munitions transports. In 1867 a refined and smaller-calibre version was produced which would detonate upon impact on the human body. It has been remarked elsewhere that:

> The Imperial Government thus found itself in the very 'modern' dilemma of having developed a military technology with a potential sufficiently appalling to suggest international restriction.[63]

Faced with this potential, and no doubt conscious that more highly industrialised potential enemies such as Britain, France or Germany could rapidly negate any initial military advantage which might be gained, the government of Tsar Alexander II called an international conference at St Petersburg, from which the 1969 Declaration emerged. It banned explosive projectiles of under 400 grammes, effectively proscribing anti-personnel explosive bullets whilst permitting larger-calibre projectiles of this type. In its Preamble, however, the Declaration of St Petersburg stated a fundamental principle, known as the 'principle of unnecessary suffering', in the following terms:

> The only legitimate objective which States should endeavour to accomplish during war is to weaken the military forces of the enemy ... this object would be exceeded by the employment of arms which uselessly aggravate the sufferings of disabled men ... [and] the employment of such arms would therefore be contrary to the laws of humanity.

A striking parallel may be seen here with the view expressed by Jean-Jacques Rousseau a century earlier.[64] The principle has a significance far beyond the law of arms control, and in its statement of the core humanitarian limitation upon legitimate military conduct it may, in so far as any single definition is possible, be taken as a formulation of the key characteristics of the humanitarian *jus in bello* in both its traditional 'Hague' and 'Geneva' dimensions.

From the conclusion of the 1864 Geneva Convention, the humanitarian protection of victims of armed conflict expanded rather slowly and uncertainly. The 1864 Convention itself addressed precisely the 'Solferino' problem of the treatment of the wounded and sick in armies in the field. It established a number of basic principles which continue to underpin modern international humanitarian law. These included the neutralisation of the wounded and sick, and the impartiality of the relief and assistance to be afforded to them, together with the protection of those charged with their treatment and assistance. Indeed, in this respect the 1864 Convention went further than current practice in prohibiting absolutely the detention of military medical personnel, a prohibition now much diluted by permitting their 'retention' for medical work with prisoners of war of their own or allied nationality.[65] The convention also established the red cross as an international protective emblem. Quite how this device was chosen is something of a mystery. The statement in 1949 Geneva Convention I that it is simply a reversal of the federal colours of Switzerland, adopted as a compliment to Switzerland[66] and its role in the development of humanitarian law, is no doubt partly true, but it also contains an element of *ex post facto* rationalisation. Pierre Boissier states:

> Dr. Appia ... suggested a white armband to be carried on the left arm [but] ... certain objections were made to his proposal. The minutes of the meeting show that, after some discussion, Dr. Appia's proposal, modified to the effect that the white armband should carry a red cross, was adopted. It seems likely that some delegate wished to avoid possible confusion with the already universally recognized white flag of truce. Tradition has it that General Dufour proposed the addition of the red cross.[67]

Jean Pictet suggests, on the basis of a letter written by Henry Dunant, that the Prussian delegate, Dr Loeffler, suggested the addition of the red cross in a private conversation during a recess in the conference.[68] Although the red cross as a neutral emblem is not intended in this usage to carry any Christian connotations, it has been found offensive in Muslim countries and in Israel. As a result, Muslim states use the red crescent as a recognised alternative.[69] This emblem was first adopted by the Ottoman Empire in the 1876 Turko-Serbian

War, and its use was reserved, without objection by other states, at the Ottoman accession to the 1906 Geneva Convention for the Amelioration of the Condition of Wounded in Armies in the Field.[70] Before the Iranian revolution, the Iranian military medical services used an emblem of a red lion and sun, which was also recognised by 1949 Geneva Conventions I and II, but this was abandoned after the revolution, and the Iranian military medical services now use the red crescent emblem. The Israeli military medical services reject both the red cross and the flag crescent emblems, and use instead a red star of David, but this has not been officially recognised. Nevertheless, during the successive Arab–Israeli wars, the red star of David emblem was accepted *de facto*, but not *de jure*, by Arab states as a protective emblem. In this respect, one may agree with Jean Pictet's comment that:

> We cannot help but regret this departure from the universality of the emblem, which has been a source of many difficulties. Up to the present, however, it has been impossible to find a solution providing for a return to the unity which is so essential. We must hope at least that there will be no further breaches in this unity through the creation of new symbols.[71]

In practice, it is unlikely that a single acceptable emblem could now be found, because almost all symbols which are simple enough to be recognisable at a distance will have acquired some cultural or historic significance which will offend in one or another country. With two recognised emblems in current use, along with one unrecognised emblem, the situation is sustainable, but, as Pictet states, it is essential that there be no further proliferation of emblems which could create potential confusion, with disastrous consequences.

Most of the major powers became party to the 1864 Convention within five years, the last, the United States, waiting until 1882. The convention was a momentous step forward, but it proved by no means perfect in practice. The reason for this lay in part outside the convention itself, in the variable effectiveness of dissemination and understanding between the various powers – a problem by no means eliminated today. The Franco-Prussian War of 1870–71 illustrated these problems. The Prussians and their allies generally understood and applied the convention effectively, but the French in many cases did not. This led the Prussian, and after 1870 the Imperial German, General Staff to demand a better organised system, and other powers rapidly came to concur. There were also serious problems with the substantive provision of the convention, which tended to be strong on general principle and rather weak on details of implementation. Geoffrey Best argues that these difficulties were the product of a perennial tension between military necessity and humanitarian endeavour.[72] Such a tension is to some degree inevitable, but it must also be strongly emphasised that if they are to be effective at all, humanitarian norms in armed conflict must be a practical regime capable of application in the real exigencies of armed conflict, and not an idealistic but impractical aspiration.

One of the issues which emerged from the Franco-Prussian War was the need for official organisation and recognition of humanitarian agencies and personnel, rather than a generalised protection of anyone who claimed to be acting under 'humanitarian' auspices – many of whom in 1870–71 were certainly not doing so, and by such abuse imperilled the whole principle of humanitarian protection. A major revision of the 1864 Convention was undertaken in 1906, which led to the 1906 Geneva Convention for the Amelioration of the Conditions of Armies in the Field, which was applied during the First World War.

Despite exaggerated claims by both sides, the 1906 Convention worked reasonably well during the First World War, but as a result of the war experience it was again revised in the late 1920s, leading to the 1929 Geneva Convention on the Wounded and Sick in Land Warfare, which was applied during the Second World War. This was replaced after 1945 by 1949 Geneva Convention I, with supplementary measures added by 1977 Protocol I Additional to the 1949 Geneva Conventions.

After the original 1864 provision for the wounded and sick in land warfare, the next obvious step – extension to warfare at sea – was delayed for a surprisingly long period, being finally taken thirty years later. Medical care for personnel at sea found expression in the Judgements of Oleron of *circa* 1194, and by the Tudor age it was well established practice for British warships to carry a surgeon.[73] The recovery of the surgeon's equipment from the Tudor warship *Mary Rose*, sunk off the Isle of Wight in 1545 and salvaged in 1982, confirms the relative contemporary sophistication of this provision.[74] However, none of this implied humanitarian provision in any modern sense, in particular for wounded enemies.

An early attempt was made to extend humanitarian provision in land warfare to warfare at sea following the victory of an Austro-Hungarian fleet commanded by Admiral Teggethof over an Italian fleet at the second battle of Lissa[75] on 20 July 1866 during the Austro-Italian War, in which many sailors drowned for lack of post-combat rescue provision. In the light of this experience, a convention was drafted extending the principles of the 1864 land convention to war at sea, but nothing came of this. It was only after the maritime death toll in the 1898 Spanish–American War that humanitarian protection was extended to the wounded, sick and shipwrecked in naval warfare by 1899 Hague Declaration 3. It may be noted that this was a pointed example of the close linkage between the 'Hague' and 'Geneva' sectors of the *jus in bello*. This was supplemented by a 1904 Convention relating to hospital ships, and the law was consolidated by 1907 Hague Convention X which, together with the 1909 London Declaration on the Rules of Naval Warfare, was applied during the First World War.

The war at sea between 1914 and 1918 raised a number of controversial issues, especially with regard to 'unrestricted submarine warfare'. The sinking of a number of passenger liners without warning – notably the Cunard liner *Lusitania* by U-20 on 7 May 1915, and the P&O liner *Persia* by U-38 on 30 December 1915 – caused international outrage. Attempts have been made to prove that the *Lusitania* was covertly armed as a warship and/or illegally carrying munitions, but no real evidence has been provided for this. It would seem that some confusion has arisen because the ship had, along with a number of others, been built with a view to potential conversion to an armed merchant cruiser in event of war, but this had not been carried out when the ship was retained in commercial service. Modern investigation of the wreck suggests that a much reported second explosion was an explosion of coal dust in the *Lusitania*'s bunkers, rather than munitions, following the torpedo strike.[76] Another, opposite, misconception has arisen from the sinking of the largest ship sunk in the First World War, HMHS *Britannic* in the Zea Channel in the Aegean on 21 November 1916. The *Britannic*, third sister of the *Olympic* and *Titanic*, was completed as a hospital ship during the war, and the sinking was denounced by the Allies as a criminal torpedo attack. All the available evidence now suggests that the ship had the misfortune to sail into a minefield which had been too recently laid to have had its position declared[77] – a victim of tragic accident rather than war criminality.

Similar problems arose during the Second World War, with the additional problem of establishing markings for hospital ships when seen from the air, along with a repetition of problems of submarine warfare, including the notorious 'no rescue' 'Laconia Order'[78] and attacks upon survivors from torpedoed ships, as in the Peleus Case.[79] The experience of 1939–45 was reflected in the drafting of 1949 Geneva Convention II, which is the present provision in this area, supplemented by further provision in 1977 Protocol I Additional to the 1949 Geneva Conventions.

The protection of prisoners of war by humanitarian treaties developed over the same timescale as that afforded to the wounded, sick and shipwrecked at sea. Although some customary protection existed, there was resistance in some quarters to codification and expansion. There seems to have been a feeling that excessive protective provision would destroy the fighting spirit of armed forces by making surrender too easy an option. Emperor Franz-Joseph of Austria-Hungary is reported to have warned that:

> to secure to prisoners of war great comforts and indulgences would be to hold out an inducement to cowardly or effeminate soldiers to escape the dangers and hardships of war by surrendering themselves to the enemy.[80]

The Soviet dictator Stalin apparently had a similar view; no doubt such opinions were held more readily in the Hofburg and the Kremlin than by soldiers facing the actual possibility of capture. It may be added that at the outset of the First World War, Emperor Franz-Joseph is recorded by Major T.J.D. Holmes, in a letter cited by L.C. Green, to have written to a British regiment of which he was honorary Colonel-in-Chief, the First King's Dragoon Guards, to the effect that any officer or man of the regiment who might be captured by Austro-Hungarian forces was to be considered the emperor's guest for the duration of hostilities.[81] Such chivalric archaism, commendable as it was in its own context, did not meet the needs of the general protection of the mass of prisoners of war, and it was to this end that international humanitarian law made its rather slow way.

The Lieber Code and the failed Brussels draft included protections for prisoners of war, but the major codification commenced with 1899 Hague Declaration 4, with a major expansion in the Land Warfare Regulations annexed to 1907 Hague Convention IV, articles 4–20. This included in article 4 what remains the most basic principle of prisoner of war protection:

> Prisoners of war are in the power of the hostile Government, but not of the individuals or corps who capture them. They must be humanely treated. All their personal belongings, except arms, horses and military papers remains their property.

This is a fundamentally important principle, stating clearly that it is the duty of the detaining power to guarantee humane treatment; abuses cannot simply be dismissed as the unfortunate excesses of local operatives. The 1907 provisions were applied during the First World War and, notwithstanding propaganda by both the Allies and the Central Powers, were generally applied correctly. Revised provision, with some tightening of specification, was made by the 1929 Geneva Prisoners of War Convention, the application of which during the Second World War disclosed a different and very revealing pattern. The Western Allies, the German Reich and Italy were parties to the 1929 Convention, and with some gross exceptions, such as the massacre of some 200 US prisoners by the SS at Malmédy,[82] it was correctly applied between these states. The retrospective tendency to confuse prisoner of war camps with the Nazi death camps gives an entirely false impression and, indeed, tends to obscure the real dimensions of the genocide perpetrated by the Third Reich, both within Germany and in its occupied territories. On the eastern front, a very different situation obtained. There the Nazis fought a 'total war' in the most extreme sense, in which the intended fate of the inhabitants of occupied territories was either extermination or enslavement. No place was allowed for humanitarian *jus in bello* norms. Hitler himself stated, in preparation for the notorious 'Commissar Order':

> The war against Russia will be such that it cannot be conducted in a knightly fashion. This struggle is one of ideologies and racial differences and will have to be conducted with unprecedented, unmerciful and unrelenting harshness. ... German soldiers guilty of breaking international law ... will be excused. Russia has not participated in the Hague Convention and therefore has no rights under it.[83]

The claim, in effect, that the *jus in bello* was not applicable was unsustainable. Even leaving aside the fact that the USSR was not party to the 1929 Prisoner of War Convention and the highly questionable issue of reciprocity implicitly raised by Hitler, both the former Tsarist Empire and Imperial Germany had been bound by 1907 Hague Convention IV, the basic tenets of which had, by the 1940s, attained the status of customary law. The International Military Tribunal at Nuremberg not surprisingly found that the atrocious German treatment of Soviet prisoners had violated these norms,[84] although, equally unsurprisingly, the tribunal did not comment upon the extremely harsh treatment meted out to German and Italian prisoners in the USSR.

Allied prisoners in the war in the Far East were treated with systematic and extreme cruelty by the Japanese armed forces, including the horrors of the forced construction of the Thailand–Burma Railway[85] and the Borneo death march. This cruelty has sometimes been blamed upon the survival of the *Bushido* code of the Samurai, in which capture was an ultimate disgrace for a warrior, but this is much overstated. In the Russo-Japanese War of 1904–5, the Japanese armed forces were notably correct in their implementation of international humanitarian law, and the senior commanders, General Nogi and Admiral Togo, as well as many of their subordinates, had actually lived in Samurai culture in the last days of the Tokugawa Shogunate. It seems probable that claims of *Bushido* in wartime Japan had much in common with the bizarre and highly selective fascination of the Nazis with certain aspects of medieval European culture, and that the excesses of both may be traced simply to modern totalitarian brutalism. Be that as it may, after the Second World War the 1929 Convention was radically revised and updated, and the modern provision is found in 1949 Geneva Convention IV, with some controversial updating in 1977 Additional Protocol I with particular regard to entitlement to prisoner of war status upon capture.

The final category of protected 'victims' of armed conflict, civilians, were also brought rather slowly into the ambit of modern international humanitarian law. Some basic protective norms are found in the Land Warfare Regulations annexed to 1907 Hague Convention IV and 1907 Hague Convention IX, including some important provisions with regard to occupied territories in articles 42–56 of the former. There were significant problems in the First World War, not least in relation to belligerent occupation, but little real effort was made to update the provision in the inter-war years. This was partly based on a specious contention that to expand the *jus in bello* in the supposedly peaceful League of Nations era would be wrong in principle. Despite this, the ICRC pressed strongly for reform in this area, but to little avail.[86] Ultimately, a conference was called to meet in 1940 to consider enhanced protection of civilians on the basis of proposals emerging from the 1934 International Red Cross Conference in Tokyo. This conference was aborted by the outbreak of the Second World War, and further protection of civilians was delayed by another decade. New provision was finally made by the present 1949 Geneva Convention IV, but even this may be thought to be less broad in scope than would be desirable. Further important provision was made by 1977 Additional Protocol I, not least in the development of 'Hague' principles moving beyond those developed in 1908 for the protection of civilians through norms of tactical battlefield conduct.[87] These provisions represent major advances in *jus in bello* provision for civilians, but more may still be thought necessary, not least in the protection of women[88] and of children[89] as victims of armed conflict.

A further area of difficulty arises in relation to humanitarian provision for non-international armed conflicts, or 'civil wars'.[90] Public international law prior to 1945 made little or no substantive provision for the restraint of the treatment of its own citizens by the government of a state, and whatever moral position might be adopted in relation to a given case, the response of a state to armed insurgence was not essentially within the remit of *jus in bello* norms. The experience of modern totalitarianism from the 1930s onwards which shaped the initial development of the modern law of human rights[91] also inspired basic humanitarian provision for non-international armed conflicts. Very basic provision, essentially a minimalist 'human rights' regime, is made by common article 3 of the four 1949

Geneva Conventions. This is significantly expanded by 1977 Protocol II Additional to the 1949 Geneva Conventions. Both common article 3 and Additional Protocol II seek to establish humanitarian norms without entering the vexed question of any express or implied recognition of insurgent belligerency, which would be in practice an insuperable political obstacle to the implementation of such norms. Despite this, considerable controversy still surrounds the implications of the 'internationalisation' of wars of national liberation by article 1(4) of 1977 Additional Protocol I.[92]

The development of legal norms regulating and constraining the conduct of hostilities on the battlefield has closely interlocked with the development of protective humanitarian norms, as in the questions of civilian protection referred to above, but has also involved a number of distinct considerations and factors. Reference has been made above to the foundational principle of 'unnecessary suffering' found in the Preamble to the 1868 Declaration of St Petersburg, and this has been repeated in a number of subsequent treaties, for example by articles 22 and 23(e) of the Land Welfare Regulations annexed to 1907 Hague Convention IV, and article 35(1)(2) of 1977 Additional Protocol I to the 1949 Geneva Conventions. The modern foundations of the elaboration of this basic proposition in the 'Hague' sector of the humanitarian *jus in bello* is found in the treaties which resulted from the 1899 and 1907 Hague Peace Conferences. These two conferences were convened by the Imperial Russian Government at the initiative of Tsar Nicholas II. The circular note inviting participation despatched by the Foreign Minister, Count Muraviev, on 24 August 1898 (Western date) stated:

> The maintenance of general peace and ... reduction of excessive armaments [are] ... the idea towards which the endeavours of all Governments should be directed.
>
> The humanitarian ... views of His Majesty the Emperor [of all the Russias] ... are in perfect accord with this sentiment. ... As the armaments of each Power increase so they do less and less attain the object aimed at by the Governments. Economic crises due to the amassing of armaments ... are transforming the armed peace of our days into a crushing burden. ... If this state of affairs be prolonged, it will inevitably lead to the very cataclysm which it is desired to avert, and the impending horrors of which are fearful to every human thought.[93]

Many, then and now, have doubted the genuineness of the claimed aim to establish peace,[94] and certainly, if this was the aim, it was not achieved – indeed, the 1907 Conference was delayed by the outbreak of the 1904–5 Russo-Japanese War. The reality is perhaps that the desire for peace may have been real, but it was pursued with that perilous combination of dilettantism and incompetence which was shortly to bring on the horrors of the First World War. Be that as it may, the real achievements of the 1899 and 1907 Hague Conferences lay not in the *jus ad bellum*, but in the *jus in bello*. A number of basic principles which remain in force at present were either codified or developed in relation, *inter alia*, to methods and means of warfare. These two categories are the essence of the 'Hague' dimension of international humanitarian law, the first concerning tactical conduct, and the latter, principally, weapons of warfare.

In the area of methods of warfare, the Land Warfare Regulations annexed to 1907 Hague Convention IV remain a basic code. They cover such matters as misuse of emblems,[95] ruses of war[96] (which are lawful, in contrast with perfidy), bombardment,[97] prohibition of pillage,[98] flags of truce,[99] capitulations[100] and armistice.[101] The 1907 Hague Peace Conference also made importance provision for naval warfare, including 1907 Hague Convention VI relating to the Status of Enemy Merchant Ships at the Outbreak of Hostilities, 1907 Hague Convention VII relating to the Conversion of Merchant Ships into Warships, 1907 Hague Convention VIII relating to the Laying of Automatic Submarine Contact Mines[102] and 1907 Hague Convention IX concerning Bombardment by Naval Forces in Time of War. Important treaties were also made at this time regarding the law of neutrality.[103]

The 1907 Conventions reflected the experience of warfare up to that time. Thus the provision for mine warfare at sea reflected the experience of the 1904–5 Russo-Japanese War, in which not only had a number of important belligerent warships been sunk by mines, including the Russian flagship *Petropavlovsk* at Port Arthur and the Japanese battleships *Yashima* and *Hatsuse*, but also a number of neutral merchant ships which had hit drifting, unanchored mines. The First World War, with both its much greater scale and the rapid development of new and ever more threatening military technologies, fulfilling the forebodings of Count Muraviev in 1898,[104] brought forward many new issues and questions, and reinforced many which already existed. Among the new tactical elements was the matter of air warfare. There had been earlier air warfare provisions, including 1899 Hague Declaration I and 1907 Hague Convention XIV dealing with the launching of projectiles from balloons, but by 1914 these had little more antiquarian interest except to the extent that they might be taken to include Zeppelin airships within their remit. After 1918, attention was devoted to the issue, and the 1923 Hague Draft Rules on Aerial Warfare were produced. These never entered into force as a treaty, but were widely considered to be an authoritative statement of the law as it then existed. The experience of area bombardment in the Second World War, including the mass conventional bombing of cities like London, Hamburg, Coventry and Dresden, did not inspire new treaty law after 1945. Roberts and Guelff remark:

> ... there is no formally binding agreement which exclusively addresses air warfare. However, in addition to the various treaty articles which do relate to air warfare, certain general principles underlying the laws of war are considered to be applicable in air warfare, even if in practice their application is not free from difficulty.[105]

There is still (in 1997) no specific treaty dealing with air war as such, although specific provision relating to air war has been made in a number of more general treaties, including 1977 Additional Protocol I to the 1949 Geneva Conventions, as Roberts and Guelff suggest. It is accepted that the general norms of international humanitarian law governing, in particular, discrimination in bombardment apply to air warfare as much as to warfare in any other sector.

New provision governing methods of warfare, both breaking new ground and affirming or codifying earlier principles, was made only after the Vietnam War, which, as a guerrilla war on a scale and of a type not formerly seen, generated a number of new or renewed concerns. The immediate result was the 1977 UN Convention on the Prohibition of Military or any other Hostile Use of Environmental Modification Techniques, to some extent reflecting a concern more apparent than real,[106] and 1977 Additional Protocol I to the 1949 Geneva Conventions. The latter makes provision for methods and means of warfare in articles 35–42, with additional measures relating to discrimination in bombardment in articles 48–51. The measures deal, *inter alia,* with misuse of flags and emblems,[107] a useful codification of the law relating to perfidy,[108] and the customary ban on orders of 'no quarter'.[109] These basic rules on methods of warfare are well settled, even if they are not necessarily applied consistently or without difficulty. The law relating to means of warfare – essentially arms control – raises other more problematic issues.

An initial issue of theory lies in the question of whether the law of arms control is a coherent and principled structure of norms or simply a random collection of historic responses to particular weapons and usages.[110] A common theme in arms control provision may be discerned deriving from the 'principle of unnecessary suffering' in the Preamble to the 1868 Declaration of St Petersburg,[111] possibly associated with a related but unarticulated 'principle of excessive cruelty', but the question of specificity is inevitably of central concern in such law. The idea of arms control is of some antiquity. The customary ban on poison weapons now found in article 23(a) of the Land Warfare Regulations annexed to 1907 Hague Convention IV was found in ancient Greek and Roman practice, as well as in that of ancient India. In the Middle Ages, attempts were made to proscribe the use of 'Greek Fire' (a Byzantine precursor of napalm), and the Second Lateran Council in 1139 attempted, without great success, to ban the use of crossbows and arbalests, at least in warfare between Christians.[112] It is not surprising that, apart from ancient principles such as the ban upon poison weapons, the modern era of arms control law and debate dates from the technological developments of the later 19th century. Reference has been made above to the proscription of small-calibre anti-personnel explosive bullets by the 1868 Declaration of St Petersburg, but the subsequent developments in relation to dumdum bullets illustrates an important issue in the law of arms control.

Dumdum bullets, named after the Dum Dum arsenal near Calcutta where they were first manufactured, are bullets which have only a partial or a perforated hard casing, and which therefore tend to expand upon impact on a human body, causing much worse injuries than would be inflicted by an equivalent conventional, wholly cased, bullet. Many states believed that the ban on small-calibre explosive projectiles contained in the 1868 Declaration of St Petersburg also covered expanding bullets, even though they were not strictly 'explosive'. The United Kingdom, which had swiftly adopted dumdum bullets for military use, denied this, and contended, on overtly racist grounds, that they were suitable for use in certain combat situations.[113] These arguments were decisively rejected by the 1899 Hague Peace Conference, and bullets of this type were banned by 1899 Hague Declaration 3.

The First World War brought new horrors in combat, notably the use of chemical and gas weapons, commencing with a gas attack on French troops near Ypres on 22 April 1915. Gas was widely used thereafter on the western front, and to a lesser extent on the eastern front, especially with a view to breaking the western front infantry stalemate. In this respect it was unsuccessful, the deadlock being ultimately broken by the Allied development of the tank, first used on a large scale at the Battle of Cambrai on 20 November 1917.[114] The use of gas weapons was already unlawful in 1914. Plans for the use of sulphur gas had been considered but rejected during the Crimean War,[115] and the received opinion developed that gas weapons violated the customary ban on poison weapons and the general 'St Petersburg principle of unnecessary suffering'. This was affirmed by 1899 Hague Declaration 2, which banned the use of projectiles having the sole object of diffusing asphyxiating gases. The violation of 1899 Hague Declaration 2 in the First World War was denounced by the International Committee of the Red Cross on 6 February 1918,[116] and condemned after the war by article 171 of the Treaty of Versailles. The proscription was reiterated by the 1922 Treaty of Washington, and finally a new and more comprehensive ban was instated by the 1925 Geneva Protocol for the Prohibition of the Use in War of Asphyxiating, Poisonous or Other Gases, and of Bacteriological Methods of Warfare, known as the 1925 Geneva Gas Protocol. This Protocol shares with the 1868 Declaration of St Petersburg and 1899 Hague Declaration 3 a very considerable record of success in the field of arms control.[117]

The 1925 Geneva Gas Protocol also proscribes the use of biological weapons, a means of warfare that has a rather longer history than is commonly supposed. In the Middle Ages the bodies of plague victims were catapulted into besieged towns in order to spread the disease amongst the defenders. Experiments with biological toxin weapons were undertaken in 1930s, it is possible that such weapons may have been used by Japanese forces in Manchuria,[118] and there was somewhat misinformed debate in the 1990s upon the nature and causes of 'Gulf War Syndrome',[119] but this ban too has achieved a considerable measure of success in practice. There have been recent extensions of the bans on chemical and biological weapons, specifically to include proscriptions on the manufacture and stockpiling of such weapons, respectively in the 1972 UN Convention on Prohibition of the Development and Stockpiling of Bacteriological, Biological and Toxin Weapons and their Destruction, and the 1992 UN Convention on Prohibition of the Development and Stockpiling of Chemical Weapons and their Destruction. The difficulty with these conventions lies in the areas of policing and verification, although the enunciation of the principle must be considered positive.[120]

The most difficult issue in post-1945 arms control law has been that of the status of nuclear weapons. The belligerent powers in the Second World war were engaged in considerable military nuclear research, and the widely disseminated myth that the Axis powers were not much interested in this weaponry has conclusively been shown to be false.[121] For a variety of reasons, however, the United States was the first state to develop nuclear weapons, and bombs were dropped at the end of the Second World War upon two Japanese cities: Hiroshima on 6 August 1945, and Nagasaki on 9 August 1945. The legality of this action was questioned in *Ryuichi Shimoda et al.* v. *The State*,[122] and the United Nations General Assembly has condemned nuclear weapons on a number of occasions, but by small majorities.[123] The matter was finally considered by the International Court of Justice in 1996 in the *Advisory Opinion on the Legality of the Threat or Use of Nuclear Weapons*,[124] which considered most potential uses to be unlawful, whilst reserving the possibility of resort *in extremis*.[125]

Further development also occurred in the control of conventional armaments. The most notable step has been the 1981 UN Convention on Prohibitions or Restrictions on the Use of Certain Conventional Weapons Which may be Deemed to be Excessively Injurious or to have Indiscriminate Effects. This convention was originally intended to form part of 1977 Additional Protocol I to the 1949 Geneva Convention,[126] but finally emerged as a separate UN Convention. Its substantive provision is found in three protocols which, respectively, ban non-detectable fragmentation weapons (plastic mines), make provision for the protection of civilians from 'booby-trap' type weapons, and proscribe the indiscriminate or anti-civilian use of incendiary weapons. In the 1990s, the Review Conference of the 1980 UN Conventional Weapons Convention addressed the question of laser weapons used to cause blindness, and landmines. The former were banned by a new Fourth Protocol to the 1980 Convention, adopted on 13 October 1995.[127] Severe restrictions were decided upon with regard to landmines, largely because a weapon which was originally designed to provide 'passive' defence in clearly marked minefields had in practice become a means of indiscriminate warfare causing mass civilian injury, in many cases long after the armed conflict had ceased.

These debates return to the question of the structural integrity of arms control law. On the one hand, the motivation for the proscription of both blinding laser weapons and landmines clearly derives directly from the 1868 Declaration of St Petersburg and the 'unnecessary suffering' principle. On the other hand, the tense international negotiation involved made very clear the fact that general principles will not suffice to impose controls which can be rendered effective only by very specific provision, as was shown in the 19th century by the inability of the 1868 Declaration of St Petersburg to cope with dumdum bullets.

International Humanitarian Law and the Changing Pattern of Warfare

All law, if it is to avoid practical desuetude, must meet the developing demands of the sector of human activity which it seeks to regulate. The humanitarian laws of armed conflict are no exception to this. L.H. Addington has written:

> ... the history of warfare is best understood as a process of change in war's socio-political, technological, and organizational aspects.[128]

The laws of armed conflict must necessarily change and develop to take account of the new humanitarian imperatives which may be generated by such evolution in the conduct of armed conflict itself. However, it would be a grave error to imagine that armed conflict follows linear patterns of development to which legal development can in any way simply be matched. For example, it was widely felt in the 1960s and early 1970s that the future pattern of warfare was likely to be one of 'informal' guerrilla war following the model of Vietnam. Since that time there have indeed been guerrilla conflicts, but there have also been other and much different forms of armed conflict. Thus the 1980–88 Gulf War between Iran and Iraq had much in common with the First World War, including an appalling infantry stalemate and the use of gas weapons in unsuccessful attempts to break the front. In its essential dynamics, the 1982 Anglo-Argentine Falklands Conflict had, apart from the technology, much in common with the so-called 'small wars' of the 19th century, bearing in mind an aphorism attributed to H.G. Wells that no war is 'small' to one who dies in it. The 1990–91 Gulf Conflict represented, in its ultimate impact at least, an example of UN-authorised international response to military aggression enacted with some immediate success. A quite contrasting picture is offered by the armed conflicts which accompanied the dissolution of former Yugoslavia and the eventual replacement of an under-resourced and ill-mandated UNPROFOR with the successive NATO-led IFOR and SFOR forces. It may be suggested that there is in fact no stable 'pattern', but rather a phenomenon of armed confrontation in many guises, for which international humanitarian law must make the broadest possible provision. Even then, attempts to provide an adequate basis may always face the unexpected, as the military operations in the US Operation Restore Hope and later by UNOSOM in Somalia in the 1990s made graphically clear. For all practical purposes, governmental authority collapsed in Somalia, and had dissolved at latest by January 1991.[129] The multiple conflicts which then raged in Somalia were essentially without precedent, in that the country simply collapsed into violent anarchy between various factions, ranging from contenders for governmental authority over all or part of the country to mere bandits. The ICRC Commentary on 1977 Protocol II Additional to the 1949 Geneva Conventions, expanding the provision of common article 3 of the conventions for non-international armed conflicts, reveals that the ICRC draft for the Protocol had taken such a possible situation into account, but the idea had been dismissed by the Diplomatic Conference as a 'theoretical textbook example'.[130]

Within the broad framework set out by existing treaty provision, the continuing development of international humanitarian law continually brings forward new, or renewed, issues for consideration. Since 1977, such diverse problems as blinding laser weapons, mercenarism, the adequacy of protection of women in armed conflict, detailed protection of the environment in armed conflict – an issue covered by 1977 Additional Protocol I in the light of the Vietnam experience, but raised anew following oil pollution during the 1990–91 Gulf Conflict – the application of international humanitarian law by and to United Nations forces in the context of increased UN military activism in the post-1991 so-called 'new world order', and modes of maintenance and enforcement, as in the context of former Yugoslavia and Rwanda, have all demanded attention. These set a continuing agenda, but cannot be a fixed framework for foreseeable future requirements, since in many cases they were themselves unforeseen.

Finally, there remains the question of the fundamental imperatives of future development in international humanitarian law. In the first edition of this work, it was suggested that:

> Although cultural and technological forms vary widely according to both time and place, the fundamental issues raised by attempts to impose moderating norms upon the conduct of armed conflicts do not much change in their essential nature. ... Experience from 1864 onwards demonstrates that clearly stated provision is far more valuable than worthy aspiration ... if this is remembered then one may hope that progress may continue to be made and the calamities of armed conflict, while it occurs, may be reduced so far as may be possible.[131]

This remains true – indeed, in some respects it has become even more so. International humanitarian law faces perhaps the most difficult task of regulation of any sector of law, international or municipal, and its clear-sighted direction in the light of a practical vision of what may really be achieved is vital to maximise its efficacy. The price of failure is all too obvious, and should never be incurred where it can be avoided.

Notes

1 See, for example, Geza Herczeg, *Development of International Humanitarian Law*, trans. Sandas Simon and Lajos Czante (Akademiai Kiado, 1984).

2 For discussion, see N.D. White, *Keeping the Peace: The United Nations and the Maintenance of International Peace and Security* (Manchester University Press, 1993); H. McCoubrey and N.D. White, *The Blue Helmets: Legal Regulation of United Nations Military Operations* (Dartmouth, 1996), Chapters 1 and 2; D.W. Greig, 'Self-Defence and the Security Council: What Does Article 51 Require?' (1991) 40 *International and Comparative Law Quarterly*, p. 336; W. Rostow, 'Until What? Enforcement Action or Collective Self-Defence' (1991) 85 *American Journal of International Law*, p. 506.

3 See Chapter 2.

4 H. Lauterpacht, 'The Revision of the Law of War' (1952) 29 *British Yearbook of International Law*, pp. 381–2.

5 C. von Clausewitz, *On War* (1832), ed. and trans. M. Howard and P. Paret (Princeton University Press, 1976), Book I.3, p. 76.

6 L. Tolstoy, *War and Peace* (Moscow, 1868–69), trans. L. and A. Maude (Macmillan, 1943), Book XIV, Chapter 1 at p. 1, 139.

7 G. Schwarzenberger, *International Law, Vol. II: Armed Conflict* (Stevens, 1968), p. 10.
8 Aristotle, *The Ethics*, 1253a 7, using the term *politikon zoon*, meaning, in a general sense, 'political animal'.
9 See the ICRC report by S. Junod, *Protection of the Victims of Armed Conflict, Falkland Malvinas Islands* (2nd edn) (ICRC, 1985). Subsequent allegations made against British forces have not been found to have serious foundation.
10 For discussion of the emergence of human rights law, see A. Cassese, *Human Rights in a Changing World* (Polity Press/Blackwell, 1990), Chapter 1.
11 See below.
12 These included, most importantly, the first humanitarian Geneva Convention of 1864, and the 1868 Declaration of St Petersburg.
13 G.I.A.D. Draper, 'Humanitarian Law and Human Rights', in Forsyth, C.F. and Schiller, J.E. (eds) *Human Rights: The Cape Town Conference* (Juta, 1979), p. 193, at pp. 194–5.
14 See Chapter 9.
15 G. Herczeg, op.cit.
16 See pp. 1–2.
17 This might be argued to be subject to controversial claims of rights to 'humanitarian intervention', but even if such a right exists, it could only be validated within a UN framework of maintenance of international peace and security.
18 For discussion of this, see D.W. Greig, op.cit.
19 R. Dworkin, *Taking Rights Seriously* (Duckworth, 1987), Introduction, p. xi.
20 G. Herczeg, op.cit.
21 I.P. Blishchenko, 'Humanitarian Norms and Human Rights', in the Independent Commission on International Humanitarian Norms Report, Abi-Saab, R., El Kouhene, M. and Z. Vivi (eds), *Modern Wars: The Humanitarian Challenge* (Zed Books, 1986), p. 142, at p. 143.
22 See I. Shaw, *Egyptian Warfare and Weapons* (Shire Egyptology, 1991), Chapter 2.
23 Numbers 31:7, 10, 15–19. All biblical passages are taken from the Revised Standard Version (Collins, OT 1952, NT 1971).
24 2 Kings 6:21–2.
25 For analysis, see G.I.A.D. Draper, ed. M.A. Meyer, 'The Contribution of the Emperor Asoka Maurya to the Development of the Humanitarian Idea in Warfare' (1995) 35 *International Review of the Red Cross* , pp. 192–206.
26 Ibid., at p. 195, citing Edict XIII, known as the 'Rock' or 'Conquest' Edict.
27 *The Laws of Manu*, trans. W. Doniger and B.K. Smith (Penguin Classics, 1991), Chapter 7: 90–2, at pp. 137–8.
28 See L.C. Green, *The Contemporary Law of Armed Conflict* (Manchester University Press, 1993), p. 19.
29 *Mencius*, trans. D.C. Lau (Penguin Classics, 1970), IV.A.14, at p. 124.
30 Ibid., VII.B.2.
31 Da Diu, *The Tao and Chinese Culture* (Routledge and Kegan Paul, 1981), p. 41. This book was drawn to the attention of the author by one of his PhD students, Ms S. Huza.
32 Zhu Li-Sun, 'Traditional Asian Approaches to the Protection of Victims of Armed Conflict – The Chinese View' (1985) 9 *Australian Yearbook of International Law*, p. 143, at pp. 145–6.
33 See G.I.A.D. Draper, 'The Origins of the Just War Tradition (1964) 46 *New Blackfriars*, p. 82, at pp. 82–4.
34 For discussion of this concept in a range of faiths and cultures, see S.S. Ali, S. Subedi and H. McCoubrey, *Ideas of 'Just War' in World Faiths* (University of Hull Press, 1997).

35 See ibid., Chapter 3.
36 Doubts about this arose at various times: see, for example, the work of Emer de Vattel *Le Droit des Gens, ou Principes de la Loi Naturelle appliqués à la Conduite et aux Affaires des Nations et des Souverains*, mod. edn, ed. J.B. Scot, trans. G.G. Fenwick, in The Modern Classics of English Law series (Carnegie Institute of Washington, 1916).
37 J. Pictet, *Development and Principles of International Humanitarian Law* (Martinus Nijhoff, 1985), pp. 13–14.
38 See St Augustine of Hippo, *Contra Faustem*, LXXIV, and St Thomas Aquinas, *Summa Theologica*, 1a2ae.40,1.
39 P. Contamine, trans. M. Jones, *War in the Middle Ages* (Blackwell, 1984; originally published as *La Guerre au Moyen Age* by Presses Universitaires de France, 1980), p. 290.
40 For discussion, see G.I.A.D. Draper, 'Penitential Discipline and Public Wars of the Middle Ages' (1961) 31 *International Review of the Red Cross*.
41 See T. Meron, *Henry's Wars and Shakespeare's Laws* (Clarendon/Oxford, 1993), Chapter 9; see also M. Walzer, *Just and Unjust Wars* (2nd edn) (Basic Books/HarperCollins, 1992; 1st published 1977), pp. 17–19.
42 See G. Schwarzenberger, *International Law, Vol. II: Armed Conflict* (Stevens, 1968), pp. 462–6; see also R.K. Worzel, *The Nuremberg Trials in International Law* (Stevens, 1962), pp. 19–21. For further discussion, see Chapter 10.
43 For discussion of the 1621 Articles of War, see K. Ogren, 'Humanitarian Law in the *Articles of War* Decreed in 1621 by King Gustavus II Adolphus of Sweden' (1996) 36 *International Review of the Red Cross*, pp. 438–42.
44 Muhammad Hamidullah, *The Muslim Conduct of State* (Sh. Muhammad Ashraf, 1981), pp. 205–8.
45 Ibid., at p. 214.
46 See Chapter 6.
47 J. Picket, op.cit., at p. 22.
48 This figure is derived from those set out by Jean Pictet, op.cit, at p. 22.
49 J. Rousseau, *Du Contrat Social* (1762), Book 1, Chapter IV (Garnier-Flammarion, 1966), p. 48.
50 Ibid., at pp. 21–2.
51 See H. McCoubrey, 'Before Geneva Law: A British Surgeon in The Crimean War' (1995) 35 *International Review of the Red Cross*, pp. 69–80.
52 E.M. Wrench, 'The Lessons of the Crimean War', *The British Medical Journal*, 22 July 1899, quoted in H. McCoubrey, op.cit., at p. 71.
53 Reported in a letter to his family dated 13 June 1855, and preserved in the Wrench Collection at the University of Nottingham Library Department of Manuscripts and Special Collections. See also H. McCoubrey, op.cit., at p. 73.
54 See H. Seton-Watson, *The Russian Empire 1801–1917* (Oxford, 1967), p. 388.
55 P. Boissier, *History of the International Committee of the Red Cross, Vol. I: From Solferino to Tsushima* (Henry Dunant Institute, 1985), pp. 20–1.
56 See A. Fraccaroli, *Italian Warships of World War I* (Ian Allan, 1970), p. 253.
57 Republished in English translation by the American National Red Cross in 1959.
58 Ibid., p. 66.
59 Ibid., p. 72.
60 For discussion, see Chapter 2.
61 For discussion, see Chapter 4.
62 G. Best, *Humanity in Warfare* (Methuen, 1983; 1st published by Weidenfeld and Nicolson, 1980), pp. 155–6.
63 H. McCoubrey and N.D. White, *International Law and Armed Conflict* (Dartmouth, 1992), p. 219.

64 See above, p. 14.
65 See 1949 Geneva Convention I, article 28, and 1949 Geneva Convention II, article 37.
66 See 1949 Geneva Convention I, article 38, and 1949 Geneva Convention II, article 41.
67 P. Boissier, op.cit., p. 77.
68 J. Pictet, op.cit., p. 30.
69 See 1949 Geneva Convention I, article 38, and 1949 Geneva Convention II, article 41.
70 See A. Durand, *History of the International Committee of the Red Cross, Vol. II: From Sarejavo to Hiroshima* (Henry Dunant Institute, 1978), p. 14.
71 J. Pictet, op.cit., p. 32.
72 G. Best, op.cit., pp. 47–9.
73 See G. Clark, *'Doc': 100 Year History of the Sick Berth Branch* (HMSO, 1984), Chapter 1, at pp. 1–3.
74 See M.H. Rule, *The Mary Rose, The Excavation and Raising of Henry VIII's Flagship* (Conway Maritime Press, 1982).
75 The first battle of Lissa was fought between a British and a Franco-Venetian fleet on 13 March 1811.
76 See R.D. Ballard with S. Dunmore, *Exploring the Lusitania* (Weidenfeld and Nicolson/Madison, 1995), pp. 194–5.
77 See S. Mills, *HMHS Britannic: The Last Titan* (Waterfront Publications, 1992), Ch. 6, also *The Titanic Commutator*. This view seems to be confirmed by dives made upon the wreck by Commander Cousteau and his team: see *The Titanic Commutator*, Winter 1977 and Winter 1978.
78 See Chapter 10.
79 See *War Crimes Trials*, Vol. 1, (William Hocky, 1948). For discussion, see Chapter 10.
80 See G. Best, op.cit., at p. 157, citing a note of Lord Lyons to Lord Derby, 13 July 1874, PRO, FO 881/2485 No.48.
81 Letter to *The Times* (London), 24 July 1984, cited by L.C. Green, *The Contemporary Law of Armed Conflict* (Manchester University Press, 1993), p. 18, note 3.
82 See T. Bowyer, *Blind Eye to Murder* (André Deutsch, 1981), pp. 133–5.
83 W.L. Shirer, *The Rise and Fall of the Third Reich* (Pan, 1964; 1st published in the UK by Secker & Warburg, 1960), p. 993, citing notes taken by General Halder, Halder Affidavit, 22 November 1945, Nuremberg Documents, *Nazi Conspiracy and Aggression*, VIII, at pp. 645–6.
84 See Chapter 10.
85 See A.C. Brackman, *The Other Nuremberg* (Collins, 1989), pp. 278–87.
86 See G. Best, op.cit, at pp. 232–3.
87 See the Land Warfare Regulations annexed to 1907 Hague Convention IV, articles 25–8, and 1977 Additional Protocol I, articles 48–60.
88 For discussion, see J. Gardam, 'Women and the Law of Armed Conflict: Why the Silence?' (1997) 46 *International and Comparative Law Quarterly*, pp. 55–80.
89 For discussion, see G. Goodwin-Gill and I. Cohen, *Child Soldiers: The Role of Children in Armed Conflicts* (Clarendon/Oxford, 1994), especially Chapter 6.
90 See Chapter 9; for further discussion, see H. McCoubrey and N.D. White, *International Organizations and Civil Wars* (Dartmouth, 1995), Chapters 6 and 7.
91 See above.
92 For discussion, see pp. 58 ff.
93 For full text, see J.B. Scott (ed.), *The Reports to the Hague Peace Conferences of 1899 and 1907* (Oxford University Press, 1917), pp. 1–2.
94 See G. Best, op.cit., at pp. 139–40.
95 Article 23(f).

96 Article 24.
97 Articles 25–7.
98 Articles 28 and 47.
99 Articles 32–4.
100 Article 35.
101 Articles 36–41.
102 This remains in force, but is perhaps now somewhat dated: see A.G.Y. Thorpe, 'Mine Warfare at Sea – Some Legal Aspects of the Future', 18 *Ocean Development and International Law*, p. 272.
103 In particular 1907 Hague Conventions V and XIII.
104 See above.
105 A. Roberts and R. Guelff, *Documents on the Laws of War* (2 edn) (Oxford, 1989), pp. 122–3.
106 See Chapter 8.
107 Articles 38 and 39.
108 Article 37.
109 Article 40.
110 For discussion, see H. McCoubrey, *Modern Perspectives upon the Law of Arms Control* (University of Hull Centre for International Defence Law Studies, forthcoming 1999), Chapter 1.
111 See above.
112 See P. Contamine, trans. M. Jones, *War in the Middle Ages* (Basil Blackwell, 1984; 1st published as *La Guerre au Moyen Age* by Presses Universitaires de France, 1980), pp. 71–2.
113 See G. Best, op.cit., p. 162.
114 See M. Gilbert, *First World War* (HarperCollins, 1995; 1st published by Weidenfield and Nicolson, 1994), pp. 378–9.
115 For a historical review of the use of chemical means of warfare, see W. Moore, *Gas Attack: Chemical Warfare 1915–1918 and Afterwards* (Leo Cooper/ Heinemann, 1987), pp. 2–6.
116 *Appeal to the Belligerents*, 6 February 1918; see the Stockholm International Peace Research Institute analysis, *The Problem of Chemical and Biological Weapons* (Almqvist and Wiksell, 6 vols, 1971–75), Vol. VI, p. 44; see also V. Adams, *Chemical Warfare, Chemical Disarmament* (Macmillan, 1989), p. 168.
117 For discussion, see below at pp. 240–3; see also H. McCoubrey, 'The Regulation of Biological and Chemical Weapons', in H. Fox and M.A. Meyer (eds), *Armed Conflict and the New Law, Vol. II: Effecting Compliance* (The British Institute of International and Comparative Law, 1993), pp. 123–39.
118 See V. Adams, op.cit., p. 11, citing A.H. Westing, 'The Threat of Biological Warfare', (1985) 35 *Bio-Science*, p. 627.
119 See pp. 241–2.
120 See H. McCoubrey, op.cit.
121 See G. Brooks, *Hitler's Nuclear Weapons* (Leo Cooper, 1992).
122 (1984) *Japanese Annual of International Law*, p. 212; see also R.A. Falk, 'The Shimoda Case: A Legal Appraisal of the Atomic Attack upon Hiroshima and Nagasaki' (1965) 59 *American Journal of International Law*, p. 759; see also L. Friedman, *The Laws of War: A Documentary History* (Random House, 2 vols, 1972), Vol. II, p. 1688.
123 UN General Assembly Resolution 1653 (XVI) of 1961, and UN General Assembly Resolution 1936 of 1972.
124 See (1996) 35 *International Legal Materials*, p. 1343.
125 For discussion, see D. Kritsiotis, 'The Fate of Nuclear Weapons after the 1996 Advisory Opinions of the World Court' (1996) I *Journal of Armed Conflict Law*, pp. 95–119.

126 See A. Roberts and R. Guelff, op.cit., p. 471.
127 For discussion, see L. Doswald-Beck, 'New Protocol on Blinding Laser Weapons' (1996) 36 *International Review of the Red Cross*, pp. 272–98.
128 L.H. Addington, *The Patterns of War Since the 18th Century* (Croom Helm, 1984), Preface, p. xiii.
129 See P. Brogan, *World Conflicts* (2nd edn) (Bloomsbury, 1992), pp. 80–85.
130 Y. Sandoz, C. Swinarski and B. Zimmermann (eds), *Commentary on the Additional Protocols of 8 June 1977 to the Geneva Conventions of 12 August 1949* (ICRC (Martinus Nijhoff, 1987), p. 1,351, para. 4 461, note 8.
131 H. McCoubrey, *International Humanitarian Law* (Dartmouth, 1990), pp. 19–20.

2 Institutions

The institutional structures of general public international law and their comparison with the typical structures of municipal legal systems have long raised controversial questions in legal theory. In 1832, the effective absence of a contemporary institutional framework led John Austin to assert that international law was not really 'law', but rather a form of 'positive morality'.[1] This argument may have had some force in the first half of the 19th century, although even then it may be contended that it was founded upon an inappropriate institutional comparison rather than upon more fundamental questions of *function*,[2] but since that time the institutional base of public international law has greatly developed. This has particularly been the case in the 20th century, during which, faced with the experience of two immensely destructive world wars, institutions have developed in an endeavour to redirect international relations into more constructive paths of development, and especially into peaceful modes of dispute-resolution. The successive developments of the League of Nations and United Nations eras, including the appearance of their respective judicial organs, the Permanent Court of International Justice and the International Court of Justice – the jurisdiction of which has been treated as in essence continuous – has gone far to strengthen the institutional claims of international law.

International humanitarian law is a sector of public international law, and thus shares its institutional base. It derives primarily from multilateral treaties, international custom and, in a subsidiary way, from judicial decisions and the writings of publicists.[3] It developed in the conduct of the international relations of states and by the activities of certain non-governmental organisations, and its development does not differ much in technical principle from the manner of generation of international legal norms in general. However, the peculiarly extreme circumstances in which the international humanitarian laws of armed conflict are required to be applied has from an early stage demanded the development of specialised institutions.

For this reason, rapid, modern, specialised institutional development in this area pre-dates the general institutional development of modern public international law by half a century.

There are a number of non-governmental agencies (NGOs) which in varying degrees deal with issues of international humanitarian law. Pre-eminent amongst these, and much the most important organisation in this area, is the international Red Cross movement, but various United Nations agencies must also be considered, including the United Nations High Commissioner for Refugees, medical relief agencies such as Médecins sans Frontières, and campaigning organisations such as Amnesty International. Their roles may interlock, and may also on occasion appear to conflict, but all have a significance to a greater or lesser degree in maintaining humanitarian norms in the crisis of armed conflict.

The Elements of the International Red Cross Movement

The international Red Cross movement is of fundamental importance to the practical operation and development of international humanitarian law, having been the fruit of Henry Dunant's first proposal, for a medical relief agency in armed conflict, made in his pamphlet, *Souvenir de Solferino*, following his volunteer relief effort after the Battle of Solferino in 1859.[4] The international Red Cross movement, as it is presently constituted, comprises four elements: the International Committee of the Red Cross (ICRC), the various national Red Cross and Red Crescent societies, the Federation of Red Cross and Red Crescent Societies, and the International Red Cross Conference. A brief outline of their respective functions follows, before subjecting their operation to more detailed examination.

The International Committee of the Red Cross is a private Swiss organisation whose membership is Swiss, being 'international' in function rather than identity. It acts as a neutral intermediary in armed conflicts, seeking to ensure and monitor the maintenance of humanitarian standards in the treatment of victims of conflicts, by diplomatic pressure, through visits to internment camps by ICRC Delegates, and through the operation of such offices as the Central Tracing Agency. It also acts as a central co-ordinating body in the Red Cross movement as a whole, approving new national societies, for example. The committee also plays a highly significant role as a non-governmental agency in the development of international humanitarian law, for example campaigning in the 1990s for new restrictions on landmines.[5]

The national Red Cross and Red Crescent societies were set up in the various countries over the years after the original establishment of what became the ICRC. Their original function was precisely that outlined by Henry Dunant in his second proposal in *Souvenir de Solferino*[6] – supplementing and supporting the military medical services in time of armed conflict. This function remains central, but its major medical and other relief potential obviously cannot be left dormant unless and until an armed conflict occurs. In peacetime, therefore, national societies engage in a wide range of health and health-rated work, together with programmes to disseminate international humanitarian law principles to suitable target groups, and they will also assist in international disaster relief work when necessary.

The International Federation of Red Cross and Red Crescent Societies (originally called the League of Red Cross and Red Crescent Societies) co-ordinates international relief efforts by national societies – not least to avoid overlap and to ensure the appropriateness of relief offered. It also offers encouragement and counsel in setting up new national societies.

The International Red Cross Conference is an international meeting of government representatives of states party to the 1949 Geneva Conventions and members of the ICRC. It considers issues relevant to international humanitarian law at the level of diplomatic relations, and plays a large part in the development of international law, for example by drafting the two 1977 Additional Protocols to the 1949 Geneva Conventions.

The International Committee of the Red Cross

The ICRC is the direct successor of the original Committee of Five set up in Geneva as a result of Henry Dunant's initiative after the Battle of Solferino.[7] It is a private Swiss organisation, being international in function rather than corporate identity. Its Swiss identity, which is the result of historical accident rather than original, fixed policy, has proven very fortunate, since it effectively preserves the overt neutrality which plays a vital role in securing the trust of parties to armed conflicts in the performance of its humanitarian functions. The Swiss Federation is constitutionally neutral, although legally and practically well prepared to defend itself if Switzerland were ever to be attacked. Such a situation would cause much difficulty for the ICRC, but fortunately, it may be considered extremely unlikely – Switzerland was not attacked by either side, even during the Second World War. The ICRC also jealously guards its independence from all national governments, including that of Switzerland.

The committee itself has a maximum membership of 25, which meets as an Assembly approximately eight times per year, and acts, in effect, as a general board of management, formulating general policy and maintaining an overview of action undertaken by the ICRC. Supervisory administration of ICRC activities is undertaken by an Executive Board with a maximum membership of seven, chaired by the President of the ICRC. Administration in detail is conducted through a tripartite Directorate dealing with General Affairs, Operational Activities and Administrative Affairs. The ICRC has a large operational and administrative staff based at the ICRC Headquarters in Geneva.

The funding of the ICRC comes from three principal sources: contributions from the various national Red Cross and Red Crescent societies, from governments of states party to the 1949 Geneva Conventions,[8] and from public collections and private benefactions. The ICRC will also make international appeals for support for specific relief operations where this seems necessary and appropriate.

The functions of the ICRC cover a broad spectrum of activity, but the central concern is implementing and maintaining humanitarian provision in armed conflict. Article VI of the Statutes of the International Red Cross provides with regard to the ICRC, *inter alia*, that:

> (4) It undertakes the tasks incumbent on it under the Geneva Conventions, works for the faithful application of these Conventions and takes cognizance of complaints regarding alleged breaches of the humanitarian Conventions.
> (5) As a neutral institution whose humanitarian work is carried out particularly in time of war, civil war or internal strife, it endeavours at all times to ensure the protection of and assistance to military and civilian victims of such conflicts and of their direct results. It contributes to the preparation and development of medical personnel and medical equipment, in co-operation with the Red Cross organisations, the medical services of the armed forces, and other competent authorities.
> (6) It takes any humanitarian initiative which comes within its role as a specifically neutral and independent institution and intermediary and considers any question requiring examination by such an institution.

This remit combines the functions of supervision, neutral intermediation and provision of relief.

Supervision and intermediation are distinct functions, but in practice overlap to a significant degree. In principle, parties to an armed conflict will appoint 'Protecting Powers': neutral governments which are willing to oversee the interests of the appointing power under the Geneva Conventions and Protocols, where relevant. In reality, it is very rare for Protecting Powers to be appointed, the 1982 Anglo-Argentine Falklands Conflict being an exception in which the United

Kingdom appointed Switzerland, and Argentina appointed Brazil. Where no Protecting Power is appointed, 1949 Geneva Convention III, article 10, and 1949 Geneva Convention IV, article 11, each provide that:

> The High Contracting Parties may at any time agree to entrust to an organization which offers all guarantees of impartiality and efficacy the duties incumbent on the Protecting Powers by virtue of the present Convention.

In practice, the organisation thus entrusted is invariably the ICRC. This point is expressly made by the equivalent provision in 1977 Additional Protocol I, article 5(4), which provides that:

> If ... there is no Protecting Power, the Parties to the conflict shall accept without delay an offer which may be made by the International Committee of the Red Cross or by any other organization which offers all guarantees of impartiality and efficacy, after due consultations with the said Parties and taking into account the result of these consultations, to act as a substitute.

It will be noted that the 1977 provision is mandatory in tone, in contrast with the permissive phrasing of the 1949 provision, subject to the obvious necessity for consultation. Even if the tasks of a Protecting Power are not undertaken, the ICRC will still play a large role in securing humanitarian observance in an armed conflict. 1949 Geneva Convention III, article 9, and 1949 Geneva Convention IV, article 10, provide that:

> The provisions of the present Convention constitute no obstacle to the humanitarian activities which the International Committee of the Red Cross or any other impartial humanitarian organization may, subject to the consent of the Parties to the conflict concerned, undertake for the protection of [prisoners of war or civilian persons] and for their relief.

The supervisory work of the ICRC during armed conflicts involves visiting prisoners of war, civilian internees and occupied territories to monitor and encourage the proper implementation of international humanitarian norms. This work is performed by ICRC Delegates. Delegates may be specialists engaged, for example, in medical relief work, but their general functions include visiting prisoners of war and internees in order to inspect their conditions of detention. In doing this, they will also conduct 'interviews without witnesses', which enable the people interviewed to speak more freely than might otherwise be the case, and which may bring to light abuses which would otherwise remain hidden. The right of visitation and interview without witnesses is guaranteed by 1949 Geneva Convention III, article 126, and 1949 Geneva Convention IV, article 143, subject only to 'imperative military necessity'.[9] The work of ICRC Delegates is both important and sensitive, and the Delegates are frequently placed at considerable risk. On 17 December 1996, six ICRC Delegates working in the Red Cross hospital at Novye Atagi in Chechnya were murdered by masked gunmen.[10] On 7 May 1997, ten Zairian Red Cross volunteers were killed at Kenge in Zaire. As was stated at the time:

> This ... highlights the fact that death does not discriminate among Red Cross and Red Crescent workers. Volunteers from National Societies, expatriate (international) Red Cross delegates and locally hired staff are equally vulnerable when violence strikes those who bring aid.[11]

Because ICRC Delegates may discover outrages and abuses which the perpetrators would wish to conceal, they are clearly at risk, as are other staff who assist them. Their only real protection lies in the fact that a receiving state in conflict knows that it, like its enemy, needs the humanitarian aid of the ICRC, and in this there is an implicit reciprocity of acceptance, even though reciprocity is not in a formal sense any part of the principle and operation of international humanitarian law;[12] furthermore, molestation of ICRC Delegates will drawn odium upon the responsible state or organisation, to the detriment of its conduct of general international relations.

If ICRC Delegates discover abuses or infractions of international humanitarian law in the course of their duties, they will first urge the responsible authorities to comply with the humanitarian norms in question, and report the matter to the ICRC in Geneva. The International Committee will then make a confidential report to the defaulting authority, similarly urging it to comply. The ICRC only very rarely issues public denunciations. Examples may be seen in the denunciations of chemical warfare issued in the First World War and in the 1980–88 Gulf War, and of the conditions in internment camps in the conflicts in former Yugoslavia in the 1990s. Even then, delinquent states are not identified, and the complaint is phrased in carefully neutral language, to the effect that belligerents in general are urged to desist from a particular objectionable practice. This approach of quiet diplomacy has on occasion led to misunderstandings with more confrontational organisations such as Amnesty International, but the difference is essentially one of approach so far as humanity in warfare is concerned. The ICRC is properly concerned that its role as a neutral intermediary, enabling it to maintain access to the victims whose protection it seeks to advance and facilitate and to urge full compliance with humanitarian law, should be preserved, and not compromised or destroyed by the adoption of an adversarial posture. This approach has over the years achieved many notable successes, as well as meeting with some inevitable failures.[13]

In the late 1990s, the ICRC has faced criticism over its silence regarding the Nazi concentration camps in the 1940s. Some have even alleged Nazi penetration of the organisation during that period. A detailed investigation was undertaken by the ICRC, and only one case of illicit activity by a delegate was sustained by the investigators, and in that case the ICRC severed its contact with the wrongdoer as soon as it became known that he was behaving improperly.[14] More relevantly, in October 1997, documentation which the ICRC released to the Yad Vashem Holocaust Memorial in Jerusalem shows that some Delegates were readily duped about conditions in the camps, and others seem to have been extraordinarily unsuspicious when denied access to sections of them. The desire to retain maximum contact with prisoners and detainees in the Third Reich, which might readily have been cut off, is understandable in terms of the ICRC's function but failure to speak out – even in non-specific but contextually obvious terms, as has been done before and after the Second World War – was unjustifiable, as is now accepted.[15] A contrast may be made with the ICRC's constructive and proper response to the conditions discovered in internment camps during the armed conflicts in former Yugoslavia in the 1990s.

The maintenance of neutrality in the context of actual or alleged abuses may raise delicate questions about the response of other organisations, such as the United Nations. For example, it is possible that an ICRC Delegate might witness events in relation to which his or her evidence at a subsequent war crimes trial might be useful. In the immediate context, a strong case may be made out that the Delegate should be required to give such evidence. In the longer term, the idea that Delegates would do so could well serve to restrict their access to victims of armed conflict, to their severe detriment. It has been remarked elsewhere that:

> [ICRC delegates'] effectiveness depends to a significant degree on observance of the basic principles of Impartiality and Neutrality in relations with the parties engaged in conflict. That might obviously be put in danger if they came to be regarded as playing an adversarial role. For this reason, requiring evidence from [them] ... could be counter-productive.[16]

In practice, the extent to which ICRC personnel would be given practical immunity from giving evidence might vary; certainly, no such formal privilege is granted in most national jurisdictions, but the ICRC itself, in conjunction with the states party to the 1949 Geneva Conventions, would probably be able to avert this matter arising as a practical problem.

The supervisory work of the ICRC also involves the highly significant services of its Central Tracing Agency (CTA). In practice, the CTA plays the role of the 'Central Prisoners of War Agency' provided for in article 123 of 1949 Geneva Convention III, and the 'Central Information Agency for Protected Persons' provided for in article 140 of 1949 Geneva IV. The CTA maintains, so far as possible, records of all persons captured, detained, killed or injured in armed conflict, and will pass on the information to their families, via the national authorities in their home countries. The CTA will also transmit messages to families of detainees and other missing persons. Voluminous records are kept by the ICRC in Geneva, and even in the 1980s and 1990s, enquiries are still received about people with whom their families lost contact in the Second World War. Each year, tens of thousands of enquiries and an even greater number of messages may be received or transmitted, obviously with some fluctuation in numbers according to the hostilities under way at any given time.

As a relief agency *stricto sensu*, the ICRC plays a major role in organising relief aid to victims of armed conflict. This includes the well-known supply of 'Red Cross parcels' to prisoners of war.[17] General relief work is carried out under the provisions admitting this work,[18] subject only to 'measures which the Detaining Powers may consider essential to ensure their security or to meet any other reasonable need'. The difficulties which may be encountered in delivering relief supplies were pointedly illustrated in the experience of the conflicts in former Yugoslavia in the 1990s. The Red Cross and other humanitarian relief organisations sent relief supply convoys to beleaguered enclaves, and these frequently came under attack from forces attached to other communities in former Yugoslavia. As a result, protection was supplied by UNPROFOR,[19] which was necessary, but in itself a further cause of the 'adversarial' situation which the relief organisations wanted to avoid. The resulting controversies led to ill feeling between UNPROFOR and some of the relief agencies. In November 1993, Médecins sans Frontières published a report, *Life, Death and Aid*, which virtually accused UNPROFOR of non-compliance with international humanitarian law, and of bargaining with the parties in conflict in order to secure the passage of relief convoys at the expense of the principles of impartiality.[20] It has been commented elsewhere that:

> The difficult implications of such bargaining are in principle obvious enough but, in the immediate circumstances, the practical alternatives might seem somewhat less clear.[21]

Such situations present profound difficulties of both principle and practice, no perfect solution is likely to be found, and *ad hoc* responses, however problematic, are probably the best that may reasonably be hoped for.

In aiding victims of armed conflict the ICRC is not limited to the specific matters considered above, as article VI(6) of the Statutes of the International Red Cross makes clear.[22] The need to provide humanitarian aid to prisoners of war, internees, displaced persons and refugees[23] will often continue for some considerable time after the cessation of hostilities.[24] Work with refugees is also beset by particular difficulties which are inevitable in the context of post-conflict confusion. Some of these, in the especially problematic aftermath of the Second World War, are illustrated by the Klaus Barbie affair. Barbie, a German SS officer, was accused of having committed serious crimes in Lyons during the occupation of France, in particular of being involved in a massacre at an orphanage. He left Germany after the war with papers under the false name of Klaus Altmann, issued by the Allied Forces High Commission in Munich. He was then issued with ICRC travel documents in that name, and travelled under their protection, as a displaced person, to South America. Such travel documents are issued to people who have no passport but who do have valid departure and entry papers for the countries between which they are in transit. These facts emerged after Barbie's arrest and return to France for trial in 1987, and allegations were then made of ICRC 'connivance' in his original escape. To counter these damaging allegations, the ICRC issued a statement which, very reasonably, argued that in the year of his departure to South America, the ICRC issued 2,259 travel documents to the many refugees applying for them, and:

> It was impossible for ICRC delegates to verify the statements of those applying for travel documents. The ICRC believes that certain risks had to be accepted in the interests of the vast majority.[25]

In these circumstances, it must seem reasonable that the ICRC relied upon the erroneous papers issued, by similar accident, by the Allied military authorities in Munich.

The ICRC has general responsibilities for maintaining the fundamental principle of the Red Cross movement, including, in particular, impartiality of action, the universality of the Red Cross and the equality of national Red Cross and Red Crescent societies,[26] recognition of new national societies which fulfil the requisite conditions,[27] and improvement and dissemination of international humanitarian law.[28] The work of dissemination, in association with national Red Cross and Red Crescent societies, is of very great importance, and is considered in Chapter 3. It may be added that the *International Review of the Red Cross,* to which frequent reference is made in this book, is itself a valuable instrument of dissemination. In 1996, the ICRC also set up an Advisory Service on national implementation of international humanitarian law, with the aim of assisting and encouraging states to implement and disseminate knowledge of international humanitarian law.[29] The ICRC also plays a significant role in co-ordinating civil disaster relief by the international Red Cross organisation, along with the Federation of Red Cross and Red Crescent Societies.

More recently, and especially in the 1990s, the ICRC has begun to play a much greater role in public advocacy. Its campaign for a complete ban on landmines in the context of the Review Commission of the 1980 UN Conventional Weapons Convention has been a prominent example.[30] There is obviously a strong case to be made for this type of advocacy in some cases, subject always to the imperative caveat that impartiality must not thereby be compromised. More traditionally, the ICRC plays a very important direct role in the development of international humanitarian law by proposing ideas and presenting drafts for consideration by the International Red Cross Conference.[31]

The Federation of Red Cross and Red Crescent Societies

The Federation of Red Cross and Red Crescent Societies (formerly known as the League of Red Cross and Red Crescent Societies) was established in 1919 to assist national societies in developing their community services, to co-ordinate and direct international disaster relief, and to assist refuges outside zones of armed conflict, including developing national disaster preparedness planning, and encouraging the establishment of new national societies where none have formally existed.[32] It has an Assembly and an Executive Council, and the membership of the federation comprises the recognised national societies.

In the context of disaster relief, the role of the federation as a directing and co-ordinating body is of self-evident importance: to take a hypothetical example, if in the case of a natural disaster both food and medical relief are required, it is obviously not desirable that all the contributing national societies should offer medical supplies or assistance and none of them contribute food relief. The federation may also play an important role in ensuring the *suitability* of the relief offered, in both practical and cultural terms.

In circumstances of armed conflict, rather difficult legal questions could potentially arise, and this matter is therefore the subject of an agreement between the ICRC and the federation signed on 25 April

1969. Article 2 of this agreement deals with 'Red Cross Action in the Event of a Conflict', and provides, *inter alia*, that:

> In countries where there is an international war, civil war, blockade or military occupation, the ICRC, by virtue of the functions of a neutral intermediary devolving on it ... shall assume the general direction of the Red Cross international action.
>
> If ... as a result of special circumstances or in the event of a natural disaster, the [Federation] is, at the request of a National Society, called upon to give assistance to the civilian population ... the ways and means of the intervention of the [Federation] ... shall be defined from case to case ...
>
> When the intervention of a neutral intermediary is not or is no longer necessary, the ICRC shall reach agreement with the [federation] with a view to associating it with the relief action or even handing over to it the entire responsibility.

The importance of agreement on this point will be self-evident. In essence, the federation will not play a role in the direction of humanitarian activity in armed conflict, although it can and will play a part in co-ordinating relief efforts by neutral national societies. In peacetime, the federation can and does play a positive part in supporting national societies' endeavours to disseminate international humanitarian law and principles.

National Red Cross and Red Crescent Societies

National Red Cross and Red Crescent societies were established with the primary purpose of supplementing military medical services in the event of armed conflict, and this remains their essential purpose today. Of course, national societies perform many other functions, not least all the very valuable first aid work and general support services with which the Red Cross is especially associated in the general public perception. However, this has resulted from the fact that a society set up to assist the victims of war has a body of skilled personnel and useful resources which it would be bizarre to keep inactive unless and until the particular tragedy – armed conflict – with which it was originally designed to deal occurs.

In armed conflict, the national Red Cross or Red Crescent societies of the parties to the conflict perform a wide range of humanitarian duties, which are referred to in Chapters 4 and 5. The combined general functions of the national societies are set out in detail in the Principles of the Red Cross, and include the dissemination of humanitarian ideas, the practical alleviation of suffering and, if war should break out, 'lessening the distress caused by the war', in particular by working to improve the conditions of the wounded, sick and/or shipwrecked, prisoners of war and civilians, such work supplementing government provision, in agreement with the defence, health and other relevant authorities.[33]

National societies play an important role in disseminating humanitarian principles, and have also begun to play an important part in public campaigns for the development of humanitarian law, including urging the ratification of relevant treaty provisions in their own state, and campaigning actively for further development. The involvement of national societies in the campaign for a complete ban upon landmines in the 1990s is a clear example of this field of activity.

As for the ICRC,[34] national societies can play a most positive role here, but must also consider their approach with great care in order to avoid confrontational or apparently 'politicised' activities which could compromise the performance of their fundamental purposes. A move towards more public advocacy, in contrast with the tradition of 'discreet diplomacy', requires very delicate judgement in this context. As Michael Meyer remarks:

> The International Red Cross and Red Crescent Movement has a reputation for neutral and impartial humanitarianism, earned through its long record of distinguished service and strict adherence to its principles. Regardless of the formal legal position, components of the Movement are often only able to act because of the confidence they inspire. Public advocacy, unless carefully considered and executed, will put this in jeopardy and ultimately will lead to the Red Cross and Red Crescent, including the ICRC, being treated as just another non-governmental organization.[35]

Of course, this is not to say that national societies, or indeed the ICRC, should not engage in public advocacy, merely that very careful judgement must be exercised in determining the method and tone of doing so, in order to protect the movement's position and efficacy.

The International Red Cross Conference

These conferences play a very important part in the development of international humanitarian law. The International Conference of the Red Cross normally meets every four years, although this date may be advanced in case of need, and provides the essential interface between the institutional elements of the international Red Cross movement. According to article 1 of the Rules of Procedure of the International Conference of the Red Cross, the members with participatory and voting rights are:

- delegates of recognised national societies
- delegates of states party to the Geneva Convention for the Amelioration of the Condition of the Wounded and Sick in Armed Forces in the Field[36]
- delegates of the ICRC and the Federation of Red Cross and Red Crescent Societies.

The agenda is determined by a Council of Delegates, including matters referred to it by the Standing Commission set up under article IX of the Statutes of the International Red Cross. The matters to be considered by the conference may include proposed additions or amendments to humanitarian treaty provision. The processes which ultimately led to the two 1977 Additional Protocols was initiated by a resolution adopted by the XXI International Conference of the Red Cross in Istanbul in 1969.

The UN High Commissioner for Refugees

The United Nations High Commissioner for Refugees (UNHCR) derives ultimately from the High Commissioner for Refugees established by the League of Nations in 1921, and the post was established in its present form in 1951. The functions of the UNHCR are stated in its Statute, in the 1951 Convention of Refugees, and in the 1967 Protocol on Refugees. The general functions are set out in paragraph 1 of the UNHCR Statute:

> The United Nations High Commissioner for Refugees ... shall assume the function of providing international protection, under the auspices of the United Nations, to refugees ... and of seeking permanent solutions for the problem of refugees by assisting Governments and, subject to the approval of the Governments concerned, private organizations to facilitate the voluntary repatriation of such refugees, or their assimilation within new national communities.

Article 8 of the Statute then sets out nine specific ways in which the UNHCR is required to make provision for refugees:

1. promotion of international treaties for the protection of refugees
2. promotion of measures to ameliorate their condition through special agreements with governments
3. assisting governmental and private efforts to promote voluntary repatriation or assimilation
4. promoting admission of refugees
5. securing permission for transfer of assets

6 gathering information from governments regarding numbers of refugees
7 liaising with governments and relevant inter-governmental agencies
8 maintaining contact with private organisations active in refugee protection
9 facilitating co-ordination in the activities of such organisations.

There have been large movements of refugees in the years following the Second World War – many, but by no means all, occasioned by the exigencies of armed conflict. The upheavals in Afghanistan, Iraq, Somalia, Haiti and former Yugoslavia may be cited as examples in the later 20th century. In all these situations, the UNHCR has played a vital role in the settlement or resettlement of refugees, often in the face of resistance from states.

Other Humanitarian Organisations

Many other organisations engage in humanitarian activity directly or indirectly associated with the problems of armed conflict, including specifically medical relief organisations, such as the French Médecins sans Frontières, which has done notable work in many modern conflicts, and organisations such as Oxfam, which are engaged in general relief and assistance in the broadest range of human disasters. Amnesty International, an organisation dedicated to campaigning for the release of non-violent political prisoners, is not directly concerned with armed conflict as such, but may obviously become involved with persons whose penal incarceration results from such conflict.

Finally, but by no means least, there are the various educative and disseminatory institutions which are directly concerned with international humanitarian law. These include the International Institute of Humanitarian Law at San Remo, and the Henry Dunant Institute at Geneva, both of which are considered in Chapter 3.

Notes

1 J. Austin, *The Province of Jurisprudence Determined* (1832), Lecture V (Weidenfeld and Nicolson, 1954), at p. 187.
2 For discussion, see D.J. Harris, *Cases and Materials on International Law* (4th edn) (Sweet and Maxwell, 1991), pp. 1–17; see also H. McCoubrey and N.D. White, *Textbook on Jurisprudence* (2nd edn) (Blackstone, 1996), pp. 26–8.
3 These are three of the principal formal sources of international law recognised by article 38 of the Statute of the International Court of Justice. The Statute also recognises general principles of law recognised by civilised nations, but this is

now a very limited source whose essential substance has entered international humanitarian law by other means, notably in the context of requirements of due process.
4 See pp. 16–17.
5 See Chapter 8.
6 See p. 17.
7 See Chapter 1.
8 The largest proportion of this element comes from Switzerland.
9 For discussion of 'military necessity', see below.
10 For response to this tragedy, see commentaries in (1997) 37 *International Review of the Red Cross*, at pp. 311–23.
11 Ibid., p. 311.
12 See Chapter 1.
13 For an interesting account of the work of ICRC Delegates, see M. Junod, *Warrior Without Weapons* (ICRC, 1984).
14 See ICRC Press Division, 'ICRC Activities During the Second World War' (1996) 36 *International Review of the Red Cross*, pp. 562–7.
15 See *Daily Telegraph* (London), 19 October 1997.
16 F. Hampson and H. McCoubrey, 'Evidence in Cases Involving Proliferation Issues', in J. Dahlitz (ed.), *Arms Control and Disarmament Law, Vol. III: Future Legal Restraints on Arms Proliferation* (United Nations, 1996), p. 273, at p. 292.
17 See 1949 Geneva Convention III, article 125, and 1949 Geneva Convention IV, article 142.
18 Ibid.
19 The United Nations force in former Yugoslavia.
20 See *Independent* (London), 23 November 1993.
21 H. McCoubrey and N.D. White, *International Organizations and Civil Wars* (Dartmouth, 1995) p. 131.
22 See above.
23 For discussion of this, see J. Lavoyer, 'Refugees and Internally Displaced Persons: International Humanitarian Law and the Role of the ICRC' (1995) 35 *International Review of the Red Cross*, pp. 162–80.
24 For general discussion of the work of the ICRC since 1945, see F. Bugnion, 'From the End of the Second World War to the Dawn of the Third Millennium – The Activities of the International Committee of the Red Cross during the Cold War and its Aftermath: 1945–1995' (1995) 35 *International Review of the Red Cross*, pp. 192–224.
25 International Committee of the Red Cross Press Release 1539, 5 May 1987.
26 Statutes of the International Red Cross, article VI(2).
27 Ibid., article VI(3).
28 Ibid., article VI(7).
29 See P. Berman, 'The ICRC's Advisory Service on International Humanitarian Law: The Challenge of National Implementation' (1996) 36 *International Review of the Red Cross*, pp. 338–47.
30 See Chapter 8.
31 See below
32 See the Constitution of the Federation of Red Cross and Red Crescent Societies, article 5.
33 Principles of the Red Cross, paras 2, 4 and 6.
34 See above.
35 M.A. Meyer, 'Public Advocacy: Why the Red Cross and Red Crescent Should Look Before it Leaps', (1996) 36 *International Review of the Red Cross*, p. 614 at p. 626. For an alternative view, see H. Haug, *Humanity for All: The International Red Cross and Crescent Movement* (Henry Dunant Institute/Paul Haupt Publish-

ers, 1993), pp. 461–4, reproduced without footnotes in H. Haug, op.cit., at pp. 627–30.

36 This refers to the conventions of 1864, 1906, 1929, or 1949 Geneva Convention I – in almost all, if not all, cases it is the latter which is now principally referred to.

3 Implementation of International Humanitarian Law

A number of questions arise in the context of the implementation of international humanitarian law, the most basic – at first sight, rather surprisingly – being the circumstances in which it is to be applied. The general answer to this is, of course, 'during armed conflicts'. Unfortunately, the definition and categorisation of levels of armed conflict have in the past caused some difficulty, and the specification of clear criteria of application has not been easy to achieve. Even now there remain some peripheral areas of debate in this context, although the basic issue appears to have been resolved satisfactorily.

Assuming satisfactory criteria of identification and application, the broader issues of practical implementation need to be considered. The implementation and enforcement of law are often seen as essentially coterminous processes, and it is true that the two do to a degree overlap, in the sense that both are ultimately concerned with the maintenance of legal norms. Nevertheless, a major distinction must be drawn between the two processes.

Enforcement is, by definition, a retrospective response to the violation of norms, which therefore presupposes failure in the primary endeavour of legal prescription to establish and maintain whatever normative standards may be in question. All law may fail in its primary purpose in given situations, and in such cases *enforcement* may well be an appropriate response. This is as much true for international humanitarian law as for any other areas of law, and the relevant national and international legal processes are considered below.[1]

The processes of implementation – meaning measures to ensure the observance of law in prospect, rather than penalisation of violations – are important for all law, however, and by no means least for international humanitarian law. To secure the effective application of the law is far more beneficial for actual and potential victims of armed conflict than to punish war criminals after 'unnecessary suffering' and atrocities have been inflicted. This point was emphasised in a lecture given by the late Professor-Colonel G.I.A.D. Draper at the Hague Academy of International Law in 1979, in which he stressed that proper training in the armed forces in particular is a prerequisite for the effective operation of the 1949 Geneva Conventions in armed conflict.[2] Training and discipline within the armed forces of nations engaged in an armed conflict self-evidently constitute a *sine qua non* for the practical operation of international humanitarian law, but there is also a case to be made for a much wider programme of dissemination. This may be thought to be especially the case at present, in view of the commonplace denigration and widespread ignorance of the laws of armed conflict by modern journalists, and even by some specialist writers on the subject of war.

Criteria of Application

That the laws of armed conflict are to be applied in armed conflicts might seem too obvious a proposition to require statement. The criteria of application of the international humanitarian laws of armed conflict have nevertheless, at various times, proved to be problematic, largely concerning the technical meaning of the term 'war'. The *Oxford Reference Dictionary* defines 'war' as, *inter alia*:

> strife (especially between countries) involving military, naval or air attacks; the period of this.[3]

This would seem a reasonable and factual definition for most purposes, but the term has unfortunately become bound up in legal technicalities of definition which have rendered it increasingly less suitable as a criterion for the application of international humanitarian law.

The difficulties flow from the fact that as a matter of international law, 'war' has come to be interpreted as a *declared* state of international relations, and most military hostilities have not been subject to declaration. In modern circumstances it is highly unlikely that they ever would be, granted that the current *jus ad bellum*, as founded upon articles 2(3)(4) and Chapter VII of the United Nations Charter, clearly provides that war, and indeed armed conflict, are not a lawful condition of international relations as distinct from a defensive use of force in response to aggression or under the direction of the United Nations Security Council. Any modern state which chose to take the formal step of 'declaring war' would risk presenting itself as the aggressor, and this is therefore most unlikely to happen.

The difficulties of definition potentially generated by 'undeclared wars' may readily be illustrated by reference to English municipal case experience. In litigation in the United Kingdom, the state of international relations is a matter in which in general, although not invariably, the courts rely upon certification from the Foreign Office. McNair and Watts remark pertinently that:

> ... in many cases the view of the Executive is not sought or, if sought, is temporizing. The Courts must then proceed as best they can to determine whether or not a state of war exists between two foreign States, and it may be assumed that they will not be unmindful of the rules of international law in this matter.[4]

The leading English case in this area is *Kawasaki Kisen Kabushiki Kaisha* v. *Bantham Steamship Company*,[5] in which a British company had hired one of its ships, the *Nailsea Meadow*, to a Japanese company on a charterparty, subject to a cancellation clause activated 'if war breaks out involving Japan'.[6] The Japanese invasion of Manchuria in 1937 was clearly an outbreak of international hostilities, but neither side formally declared 'war'. When the British company sought to cancel the charterparty under the 'war' cancellation clause, the Japanese company claimed that there was no 'war', that the cancellation was therefore unlawful, and upon this basis sought an award of damages. The opinion of the British Foreign Office regarding the condition of Sino-Japanese relations was that:

> the current situation in China is indeterminate and anomalous and His Majesty's Government are not at present prepared to say that in their view a state of war exists.[7]

This equivocal view followed precisely from the fact that no 'war' had been declared. Fortunately for the practical determination of the case, the Foreign Office went on to state:

> the meaning to be attached to the term war as used in a charterparty may simply be one of interpreting the relevant clause, and the attitude of His Majesty's Government may not necessarily be conclusive [as to] ... the meaning of the term 'war' as used in particular documents or statutes.[8]

Both the court of first instance and the Court of Appeal chose to interpret the charterparty in the light of the apparent intention of the parties, concluding that the essence of the matter lay in the likelihood of the ship being placed at risk in hostilities, and therefore declared the charterparty to have been properly cancelled.

This decision may readily be contended to have followed the commonsense implications of the commercial document under consideration, but it may readily be appreciated that the application of humanitarian laws in the fraught exigencies of armed hostilities allows no leisure for technical debate about the meaning of 'war' as a term of art. The point arose directly in the early stages of the 1982 Anglo-Argentine Falklands Conflict, when on 26 April 1982, Sir Bernard Braine MP asked the then British Prime Minister, Margaret Thatcher, in the House of Commons about arrangements for the eventual repatriation of Argentine prisoners of war. The Prime Minister replied:

> They are not prisoners of war. A state of war does not exist between ourselves and the Argentine. They are prisoners and they will be repatriated as soon as possible.[9]

The implications of this were alarming. If captured Argentine military personnel were not 'prisoners of war', what sort of prisoners were they, and what legal rules applied to them? By the same token, what would be the status of any British military personnel in Argentine hands? The Prime Minister was quite right in stating that there was no technical state of 'war' between the United Kingdom and Argentina, and utterly wrong in concluding that captured enemy personnel were therefore not 'prisoners of war'. This dangerous mistake was quickly corrected by a Ministry of Defence statement confirming that captured Argentine military personnel were indeed entitled to prisoner of war status and enjoyed the protection of 1949 Geneva Convention III.[10] A much more serious instance of this type occurred during the 1950–53 Korean War, during which, upon the basis that no technical 'war' existed in Korea, China refused to accord captured USAF pilots prisoner of war status, and treated them instead as 'spies' – an attitude expressly condemned in UN General Assembly Resolution 906(ix) of 1954. In the light of these potential and actual difficulties of application, the use of the term 'war' as a criterion for the application of international humanitarian law has come to be seen as inadequate in modern practice and usage.

In fact, the terminology of 'war' as such is not necessarily found as a criterion of application even in some of the older international humanitarian treaties. 1907 Hague Convention IV, to which are annexed the highly significant Land Warfare Regulations,[11] states in its Preamble:

> ... while seeking means to preserve peace and prevent armed conflict between nations, it is likewise necessary to bear in mind the case where the appeal to arms has been brought about by events which their care was unable to avert; [a]nimated by the desire to serve, even in this extreme case, the interests of humanity ... the High Contracting Parties ... have agreed upon the following: ...

It will be noted that the reference here is actually to *armed conflict*, and not to *war*, even though the annexed Regulations are termed the Land *Warfare* Regulations. It may be added that the 1904–5 Russo-Japanese War was not at its outset a declared 'war', but at no time in its course was the applicability of the prevailing laws of armed conflict called into doubt.

In an effort to avoid all doubt, the criteria for application of the four 1949 Geneva Conventions are set out in somewhat convoluted form in common article 2 to the conventions as follows:

> In addition to the provisions which shall be implemented in peacetime, the present Convention[s] shall apply to all cases of declared war or of any other armed conflict which may arise between two or more of the High Contracting Parties, even if the state of war is not recognized by one of them.

This phrasing refers both to declared war and to (undeclared) armed conflict, and thus seeks to avoid the problems of technical usage referred to above. However, it must be noted that, even so, the phrasing is less than fortunate, because it refers to armed conflict 'even if the state of war is not recognized by one of [the parties]', which seems to imply that it must be recognised as 'war' by at least one of the others. This is manifestly not the intention which informs the conventions, but the point was pursued by the Netherlands in the 1950s in the conflict between the Netherlands and Indonesia over (now) Irian Barat.[12] There is indeed good reason to think that this particular section of common article 2 is a product of misdrafting.[13] It is now accepted that armed conflict as a factual condition of hostilities is a sufficient trigger for the application of the humanitarian laws of armed conflict. As Christopher Greenwood remarks:

> Although the final phrase [of common article 2] does not deal expressly with the situation in which *neither* party to an armed conflict admits that it is in a state of war, it is generally believed that the Conventions were intended to apply in such a case, so that the last phrase of Art.2, para. 1 should be read as if it said 'even if the state of war is not recognized by one *or both* of them'. That is certainly the way in which it has been interpreted: in practice in most conflicts since 1949 neither side has admitted that it was in a state of war, yet they have treated the Geneva Conventions as applicable.[14]

Significantly, this phrasing is used by article 18 of the 1954 Hague Convention for the Protection of Cultural Property in the Event of Armed Conflict, dealing with the scope of the application of the convention.

State practice has clearly established the rational interpretation of the 1949 Geneva Conventions as applicable wherever international armed conflict, whether or not declared to be 'war', occurs. The question then arises of other and earlier treaties comprised within the body of international humanitarian law. The criteria of application formally stated by these treaties varied considerably; but, as in the instance of the 1904–5 Russo-Japanese War referred to above, the absence of a formally declared state of war was not in practice treated as an impediment to the application of the laws of such treaties. The end result is that the criterion for the application of the humanitarian *jus in bello* is not a formal declaration of war, but the factual occurrence of international armed conflict. As Christopher Greenwood has remarked:

> For the purposes of bringing into operation the rules regulating the conduct of hostilities, it no longer matters whether those hostilities are characterized as war. It is the factual concept of armed conflict rather than the technical concept of war which makes those rules applicable.[15]

This factual criterion obviously avoids most of the potentially dangerous ambiguities inherent in more technical criteria of application, such as the existence of a formal condition of 'war'. There are, nevertheless certain matters of observation which should be understood from the outset. Very clearly, any actual international hostilities will amount to a factual condition of armed conflict, to which the rules and principles of the humanitarian *jus in bello* will apply, but it must not be thought that this means that the law applies only when actual combat is in progress, with intermissions when it is not. Writing in 1954, at a time when the terminology of 'war' was still the conventional mode of discourse in this area, Erik Castren made the useful observation:

> We might say that war exists, first when such *armed activities* occur as are *intended* to constitute *war*, even though they may be carried out by only one party and, secondly, when either party takes measures which *only a belligerent is entitled* to take ...[16]

The first part of this formulation may usefully be termed as *animus belligerendi*. In almost all cases of hostile military activity, this can simply be presumed, but it may still afford useful guidance in rare cases of ambiguity. A historic instance may be seen in the carefully staged incidents on the German–Polish border in August 1939, including in particular a faked 'Polish attack', conducted by German personnel, upon the radio transmitter in the frontier town of Gleiwitz on 31 August, which Hitler used as a pretext for his invasion of Poland.[17] Border 'incidents' may result from many causes; in this particular case the *animus belligerendi* was unequivocal, and had any confrontation with Polish military or civilian personnel occurred in the course of the Gleiwitz 'incident', it must be taken that the laws of armed conflict would be held to have been applicable.

The second element in Castren's formulation refers simply to the fact of military action, but in its reference to belligerent 'measures', it is usefully broader than combat *stricto sensu*. To take examples from the 1980s and 1990s: after the Argentine invasion of the Falkland Islands in 1982, an interval elapsed before British forces arrived to retake the islands, during which there was a military occupation but no actual combat; the same point may be made in relation to the sequence of the Iraqi invasion and occupation of Kuwait in 1990 (without for a moment equating the conduct of the two occupations). There was an inevitable time lapse between the departure of the Emir and his government in the face of Iraqi attack and the arrival of the Coalition Forces in response. In each case, the condition of armed conflict was continuous, notwithstanding intervals of absence of actual combat, essentially because of the fact of 'belligerent measures' – measures for the maintenance of, or taken in preparation for, hostile military action.

If a description, rather than a 'definition', of armed conflict as a criterion for the application of the humanitarian *jus in bello* is sought, one advanced elsewhere may be found acceptable:

> International armed conflict involves resort by states to active and hostile military measures in the conduct of their international relations [for] ... the attainment of policy objectives or defence against the same, whether or not a state of 'war' is declared or recognized to exist.[18]

In most cases, the fact of hostile military action will hardly be a matter for debate, and the applicability of international humanitarian law should similarly be unequivocal, even where specious attempts are made to dispute it – as in the Iraqi claim that its occupation of Kuwait was not an 'occupation'.[19]

Somewhat more interesting questions arise in determining when the humanitarian laws of armed conflict cease to apply in a given situation. The termination of the application of the humanitarian *jus in bello* is at least as important a question as that of its commencement, and one in which unduly technical or obfuscatory criteria would be no less potentially dangerous. It is also a somewhat more complex question than that of commencement, because whilst the beginning of hostilities may in most cases be the subject of fairly ready factual observation, the ending of the effects of armed conflict calling for the regulation of the humanitarian *jus in bello* is not necessarily a simple 'event', nor one that necessarily occurs at the same time for all parts of the law.

A condition of armed conflict may be formally announced to have ended, or simply cease to continue. The ratification of a peace treaty clearly signals the formal end of conflict, although actual hostilities will usually have ended considerably before this. In the First World War, hostilities ended, following the acceptance by Germany of the Armistice, at 11.00 a.m. on 11 November 1918. The formal termination of the state of war waited until the ratification of the peace treaties between the Allies and the Central Powers considerably after this – a matter specifically provided for in the United Kingdom by the Termination of the Present War (Definition) Act 1918. The Second World War ended rather differently in the European and Far Eastern sectors: both the Third Reich and Japan signed instruments of unconditional surrender, and in the Far East a Peace Treaty with Japan was entered into; in Europe, however, the formal condition of war simply withered away. This was in part because there was no *Reich*-government (apart from the fatuous rump presided over by Grand Admiral Dönitz in a school classroom at Flensburg until the arrest of its members) with which the Allies could or would deal. In most armed conflicts since 1945, the conflict has ended with even less formality.

So far as the humanitarian *jus in bello* is concerned, the most useful formula may be be the one given elsewhere to the effect that:

> In general it may be suggested that the provisions of the *jus in bello* will remain applicable as long as the situation in contemplation of which they were made endures, and this may of course vary somewhat according to context.[20]

This point is made strongly by reference to the provisions for duration of application set out respectively by the four 1949 Geneva Conventions. Article 5 of 1949 Geneva Convention I relating to the wounded and sick in land warfare provides that:

> For the protected persons who have fallen into the hands of the enemy the present Convention shall apply until their final repatriation.

The second convention relating to the wounded, sick and/or shipwrecked at sea does not repeat article 5 of the first convention, but it would obviously apply throughout the period of the conditions set out by common article 2 – during the practical continuance of hostilities at sea – and so far as any enemy personnel on hospital ships were concerned, they would remain protected by the convention until they reached land, at which point article 5 of the first convention would become applicable.

The same basic principle is, not surprisingly, stated by article 5 of the third Geneva Convention relating to prisoners of war, which states in its first paragraph that:

> The present Convention shall apply to [prisoners of war] ... from the time they fall into the power of the enemy and until their final release and repatriation.

By the nature and range of the situations to be dealt with, somewhat more complex provision is set out for the termination of the application of 1949 Geneva Convention IV in relation to the protection of civilians by article 6 of the convention. It provides in relation to termination of application that:

> In the territory of Parties to the conflict, the application of the present Convention shall cease on the general close of military operations.
>
> In the case of occupied territory, the application of the present Convention shall cease one year after the general close of military operations; however, the Occupying Power shall be bound, for the duration of the occupation, to the extent that such Power exercises the functions of government in such territory, by the provisions of [specified] ... Articles of the present Convention ...
>
> Protected persons whose release, repatriation or re-establishment may take place after such dates shall meanwhile continue to benefit by the present Convention.

It may be noted that since 1928 and the conclusion of the Pact of Paris, or at the very latest 1945, conquest is not a legitimate means of acquiring territory in international law. This is the case even where a state asserts a legal claim to the territory in question, since article 2(3) of the United Nations Charter requires that states settle their disputes by peaceful means. The point was expressly affirmed by the 1970 UN General Assembly Declaration on Principles of International Law Concerning Friendly Relations and Co-operation Among States,[21] which provides, *inter alia*, that:

> The territory of a State shall not be the object of acquisition by another State resulting from the threat or use of force. No territorial acquisition resulting from the threat or use of force shall be recognised as legal.

In this respect, the resolution simply draws out the manifest implication of article 2(3)(4) of the Charter. Thus, in the 1990–91 Gulf Conflict, Iraq's dubious claim to the territory of Kuwait was in no way legitimised by the fact of Iraqi military occupation.[22] Lengthy 'occupation' may sometimes be retrospectively legitimised by international recognition, in effect curing an original defect in title, India's military seizure of Goa, formerly the last (Portuguese) colony on the subcontinent, in 1961 being one of the few examples. Unless and until that time, the occupation remains a *de facto* and *prima facie* unlawful, temporary regime. The references to extended occupation found in article 6 of 1949 Geneva Convention IV do not contradict this proposition by the formal limitation of application to one year following the close of hostilities. The point is rather that in such a long occupation, there is little to be gained by a perpetuation of the *jus in bello* regime as such, with certain major caveats covered by the excepted articles, but other limiting norms clearly remain in force.

The ultimate conclusion must be that the termination of application of the norms of international humanitarian law in a given conflict will be determined by factual criteria, as is the commencement of their application, but this will be a more complex and varied observation than the initial commencement of hostilities. In many respects, the primary criterion will be the end of hostilities, but in many other cases the criterion will simply be the end of the situation calling for humanitarian protection to which a treaty of provision refers, and this may be long after the end of hostilities.

Dissemination of International Humanitarian Law Principles

For any sector of law, municipal or international, effective dissemination of knowledge of its requirement is a prerequisite for its efficacy. A law which is not known will, *ex hypothesi*, not be obeyed. This rather obvious proposition is sometimes lost sight of in the light of the emphasis commonly placed upon *enforcement*, in the narrow sense of coercive imposition and penalisation of default, in discussions of the implementation and efficacy of law. It is certainly the case that enforcement has its importance,[23] not least in so far as a law which may routinely be flouted with utter impunity is in manifest danger of practical, if not theoretical, desuetude; however, an excessive emphasis on this factor is not necessarily positive in its implications. This aspect of argument may be especially noticeable in the common law tradition, which remains much influenced by a vastly oversimplified understanding of the early 19th-century sanctions-based analytical positivism advanced by Jeremy Bentham and John Austin,[24] but his emphasis is also found across the range of legal and jurisprudential traditions.

In reality, enforcement can only ever be a secondary office of law, although the fundamental purposes of law may be defined.[25] In the case of the international humanitarian laws of armed conflict, the primary purposes clearly include the mitigation of the effects of armed conflict, and the protection of its defined victims. Before any question of 'enforcement' arises, failure in one or both of those primary endeavours must be supposed. The capture and punishment of war criminals after war crimes have been committed may be both important and in itself beneficial as an example and deterrent, but the fact remains that the war crime has been committed, and the victims have not been protected. Better to disseminate and afford training so that violations are averted than to emphasise unduly the objective of punishing the perpetrators of serious breaches of the law. A medical analogy may be found in the suggested preference for preventive rather than curative medicine wherever possible. The point is put well by Frits Kalshoven in his comment that:

> Among the available methods [of implementation, dissemination] ... is probably the most promising one: at all events, all other methods, unless combined with instruction and education are doomed to failure. ... [How] could one expect that its rules [that is, those of international humanitarian law] will be respected and, for instance, a soldier will recognize as unlawful an order to kill prisoners of war or unarmed civilians, if adequate information has not been spread in advance and on the widest possible scale?[26]

The importance of this imperative is recognised both in the requirements of the 1949 Geneva Conventions and the 1977 Additional Protocols and in the practice of the international Red Cross movement.

The four 1949 Geneva Conventions expressly require states to engage in dissemination of international humanitarian legal norms and to make appropriate training provision, at the very least in their armed forces and, if possible, to a wider audience. Article 47 of 1949 Geneva Convention I relating to the wounded and sick in land warfare provides that:

> The High Contracting Parties undertake, in time of peace as in time of war, to disseminate the text of the present Convention as widely as possible in their respective countries, and, in particular, to include the study thereof in their programmes of military and, if possible, civil instruction, so that the principles thereof may become known to the entire population, in particular to the armed fighting forces, the medical personnel and chaplains.

This basic provision is common to all the four 1949 Conventions. It is repeated by 1949 Geneva Convention II, article 48, 1949 Geneva Convention III, article 127 (with an additional requirement that the text be made available to those with responsibility for prisoners of war), and 1949 Geneva Convention IV, article 144 (again with a requirement that the text be supplied to relevant authorities). The same provision is made by article 83(1) of 1977 Additional Protocol I. 1977 Additional Protocol II, making further provision for non-international armed conflicts, requires by article 19 simply: 'This Protocol shall be disseminated as widely as possible'.

The purport of these provisions, especially with regard to international armed conflicts, is obvious enough. The primary emphasis is on the provision of training to those most likely to be required to implement international humanitarian norms, in particular to members of the armed forces and military medical services. Inclusion in programmes of civilian education, such as university law courses, is suggested to be desirable, but much less of a priority.

The imperative of dissemination is not limited to the 1949 Geneva Conventions and the 1977 Additional Protocols. 1907 Hague Convention IV, to which is annexed the still highly significant Regulations Respecting Land Warfare, provides by article 1 that:

> The contracting Powers shall issue instructions to their armed land forces which shall be in conformity with the Regulations respecting the laws and customs of war on land, annexed to the present Convention.

Whilst there is a clear difference between 'instructions' in this sense of 'orders' and 'instruction' in the sense of 'education', such instructions can only be disseminatory in practical effect. Even where no specific requirement of dissemination is included in treaty provision, the obligations assumed by states in respect of the humanitarian *jus in bello* can in any event only be fulfilled through processes of military regulation and training. On this basis, it seems uncontroversial to suggest that, explicitly and implicitly, a duty is laid upon states to undertake appropriate dissemination and training amongst their armed forces and other personnel directly concerned.

From this flow two basic questions. First, to what extent and by whom is this requirement met? Second, what liabilities may arise where training is either inadequate or even contrary to the requirements of humanitarian norms?

It cannot be repeated too often that the primary responsibility for the maintenance of international humanitarian law is laid upon states, and this includes provision for dissemination and training. In many but by no means all national armed forces, training in *jus in bello* norms forms part of the regular programmes of military training. Self-evidently, this will be upon a 'need to know' basis.

Ordinary soldiers need to know what they are required or can in practice do upon the battlefield or in any other situations, such as guarding prisoners of war, which they may be likely to encounter. At this level, instruction can take the form of education in a set of rules, most of which are fairly obvious. This level of educated 'lay' knowledge of legal requirements, and prohibitions, is essential for the effective implementation of international humanitarian law in such matters as the immediate treatment of captured or surrendered enemy personnel, treatment of civilians, and use of weapons. These are matters where a soldier may well be required to make instant decisions which may have considerable legal significance and consequences. This is not to advocate a system of 'barrackroom lawyers', but to require an essential dimension of practical knowledge. Similar statements may be made about any area of law – a driver needs to have a practical working knowledge of road traffic law, and will not pass a driving test, or retain a licence for long, without it. At ascending levels of command responsibility, more detailed knowledge, and therefore training, will be required. Major-General A.P.V. Rogers remarks in this context that:

> Commanders and staff officers require manuals which are written in clear straightforward and non-legal language, [in some cases with explanatory examples] ... [j]unior officers probably need a pamphlet explaining the basic principles of the laws of war. Soldiers and junior non-commissioned officers do not need a manual at all, a brief summary being all that is required. Rules of engagement cards may well suffice.[27]

At the higher levels of command, at which general objectives and decisions about policy regarding methods and means of warfare will be made, professional legal advice will become both possible and necessary. 1977 Additional Protocol I requires by article 82 that:

> The High Contracting Parties at all times, and the Parties to the conflict in time of armed conflict, shall ensure that legal advisers are available, when necessary, to advise military commanders at the appropriate level on the application of the Conventions and this Protocol and on the appropriate instruction to be given to the armed forces on this subject.

The role and availability of military legal advisers is vital in securing the implementation of international humanitarian law. This work clearly involves giving advice on the legality or otherwise of proposed action when that is sought, and on the detailed application and interpretation of law. As G.F. Walgemoed has remarked:

> From the earliest stage onwards the law of war should be included in the estimate of a situation. Only then can a sound, integrated planning process come to fruition.[28]

This function is evidently essential if the the conduct of armed conflict is to be correctly legally informed.

There is also, another proactive role, however. One of most important roles of any institutional legal adviser – whether one is speaking of central or local government, companies, charities, universities or, in this case, the armed forces – is to point out legal problems which may not have been recognised by other personnel, not least on the basis that the worst legal problems are almost always those that were detected too late for effective corrective action. This point is, again, made by Major-General Rogers in his remark that:

> The legal adviser must also be pro-active. Legal problems may not be recognized by commanders and their staff. ... Here the legal adviser can perform a useful function by briefing commanders about likely pitfalls and in advising them on procedures to be adopted to ensure compliance with the law.[29]

Thus a headquarters of any significance should have access to the advice of a military lawyer, usually a specialist career officer, for legal guidance in order to avoid error and the inadvertent commission of war crimes.[30]

The model so far set out is essentially one for armies; the needs of navies and air forces are obviously parallel in nature, but each of these services also has its own distinct requirements in terms of legal training and advice. The legal training requirements of 'lay' officers and ratings in a navy are not essentially different from those of other branches of armed forces, but the availability of legal advice in the context of naval operations raises rather more complex questions. In many cases, naval units are likely to be very much more remote from central control than army and air force units, and are also likely to encounter significant international legal problems, not only in combat, but in such matters as rights of search and seizure, and even potentially, in peacetime, such questions as 'hot pursuit'. One solution to this is for naval officers who are suitably qualified upon entry to the service to be put through appropriate legal training; they will then have a sufficient base of legal skill to ensure that, in normal service, ships at sea should be within range of informed advice even if they do not have a legally trained officer on board. This is the type of approach adopted by a number of navies, including the British Royal Navy, and clearly represents a practical approach to the difficulties of widely scattered operational roles in this context. At higher command levels, navies will require specialist legal advisers in exactly the same manner as other armed forces.

Air forces represent, to some extent, the opposite end of the spectrum from navies regarding legal advice requirements. Air force personnel are unlikely to encounter much in the way of personal decision-making relevant to international humanitarian law, except in the case of relatively rare requirements of individual target selection, which should obviously form a part of basic training. They might also conceivably find themselves assigned to guard duty at prisoner of war camps, in which case training in the relevant legal requirements would self-evidently be necessary. By and large, however, the legal issues confronting air forces will be at the level of target pre-selection and weapons use, and here the specialist headquarters staff lawyer has an obvious and vitally important role to play.

Dissemination to the Mass Media

The media can have an enormous impact on attitudes to the conduct of armed conflict, and indeed, to the idea of armed conflict itself. As Alain Modoux has remarked:

> public opinion, conditioned by the media, is an excellent means of bringing pressure to bear on belligerents and is capable of favourably modifying the attitude of combatants to victims protected by humanitarian law.[31]

The media's role, both in the past and at present, has been highly variable in intent and effect. An early example can be seen in the reporting of William Howard Russell from the Crimean War to *The Times* of London. Russell's revelations of the appalling state and organisation of army service in that war led to his being regarded by some establishment figures, such as Prince Albert, as a 'traitor', but also served to alert public opinion to the need for the extensive military reforms which followed after the war.[32] Paradoxically, however, Russell's concerns were not originally by any means humanitarian: on the contrary, *The Times* had been an enthusiastic advocate of the wholly pointless Crimean conflict, and his fear had been that 'their' war might not be run to best advantage. The vast power of the modern press is clearly illustrated by its much discussed role in the Vietnam War, when the scenes of carnage beamed daily into the living rooms of the USA are argued to have had a significant effect in hastening US withdrawal from the conflict.

In assessing the effect of reporting of armed conflict in the press, there are a number of potentially conflicting factors to be taken into account. On the one hand there is the proper balance to be drawn between military security and public information. Clearly, soldiers' lives and national defence are far more important than the scale of newspaper profits or television channel ratings. At the same time, the blanket of 'security' should not be used as a means of covering up matters which are of genuine public concern: these issues of public and political accountability fall within the areas of constitutional, administrative and media law rather than international humanitarian law *stricto sensu*. Of direct humanitarian concern, however, are the issues on the one hand of mode and volume of coverage, and on the other of the degree to which coverage is well informed.

The quality of reporting of war and armed conflicts is very uneven. The British press in the 1982 Falklands Conflict varied between a bellicose 'wargames' approach which tended to obscure the fact that real soldiers were dying in a distant territory, and a sometimes simplistic dismissal of the whole concept of defensive action, typified in some of the analyses of the action between HMS *Conqueror* and ARA *General Belgrano*. Neither of these extremes, which bracketed a considerable volume of responsible reporting, can be thought to have been very helpful from the practical viewpoint of public understanding of international humanitarian law.[33] A much more generally positive picture can be found in the general response of the free international press to the armed conflicts in former Yugoslavia. Humanitarian abuses in former Yugoslavia, notably the appalling conditions in a number of internment camps, including gross malnutrition and torture of internees, were brought to international attention by press reporting in August 1992.[34] Similarly, the horror of forced prostitution in military 'brothels' in that conflict was also brought to public attention by press reporting.[35] These reports had significantly beneficial effects, in that formerly ignorant or intransigent authorities in the area were forced to act, and also finally to facilitate entry into some of the camps by Delegates of the International Committee of the Red Cross, providing here graphic illustration of Alain Modoux's basic proposition.[36]

The quality of reporting from this point of view depends on a number of factors, including the freedom of the press in general, the political agenda of the media outlets concerned and, fundamentally, the degree of knowledge of the journalists doing the reporting. Journalists are clearly among the target groups for dissemination of knowledge of international humanitarian law and a number of Red Cross and Red Crescent Societies make efforts in this direction. The annual seminars conducted by the British Red Cross Society for trainee independent television journalists are a laudable instance of this kind of work.

As has been suggested above, the press can play a profoundly significant role, for good or ill, in informing the attitudes of the general public to issues arising from the implementation, or failure thereof, of international humanitarian law. Dissemination to civilians is at once the most general and perhaps the least effective of the areas of this kind of education, and the one which may properly give rise to most concern.

The four 1949 Geneva Conventions require dissemination of international humanitarian law and principles to the general public 'if possible'. There are some sectors of civilian service whose personnel obviously require detailed training in relevant rules and principles of international humanitarian law, including civil defence workers and, as outlined below, Red Cross personnel themselves. Clearly, however, large-scale and detailed dissemination to the public as a whole is a somewhat unrealistic aspiration, and it is doubtful whether there is room for the subject in many countries' already crowded school curricula. Having said this, there is some room for development in this area, as shown, for example, by the British Red Cross Society's schools information packs. At the level of university study, more intensive provision may be hoped for, and to take again the example of the United Kingdom, the relatively small number of law schools which offered courses or modules in this area twenty years ago has at the very least trebled, both as a result of increasing general interest and the urging of the Red Cross. Instruction is also offered in other relevant academic areas, such as strategic studies and international relations.

The Role of the International Red Cross Movement in Dissemination

The XXIVth International Conference of the Red Cross held in Manila in 1981, by Resolution X:

> 1. urges the Governments of States Parties to the Geneva Conventions ... to fulfil entirely their obligation to disseminate knowledge of international humanitarian law among their armed forces, ministries, academic circles, schools, medical professions and general public ...
> 2. notes the special responsibilities of National Societies to assist their Governments in this work...
> 3. asks the ICRC and the League [now the Federation[37]] to draw up and implement national and regional dissemination programmes. ...[38]

The international Red Cross and Red Crescent movement plays a significant role in general dissemination of knowledge of international humanitarian law.[39] The means whereby this is done include holding instructional courses. In this regard, the XXIVth International Conference of the Red Cross at Manila also, by resolution XI(1):

> recommends the ICRC conduct and/or sponsor the conduct of, international courses on the [1949 Geneva] ... Conventions and other rules, annually or as often as possible, and request States to send legal officers and commanders of their armed forces to attend these courses ...[40]

International training courses for members of armed forces are conducted regularly by the International Institute of Humanitarian Law at San Remo[41] but the ICRC itself holds annual Summer Schools jointly with the Polish Red Cross Society in Warsaw. These courses involve instruction by international experts in the field, last approximately ten days, and are directed at persons with relevant qualifications or previous study who wish to engage professionally with international humanitarian law in their continuing or future careers. This must be considered an aspect of 'seedcorn' dissemination, in that those who attend may themselves, in one way or another, be hoped to engage in disseminatory work.

National Red Cross and Red Crescent societies are also encouraged to conduct training courses. To take the example of the British Red Cross, a Summer School on international humanitarian law is held regularly, usually at Cambridge, with Red Cross, military and academic speakers, and has attracted significant interest from both the military and civilian sectors. The British Red Cross also holds seminars for particular target groups, including those for trainee television journalists referred to above.

In all countries, there is also the important question of training of Red Cross and Red Crescent staff themselves. It is vitally important that these people who may be called upon to operate under international humanitarian rules in armed conflict in association with the military medical services are fully conversant with the standards and procedures demanded of them. This is true for obvious reasons of service; it is also important in ensuring the continuing viability of the institutional role of the Red Cross in international humanitarian law, as the early unfortunate experience of the 1870 Franco-Prussian War made abundantly clear.[42]

The International Committee of the Red Cross may offer direct assistance in national dissemination of knowledge of international humanitarian law, an authority deriving ultimately from article 4 of its Statute, which provides, *inter alia*, that:

> (1) The special role of the ICRC shall be: ...
> (g) to work for the continual improvement of international humanitarian law and for the better understanding and dissemination of the Geneva Conventions ...
> (2) The ICRC may also take any humanitarian initiative which comes within its role as a specifically neutral and independent institution ...[43]

Such assistance can clearly only be afforded to a state at its request, or at least with its consent and co-operation. To take a specific example, in 1980 the ICRC was granted permission to provide instruction in international humanitarian law to the armed forces of El Salvador.

This was a vital and very difficult task in the context of the cruel conflict which raged in that country from 1979 to 1992[44] from which some encouraging suggestions of progress did emerge.[45]

The ICRC, the Federation of Red Cross and Red Crescent Societies and national Red Cross and Red Crescent societies may also offer *ad hoc* assistance in the area of dissemination from time to time, on request. A minor example of this kind of work is a series of lectures on international humanitarian law given by the author in Albania, the Former Yugoslav Republic of Macedonia and Federal Yugoslavia (Serbia-Montenegro) in 1995. This initiative, involving co-ordination between the ICRC, the federation, the British, Albanian, FYROM and Yugoslav Red Cross Societies, with assistance from the British Council[46] for the lecture in Federal Yugoslavia, is not untypical of activity of this type, including the complex international organisation which may be necessary.

Institutions Engaged in International Dissemination

This is potentially a vast category, including many universities which receive postgraduate students from other countries. From a rather narrower perspective, however, two particular institutions demand comment: the Henry Dunant Institute and the International Institute of Humanitarian Law at San Remo.

The Henry Dunant Institute, named after the founder of the international Red Cross, was established in 1965 jointly by the International Committee of the Red Cross and the League (now Federation) of Red Cross and Red Crescent Societies. Its basic objects are stated by article 3 of its Statute:

> the object of the Institute shall be to make available to the member institutions ways and means of carrying out studies, research, training and instruction in all branches of Red Cross activities and thus to contribute to the strengthening of Red Cross unity and universality.[47]

The institute is a major research centre, and publishes papers and other materials for the study and advancement of international humanitarian law.

The International Institute of Humanitarian Law at San Remo was established in 1970 with the objectives of promoting and diffusing the development of international humanitarian law, and working for its implementation.[48] The institute plays a highly significant role in offering training courses in international humanitarian law, which are attended by officers from the armed forces of many countries, as well as courses for the other involved groups, and also publishes a wide range of papers and other materials on aspects of international humanitarian law. In relation to this, Professor Patrnogic, the President of the San Remo Institute, has written:

> Education and training in international humanitarian law is one of the ... most important aspects of the Institute's work. It began with courses on the law of war, conducted in close cooperation with the ICRC and bringing together officers of the armed forces of many countries ... and with seminars to spread knowledge of international humanitarian law and on dissemination methods. ... To date 54 such courses have been held with more than 200 participants from 125 countries.[49]

The statistics quoted speak for themselves, and since the above was written in 1995, the figures have increased significantly. The institute also holds an annual round table conference of experts in the field of humanitarian law and human rights to focus on a particular issue of current concern.

The Problem of Counter-dissemination

It may finally be remarked that there is a significant danger in what might be termed inadvertent counter-dissemination. This arises especially in the context of war and other books and films, where very negative messages can be sent out with considerable effect in societies whose culture is increasingly dominated by televisual images. This is especially, but not only, the case in relation to misuse of the protective emblems,[50] and is an area in which vigilance is required if serious damage is not to be done to the rather limited public understanding which often exists. Both positive and negative responses to this problem are possible. The whole process of dissemination considered in this chapter may be considered the principal positive response. The negative response lies in such matters as legal action over, for example, abuses of the protective emblem,[51] and alert rebuttal in the media of false or misleading information, whether this be inadvertent or malicious in origin.

Notes

1 See Chapter 10.
2 G.I.A.D. Draper, 'The Implementation of the Geneva Conventions of 1949 and the Additional Protocols of 1977, *Recueil des Cours* (Hague Academy of International Law, 1979).
3 J.M. Hawkins (ed.), *The Oxford Reference Dictionary* (Clarendon/Oxford, 1986), p. 923.

4 Lord McNair and A.D. Watts, *The Legal Effects of War* (Cambridge University Press, 1966), p. 44.
5 [1939] 2 KB 544.
6 Ibid., at p. 545.
7 Ibid., at p. 546.
8 Ibid.
9 *Hansard* [1982] Vol. 22, col. 616.
10 *The Times* (London), 3 May 1982.
11 See Chapter 1.
12 See F. Kalshoven, *Constraints on the Waging of War* (2nd edn), (ICRC, 1991), p. 27.
13 See J. Pictet, *The Geneva Conventions of 12 August 1949: Commentary* (ICRC, 1952–60), on common article 2; see also J. Gutteridge, 'The Geneva Conventions of 1949' (1965) 26 *British Yearbook of International Law*, p. 298, and J. Detter de Lupis, *The Law of War* (Cambridge, 1987), p. 12.
14 C. Greenwood, 'Scope of Application of Humanitarian Law', in D. Fleck (ed.), *The Handbook of Humanitarian Law in Armed Conflict* (Oxford, 1995), p. 39, at p. 41.
15 C. Greenwood, 'The Concept of War in Modern International Law' (1987) 36 *International and Comparative Law Quarterly*, at p. 283.
16 E. Castren, *The Present Law of War and Neutrality* (Summalaisen Tiedeakatemian Taimituksia Annales Academiae Scientiasrum Fenniciae, Helsinki, 1954), p. 31.
17 See M. Gilbert, *Second World War* (Weidenfield and Nicolson, 1989; Phoenix, 1955), p. 1.
18 H. McCoubrey and N.D. White, *International Law and Armed Conflict* (Dartmouth, 1992), p. 194.
19 See Chapter
20 H. McCoubrey and N.D. White, op.cit., at p. 204.
21 United Nations General Assembly Resolution 2625 (XXV), 24 October 1970.
22 For discussion, see H. McCoubrey and N.D. White, 'International Law and the Use of Force in the Gulf' (1991) X *International Relations*, p. 347, at pp. 348–9.
23 For detailed discussion, see Chapter 10.
24 For critical discussions, see H. McCoubrey, *The Obligation to Obey in Legal Theory* (Dartmouth, 1977), pp. 15–33; see also R.N. Moles, *Definition and Rule in Legal Theory* (Basil Blackwell, 1987), Chapters 1 and 2; and H. McCoubrey and N.D. White, *Textbook on Jurisprudence* (2nd edn), (Blackstone, 1996), Chapter 2.
25 In this respect, the 'law jobs' approach advanced by Karl N. Llewellyn may be recommended: see K.N. Llewellyn, 'The Normative, the Legal and the Law Jobs: The Problem of Juristic Method' (1940) 49 *Yale Law Journal*, pp. 1,355.
26 F. Kalshoven, *Constraints on the Waging of War* (2nd edn), (ICRC, 1991), p. 70
27 A.P.V. Rogers, *Law on the Battlefield* Manchester University Press, 1996), p. 152.
28 G.F. Walgemoed, 'Law of War in Operational Planning: A View from the Netherlands' (1996) XXXV *Revue de Droit Militaire et de Droit de la Guerre* ('The Military Law and the Law of War Review), p. 97, at p. 105.
29 A.P.V. Rogers, op.cit.
30 For an interesting discussion of the role of military legal advisers, see K. Thelin, 'Legal Advisers to the Armed Forces – The Swedish Experience' (1994) 30 *International Review of the Red Cross*, pp. 255–65.
31 A. Modoux, 'International Humanitarian Law and the Journalists' Mission', delivered at the Round Table and Red Cross Symposium at the San Remo Institute of International Humanitarian Law in September 1982, printed in the *International Review of the Red Cross* (January–February 1983), Extract Offprint, p. 19, at p. 20.
32 For discussion, see Chapter 1.

33 For discussion of the British press in the Falklands Conflict, see R. Harris, *Gotcha! The Media, the Government and the Falklands Crisis* (Faber and Faber, 1983).
34 See, for example, *Guardian* (London), 7 August 1992, and *Independent* (London), 7 August 1992.
35 See, *The Times* (London) 14 August 1992.
36 See above.
37 See Chapter 2.
38 The full text can be found in the *International Red Cross Handbook* (12th edn), (ICRC/Federation of Red Cross and Red Crescent Societies, 1983), at pp. 634–5.
39 For further discussion, see below.
40 The full text can be found in the *International Red Cross Handbook* (12th edn), at p. 640.
41 See below.
42 See Chapter 1.
43 See the *International Red Cross Handbook* (12th edn), at p. 422.
44 For discussion, see P. Brogan, *World Conflicts*, (2nd edn) (Bloomsbury, 1992), pp. 447–60.
45 See *Dissemination* (ICRC) No. 6, April 1987, pp. 3–4.
46 The British Council is a government organisation concerned with international British cultural and educational activity.
47 See *International Red Cross Handbook* (12th edn), p. 524.
48 See IIHL, *Twenty Years of Humanitarian Dialogue 1970–1990* (International Institute of Humanitarian Law, San Remo, 1990), pp. 7–13.
49 J. Patrnogic, 'The International Institute of Humanitarian Law: 25 Years of Humanitarian Dialogue' (1995) 35 *International Review of the Red Cross* 307, p. 469, at pp. 472–3.
50 See pp. 105–8.
51 See pp. 108.

4 Protection of the Sick and Injured on Land

The first humanitarian Geneva Convention of 1864 was concerned with the amelioration of the condition of wounded and sick, in armies in the field, following directly from Henry Dunant's initiative in the aftermath of the Battle of Solferino in 1859,[1] and this is therefore the oldest established sector of modern international humanitarian law. The principal present provision is found in 1949 Geneva Convention I and in 1977 Additional Protocol I, Part II. The basic principle of protection is the same as that advocated by Henry Dunant in 1859: the impartial rendition of medical assistance to the wounded and sick in armed conflict, friend and foe alike, based solely upon the nature and urgency of their need, provided its beneficiaries are not engaging in continuing hostile action.[2] The principle seems to be, and indeed is, in itself perfectly simple. Some of the details of its application are not, however, and effective implementation involves not only consideration of *jus in bello* norms, but also, *inter alia*, substantive issues of law and medical ethics which must, as ever, be interpreted and applied in the context of the sometimes harsh exigencies of the battlefield if they are to be practically sustainable.

The Basic Principle of Protection

The people benefiting from the protection of 1949 Geneva Convention I and 1977 Additional Protocol I, Part II, in land warfare fall into two broad categories: the wounded and sick themselves and the medical and associated support staff charged with their care.[3]

The wounded and sick protected by 1949 Geneva Convention I are defined by article 13 of the Convention as falling into six categories:

1 members of the armed forces of parties in conflict, including militias and volunteer corps
2 members of other militia and volunteer corps, including resistance movements in occupied territories, so long as they
   - are under the command of a person answerable for the conduct of his or her subordinates

- carry a 'fixed distinctive sign recognisable at a distance'
- carry arms openly
- conduct their operations 'in accordance with the laws and customs of war'

3 members of the regular forces of an authority not recognised by a detaining power
4 authorised civilians accompanying armed forces, including labour units, welfare workers and war correspondents
5 crews of merchant ships and civil aircraft not benefiting from any more advantageous legal protection
6 those forming part of a *levée en masse* resisting invasion who carry arms openly and otherwise observe the laws and customs of war.

It will be observed that this list of protected persons essentially comprises combatants and varieties of analogous or support personnel, with the exception of merchant ship and civil aircraft crews. These 1949 categories were significantly expanded by 1977 Additional Protocol I, article 8(a), which defines the 'wounded and sick' for this purpose as:

> persons, whether military or civilian, who because of trauma, disease or other physical or mental disability, are in need of medical assistance or care and who refrain from any act of hostility. These terms also cover maternity cases, new-born babies and other persons who may be in need of immediate medical assistance or care, such as the infirm or expectant mothers, and who refrain from any act of hostility:

Under this extended provision, any person who is wounded or sick in land warfare and in need of medical care or assistance comes within the protective provision afforded by 1949 Geneva Convention I and 1977 Additional Protocol I. It should be added that the significance of the extended definition given by article 8(a) of the Additional Protocol is not that civilians would not previously have been assisted, for example by a field hospital, if found injured on the battlefield, but rather that it is now *required* that they be assisted. The caveat that in order to benefit from this protection a wounded or sick person must refrain from 'acts of hostility' is obvious, in that a person actively engaging in combat cannot expect simultaneously to benefit from humanitarian medical relief. As for the generality of 'Geneva' protective provisions, these are founded upon a presumption that the protected victims have been rendered *hors de combat* in the given context.

The basic principle of protection is the same as that advocated by Henry Dunant in the mid-19th century, arising from his own experience of relief work after the Battle of Solferino: the impartial rendition of medical assistance to all the wounded and sick, friend and foe alike, based solely upon the criterion of priority of medical need. This principle is simply expressed by article 12 of 1949 Geneva Convention I, which provides, *inter alia*, that:

> [The] wounded or sick, shall be respected and protected in all circumstances. They shall be treated humanely and cared for by the Party to the conflict in whose power they may be, without any adverse distinction founded on sex, race, nationality, religion, political opinions, or any other similar criteria. ... Only urgent medical reasons will authorize priority in the order of treatment to be administered.

This fundamental principle is in essence restated with further emphasis by article 10(2) of 1977 Additional Protocol I, which provides that:

> In all circumstances they shall be treated humanely and shall receive, to the fullest extent practicable and with the least possible delay, the medical care and attention required by their condition. There shall be no distinction among them founded on any grounds other than medical ones.

These general principles of protection require some further explanation. The requirements that the wounded and sick be 'respected' and 'protected' are not identical: the former imposes a duty of relief and non-molestation upon the party into whose power a wounded or sick person may have fallen, whereas the latter imposes a duty upon parties to the conflict to prevent molestation by others, including by looters who are still to be found in the aftermath of battle. The duty of non-discrimination upon any other than objective medical grounds in prioritisation for medical treatment should be obvious enough, and is a simple expression of one of the basic elements of Henry Dunant's original 'Solferino' propositions. Other matters require further discussion. These include the question of the duty of search and rescue, which is manifestly a prerequisite for the performance of any other duty of medical care, the nature of the 'urgent medical reasons' which are a legitimate ground for prioritisation in treatment, and the more detailed issues of law and medical ethics in battlefield medicine as the most extreme form of 'emergency' medical practice, which are considered below.

Collection and Identification of the Wounded, Sick and Dead

The collection of the injured and sick is an obvious prerequisite for their adequate treatment in medical facilities. 1949 Geneva Convention I provides by article 15 that:

> At all times, and particularly after an engagement, Parties to the conflict shall, without delay, take all possible measures to search for and collect the wounded and sick, to protect them against pillage and ill-treatment, to ensure their adequate care, and to search for the dead and prevent their being despoiled.

This, like a number of other basic principles set out by 1949 Geneva Convention I, derives directly from Henry Dunant's experience on the battlefield of Solferino in 1859, where many had been had been left to die where they lay because of simple neglect. The requirement, it will be noted, is that parties take all *possible* measures, which means, *inter alia,* that there is no demand for military medical personnel, including stretcher bearers, should be exposed to unreasonable danger from enemy fire and other military hazards. This matter raises even more pointed questions in warfare at sea, especially regarding submarines.[4] Stretcher bearers have a degree of humanitarian protection while acting in that capacity under 1949 Geneva Convention I, article 25,[5] but this cannot be an absolute guarantee against all dangers of combat, and some element of risk assessment necessarily enters into the practice of rescue. Clearly, these dangers recede once actual combat in a given sector has ceased temporarily or permanently, and it may be noted that article 15 of the 1949 Geneva Convention I also requires that:

> Whenever circumstances permit, an armistice or a suspension of fire shall be arranged, or local arrangements made, to permit the removal, exchange and transport of the wounded left on the battlefield.

How practically possible this may prove to be will naturally depend upon the circumstances of the combat in question. Whilst there may be circumstances of modern warfare where this is not possible, it is clearly not to be ruled out as a prospect at all, especially at the level of the 'local' arrangements in a given sector to which reference is specifically made by the article.

No specific provision is made for the collection of the dead on the field of battle. However, the provision for the honourable interment or cremation of the dead made by article 17 of 1949 Geneva Convention I presupposes that appropriate arrangements for their collection will be made wherever and to the extent that this is possible.[6]

Prioritisation of Medical Treatment

The neutralisation of the wounded and sick – their entitlement to treatment and care without discrimination on non-medical grounds

– is a fundamental norm of international humanitarian law. However, the medical grounds on which decisions of prioritisation in treatment will inevitably have to be made can still raise very difficult questions of both law and medical ethics. The medical capacities of a military field hospital or medical unit will, however relatively extensive its facilities may be, be much less than those of an advanced city hospital, and it is entirely possible that some of the wounded brought into such a facility who might be saved in a civilian hospital in peacetime cannot be saved in a field hospital in a combat zone. The medical staff may therefore be faced with very difficult medical and ethical decisions to which 1949 Geneva Convention I and 1977 Additional Protocol I do not offer any easy answers. Article 12 of 1949 Geneva Convention I, it will be recalled, forbids discrimination in priority of treatment on basis of 'sex, race, nationality, religion, political opinions, or any other similar criteria', but the reference in the article to 'urgent medical reasons' might *prima facie* be read to imply that the most badly wounded patient should receive priority in treatment even though he or she is clearly beyond help, even though others who might be saved thus suffer delays in receiving attention. This would seem to be an absurdly literal reading of the convention, and that view is encouraged by article 10(2) of 1977 Additional Protocol I, which requires that the wounded and sick:

> shall receive, to the fullest extent practicable and with the least possible delay, the medical care and attention required by their condition. There shall be no distinction among them founded on any grounds other than medical ones.

This is obviously a broad restatement and elaboration of the principle set out in this regard by article 12 of 1949 Geneva Convention I, and also the virtually identical article 12 of 1949 Geneva Convention II in relation to the wounded, sick and shipwrecked at sea. However, the elaboration is very valuable in the present context. The ICRC Commentary on article 10(2) states usefully that:

> It is obvious that some wounded or sick persons could be saved, or at any rate be better cared for, in the clinics of wealthy countries which have the most advanced resources at their disposal. However, the requirement imposed here relates to the material possibilities existing in the place and at the time that the wounded person is cared for.[7]

In other words the prioritisation of treatment is to be determined by medical need, but also, impartially and objectively, by the practical possibilities for treatment which are available. The practical implications were well stated by Colonel Kaj Mollefors, who commanded a

Swedish military medical unit sent to Saudi Arabia during the 1990–91 Gulf Conflict. He stated in a newspaper interview:

> Obviously, those who have no chance of survival will be treated after those who have a chance of survival. ... But, however badly a patient is hurt, even if he is dying, he will be properly cared for [and] made comfortable.[8]

Some degree of such selectivity is inherent in much emergency medical practice, of which battlefield medicine may be taken as an extreme case. Various criteria of selection may be adopted,[9] but perhaps the most obvious is *triage*: the separation of casualties into priority groups for treatment is a concept which derives from military medical practice, and current British military medical practice is to divide patients into four groups, ranging from those with slight injuries apparently capable of self-help to those who cannot be expected to survive and who will therefore be afforded only basic humanitarian relief, including, in particular, pain relief. This is the only practical humanitarian policy, and concords fully with the spirit of 1949 Geneva Conventions I and II and 1977 Additional Protocol I. At the same time, an important caveat must be emphasised: acceptance of the fact that only the practically possible can be achieved – in essence a form of that narrowly defined 'military necessity' acknowledged by Jean Pictet[10] – is not a mandate for the provision of less military medical assistance than is practically possible. Assistance to the 'fullest extent practicable' demanded by article 10(2) of 1977 Additional Protocol I is a more stringent demand than merely such assistance as may be found convenient, and to fall below this standard could readily be interpreted as equivalent to culpable neglect.[11] In this context, it may be added that whilst the primary burden of immediate and emergency battlefield care will inevitably fall upon field hospitals, this does not mean that more sophisticated resources, including those in the home country, should not also play their part. As an example, it may be noted that during the 1990–91 Gulf Conflict the United Kingdom made arrangements for wounded to be flown from military hospitals in the Gulf and Cyprus to nominated hospitals in each of the 14 regional health authority areas in the UK.[12] At the same time, plans were made to re-open 'mothballed' US military medical facilities with a 3,000-bed capacity for any injured US military personnel from the Gulf.[13] This raises by implication the important point that the duty of medical support is not in all cases limited to the immediate resources of military medical facilities in the field. The requirement of search and rescue may here be read in the light of the general requirement of article 10(2) of 1977 Additional Protocol I, that the wounded and sick:

> shall receive, *to the fullest extent practicable and with the least possible delay*, the medical care and attention required by their condition. [emphasis added]

This at least suggests that where suitable transport is available to convey a seriously wounded patient to the advanced medical facilities which the treatment of his or her condition demands, this should be done. It may be remarked that during the 1980–88 Iran–Iraq Gulf War, Iran sent a number of victims of chemical attacks to European capitals, including London, for treatment, both for the victims' advantage and, no doubt, to draw international attention to the Iraqi deployment of chemical weapons. As far as parties to an armed conflict are concerned, this will obviously involve advance preparation of home and/or allied medical reception facilities, as in the case of the 1990–91 Gulf Conflict referred to above.[14] The practicalities of the situation include the availability of transport, the question of its other use, such as the immediate rescue of possibly large numbers of other wounded and sick, the capacity of the patient to survive a long journey at all, and the general exigencies of what may for this purpose be termed 'military medical necessity'. All that may reasonably and practically be done must be done; anything less may be considered culpable neglect. But help rendered in extreme cases to the few at the possibly terminal expense of the many would also constitute neglect. In the end, hard decisions must be made as to what can be done in the prevailing circumstances.

Such questions of judgement in what may be considered a very extreme form of accident and emergency medical practice raise more general but very important issues. Whatever system of prioritisation of treatment is adopted – *triage* or otherwise – the decisions made must concord with both the principle of impartiality and the requirements of general medical ethics.

Military Medical Ethics and Standards of Treatment

The discussion of this subject is not intended to suggest that the ethical base of military medical practice is, or should be, different from or less stringent than that applicable to any other area of medical practice. The matter arises as a distinct issue, as in many other questions of military medicine, because the very particular and extreme circumstances of application raise questions not otherwise commonly encountered. The reference to medical ethics in 1949 Geneva Conventions I and II and 1977 Additional Protocol I are not very extensive. In 1949 Geneva Convention I, the general standard outlined by article 12 implicitly provides for ethical standards in practice. Explicitly, it is provided that:

> Any attempts upon their lives, or violence to their persons, shall be strictly prohibited; in particular, they shall not be murdered or exterminated, subjected to torture or to biological experiments; they shall not wilfully be left without medical assistance and care nor shall conditions exposing them to contagion or infection be created.

The most clear and extensive provision is offered by 1977 Additional Protocol I, article 11. Article 11(1) provides that:

> The physical or mental health and integrity of persons who are in the power of the adverse Party ... shall not be endangered by any unjustified act or omission. Accordingly, it is prohibited to subject ... [such] persons ... to any medical procedure which is not indicated by the health of the person concerned and which is not consistent with generally accepted medical standards which would be applied under similar medical circumstances to persons who are nationals of the Party conducting the procedure and who are in no way deprived of liberty.

Article 11(2)(b) repeats and reinforces the ban on conducting 'medical or scientific experiments' upon protected persons. The basic criterion of 'generally accepted medical standards' is not closely defined, but the substantive provisions of both 1949 Geneva Conventions I and II and 1977 Additional Protocol I make plain that it is not simply a validation of whatever, possibly abysmal, standards might happen to be accepted by any given state or group of states. In reference to this, F.J. Hampson makes the important point that:

> ... the concept of 'medical ethics' has varied over time and between different places, religions, and political systems. These variations are likely to raise new problems for the *application* of medical ethics but do not, of themselves, suggest that no common denominator can be found. So, for example, life support machines raise the possibility of sustaining a form of existence that was not available fifty years ago. The problem is new but the basis for action, the best interests of the patient, is not.[15]

The ICRC Commentary on the Protocol remarks in specific reference to the criterion of generally accepted medical standards that:

> Unfortunately 'generally accepted medical standards' have not been assembled in a universally adopted international instrument, and it is certainly beyond the scope of this commentary to attempt to list these standards. At most it is possible to mention certain instruments which

> give some indications of this matter. However, it is clear that some standards are undeniable, such as that ... which requires that medical procedures are performed in the interests of the patient.[16]

The international instruments referred to by the Commentary are the 1948 Declaration of Geneva, the 1949 International Code of Medical Ethics, the 1962 Rules of Medical Ethics in Time of War and the 1962 Rules to Ensure Aid and Care for the Wounded and Sick, particularly in Time of Armed Conflict. All these have been adopted by the World Medical Association.[17] The 1949 Geneva Declaration, which is essentially an updated version of the classical Hippocratic oath, requires, as amended at Sydney in 1968, that a doctor undertakes that:

> The health of my patient will be my first consideration ... I will not permit considerations of religion, nationality, race, party politics or social standing to intervene between my duty and my patient; I will maintain the utmost respect for human life from the time of conception, even under threat, I will not use my medical knowledge contrary to the laws of humanity.

It does not seem that such formulations can in themselves claim the status of customary international law, although the standard set out by this provision is in any case clearly reflected in the relevant substantive articles of 1949 Geneva Conventions I and II and 1977 Additional Protocol I cited above.

The most immediately important principle after neutrality in prioritisation of treatment is treatment for the patient's benefit. The requirement of article 11(1) of 1977 Additional Protocol I, that '... any medical procedure which is not indicated by the state of health of the persons concerned [is prohibited] ...' derives ultimately from the tenets of the classical Hippocratic oath and is self-evidently of fundamental significance in military as in any other area of medical practice. The background to this specific provision, and to the references to 'biological experiments' and 'exposure to contagion' in article 12 of 1949 Geneva Conventions I and II, and to 'medical or scientific experiments' in article II(2)(b) of 1977 Additional Protocol I lies in large part in the appealing medical experimentation carried out by the Nazis during the Second World War. The obscene genetic 'research' carried out by Dr Mengele upon infant identical twins at the Auschwitz death camp is one example; another can be seen in the 'research' carried out into the treatment of hypothermia on behalf of the *Luftwaffe*. The 'subjects' were repeatedly thrown into icy water, dragged out, revived and thrown in again until they died, in order to gather data on the best means of protecting pilots who might be forced to bale out into Arctic waters. Such action would be manifestly illegal now, as it was then. It is worth mentioning, however, that the hypothermia 'research' in particular continues to pose serious ethical questions: appalling as the experiments were, they yielded results which are of value in the treatment of hypothermia – should they therefore be used for the benefit of modern hypothermia victims, or should they be expunged from the records because of their origin? There was an extensive discussion of this issue in the 1988 *New Scientist* correspondence columns. So far as this is concerned, a tenable ethical position may be thought to lie in the proposition that the victims of the Nazi experiments cannot be restored to life, and the saving of modern hypothermia victims is perhaps a more fitting memorial to their suffering than a shamefaced attempt to destroy all reference to it. The matter remains open to argument.

Any future 'research' of this nature would be unequivocally criminal, but more complex issues of 'research' in medical practice pose much more difficult legal questions. In one sense, some element of 'experimentation' comes into many areas of medical assessment and treatment beyond the level of setting broken limbs or repairing open wounds. Certainly, in any medical process there is some element of waiting to see whether the patient's condition improves or not. In this respect, a clear distinction can be drawn between clinical and non-therapeutic research, which J.K. Mason and R.A. McCall-Smith define as follows:

> Research activities can be broadly categorised as clinical research, which is aimed at the improved treatment of a patient or a group of patients and as non-therapeutic – in which the essential object is the furtherance of purely scientific knowledge which may, eventually, have a wider application than patient care.[18]

In the context of military medicine within the terms of the 1949 Geneva Conventions and 1977 Additional Protocol, 'clinical research' for immediate patient benefit may not only be lawful but, within the limits of the practically possible and the likely benefit and risk, may actually be required. 'Non-therapeutic research', even within the benign terms considered by Mason and McCall-Smith, would be unequivocally unlawful in military medicine under the conventions and Protocol.

Creation of conditions of contagion expressly forbidden by article 12 of 1949 Geneva Conventions I and II refers ultimately to the conditions discovered by advancing Allied armies at the Bergen-Belsen concentration camp in 1945. This was not in theory a death camp, but such appalling conditions of malnourishment and sanitation had been created that mass death from starvation, typhus and similar diseases had resulted. It might have been hoped that such conditions were an isolated nightmare of the mid-20th century, but, tragically, the experience of former Yugoslavia has called any such hope into question. The appalling conditions discovered in a number of 'internment' camps during the conflicts in former Yugoslavia in the first half of the 1990s included gross malnourishment, supported by incontrovertible photographic evidence. Early evidence came in August 1992 in press reports from the Bosnian Serb-run camp at Omarska, which was officially described as an 'investigation centre', with photographs of grossly malnourished prisoners and clear evidence of brutality.[19] Worrying accounts also emerged at the same time from the camps at Brcko and Trnoplje. Counter-allegations were made by the Bosnian Serbs about camps run by other factions and parties, including camps at Tuzla, Bihac and Zenica.[20] Whatever view may be taken of any particular claim – and it must not simply be assumed that all allegations are necessarily or wholly correct – the evidence for serious violations of the principles considered here in a number of camps is all too considerable. Significantly, and unusually, the International Committee of the Red Cross publicly condemned the conditions in all these camps on 14 August 1992 as violating the relevant requirements of the 1949 Geneva Conventions.[21]

A more difficult question in the context of 'creation of conditions of contagion' arises in the context of HIV infection and AIDS, especially with regard to blood transfusions. The receipt of blood donations in battlefield medicine is in itself the subject of significant and detailed legal provision,[22] but once received, the quality of the blood becomes an issue. HIV infection from donated and inadequately screened blood administered to surgical cases and haemophiliacs has been the subject of legal proceedings in a number of countries, and it would seem difficult to deny in routine civil medical practice that any such failure could constitute culpable medical negligence.[23] A military field hospital is obviously in a rather different situation from that of a Western city hospital in peacetime. Many of the patients it is dealing with will have serious wounds, and in many cases dangerous blood loss, and in such a case transfusions of locally donated blood may well be a necessity, and the capacity to test the donated blood for HIV or any other infection may not exist. In such a case, it may be suggested that where there is a slight but real risk of HIV infection from transfusion, in contrast with a virtual certainty of death from blood loss, that risk may legally and ethically be taken. A different view would be taken of any procedure in which contamination might be avoided by simple and available action. It has been remarked elsewhere that:

> The matter is essentially subject to the legal ethical test of what may best be done in the circumstances, emphasising that it must, of course,

> be the *best* possible. If this standard is met it would seem difficult to sustain any charge of creating conditions of exposure to contagion or infection within the meaning of article 12 of 1949 Geneva Conventions I and II or of failure to maintain controls for the benefit of donors and recipients within the meaning of article 11(3) of 1977 Additional Protocol I. It may be added that the sterilisation of needles and other blood extraction and transfusion equipment would clearly fall within the requirements of both 1949 Geneva Conventions I and II article 12 and 1977 Additional Protocol I Article 11(3). Failure in this respect would seem, at least, negligent and grossly culpable.[24]

By the same token, omission of such readily possible procedures as the decontamination of surgical instruments would clearly be culpable.

Exceptions to the Requirement of Patient Benefit

The requirement that military medical procedures be carried out for the patient's benefit is in itself both fundamental and obvious. However, there are two limited exceptions to this: donations of blood for transfusion and skin for grafting. Both of these, which are obviously carried out for the benefit of patients other than those subjected to the procedure, are expressly admitted by 1977 Additional Protocol I, article 11(3), as an exception to the ban in article 11(2)(c) on 'removal of tissue or organs for transplantation'. Article 11(3) provides that:

> Exceptions to the prohibition in paragraph 2(c) may be made only in the case of donations of blood for transfusion or of skin for grafting, provided that they are given voluntarily and without any coercion or inducement, and then only for therapeutic purposes, under conditions consistent with generally accepted medical standards and controls designed for the benefit of both the donor and the recipient.

The basic reason for this exception lies in the nature of battlefield medicine as, in effect, an extreme branch of accident and emergency practice. The ICRC Commentary on the Protocol states in reference to this provision that:

> In both cases such removal may be invaluable from the medical point of view, and of considerable practical importance. Large numbers of the wounded may die for lack of blood for transfusion and skin grafts can also save lives, especially in cases of severe burns. Thus it seemed to be going too far to totally ban [such] donations ... especially as the risk of abuse in such cases is not ... great. Besides, the article itself imposes very rigorous rules on such removals.[25]

The protection of donors set out in article 11(3) falls into two distinct areas. In the first place, the donation must be *voluntary*, this means that in dealing with slightly wounded enemy personnel when requesting donations, medical staff must be very sure that the request is conveyed precisely as such, and not, for example when being transmitted via one of their officers, as an apparent or actual order. The other protection lies in the requirements of 'standards and controls designed for the benefit of both the donor and the recipient'. This raises again the question of infected blood considered above. The difficulties of screening blood for potential HIV, hepatitis or other contamination have already been discussed; however, it is worth mentioning that the use of infected needles or other equipment in either the process of donation or that of transfusion would be inexcusable in almost any rationally conceivable situation.

The ban on other removal of tissues or organs for transplant in article 11(2)(c) is absolute. The reasons for this in principle are obvious enough. There are nevertheless hypothetical situations which might give rise to serious humanitarian difficulties: for example, what if two siblings are held as prisoners of war by the same adverse party and one of them suffers renal failure, in which case the only long-term chance of survival lies in transplanting a new kidney from his or her sibling, which the other is willing and eager to donate. According to the wording of the Protocol, such an offer would have to be refused by the medical authorities. On the other hand, where the humanitarian interests of protected persons are not served by the precise wording of the conventions and Protocols in a particular case, there may be some room for manoeuvre, although in such a case the approval of the relevant authorities, including the ICRC, and through them or the Protecting Power, if any, the home authorities of the donor, should be obtained for the *prima facie* unlawful procedure. It should be remembered that the consent of the prospective donor is not enough, since he or she is in all cases not legally capable of waiving the rights conferred on her or him by the conventions and Protocols.[26]

The Question of Patient Consent

In much medical practice, a patient's consent is necessary before many medical procedures can be carried out, not least because invasive procedures such as surgery would otherwise constitute a *prima facie* assault. 1977 Additional Protocol I provides by article 11(5) that protected persons have the right to refuse surgical procedures, but that if this is done, medical personnel should try to obtain a *written* statement of refusal, 'signed or acknowledged' by the patient. This latter element of the provision is designed essentially to protect medical personnel from subsequent allegations of culpable neglect under article 12 of 1949 Geneva Conventions I or II. If the patient is conscious and capable of expressing his or her wishes clearly, this provision is not necessarily problematic, except possibly in cases of misunderstanding where a soldier may have been told as a matter of propaganda that enemy medical personnel routinely torture or kill people on the opposing side. In such a case, clearly, every practically possible effort should be made to reassure the patient about what is intended, possibly with the assistance of one of his or her own officers if any are available. Potentially more difficult questions arise where a patient is unconscious or otherwise incapable of expression and his or her comrades insist that a given procedure is contrary to her or his religious or ethical beliefs. In such a case, the only safe counsel must be to proceed with the requisite medical action, since the patient's comrades have no necessary or implicit authority to speak in such a matter on his or her behalf. Even if their assertions subsequently prove to be correct, it must be thought better to save a patient's life in error than to let her or him die in circumstances where, if the comrades are wrong, there might be a very clear case of culpable neglect.

Treatment of the Dead

Parties to an armed conflict are required by article 17 of 1949 Geneva Convention I, so far as is possible, to bury or cremate the dead, and therefore, by implication, to collect bodies from the battlefield. If possible, burial or cremation must be carried out individually, and must be preceded by medical examination in order to enable a report to be made upon the death. Where a standard double identity disc is worn, one half is removed to be sent to the ICRC Central Tracing Agency, and the other half is left on the body. If there is only a single identity disc, it is left on the body. Article 33(4) of 1977 Additional Protocol I enjoins parties in conflict to agree upon arrangements for the recovery and identification of the dead from the battlefield. This provision requires that recovery teams be respected and protected while exclusively engaged on this duty.

Article 17 of 1949 Geneva Convention I makes a presumption in favour of burial, unless the apparent religion or national custom of the deceased or the immediate requirements of hygiene indicate cremation. This is perhaps a slightly curious provision, in that some religious and cultures demand inhumation, and some, such as Hinduism, demand cremation, whilst in many cases either practice is acceptable. However, it is obviously necessary that there should be some governing presumption for cases of doubt or ambiguity. In any event, obsequies must be conducted honourably and, where possible, in accordance with the rites of the religion, if any, of the deceased, where this is known.

Article 17 also sets out stringent requirements for the arrangement and reporting of war graves, which, wherever possible, should be grouped according to the nationality of the deceased, and be respected and properly identified. A graves registration service should be set up at the outset of hostilities, and the parties should exchange information on the location and identity of war graves as soon as possible. In this respect, article 17 refers to the bureau mentioned by article 122 of 1949 Geneva Convention III, which role is in fact played by the ICRC Central Tracing Agency, through which all such information is passed.

Article 34(2)(a)(b) of 1977 Additional Protocol I requires parties in whose territory grave sites are located to enter into agreements for their permanent maintenance and for access to them by relatives and representatives of the official registration services as soon as possible. Article 34(2)(c) requires that the return of remains and personal effects to the home country of the deceased should be facilitated where that country requests it or, unless the home government objects, the relatives of the deceased request it.

The 1982 Falklands Conflict raised a number of issues in relation to 'war graves' and, whilst 1977 Additional Protocol I was not applicable, they do throw an interesting light on some of the implications. There are numerous graves of Argentine service personnel in the Falkland Islands, and the Argentine Government has pressed for relatives to be allowed access to them. Protocol I would require that such access be permitted as soon as practically possible, but also recognises that 'relations between the adverse parties' may be an obstacle to this. In fact, some such visits have been arranged, although there remains inevitable sensitivity between the United Kingdom and Argentina on the subject of the islands. Much more serious difficulties arose in the mid- to late 1990s over visits to grave sites in territory held by adverse parties in former Yugoslavia. Bus parties arranged for relatives to visit grave sites were subjected to abuse and stone-throwing by local civilians.

International humanitarian law as it is applied to international armed conflicts does not purport to create obligations between a state and its own citizens, although many governments and veterans' associations, such as the Royal British Legion in the United Kingdom, do make arrangements for visits to grave sites located in foreign countries. There can be considerable sensitivities in this area. During the mid-1990s, in a number of incidents, monuments and headstones at Allied war graves in European countries were defaced with neo-Nazi slogans as part of an upsurge of Hitlerite revisionism. Rather different sensitivities arise from disturbance of sunken warships which are classified as war graves at sea, and this is considered below.[27]

Tracing of the Injured, Sick and Dead

The collection and transmission of information about missing and dead persons is recognised as an important humanitarian consideration for the families of the people concerned. This imperative is now stated as a general humanitarian norm by article 32 of 1977 Additional Protocol I. Specifically, article 33(1) of the Additional Protocol requires that:

> As soon as circumstances permit, and at the latest form the end of active hostilities, each Party to the conflict shall search for the persons who have been reported missing by an adverse Party. Such adverse Party shall transmit all relevant information concerning such persons in order to facilitate such searches.

The details of the information to be recorded by an adverse party into whose hands the injured, shipwrecked or dead may fall is set out in article 16 of 1949 Geneva Convention I. Eight elements of information are required if obtainable: name, rank, serial number, nationality, date of birth, date and place of capture or death, and details of wounds, illness or cause of death. In the case of military personnel, personal details should be obtainable from identity discs where appropriate questioning is not possible. This information will be passed on to the ICRC's Central Tracing Agency so that it may be sent to the home state. If a Protecting Power has been appointed, it should be informed too.

Protecting of Medical Personnel

The status and protection of medical personnel is an area in which the law applicable on land differs significantly in certain respects from that applicable at sea. The discussion which follows is therefore primarily addressed to practice on land, and the rules and principles applicable at sea which diverge from these are considered in Chapter 5.

For the purpose of 1949 Geneva Convention I, protected medical personnel fall into three broad categories: permanent medical personnel,[28] auxiliary medical personnel[29] and personnel of voluntary aid societies.[30] The scale and type of protection afforded to these categories of personnel differs somewhat in accordance with their different duties and needs. In addition to these, parallel protection is afforded to chaplains and other religious personnel, but this raises other questions, so it is considered separately below.[31]

Medical personnel in armed conflict are potentially placed in difficult circumstances from a variety of points of view. The protection offered is designed to ensure that medical personnel are enabled to perform their medical duties without threat or coercion, beyond the level of accidence unavoidably attendant upon anyone's presence in a combat zone. 1949 Geneva Convention I requires by article 24 that medical personnel exclusively so engaged, including administrators of medical units and establishments, are to be 'respected and protected in all circumstances'. As for the wounded and sick themselves, this means that they must not only not be molested, but must also be protected from molestation by others. Article 25 requires that auxiliary staff, including orderlies, auxiliary nurses and stretcher bearers who are trained to undertake these duties in case of necessity, are to be respected and protected 'if they are carrying out these duties at the time when they come into contact with the enemy or fall into his hands'. If they are engaged upon other duties, they will not fall within this protection. Article 26 provides that staff of recognised voluntary aid societies, including in particular national Red Cross or Red Crescent societies, who are employed in the same way as permanent medical personnel under article 24 and so authorised by their government, receive the same level of legal protection as that set out by article 24, provided that the staff of such societies are subject to military law and regulation. Any such authorised use of voluntary aid society personnel to assist the military medical services must, under article 26, be notified in advance to the opposing side. The requirements of authorisation and regulation are of obvious importance, and derive specifically from experience in the 1870 Franco-Prussian War, when a number of alleged relief organisations engaged in hostile activity under a 'humanitarian' cover.

Detailed specification of protection for the performance of medical duties is set out by article 16 of 1977 Additional Protocol I, although this for the most part simply makes explicit what was at least implicit in article 12 of 1949 Geneva Conventions I and II with regard to the treatment of patients. Article 16(1) forbids under all circumstances the punishment of anyone for medical action which is compatible with medical ethics, 'regardless of the person benefiting therefrom'. This derives from early 19th-century experience, when in some cases doctors were severely punished for rendering medical aid to enemy personnel, as in the case of Dr Palasciano at the siege of Messina in 1848. It may be noted that this provision is not limited to medical personnel *stricto sensu*. A soldier with basic first aid skills who renders assistance to an injured enemy could not lawfully be punished for doing so.

Article 16(2) makes the obvious provision that medical personnel must not be compelled to act in any way contrary to medical ethics or the requirements of 1949 Geneva Conventions or 1977 Additional Protocol I, or by the same token, to refrain from acts required by those treaties. This is implicit in the protection afforded to the wounded and sick by article 12 of 1949 Geneva Conventions I and II, and by 1977 Additional Protocol I, articles 10(2) and 11. An unusual question in this context arose in *US* v. *Levy*.[32] Captain Levy had been ordered to provide dermatological training for special forces paramedics in US forces during the Vietnam War, and had neglected to do so. Apparently, he believed that to obey the order and to provide medical training to non-medical military personnel engaged in a conflict of which he strongly disapproved in general, and in which he disapproved especially of the conduct of US special forces, would violate his sense of medical ethics. These arguments were rejected, and his conviction for wilful disobedience was upheld in a series of appeals. In the context, this was hardly surprising, and an examination of the circumstances of the case suggests that the central concern was more one of conscientious objection than of military medical ethics *stricto sensu*. However, it is possible to imagine situations in which this question would be far from academic. If it was clearly and objectively established that a given unit was engaging in medical crimes, affording training to its personnel might very well be considered an act violating medical ethics, or at least lending aid and assistance to such violation. For example, what would now be the legal position of one who provided medical training for the SS doctors who in the Second World War perpetrated appalling criminal 'medical' experimentation at the Auschwitz concentration camp? Even in the light of what is now known, such a question does not lend itself to easy answers. Much would depend upon what was actually known, or might reasonably have been known,[33] to the provider of such training at relevant times.

Article 40 of 1949 Geneva Convention I and article 42 of 1949 Geneva Convention II require that protected medical personnel demonstrate their status by wearing upon the left arm a water-resistant armband bearing the protective emblem, either red cross or red crescent in accordance with their national practice. Protected personnel must also, under the same provisions, carry both the standard form of identity disc carried by service personnel and a water-resistant, pocket-sized identity card carrying the appropriate protective emblem and stating, *inter alia*, in what capacity the bearer is entitled to protected status. A model for such identity cards can be found in 1949 Geneva Convention I, Annex II. It must be stressed that failure to wear the protective emblem is in itself wrongful, and clearly compromises the practical protection of medical personnel, although, as for buildings and transport, it does not necessarily deprive them of protection as a matter of principle.[34]

Medical personnel should desist from hostile activity, and would lose protected status, in the same way as medical establishments under article 21 of 1949 Geneva Convention I, if they were to engage in attacks. However, it is specifically stated by article 22(1) of the convention that an establishment will not forfeit its protected status simply because its medical personnel are armed and 'use the arms in their own defence or in that of the wounded and sick in their charge'. This may be taken to refer to small arms.

There remains the question of capture. The first humanitarian Geneva Convention of 1864 forbade the capture of medical personnel by the adverse party, and under 1949 Geneva Convention I, this remains technically the case. Permanent medical personnel under articles 24 and 26 of the convention may not be 'captured' *stricto sensu*, but, article 28 of the convention provides that:

> Personnel designated in articles 24 and 26 who fall into the hands of the adverse Party, shall be retained only in so far as the state of health … and the number of prisoners of war require.
> Personnel thus retained shall not be deemed prisoners of war. Nevertheless they all at least benefit by all the provisions of [1949 Geneva Convention III] … . Within the framework of the military laws and regulations of the Detaining Power, and under the authority of its competent service, they shall continue to carry out, in accordance with their professional ethics, their medical … duties on behalf of prisoners of war, preferably those of the armed forces to which they themselves belong.

Apart from the highly significant reservation of function, the practical distinction between 'capture' and 'retention' is obviously rather slight. Medical personnel are nevertheless to be retained only for the performance of their medical duties for prisoners of their own country, or at least their own side, and are treated in terms of protection 'as if' they were prisoners of war, without actually being so. Medical personnel at sea are treated differently, and may be neither 'captured' nor 'retained'.[35]

Article 6 of 1949 Geneva Convention I permits special agreements between parties in conflict, but states that they may not adversely affect the position of the wounded and sick, or medical personnel. In short, such agreements may only *increase* the protection offered, and may never *diminish* it. Similarly, under article 7 of the convention, the wounded and sick and medical staff cannot legally renounce their rights under 1949 Geneva Convention I.

Protection of Medical Establishments

An extended definition of such establishments is offered by 1977 Additional Protocol I, article 8(e):

> establishments and other units, whether military or civilian, organized for medical purposes, namely the search for, collection, transportation, diagnosis or treatment – including first aid treatment – of the wounded, sick and shipwrecked, or for the prevention of disease. The term includes ... hospitals and other similar units, blood transfusion centres, preventive medicine centres ... medical depots and [their] ... medical and pharmaceutical stores ... Medical units may be fixed or mobile, permanent or temporary.

It will be noted that this definition is much wider than 'hospitals' *stricto sensu*, and includes the broad range of medical facilities. The inclusion of civilian medical establishments and units within these provisions was an innovation of 1977 Additional Protocol I, the relevant provisions of 1949 Geneva Convention I having been framed in terms of military establishments and units only. However, this would not mean that civilian medical establishments would be without legal protection in an armed conflict involving a state or states nor party to the Protocol. Civilian hospitals are expressly protected by article 18 of 1949 Geneva Convention IV.[36]

The general scheme of protection of medical establishments is set out by article 19 of 1949 Geneva Convention I. Medical establishments must be respected and protected at all times. If they fall into the hands of an adverse party to the conflict, their continuing performance of their medical functions must be not inhibited until such time as the adverse party has itself established adequate medical services for the care and treatment of the wounded and sick. This protection also extends to the material and stores of both fixed and mobile medical establishments, which, under article 33 of 1949 Geneva Convention I, must not, in the hands of an adverse party, be diverted from use for the care of the wounded and sick. Commanders of forces in the field may make use of them 'in case of urgent military necessity', however, so long as previous arrangements are made for the continuing care of the wounded and sick for whose benefit and treatment they were originally used. Under article 34 of the convention, the real and personal property of aid societies, which is protected under the convention, is considered private property, but may still be requisitioned in cases of 'urgent necessity' for the welfare of the wounded and sick, again with the caveat that proper provision for the continuing care of those currently being treated must be made.

Article 19 of 1949 Geneva Convention I also requires that, 'so far as is possible', medical establishments shall not be located in places where attacks upon military objectives may imperil their safety. This may not always be fully possible, but the provision clearly excludes the use of hospitals as 'human shields' for military objectives, and, indeed, a hospital so used would be exposed to collateral damage, which, providing this was minimised to the greatest practical degree, would be the responsibility of the party which sited the establishment. The question of 'human shields' became an important legal issue in the 1990–91 Gulf Conflict so far as prisoners and internees in Iraq were concerned, although not in respect of hospitals as much.[37]

Medical units entitled to protected status under 1949 Geneva Convention I are indicated by flying a flag displaying the protective emblem of red cross or red crescent. When under the control of its own state, the establishment may fly its national flag along with the protective emblem, but if under adverse control, it should fly only the flag displaying the protective emblem.[38] The same applies to medical establishments from neutral countries which have been authorised to lend their aid to a belligerent, except that when under friendly control, they may fly the flag of the belligerent to which they are attached, rather than that of their own state.[39] The marking of medical establishments with the protective emblem is the duty of the party responsible for them. Article 42 of 1949 Geneva Convention I provides, *inter alia*, that:

> Parties to the conflict shall take the necessary steps *in so far as military considerations permit*, to make the distinctive emblems indicating medical units and establishments clearly visible to the enemy land, air or naval forces, in order to obviate the possibility of any hostile action [emphasis added].

It is possible to imagine circumstances in which such display might not be possible in practice but whilst in such a case deliberate and knowing attack upon the medical establishment would clearly remain unlawful, the dangers of unknowing attack or serious collateral damage might be significantly increased. In any event, the possibility of excusable collateral damage is not a licence for indiscriminate bombardment of the type that was practised all too widely in the conflicts in former Yugoslavia in the early 1990s.

Medical establishments lose their legal protection only if, according to article 21 of 1949 Geneva Convention I:

> they are used to commit, outside their humanitarian duties, acts harmful to the enemy. Protection may, however, cease only after a due warning has been given naming, in all appropriate cases a reasonable time limit and after such warning has remained unheeded.

Article 22 goes on to list a number of circumstances which do not deprive a medical establishment of legal protection:

1 if the medical personnel are armed, and use their weapons in defence of themselves or their patients
2 if the unit is defended, in the absence of armed orderlies, by sentries or a picket
3 if small arms and ammunition taken from patients and not yet handed over to the proper authorities are found in the unit
4 if members of the military veterinary service are found in the establishment without forming an integral part of it
5 if civilian wounded are being cared for in the establishment

In relation to this, it may be remarked that in a field hospital there may well be significant quantities of weapons taken from patients, so the point at which a hospital becomes an illegal weapons store is a matter for quantitative and circumstantial judgement. Since for such a judgement to be made the establishment would presumably have to be already under adverse control, such a decision could not in any event justify attack. Of course, if offensive military vehicles were parked in the vicinity of a hospital, that would not deprive the hospital of protection, but it would render it liable to collateral damage, since the vehicles themselves would unequivocally be military vehicles.[40] The military veterinary service may seem a rather outdated concept in modern hostilities, but in some types of terrain, pack animals may still be used. In this context, however, veterinary service is seen essentially as a matter of military utility rather than a 'humanitarian' service as such. The reference to civilian wounded has been rendered otiose in any situation to which 1977 Additional Protocol I applies, since the protocol brings all wounded and sick, military or civilian, within the same protective remit.

Hospital Zones

Under article 23 of 1949 Geneva Convention I, states may at any time, whether or not they are engaged in armed conflict, establish within their own territories or, if necessary, in territories under occupation, hospital zones for the protection of the wounded and sick and those charged with their care from the effects of conflict. When armed conflicts occur, parties thereto are urged, possibly through the good offices of the International Committee of the Red Cross or a Protecting Power, to conclude agreements with adverse parties for the mutual respect and recognition of hospital zones. A model agreement of this sort is set out in Annex I to 1949 Geneva Convention I.

Amongst other points covered by the model agreement, it is provided that such zones should cover only a small proportion of the territory of the state concerned, and should be far removed from military objectives and large industrial and administrative facilities. Further, although previously resident populations need not be evacuated from a designated hospital zone, no work directly related to military operations or munitions production may be done within it. These are obvious limitations, designed to avert abuse of hospital zones as 'human shields' for legitimate military targets. The concept of hospital zones is of obvious potential humanitarian utility, but has not in practice found significant use in modern armed conflicts.

Medical Transport on Land

Medical transport is entitled to respect and protection in exactly the same way as mobile medical units.[41] Protected transport, such as an ambulance, is marked with the protective emblem in the same way as other protected establishments and equipment. In the case of trucks or ambulances, this will usually involve marking appropriate flat surfaces, including the top for identification from the air, and possibly also flying a flag bearing the protective emblem. In the case of temporary medical transports, the emblem may only be used during the period of such assignment. It should be stressed that military vehicles such as tanks or armoured cars are not entitled to protected status on the battlefield, even if they do engage in any *ad hoc* rescue work.

Medical transport is 'subject to the laws of war' if it falls into adverse hands according to article 35 of 1949 Geneva Convention I. This somewhat delphic phrase means that such transport may legitimately be captured. Where this occurs, however, the adverse party must ensure the continued care of any wounded and sick who are being transported.

As for all protected facilities, medical transport must not be used to damage the enemy. Thus to use a protected ambulance for the conveyance of uninjured troops for the furtherance of hostile action would lead to discontinuance of protected status in the same way as for similar misuse of protected medical units.[42]

Medical Aircraft

Medical aircraft have come into increasing prominence since 1949 as air technology, and especially helicopters, has developed. Little use was made of medical aircraft in the Second World War, and little if any legal account was taken of them, no reference being made to them by the 1923 Hague Draft Rules on Aerial Warfare. During the Second World War there was some controversy over occasional medical use of aircraft, including non-recognition by the United Kingdom of the activities of German 'ambulance planes' during Operation Sealion (the planned Nazi invasion of the United Kingdom). Later experience, in guerrilla wars such as those in Vietnam, in Afghanistan and in Central and South America, as well as in conventional conflicts such as the 1982 Falklands Conflict, have proved the value of aircraft in medical rescue. This applies especially to medical helicopters, with their capacity to land in otherwise inaccessible terrain and effect a rapid evacuation of casualties. The provision made by 1949 Geneva Convention I for medical aircraft is found in article 36, but it dates from an era when the suitability of aircraft for medical use was little developed, and is fairly minimal. The article provides that:

> Medical aircraft ... exclusively employed for the removal of wounded and sick and for the transport of medical personnel and equipment, shall not be attacked, but shall be respected by the belligerents, while flying at heights, times and on routes specifically agreed upon between the belligerents concerned.

It also requires that such aircraft be clearly marked with the protective emblem as well as their national colours on their 'lower, upper and lateral surfaces'. Flights over enemy or enemy-occupied territory without prior permission are forbidden. Medical aircraft are also required by article 36 to obey a summons to land, but should be allowed to continue their journey after inspection, presuming the inspection has confirmed the claimed medical status of the aircraft in question. In the event of involuntary landing in enemy territory, the military wounded, the sick and the flight crew will be prisoners of war, and the medical personnel may be retained as for land medical personnel. The wounded and sick captured in such circumstances would, of course, have the same rights of respect, protection, care and humanitarian treatment as any other wounded or sick persons in land warfare.

Much more extensive provision is made by 1977 Additional Protocol I, which, in this as in many other areas, built substantially upon the experience of the Vietnam War. Article 24 of the Additional Protocol reasserts the basic principle that medical aircraft are to be respected and protected, but the operations of medical aircraft are subjected to certain restrictions designed to rule out misuses to which they are, by their nature, especially well suited. The main point of this is that medical aircraft may not be used to acquire military advantage over the enemy. Article 28 of the Additional Protocol specifically forbids the use of medical aircraft to immunise military objectives from attack,[43] their use for the collection or transmission of intelligence data, or the carriage of persons or cargo not having protected status,[44] the carriage of armaments, apart from small arms and ammunition taken from patients and not yet handed over to the proper service and light arms carried by medical personnel for the defence of themselves and their patients.[45] The article finally forbids use of medical aircraft to search for wounded and sick over enemy-held or enemy-controlled territory except by prior agreement.[46] The reasoning behind this restriction relates to the possibility of dangerous misunderstanding of such activities by observers from the adverse party. A circling aircraft or hovering helicopter might be thought to be engaged in hostile activity, especially bearing in mind the practical difficulties of visual identification, and become an object of attack under misapprehension.

The detailed regime for the protection of medical aircraft varies according to the nature of the territory or sea which is overflown. Three categories of area are recognised by 1977 Additional Protocol I for this purpose: those under friendly control, contact or similarly disputed zones, and territory under hostile control.

Under article 25 of 1977 Additional Protocol I, no agreement is necessary for flights over land under friendly control, or sea which is not under hostile control. However, it is urged that adverse parties be notified of the presence of such aircraft, especially when their flight paths may bring them within range of surface-to-air missiles.

In a 'contact zone' – an area where there is hostile military contact and especially danger of direct fire from the ground – under article 27 of 1977 Additional Protocol I, fully effective protection of medical aircraft can be obtained only by agreement between the parties in conflict. In the absence of such notification and agreement, medical aircraft fly at their own risk, but they will still be required to be respected once their identity has been established. The point of this provision was illustrated by analogy by an accident in the 1980–88 Gulf War. USS *Vincennes* was engaged in providing protection for tanker convoys in the Gulf when it was attacked by Iranian Revolutionary Guard units. An aircraft was observed approaching from Iran, and was shot down in the belief that its intentions were hostile, but tragically, it turned out to be a civil airliner.[47] In relation to medical aircraft over contact zones, the dangers resulting from difficulties of recognition and rapid-reaction automated weapons systems will be all too obvious. The formal procedures for notifications of overflights or requests for them are set out in article 29 of the Additional Protocol, and it is noted that an adverse party may respond with alternative or varied proposals for the intended overflight.

Under article 27(1) of 1977 Additional Protocol I, medical aircraft overflying enemy-controlled territory or sea will be protected only if prior permission for the overflight has been obtained. Article 27(2) provides that in cases of overflight without permission, whether through navigational error or flight emergency, a medical aircraft is required to identity itself and the cause of the overflight to the adverse party. As soon as it recognises such an aircraft, the adverse party may undertake all reasonable measures to require it to land or take other measures to protect its interests, allowing the aircraft time to comply before attacking it. Again, guidance may be found by analogy, in this case from the shooting down of Korean Airlines Flight KA007 on 1 September 1983. The airliner, on a scheduled flight from Japan to Korea, strayed, for reasons undetermined, over military sensitive Soviet territory, and after ignoring a number of orders to land of varying potential efficacy, was shot down with heavy loss of life.[48] The Soviet action was much criticised as excessive and preceded by too little or inefficacious warning procedures, and the ultimate result was the adoption of a new article 3 to the 1944 Chicago Convention on International Civil Aviation which bans use of weapons against civil aircraft in flight and requires that interceptions be carried out without endangering the lives of persons on board or the safety of the aircraft. This is made subject to non-derogation from rights set out in the UN Charter, clearly including the right of individual and collective self-defence preserved by article 51 of the charter. None of this applies directly to military aircraft of an adverse party in armed conflict, but the implications of the Flight KA007 incident are clear by analogy with the relevant provisions of 1977 Additional Protocol I. At the very least, every endeavour should be made to force the aircraft to land for inspection before any attack is made.

In relation to the identification of military medical aircraft, there are obvious difficulties with the visibility of protective emblems painted on wings, etc., or on the bodies of helicopters, at least when flying at any considerable height. For this reason, 1977 Additional Protocol I, Annex I, article 7, provides for the use by medical aircraft of a flashing blue light, as defined in the Airworthiness Technical Manual of the International Civil Aviation Organisation, Doc. 9051, by way of further identification. British forces experimented with this type of signal on a hospital ship in the 1982 Falklands Conflict, with encouraging results in the poor visibility of the South Atlantic. Sylvie-Stoyanka Junod comments:

> It is interesting to note ... that the experimental use by the British during the conflict of an improvised flashing blue light (police car type) enabled a ship to be identified with binoculars at a distance of seven nautical miles, whereas normal visibility was one nautical mile.[49]

This must be considered encouraging for the designated use of this type of identification upon medical aircraft. It may also be remarked that during the 1982 Falklands Conflict, radar identification of medical helicopters was adopted by tacit agreement between the United Kingdom and Argentina, with useful effect.[50]

It must finally be pointed out that military aircraft which engage in *ad hoc* rescue work are no more protected while doing so than land military vehicles engaged in the same activity. Such work was extensively carried out by military helicopters during the 1982 Falklands Conflict, and Sylvie-Stoyanka Junod remarks of this practice that:

> combat helicopters made up for the insufficient number of medical helicopters by joining in to help transport and evacuate the wounded and shipwrecked. They carried out these missions of assistance and relief at their own risk and peril because, as they were not medical aircraft properly speaking, they were not under any special protection. But such action is in the true spirit of humanitarian law ... These were measures of pressing necessity which are not governed by law.[51]

Such action falls outwith the law in so far as no provision is made for it, and it must certainly be considered an 'own risk' humanitarian act.

The Protective Emblems

It was recognised from the earliest days of 'Geneva' law that it was necessary for persons and establishments engaged in protected humanitarian activity to be distinguished by some distinctive emblem to facilitate their identification and protection. The recognised emblems are described by 1949 Geneva Convention I, article 38, as:

> the heraldic emblem of the red cross on a white ground, formed by reversing the federal colours [of Switzerland and] ... in the case of countries which already use [them] ... the red crescent or the red lion and sun on a white ground.

This is substantially repeated by 1949 Geneva Convention II, article 41, in relation to usage at sea.[52] Models of these three devices are set out in 1977 Additional Protocol I, Annex I, article 4. The origin of these emblems has been considered above,[53] but it must be said that the multiplication of emblems is to be deplored in view of the potential for confusion which it creates. In fact, the red lion and sun emblem, which was insisted upon by the former Shah of Iran, was abandoned after the Iranian Revolution, and the Iranian military medical services have since then used the red crescent emblem. On the other hand, controversy continues to surround the use by the Israeli military medical services of the red star of David, *Magen David Adom*. This is used because of the unacceptable associations of both the cross and the crescent in Israel, but for political reasons unrelated to international humanitarian law, the red star of David is unacceptable to the broad range of Arab states. The end result is that the Israeli emblem has not been accepted officially by the states party to the 1949 Geneva Conventions, but it has been accepted as a *de facto* unofficial substitute, for example in the various Arab–Israeli wars. The conclusion of Jean Pictet on the multiplication of emblems seems most reasonable:

> We cannot but regret [the] ... departure from he universality of the emblem, which has been a source of many difficulties. ... [however,] it has been impossible to find a solution providing for a return to the unity which is so essential. We must hope at least there will be no further breaches in this unity through the creation of new symbols.[54]

Fortunately, with the demise of the red lion and sun emblem, there are in practice only two protective emblems, with the unofficial *de facto* addition of the red star of David, and this is manageable. These emblems are also so well known that the establishment of a new universal emblem, even if one could be found, would cause far more confusion than is even remotely likely in the present situation. As Pictet hints in the passage quoted above, to find a new and universally acceptable emblem would be virtually impossible. The emblem would have to be simple enough to be instantly recognisable at a distance, and over the course of human cultural history almost all simple emblems have been used at various times in one way or another with connotations which would be unacceptable in some country or culture.

It is obviously of great importance that the recognised emblems should be protected from misuse, because if their significance was to become diluted through other uses, their protective value in armed conflict could be seriously diminished. The authorised use of the emblem is set out in articles 39–43 of 1949 Geneva Convention I so far as usage on land is concerned, and by articles 42–44 of 1949 Geneva Convention II so far as usage at sea is concerned.[55] The authorised uses on land are: on flags, armbands and military equipment of the military medical service,[56] and specifically on armbands worn by permanent military and religious personnel,[57] on armbands worn by auxiliary medical personnel *while they are actually engaged on protected medical activities*,[58] for marking of medical units and establishments,[59] and on medical units belonging to neutral countries which have been authorised to supply services to a belligerent. Other uses of the protective emblem are banned by article 44 of 1949 Geneva Convention I. There are only three exceptions to this, also provided for by article 44. Firstly, in peacetime national Red Cross and Red Crescent societies may, in accordance with national law:

> make use of the name and emblem of the Red Cross [or Red Crescent] for their other activities which are in conformity with the principles laid down by the International Red Cross Conferences. When those activities are carried out in time of war, the conditions for the use of the emblem shall be such that it cannot be considered as conferring the protection of the Convention: the emblem shall be comparatively small in size and may not be placed on armlets or on the roofs of buildings.

This is a provision of some importance, and serves to correct the commonly received impression that the red cross or red crescent emblem is in some fashion a corporate logo of national societies. On the contrary, the emblem is precisely a protective emblem designed for use in armed conflict; its peacetime 'indicative' use by Red Cross and Red Crescent societies is, whilst very clearly visible in usual practice, usually a legal *exception* to the principally intended use. The other exceptions set out in article 44 are for the use of emblem 'at all times' by the International Committee of the Red Cross and their duly authorised personnel and, as an exceptional measure and, with the express permission of the relevant national Red Cross or Red Crescent society, the use of the emblem in peacetime to identify ambulances and first aid stations exclusively used to provide free treatment to the wounded and sick. It may be noted that commercial medical organisations providing care upon a fee-paying basis are not entitled to this use.

Misuse of the protective emblem is required to be prohibited at all times by article 53 of 1949 Geneva Convention I. Article 54 of the convention then requires that:

> The High Contracting Parties shall, if their legislation is not already adequate, take measures necessary for the prevention and repression at all times, of the abuses referred to under Article 53.

In the case of the United Kingdom, this is done by section 6 of the Geneva Conventions Act 1957, which makes misuse of the emblem in the UK a criminal offence. The prosecuting authority is the Ministry of Defence, but in practice most instances are dealt with by the British Red Cross without prosecution, typically by a warning letter and a requirement to desist. Most instances are accidental rather than intentional, and result from an ignorant assumption that the emblem is a general designation for anything vaguely 'medical'. The author once saw a billboard for a 'dolls' hospital' in a small-town high street in the south of England (a workshop where broken toys could be taken for repair), which displayed a large red cross. The sign disappeared almost at once, but was clearly a violation of the Geneva Conventions Act 1957: dolls, even when damaged, are not protected entities under either the first or second Geneva Conventions of 1947! The point is that such inappropriate uses might in time of armed conflict compromise the protective value of the emblem in its proper and lawful uses. It is rare that matters proceed so far as actual prosecution, but a case did arise in 1988 with *R.* v. *Whitty*.[60] In a political campaign mounted by the Labour Party in opposition to the health-funding policy of the then Conservative British Government, a logo of a pound sterling sign, the central portion of which was the red cross emblem, was used. The Labour Party General Secretary was found guilty of abusing the emblem in this campaign. Another prominent abuse concerned one of the 'James Bond' films, in which a helicopter marked with the red cross emblem was portrayed in the fictional scenario in hostile use. At screenings of the film in France, it was required that the showing be preceded by an apology and a statement that this use of the red cross emblem was illegal. Other examples of response to deliberate and unintended misuses may readily be found. The precise mechanisms of penalisation and enforcement, and the degrees of their efficacy, vary considerably from country to country, but it is a treaty obligation for all states party to the 1949 Geneva Conventions to undertake such measures.

Status and Protection of Chaplains

Chaplains and equivalent religious personnel are treated by 1949 Geneva Convention I as analogous to medical staff. In most faiths, the presence of a chaplain or equivalent person is not a prerequisite for worship, but in practice the role of chaplains is well established in the armed forces of many nations.[61] The term 'chaplain' is used by 1949 Geneva Conventions I and II, but 1977 Additional Protocol I employs the rather wider term 'religious personnel' as more appropriate in view of the wide differences in confessional and national organisation, and to any damaging appearance of religious or cultural bias. The Protocol defines such personnel by article 8(d) as:

> military or civilian persons, such as chaplains, who are exclusively engaged in the work of their ministry and attached:
> (i) to the armed forces of a Party to the conflict;
> (ii) to medical units or medical transports of a Party to the conflict;
> (iii) to [permanent] medical units or medical transports [supplied by

> a neutral State or authorized aid society or an impartial international humanitarian organization];
> (iv) to civil defence organizations of a Party to the conflict.

Such attachment may be permanent or temporary. The essential requirement is one of *exclusive* engagement in ministry: a soldier who happened to exercise some form of ministry in private life would not for this purpose fall within the category of 'religious personnel'.

The protection afforded to religious personnel is similar to that provided for medical personnel, and is indeed largely stated as an adjunct thereto. 1949 Geneva Convention I provides by article 24 that:

> chaplains attached to the armed forces shall be respected and protected in all circumstances.

Article 15(5) of 1977 Additional Protocol I extends this protection to 'civilian religious personnel'. The scope of protection may be varied by special agreements between the parties in conflict, but article 6 of 1949 Geneva Convention I forbids any adverse variation, as for medical personnel. Article 7 similarly forbids renunciation of protection on the part of the religious personnel themselves. Like their medical counterparts, chaplains in armed conflict on land may not be 'captured', but may, under article 28 of 1949 Geneva Convention I, be 'retained' to perform their spiritual duties for prisoners of their own or an allied nationality.[62] In an age of what is, in many cases wrongly, termed religious 'fundamentalism', the question of religious observance in armed conflict has taken on a renewed sensitivity. The conflicts in former Yugoslavia in the early 1990s, which were at least in part defined, as between Muslim Bosnians, Orthodox Serbs and Roman Catholic Croats, make that point, although the religious divisions should not be ranked above the influence of nationalist feeling and hegemonistic aspiration amongst the sources of those conflicts. The protection of religious personnel implicitly includes, and most certainly should now include, protection from other religious personnel or lay adherents of some other faiths.

Obviously, considerable sensitivity may be required in some situations, including relations with allies which do not fall within the remit of the Geneva Conventions and Protocols. This was evident in the 1990–91 Gulf Conflict, when non-Muslim troops of Coalition forces were stationed in Saudi Arabia, where non-Muslim public worship is illegal and even private observance is severely constrained. US military chaplains in Saudi Arabia were instructed to use great discretion in wearing any clothing of non-Islamic religious significance, meaning in particular the wearing of clerical collars in public.[63]

At Christmas 1990, the British Forces Broadcasting Service refrained from broadcasting any overtly Christian material to British forces in Saudi Arabia, and even Christmas carols were played in instrumental versions only. The Archbishop of Canterbury's Christmas message to British troops in the Gulf area was not sent to Saudi Arabia, although a small number of personnel were taken on a bus, arranged by a journalist, to neighbouring Bahrain, where the message could be received.[64] If such restrictions had been applied to prisoners of war rather than to personnel of allied forces, they would have been in clear violation of 1949 Geneva Convention III.[65]

A more technical, but not wholly insignificant, question arises as to what exactly is a 'religion' for this purpose. No definition is offered by the 1949 Geneva Conventions or 1977 Additional Protocol I. The *Oxford Reference Dictionary* defines a religion as:

> 1. belief in a superhuman controlling power, especially in a personal God or gods entitled to obedience and worship; the expression of this in worship. 2. a particular system of faith.

Devotion to God, or some gods, is thus seen as *prima facie* central, although deity is not necessarily the central focus of a religion: for example, in Buddhism neither a buddha nor the boddhisatvas are seen strictly as gods, but rather as those who have achieved enlightenment, entitled to veneration though they may be. However, Buddhism is clearly a religious faith, and would universally be recognised as such, in common with faiths such as Judaism, Christianity, Islam and Hinduism.[66] What then of secular political or ethical doctrines? Are political ideologies capable of being 'religions' for this purpose, and would political commissars be considered 'religious personnel' under this heading? The answer must presumably be 'no', not least by reason of self-definition and perception.

Notes

1 See Chapter 1.
2 See p. 66.
3 See below.
4 See pp. 115–7.
5 See below.
6 For discussion, see p. 94.
7 Y. Sandoz, C. Swinarski and B. Zimmermann (eds), with J. Pictet, *Commentary on the Additional Protocols of 8 June 1977 to the Geneva Conventions of 12 August 1949* (Martinus Nijhoff, 1987), p. 147, para. 451.
8 *Independent* (London), 19 February 1991.
9 For review, see J.K. Mason and R.A. McCall-Smith, *Law and Medical Ethics* (2nd

edn) (Butterworths, 1987), p. 187ff. For the present purpose, the 2nd edition may be found somewhat fuller than the 3rd edition.

10 See J. Pictet, *Development and Principles of International Humanitarian Law* (Martinus Nijhoff, 1985), p. 88.

11 See p. 211 ff.

12 *Independent* (London), 25 February 1991.

13 Ibid., 17 February 1997.

14 For general discussion, see H. McCoubrey, 'The Wounded and Sick', in P. Rowe (ed.), *The Gulf War 1990–91 in International and English Law* (Routledge/Sweet and Maxwell, 1993), p. 171, at pp. 179–86.

15 F.J. Hampson, 'Conscience in Conflict: The Doctor's Dilemma' (1989) XXVII *The Canadian Yearbook of International Law*, p. 203, at p. 211.

16 Y. Sandoz, C. Swinarski and B. Zimmerman, op.cit., pp. 155–6, para. 476.

17 See ibid., note 11.

18 J.K. Mason and R.A. McCall-Smith, *Law and Medical Ethics* (4th edn) (Butterworths, 1994), p. 351.

19 *Guardian* (London), 7 August 1992.

20 Ibid.

21 The ICRC statement was reported in *The Times* (London), 14 August 1992.

22 See below.

23 For considerations of this in a common law context, see, for example, the Australian case of *H.* v. *Royal Alexandra Hospital for Children* [1990] 1 Med. LR 297.

24 H. McCoubrey, 'Medical Ethics, Negligence and the Battlefield' (1995) XXXIV *Revue de Droit Militaire et de Droit de la Guerre*, p. 103, at p. 113.

25 Y. Sandoz, C. Swinarski and B. Zimmerman, op.cit., pp. 157–8, para. 5.

26 See below, p.

27 See Chapter 5.

28 Article 24.

29 Article 25.

30 Article 26.

31 See pp. 108–110.

32 39 CMR, 672; see also (1973) 1 *Military Law Reporter*, p. 2,130; US Supreme Court Reports, 41 L. Ed., 2d, 439. For discussion of this case, see F.J. Hampson, 'Conscience in Conflict: The Doctor's Dilemma' (1989) XXVII *The Canadian Yearbook of International Law*, p. 203, at pp. 218–22.

33 In modern analyses, the question of culpable knowledge, and culpable avoidance of knowledge in relation to the Holocaust in the Third Reich has been investigated in some detail; see, for example, G. Sereny, *Albert Speer: His Battle with Truth* (Macmillan, 1995, 1st published by Alfred A. Knopf, 1995).

34 For discussion, see under 'The Protective Emblems' below.

35 See p. 127.

36 See p. 187.

37 For discussion in respect of prisoners of war, see Chapter 6; for discussion in respect of civilians, see Chapter 7.

38 1949 Geneva Convention I, article 42.

39 Ibid., article 43.

40 For further discussion of collateral damage, see pp.

41 1949 Geneva Convention I, article 35; 1977 Additional Protocol I, article 21.

42 1949 Geneva Convention I, articles 21 and 22.

43 1977 Additional Protocol I, articles 28(1).

44 Article 28(2).

45 Article 28(3).

46 Article 28(4).

47 For discussion, see M. Agora, 'The Downing of Iran Flight 655' (1989) 83 *American Journal of International Law*, p. 318.
48 See O.J. Lissitzyn, 'The Shooting Down of Korean Airlines Flight 007 by the USSR and the Furtherance of Air Safety for Passengers' (1983) 33 *International and Comparative Law Quarterly*, p. 712.
49 S. Junod, *Protection of the Victims of Armed Conflict, Falkland Malvinas Islands (1982)* (2nd edn), (ICRC, 1985), p. 25.
50 Ibid., p. 26.
51 Ibid., pp. 26–7.
52 For discussion, see Chapter 5.
53 See p. 20.
54 J. Pictet, *Development and Principles of International Humanitarian Law* (Martinus, Nijhoff, 1985), p. 32.
55 For discussion of use at sea, see Chapter 5.
56 Article 39.
57 Article 40.
58 Article 41.
59 Article 42.
60 Reported in *Daily Telegraph* (London), 11 November 1988.
61 For an anecdotal account of chaplaincy in the Second World War, see K. Oliver, *Chaplain at War* (Angel Press, 1986).
62 See also 1949 Geneva Convention III, article 35.
63 *Independent* (London), 13 November, 1990.
64 Ibid., 24 December 1990.
65 See pp. 157–9.
66 This is not an exclusive list, merely a citation of significant examples.

5 Protection of the Wounded, Sick and Shipwrecked at Sea

The principles applicable to the protection of the wounded, sick and shipwrecked at sea are parallel and in many cases identical with those applicable to the wounded and sick in land warfare which have been considered in Chapter 4. However, there are, sufficient distinctions resulting from the differences between activity on land and at sea to justify separate considerations of the relevant provisions. The historical background to the development of international humanitarian provision in naval warfare has been considered above,[1] and the present provision is found primarily in 1949 Geneva Convention II, with some additional provision in 1977 Additional Protocol I. The most important distinctions from the provision made for land warfare lie in the understanding of obligations of search and rescue, and the status and treatment of hospital ships (as medical transport) and their personnel.

The Category of Wounded, Sick and/or Shipwrecked

The categories of persons entitled to protection as 'wounded, sick and shipwrecked' at sea under 1949 Geneva Convention II are defined by article 13 of the convention, and are exactly the same as those entitled to protection as wounded and sick under 1949 Geneva Convention I, except that the category is expanded to include those who are shipwrecked. It is stated by article 12 of the convention that the term 'shipwreck' means 'shipwreck from any cause and includes forced landings at sea by or from aircraft'. The point is expanded and reinforced by article 8(b) of 1977 Additional Protocol I, which provides that:

> 'shipwrecked' means persons, whether military or civilian, who are in peril at sea or in other waters as a result of misfortune affecting them

> or the vessel or aircraft carrying them and who refrain from any act of hostility. These persons, provided that they continue to refrain from any act of hostility, shall continue to be considered shipwrecked during their rescue until they acquire another status under the Conventions or this Protocol.

The most obvious 'other status' will be that of prisoner of war under 1949 Geneva Convention III, in the event of rescue by an adverse party. As in the case of land warfare, 1977 Additional Protocol I extends these categories to include all persons who may be wounded, sick or shipwrecked, whether military personnel or civilians.[2] The requirements of medical care and ethical practice are identical with those applicable on land, including the same concessions to what may be practically possible in a warship's sickbay, apply to a field medical facility.[3] A hospital ship's equipment might be expected to be somewhat more elaborate and sophisticated, although here, too, there will be limitations.

The Duty of Search and Rescue

The obligations to search for and rescue the wounded, sick and shipwrecked at sea is set out by article 18 of 1949 Geneva Convention II, which provides that:

> After each engagement, Parties to the conflict shall, without delay, take all possible measures to search for and collect the shipwrecked, wounded and sick, to protect them against pillage and ill-treatment, to ensure their adequate care, and to search for the dead and prevent their being despoiled.

This is virtually identical with the equivalent provision made for land warfare,[4] but in practice a number of complications arise in the exigencies of search and rescue in warfare at sea. At one time it was envisaged that hospital ships would accompany fleets at sea and, under 'Geneva' protection, be able to search for and collect the wounded and shipwrecked in the immediate aftermath of naval engagements. This idea of medical aid in naval warfare in which specially designed vessels would play an 'ambulance' role as well as providing 'hospital' facilities was not very realistic even in the 19th century, and has certainly not been so during and after the two world wars of the 20th century. In most modern naval engagements, any immediate rescue work is most likely to be carried out by the belligerent warships, hospital ships being used as 'hospital' facilities and as medical transports rather than in an 'ambulance' role.

The performance of search and rescue functions by belligerent warships raises obvious difficulties, most particularly in that they have no protected status, and remain legitimate targets whilst so engaged. This problem is significantly increased in the context of submarine warfare, from the viewpoints of both submarines and surface vessels. The difficulties can readily be illustrated by the accounts of the sinking of the *Bismarck* and *Laconia* in the Second World War and that of the *General Belgrano* in the 1982 Falklands Conflict. The battleship KM *Bismarck* was sunk by British forces on 27 May 1941. After the sinking, the cruiser *Dorsetshire* and the destroyer *Maori* remained in the location to search for survivors. As Ludovic Kennedy describes it:

> The *Dorsetshire* had picked up some eighty men and the *Maori* some twenty ... when *Dorsetshire*'s navigating officer ... sighted ... two miles away a smoky discharge in the water. ... [T]he most likely explanation was a U-Boat ... [and] *Dorsetshire*, laying stopped in the water was a sitting target. In the circumstances ... [there was] no choice but to ring down for full speed.[5]

The point here is that, as article 18 of 1949 Geneva Convention II now requires, 'all possible measures' of search and rescue must be undertaken, but this cannot extend to placing the rescuing ship itself at rationally anticipated risk of loss, which would simply add vastly to the numbers of wounded, sick and shipwrecked. The nature of the dangers can be seen in the detail of the *Laconia* incident. The *Laconia* was a requisitioned former Cunard liner, in use as a transport carrying British and Polish troops and Italian prisoners of war, when it was torpedoed and sunk in the Mediterranean on 12 September 1942 by U-156. The commander of the U-boat *Kapitanleutnant* Werner Hartenstein, did all that, and indeed more than, could have been expected in the performance of humanitarian imperatives. He summoned aid from U-506, U-507 and the Italian submarine *Cappellini* to gather the scattered lifeboats together, and then sent a message to the Vichy French authorities in Dakar informing them of the location of the lifeboats and requesting assistance. In due course, the French cruiser *Gloire* from Dakar rescued nearly 1,000 survivors from the sinking. The dangers involved are illustrated by the fact that U-156 was attacked by an unidentified Allied plane during the rescue work, despite a message sent *en clair* specifying what was being done, and had the attack been pressed and the U-boat destroyed, it would, as a belligerent warship, have been an entirely legitimate target. The *Laconia* sinking had an important and most unfortunate consequence in the notorious '*Laconia* Order'. As a result of Hitler's fury when informed of the incident, Grand Admiral Dönitz issued an order forbidding U-boat commanders to engage in search and rescue activity under any circumstances, except to pick up captains, chief engineers and other personnel who might be capable of providing useful information. This order was an important part of the case later advanced against Dönitz before the International Military Tribunal at Nuremberg in 1945.[6] In so far as the order merely forbade submarine commanders to place their submarines at risk by engaging in search and rescue activity, it did no more than reflect the common and inevitable practice of submarine warfare. However, in so far as it went on to forbid such action in any circumstances, even if there was no rationally anticipated danger of hostile action, except for purposes of information-gathering, it went well beyond the law as it then was and as it now is. The required balance between humanity and possibility is well illustrated by the action of the submarine HMS *Conqueror* after sinking ARA *General Belgrano* on 2 May 1982. *Conqueror* did not, and could not, surface in the face of remaining Argentine surface forces, but did leave the remaining smaller Argentine vessels to engage in their own rescue work undisturbed. As Peter Rowe remarks:

> Apart from the lack of space for receiving the victims, the submarine itself will be at great risk if it surfaces to comply with this obligation [of rescue]. Thus, H.M.S. *Conqueror* was in no position to surface to assist the survivors of the *General Belgrano* ...[7]

Such responses clearly fall within the qualifying caveat, 'all *possible* measures', contained in article 18.

Although there are manifestly practical limitations upon warships' capacity for search and rescue, attacking or molesting survivors is invariably unlawful. There were a number of examples of this in both the First and Second World Wars. In this context it should be said that the more propagandist claims made in this respect should be treated with considerable caution. The submarine warfare of both world wars was governed by a number of conflicting considerations. Allied outrage in the First World War over the practice of sinking without warning must be balanced against the use of Q-ships (apparently unarmed merchant ships carrying concealed heavy armament), with which a U-boat surfacing to warn and sink by gunfire could be destroyed. This was a method which enjoyed some success in the First World War, starting with the sinking of U-36 by the Q-ship *Prince Charles* in July 1915. The practical outcome of developments in submarine warfare was considered by the International Military Tribunal at Nuremberg in 1945 in the case against Grand Admiral Dönitz. He was ultimately acquitted on matters relating to his conduct of submarine warfare, although this was not an endorsement of the '*Laconia* Order', but was convicted, *inter alia*, for his part in the notorious 'Commando Order' of 18 October 1942, by which commandos were ordered to be summarily shot upon capture – a violation of the ban on orders of 'no quarter'.

Amongst the numerous well-documented examples of attacks upon survivors, two in particular merit discussion: the *Llandovery Castle* case[8] in the First World War, and the *Peleus* case[9] in the Second World War. HMHS *Llandovery Castle* was a requisitioned former Union-Castle passenger liner in service as a British hospital ship when on 27 June 1918 it was torpedoed and sunk by U-86 under the command of *Kapitanleutnant* Patzig. Patzig had apparently formed the opinion, on no objectively demonstrable basis, that the *Llandovery Castle* was unlawfully carrying fit military personnel, specifically US airmen, and thus sunk it as having lost its protected status, despite the contrary advice of the officer of the watch, Lieutenant Dithmar. After the sinking, the U-boat surfaced, and survivors in the lifeboats were interrogated in order to secure evidence in support of Patzig's opinion of the *Llandovery Castle*. The results were entirely contrary to his opinion, and after a short time the U-boat fired upon the surviving lifeboats, at least two of which seem to have been destroyed. The third was not damaged, and the survivors from this were found and rescued some two days later by HMS *Lysander*. All the evidence suggests that, having discovered that he had unlawfully sunk a *bona fide* hospital ship, Patzig determined to eliminate the survivors in order to conceal the fact. At the post-war trial of Lieutenants Dithmar and Boldt before a German court, the Second Criminal Senate at Leipzig, it was determined upon this point that:

> Irregular torpedoings had already brought the German Government several times into complications with other [neutral] states, and there was the possibility that this fresh case might still further prejudice the international position of Germany. ... Patzig may have wished to prevent this by wiping out all traces of his action. The false entries in his log book and chart ... were intended ... to achieve this object. This illusion could be, however, of but short duration, if the passengers in the lifeboats ... were allowed to get home. It was therefore necessary to get rid of them ... Herein is to be found the explanation of the unholy decision, which he came to and promptly carried out after his fruitless examination of the boats.[10]

Dithmar and Boldt were convicted and sentenced to terms of imprisonment for their parts in the massacre, although the primary guilt was stated to lie with Patzig, who had by then absconded.

A somewhat similar incident gave rise to the *Peleus* case.[11] The *Peleus* was a Greek freighter under charter to the British Ministry of War Transport when it was torpedoed and sunk on 13 March 1944 by

U-852 under the command of *Kapitanleutnant* Heinz Eck. The sinking fell within the law of warfare at sea, but after the sinking, U-852 surfaced, and survivors were interrogated to discover the identity of the sunken ship, after which, with the aid of searchlight illumination, they were systematically massacred by machine gun fire and hand grenades. Three men survived, and were picked up on 2 April by the Portuguese ship *Alexandre Silva*. Eck and some of his personnel were tried before a British military tribunal in Hamburg, at which the judge advocate was Major Melford-Stevenson, who was later to be Mr Justice Melford-Stevenson. The tribunal conceded that in the circumstances, Eck would have acted lawfully in simply departing from the scene without attempting rescue, but in surfacing and perpetrating a massacre of survivors, he had very plainly committed a war crime. The reasoning of the tribunal closely followed that advanced in the *Llandovery Castle* case.[12] The motivation for the massacre remains obscure. The sinking itself was probably not unlawful, and the argument that the U-boat wished to protect himself by concealing its location, which would in any case not be a defence in such circumstances, will not stand, since the submarine was placed at much greater risk by surfacing in order to interrogate and then kill the survivors. Eck specifically denied that he had acted under superior orders, specifically the '*Laconia* Order', perhaps in an effort to shield Dönitz, who was then himself on trial, although Eck's action went far beyond anything demanded by the '*Laconia* Order'. The most cogent suggestion put forward was that members of Eck's family had suffered in Allied bombing, and that his action may simply have been an act of private vengeance. Eck and two others were sentenced to death and executed, and two further members of the personnel of U-852 received long sentences of imprisonment.

The overall state of the law which follows from these cases and present treaty provision is fairly simple. There is a duty to engage in search and rescue in naval warfare where that is *possible* – a qualifying term which includes not placing the rescuing ship itself in rationally anticipated danger. Where rescue is not thus possible, the practice of naval warfare and the substance of treaty provision, as well as the existing case jurisprudence,[13] all indicate that no offence is committed by instant departure. Massacre or other molestation of survivors, on the other hand, will invariably be unlawful.

Hospital Ships

Exactly when the idea of ships specifically dedicated to medical or hospital use first developed is unclear. The International Committee of the Red Cross Commentary on 1949 Geneva Convention II refers to an ancient Athenian vessel called the *Therapia* and to a Roman ship called the *Aesculapius*, which may, given their names, have been in some sense 'hospital ships'. There is little or no evidence of such dedicated medical vessels in the intervening centuries, but the use of hospital ships is a well-established aspect of modern warfare.

1949 Geneva Convention II specifies three types of hospital ships. The primary category is 'military hospital ships' of the belligerent powers; there are also hospital ships utilised by humanitarian relief societies in parties in conflict, and finally, such ships coming from neutral states. Military hospital ships are defined by 1949 Geneva Convention II, article 22, as:

> ships built or equipped by the Powers specially and solely with a view to assisting the wounded, sick and shipwrecked, to treating them and to transporting them ...

In practice, most navies do not construct permanent hospital ships, which would for the most part be unused. The United States Navy does have two permanent hospital ships, USHS *Mercy* and *Solace*, converted from other uses after a plan to convert the former record-breaking Atlantic liner *United States* was abandoned, but this is quite unusual. Other countries have vessels which are supposedly on stand-by for early conversion if needed, as, for example, was the former British Royal Yacht HMY *Britannia*. However, such status has commonly had more budgetary than practical implication, much in the manner that SMS *Hohenzollern*, the Imperial Yacht of Kaiser Wilhelm II, was officially designated a 'dispatch vessel' before the First World War. Most hospital ships are requisitioned merchant or other ships converted to military medical use for the duration of hostilities. Thus during the 1982 Falklands Conflict, the United Kingdom converted the large P&O (ex-British India S.N. Co.) liner *Uganda* and three smaller oceanographic survey ships, HMS *Herald, Hecla* and *Hydra,* into hospital ships, whilst Argentina converted the naval transport ARA *Almirante Irizar*. Argentina also proposed to convert a third vessel, the *Puerto Deseado,* for use as a hospital ship, but hostilities ended before this could be done.[14] In both world wars, the overwhelming majority of hospital ships were also converted merchant vessels. Article 33 of 1949 Geneva Convention II provides that:

> Merchant vessels which have been transformed into hospital ships cannot be put to any other use throughout the duration of hostilities.

This important prohibition derives from experience in the Second World War, when it was found that a number of valuable merchant ships were suddenly and temporarily designated hospital ships simply to avert their capture. Particular examples were the Italian ship *Ramb IV* at Massawa and the German ship *Rostock* at Bordeaux, the latter being found upon detention to carry naval codes and to be under instruction to engage in militarily useful weather reporting.[15]

Article 22 of 1949 Geneva Convention II requires that military hospital ships be notified by name and description to the parties to the conflict not less than ten days prior to their deployment as hospital ships as a condition of their protected status. Such notification must specify the ship's registered gross tonnage, overall length and number of masts and funnels. This latter information is most conveniently conveyed by the Talbot-Booth standard system for ship recognition, listing masts, kingposts and funnels in order as they occur from stem to stern. A ship with two masts, one forward kingpost and one funnel would appear on this system as MKFM.

Hospital ships supplied by relief societies, such as national Red Cross or Red Crescent societies, or private persons in a state party to the conflict are stated by article 24 of 1949 Geneva Convention II to enjoy the same protection as military hospital ships, provided they have been officially commissioned by the party on which they depend and have been notified in the same way as military hospital ships under article 22. They must be provided with a certificate from the responsible authorities stating that they have been under their control while fitting out and upon departure.

Hospital ships contributed by relief societies or private persons in neutral countries are similarly protected under article 25 of 1949 Geneva Convention II if they have been placed under the control of one of the parties to the conflict with the authorisation of that state and the consent of their own government, and have been notified to other parties in accordance with article 22.

At one time it was required that hospital ships should be of more than 2,000 tons gross. Article 26 of 1949 Geneva Convention II now states that there is no minimum tonnage for a hospital ship, but still requires parties to 'endeavour' to use ships above 2,000 tons gross to maximise the comfort and security of the wounded when carried over long distances or on the high seas. In addition to sea-going hospital ships, small craft may also engage in coastal search and rescue work. Article 27 of 1949 Geneva Convention II provides that such craft so employed by the state or a recognised lifeboat institution, such as the RNLI in the UK, will be respected and protected as long as they meet the requirements set out by articles 22 or 24 of the convention. This provision is significantly softened by article 22(3) of 1977 Additional Protocol I, which provides that such craft will be protected even in the absence of the notification required by article 27, by reference to articles 22 and 24, of Convention II, but still urges parties to make such notification for the facilitation of identification and recognition. This would appear to be an attempt to facilitate the ready availability of inshore rescue craft in what may well be unpredictable situations of emergency.

Hospital ships are required to be clearly identified. Article 43 of 1949 Geneva Convention II specifies that all exterior surfaces must be painted white, and one or more dark red crosses, or red crescents, which should be as large as possible, must be displayed on each side of the hull and other appropriate flat surfaces to maximise visibility from the sea and air. Hospital ships are sometimes depicted as carrying a broad green band round the hull: this was a style adopted under earlier provision, but is now obsolete. Article 43 also requires that hospital ships fly a white flag with a red cross or red crescent upon it as high as possible on the mainmast, and they must also fly their national flag. The article also requires that a hospital ship which belongs to a neutral state must in addition fly the flag of the party to the conflict under the direction of which it has been placed.

Article 43 also requires that lifeboats from hospital ships, coastal lifeboats and other small craft in use by the medical services follow the same general scheme of identification set out for larger vessels. Where coastal lifeboats continue to operate from a base which is under adverse control, they may, under article 43 and subject to the consent of the occupying power and with prior notice to all the parties to the conflict, continue to fly their national flag along with that displaying the protective emblem. The limitations on the use of the red cross and red crescent emblems at sea are the same as those applicable on land and in the air.[16]

According to article 22 of 1949 Geneva Convention II, a properly identified and, where necessary, notified hospital ship or relevant medical craft 'may in no circumstances be attacked or captured, but shall at all times be respected and protected'. This requirement is the same in effect and carries the same implications as the equivalent provisions for medical establishments and transport on land, except that hospital ships have a much greater degree of immunity from potential adverse control than do land medical establishments. The basic conditions of their use are set out by article 30 of 1949 Geneva Convention II in terms that they:

> shall afford relief and assistance to the wounded, sick and shipwrecked without distinction of nationality. The High Contracting Parties undertake not to use these vessels for any military purpose. Such vessels shall in no wise hamper the movements of the combatants. During and after an engagement, they will act at their own risk.

Most of this is simply an application at sea of equivalent land provision, especially with regard to non-use of protected medical facilities for belligerent purposes. The last sentence of this provision requires explanation, however. It is certainly not a licence to attack a hospital ship going about its humanitarian duties; it is rather a reference to the evident dangers of 'collateral damage'. The most obvious example of this type of situation, albeit somewhat distanced from the precise phrasing of article 30, can be seen in the instance of the largest hospital ship even to be sunk, HMHS *Britannic*, in 1916. The *Britannic* was the third sister of the White Star liners *Olympic* and *Titanic*, and one of the largest ships in the world at that time. Upon completion after the outbreak of war in 1914, the *Britannic* was immediately requisitioned as a hospital ship, and put to use ferrying wounded from the Dardanelles campaign between Mudros and Southampton. On its final such voyage, the vessel struck a mine and sank on 21 November 1916 in the Zea Channel in the Aegean while *en route* to the United Kingdom with wounded from Gallipoli. The minefield was newly sown, and there had been no time for its location to be notified as required by 1907 Hague Convention VIII, article 3. The claims made during the war that the *Britannic* had been torpedoed in a major 'war crime' had no real foundation, and later investigation of the wreck by the late Commander Cousteau[17] and by Dr Robert Ballard of the Woods Hole Oceanographic Institute have confirmed that the damage to the ship was inflicted by mines.[18] This sinking must be considered a tragic accident of war, rather than a violation of the humanitarian *jus in bello*. The protective emblems correctly displayed by the *Britannic* were, of course, of no assistance in the particular circumstances of encounter with an unknown minefield.

During the Second World War, a significant problem developed with aerial identification of hospital ships, tragically illustrated by the sinking of the German hospital ship *Tübingen* by RAF bombers in 1945. For this reason, hospital ships are now required to display the protective emblem, so that it is visible from the air as well as from sea. In relation to the *Tübingen* sinking, J.C. Mossop commented:

> Accidental air attacks on hospital ships on both sides were not infrequent during the 1939 war, and it has been suggested that some kind of radar recognition device ought to be made available to enable them to signal their identity to attacking planes.[19]

1977 Additional Protocol I makes provision for a radio recognition signal in Annex I, article 7, as well as for a light signal (primarily for medical aircraft) in Annex I, article 6, which was used experimentally on a British hospital ship in the 1982 Falklands Conflict, with encouraging results.[20] However, any means of long-range identification may still cause problems in certain circumstances. As Mossop remarked:

> a hospital ship cannot remain illuminated in a port, where it might guide enemy bombers to their target, or whilst passing through defensive minefields, when it might betray the swept channels. Similarly, it is imperative that hospital ships should not broadcast when they are following up a landing operation, such as that carried out by the Allies in North Africa since [this] ... provides a clear indication to enemy intelligence of the approximate timing and location of the landing. ... [I]t must accept the risk of accidental [but not deliberate] attack and cannot complain if [in such circumstances] it is mistaken for a legitimate target.[21]

This does not mean that a hospital ship can properly fail to display the required protective markings, nor does it mean that a deliberate attack upon a hospital ship which remains under legitimate protection by 1949 Geneva Convention II can ever be justified.

The importance of identification and then avoidance of all ambiguity was pointedly illustrated by an accident in the 1982 Falklands Conflict. Allegations were made that the British hospital ship *Uganda* might have been carrying fit troops to the combat zone, which would, if true, have been a most serious breach of terms of 1949 Geneva Convention II. This allegation was strongly denied by the then Chief Naval Judge Advocate, Captain L.W.L. Chelton RN and the ICRC representative on board *Uganda* afforded the allegation no credence. It seems that a confusion arose between the *Uganda* and the *Canberra*, a requisitioned P&O cruise liner in use as a troopship. The *Canberra*, although much bigger than the *Uganda* and very different in profile, was still in cruise-ship white during the conflict, although obviously not painted with red cross emblems, and in the very poor visibility of the South Atlantic a distant view of a large, white ship disembarking troops seems to have been dangerously misinterpreted.[22] The potential dangers of any such confusion will be obvious, and are indeed illustrated plainly by the facts of the *Dover Castle* case in the First World War.[23] Neither the *Uganda* nor the *Canberra* behaved in any way improperly or unlawfully, but the avoidance of any chance of ambiguity or false allegation must always be counselled, in this case by a coat of grey paint on the *Canberra*, whenever that may be practically possible.

Although a hospital ship is itself immune from capture, warships of the adverse power may demand that the wounded, sick and shipwrecked, of whatever nationality, on board be surrendered. In permitting this, however, article 14 of 1949 Geneva Convention II requires that any person so seized must be medically in a fit state to be moved, and that the warship has adequate facilities for any continuing treatment necessary. This provision is essentially a concession to the fears of belligerents that slightly injured personnel whom they permit to pass may very shortly return to the field as combatants.

Article 31 of 1949 Geneva Convention II permits parties in conflict to search and control hospital ships dependent upon adverse parties. An adverse party may refuse assistance from a hospital ship and order it off. This might be done, for example, to avoid wounded and sick falling into adverse, rather than friendly hands, and so becoming prisoners of war. Parties to an armed conflict may also require a hospital ship to follow a prescribed course, control the use of its means of communication and, where 'grave circumstances' justify such action, detain it for a period not exceeding seven days. The International Committee of the Red Cross Commentary on the 1949 Geneva Conventions suggests in relation to this article of Convention II that the 'grave circumstances' for this purpose would refer only to the need to maintain absolute secrecy regarding military deployments and operations by preventing the hospital ship from witnessing such deployments.[24] The time limit of seven days on the permitted period of detention of hospital ships reflects a number of abuses of unlimited detention in the Second World War, one of the most flagrant being that of the Netherlands hospital ship *Op ten Noort*, detained by the Japanese after seizure upon ill-founded suspicion of misuse.[25] Where an adverse party imposes measures of control upon a hospital ship, it may also place a temporary Commissioner, normally one of its naval officers, on board to supervise compliance. Orders given by such a Commissioner should, wherever possible, be noted in the ship's log in a language comprehensible to the commander. There was at one time a somewhat bizarre debate as to whether such a Commissioner would be liable to capture in the event of the hospital ship on which he or she has been placed falling in with a warship of its own side. The 1907 Hague Conference took the view that such a Commissioner could not be captured, because armed hospital ship personnel are immune from capture. The International Committee of the Red Cross Commentary on the 1949 Geneva Conventions takes the view that this was a confusion arising from the fact that members of a hospital's ship's personnel do not lose protected status merely by virtue of carrying small arms for their own or their patients' protection.[26] An imposed Commissioner, as an enemy naval officer, would not really be a member of the ship's personnel within the sense of the convention, and could therefore presumably be captured.[27] It is possible to argue that if the Commissioner were a medic, a case of this sort might be made out, but this seems extremely unlikely granted that the Commissioner's function would clearly be navigational rather than medical in the circumstances envisaged by article 31.

After the First World War there was an equally extraordinary debate upon the question of whether a hospital ship could legitimately be used for the transport of wounded or sick victims of armed conflict on land rather than conflict at sea. During that war, such transport had been commonplace, and some of the world's largest ships, including the *Aquitania* and *Britannic*, were used on this service during the Dardanelles campaign. In the *Dover Castle* case,[28] a hospital ship sinking which turned primarily upon issues of superior orders, the question of carriage of land wounded and sick was raised as a peripheral issue before the 2nd Criminal Senate at Leipzig. A. Pierce Higgins commented that the then applicable 1907 Hague Convention X, equivalent to 1949 Geneva Convention II, made no express reference to the carriage by sea of soldiers who had been wounded in land warfare, although it did make reference to the carriage of 'soldiers' *per se*.[29] Furthermore, the Report of the Commission which preceded the original 1899 Hague Declaration 3, the first humanitarian provision for the victims of warfare at sea, stated:

> The rules set forth should be applied from the moment that there are wounded and sick on board sea-going vessels, it being immaterial where the wound was given or the sickness contracted, whether on land or sea.[30]

Pierce Higgins concluded that it would have been better had this been made express in 1899 Hague Declaration 3 and 1907 Hague Convention X, even though the intention was quite clear.[31] In relation to an incident involving the Russian hospital ship *Orel* in the 1904–5 Russo-Jananese War,[32] A. Pierce Higgins concluded that a hospital ship could not properly be used to carry uninjured personnel of destroyed merchant ships who had been taken on board by the warship which destroyed them.[33] Some qualification must now be made, in that if they were injured, a hospital ship would be able to carry them, not least by reference now to 1977 Additional Protocol I, article 8(a), which generalises the category of 'wounded and sick' to include civilians. The uninjured would remain quite another matter, and it may be as, Pierce Higgins argued, that use, in effect, as a prisoner of war or internees' transport would remain an impermissible use of a hospital ship in such circumstances.

So far as the general issue is concerned, the matter is not expressly covered by 1949 Geneva Convention II or 1977 Additional Protocol I. However, the phrasing of article 13 common to 1949 Geneva Conventions I and II, together with the fact of its being common to both conventions, makes it clear that the service to which the wounded, sick or shipwrecked belong, or the place of their injury or infection, is not of significance for the purposes of 'Geneva' provision.

It would be normal practice for a hospital ship to disembark wounded and sick in a home or at any rate friendly port. However, for reasons of emergency or otherwise, it might be necessary for a hospital ship to call at a neutral or even hostile port. A hospital ship thus visiting a neutral port is not, by reference to article 32 of 1949 Geneva Convention II, considered a 'warship', so it will not be bound by the limitations on length of stay applicable to belligerent warships visiting neutral ports.[34] The hospital ship must therefore be allowed to proceed on its way, but under article 17 of the second Convention, if belligerent wounded and sick are landed in the neutral port, they may, in default of other arrangements, be held by the neutral power, with the costs being borne by the power upon which they depend.

Loss of Protection by Hospital Ships

According to article 34 of 1949 Geneva Convention II, hospital ships will lose their protected status only if they are 'used to commit, outside their humanitarian duties, acts harmful to the enemy'. Such 'acts' specifically include possession or use of secret codes for wireless or other modes of communication, the fear here being essentially one of abuse or protected status for purposes of intelligence-gathering. Overly hostile military action by a hospital ship would *ex hypothesi* also constitute compromising acts harmful to the enemy. Even when a hospital ship has *prima facie* forfeited its protected status, article 34 still requires that 'in all appropriate cases' a due warning should be given and a reasonable time be permitted for compliance before action can be taken against the vessel. 'Appropriate cases' here clearly means 'within the limits of practical possibility'.

Article 35 of Convention II then sets out five circumstances which will *not* deprive a hospital ship of its protected status:

1 the possession by personnel of arms 'for their own defence or that of the sick and wounded'
2 the possession on board of equipment solely for the facilitation of navigation or communication (other than secret codes)
3 the presence on board of 'portable' arms removed from patients and not yet handed over to the proper authorities
4 the presence on board of sick or wounded civilians
5 the carriage of medical personnel or equipment beyond the normal requirements.

In the light of the ending of distinctions between military and civilian wounded and sick by 1977 Additional Protocol I, article 8(a), the fourth exception cited above has lost its significance. It should further go without saying that any apparent violation of the conditions of protection by a hospital ship should be checked carefully before any adverse action in response is taken. The experience of the *Dover*

Castle case[35] and the *Llandovery Castle* case[36] in the First World War will serve to illustrate this point.

Protection of Hospital Ship Personnel

The protection of hospital ship personnel under 1949 Geneva Convention II is in some respects more extensive than that afforded to their land-based colleagues under 1949 Geneva Convention I, because of the different conditions obtaining at sea. Article 36 of the convention provides that:

> The religious, medical and hospital personnel of hospital ships and their crews shall be respected and protected: they may not be captured during the time they are in the service of the hospital ship, whether or not they are wounded and sick on board.

In this case, immunity from 'capture' is not taken to be subject to the caveat of 'retention' which is applied in land warfare, although this will apply where hospital ship personnel fall into enemy hands on land, in which case they fall within the provisions of Convention II. The principle of retention is also applied by article 37 of 1949 Geneva Convention II to medical personnel serving on ships other than hospital ships. For example, this would apply to the medical personnel of a belligerent warship. Religious, medical and hospital personnel on hospital and other ships are required by 1949 Geneva Convention II, article 42, to identify themselves by wearing an armband bearing the protective emblem, and must also carry the required identity cards and discs in the same way as equivalent land-based personnel. Article 42 of Convention II is in precisely the same form as article 40 of 1949 Geneva Convention I.

It will be noted that the protection extended by article 36 of Convention II applies not only to religious, medical and hospital personnel of hospital ships, but also to their crews. The reason for this is obvious: if those responsible for the navigation and general running of the ship could be removed by an adverse party, the ship, and the wounded and sick on board, would at the very least be placed in a situation of grave peril.

Medical Transports

According to 1949 Geneva Convention II, article 38, these are ships chartered for the conveyance of medical equipment for the treatment of wounded and sick from the armed forces, or the prevention of disease. It may be taken that 1977 Additional Protocol I, article 8(a), at least implicitly extends this to include the transport of medical equipment for the treatment of civilian wounded and sick. The reference to vessels 'chartered' for this purpose is curious. A charterparty is essentially a contract for the hire of a ship,[37] and it is difficult to see why medical transports for the present purpose should be limited by reference to this particular commercial practice. It seems a better view that it is intended that all ships taken up for this purpose, whether by charterparty or, more likely, by requisition or other such means, will fall within the meaning of the article. Article 38 of Convention II provides that as long as the particulars of its voyage have been notified to the adverse party, such a ship may not be captured nor its cargo seized. However, representatives of the adverse power may be placed on board such a ship by agreement in order to verify the equipment carried, and an adverse power may also board the vessel for inspection. Any such representative or boarding party must be granted freedom of access for the purposes of inspection while on board.

Other Medical Ships

Under 1949 Geneva Convention I, 'other medical ships and craft', meaning those not otherwise protected, are afforded the same protection as mobile medical units under 1977 Additional Protocol I, article 23. They must display the protective emblem, and may be ordered off, ordered to stop or directed as to course by 'any warship on the surface able immediately to enforce its command',[38] but may not otherwise be diverted from their medical mission as long as this is needed for the wounded, sick and/or shipwrecked on board. The protection will cease only in the same conditions as apply to hospital ships.[39] It is clear that this protective provision extends to short-term medical usages. The ICRC Commentary on 1977 Additional Protocol I remarks in this context:

> For example, a simple fishing boat requisitioned exclusively for the transport of medicines to a hospital situated on an island falls under the category of medical ships and craft as long as the transport lasts.[40]

The central point is that these are not necessarily *permanent* medical craft, and are therefore afforded protection only while actually engaged in medical work, in contrast with permanently designated hospital ships.

Article 23(6) of 1977 Additional Protocol I provides that wounded, sick and shipwrecked civilians who fall outwith any of the categories set out in article 13 of 1949 Geneva Convention II may not be removed from the ship by any party other than their own while on board such ships at sea. If they do fall into enemy hands while on land, they will be protected by 1949 Geneva Convention IV and the relevant provisions of 1977 Additional Protocol I governing civilian wounded and sick.

Warship Sickbays

Warship sickbays are afforded a level of legal protection by article 28 of 1949 Geneva Convention II. This provides that 'should fighting occur on board a warship' – a rather unlikely eventuality in most situations of modern naval warfare – the sickbay is to be 'respected and spared' as far as possible. However, the article goes on to provide that such sickbays and their equipment 'remain subject to the laws of warfare'. This means that they may be captured – indeed, since the warship itself can be captured, this is unavoidable. The sickbay and equipment must in such a case continue in use for the treatment of the wounded and sick unless they are diverted to other uses by reason of 'urgent military necessity', and, even then, the continuing proper case of the wounded and sick must be ensured. The meaning of 'urgent military necessity' in such a case is very limited, and really means circumstances which are in practice militarily unavoidable: a circumstance which is certainly not to be equated with mere tactical convenience.[41]

Medical Aircraft at Sea

There is no particular distinction between medical aircraft operating over the sea and those operating over land. The provisions governing their movements are the same as for those operating over land, and are governed by 1949 Geneva Convention II, article 39, which repeats 1949 Geneva Convention I, article 36, and by articles 24–31 of 1977 Additional Protocol I, considered above.[42] Medical helicopters attached to hospital ships were used to some effect during the 1982 Falklands Conflict, and as civilian air-sea rescue experience has demonstrated, this is a valuable humanitarian usage. There were relatively few such helicopters in the Falklands Conflict, and much rescue work was carried out by military helicopters, which, for reasons considered above, have no particular protected status while so engaged.[43]

Red Cross Boxes

Although hospital ships are not legitimate targets, and are thus legally immune from attack under 1949 Geneva Convention II, they are forbidden to hamper the movement of combatants by article 30 of the convention, and this inevitably places some restrictions on their location and movements. During the 1982 Falklands Conflict, the United Kingdom suggested, and Argentina agreed to, the establishment of a neutral maritime zone approximately 120 nautical miles in diameter to the north of the islands, which became known as the 'Red Cross Box'. The idea of this arrangement, for which no provision is made in either 1949 Geneva Convention II or 1977 Additional Protocol I, was to provide a designated safe area in which hospital ships could maintain station and, where necessary, exchange wounded between the adverse parties. The 'Red Cross Box' received favourable comment in the report on the conflict issued by the ICRC,[44] and it was clearly of great value in that particular situation. However, it must be pointed out that such an arrangement would only be of value in the rather limited range of circumstances in which geographical location renders the designation of defined 'safe zones' a practical possibility. This is relatively easy in the case of an isolated South Atlantic group, but much less viable, for example, in the Gulf, where no such arrangement was made in either the 1980–88 Gulf War or the 1990–91 Gulf Conflict. Nevertheless, the precedent may prove useful for *ad hoc* agreed action should the appropriate circumstances recur.

Notes

1 See Chapter 1.
2 1977 Additional Protocol I, articles 8(a)(b) and 22(d).
3 See 1949 Geneva Convention II, article 12, and 1977 Additional Protocol I, articles 10 and 11. For discussion, see Chapter 4.
4 See 1949 Geneva Convention I, article 15.
5 L. Kennedy, *Pursuit: The Sinking of the Bismarck* (Collins, 1975), pp. 203–4.
6 See Chapter 10.
7 P. Rowe, *Defence: The Legal Implications* (Brassey's Defence Publishers, 1987), pp. 188–9.
8 (1922) 16 *American Journal of International Law*, p. 708.
9 *Law Reports of Trials of War Criminals* (HMSO, 1947), Vol. I, p. 1. A more extended account will be found in *War Crimes Trials* (William Hocky, 1948), Vol. I.
10 (1922) 16 *American Journal of International Law*, p. 708, at p. 718.
11 See note 9.
12 See above.
13 It should be remembered that in public international law there is no doctrine of common law *stare decisis*, and cases are of no more than persuasive authority, although that persuasion may be very considerable. See article 38 of the Statute

of the International Court of Justice, which is generally accepted as a statement of the sources of public international law, albeit for a court of civil jurisdiction only. For further discussion, see Chapter 10.

14 See S. Junod, *Protection of the Victims of Armed Conflict, Falklands Malvinas Islands* (2nd edn), (ICRC, 1985), p. 24.
15 See J.C. Mossop, 'Hospital Ships in the Second World War' (1947) 24 *British Yearbook of International Law*, p. 398, at p. 404.
16 See 1949 Geneva Convention II, articles 41, 43 and 44.
17 See *The Titanic Commutator*, Winter 1977 and Winter 1978.
18 See S. Mills, *Britannic: The Last Titan* (Waterfront Publications, 1992), Ch. 6.
19 J.C. Mossop, op.cit., at p. 402.
20 See above.
21 J.C. Mossop, op.cit., at p. 402.
22 See H.S. Levie, 'The Falklands Crisis and the Laws of War', in A.R. Coll and A.C. Arend, *The Falklands War: Lessons for Strategy, Diplomacy and International Law* (George Allen and Unwin, 1985), p. 64, at pp. 67–8 and p. 77, note 3.
23 See below.
24 See J. Pictet, *The Geneva Conventions of 12 August 1949: Commentary* (ICRC, 1952–60) in reference to article 31 of Convention II.
25 See J.C. Mossop, op.cit., at p. 406.
26 See below.
27 See J. Pictet, op.cit., note 24, in relation to article 31 of Convention II.
28 See below.
29 A. Pierce Higgins, 'The Carriage of Sick and Wounded Soldiers by Hospital Ships' (1921–22) 2 *British Yearbook of International Law*, pp. 177–8.
30 Ref. Parliamentary Papers, Misc. No. 1 (1899), p. 74.
31 A. Pierce Higgins, op.cit., at p. 178.
32 Not to be confused with the battleship of the same name.
33 A. Pierce Higgins, 'Hospital Ships and the Carriage of Passengers and Crews of Destroyed Prizes' [1910] CIV *Law Quarterly Review*, pp. 408–14, especially at pp. 412–13.
34 See Ch. 6.
35 See pp. 126–7.
36 See p. 127.
37 See E.R. Hardy Ivamy, *Payne & Ivamy's Carriage of Goods by Sea* (13th edn) (Butterworths, 1989), Chapter 2.
38 1977 Additional Protocol I, article 23(2).
39 Ibid., article 23(3).
40 Y. Sandoz, C. Swinarski and B. Zimmermann (eds) with J. Pictet, *Commentary on the Additional Protocols of 8 June 1977 to the Geneva Conventions of 12 August 1949* (ICRC/Martinus Nijhoff, 1987), p. 263, para. 886.
41 For discussion, see H. McCoubrey, 'The Nature of the Modern Doctrine of Military Necessity' (1991) XXX *Revue de Droit Militaire et de Droit de la Guerre*, pp. 215–42.
42 See Chapter 4.
43 See p. 105.
44 See S. Junod, op.cit.

6 Protection of Prisoners of War

Of all the victims of armed conflict, prisoners of war are perhaps the most vulnerable. Interned in a country with which the state on which they depend is in armed conflict, they are an inevitable target for hostility. They tend to be detained in camps guarded by second-line troops who are not likely to have any other opportunity for confrontation with representatives of the enemy. The problem is not a new one, indeed the treatment of prisoners taken in war is considered in the Old Testament.[1]

This is of considerable interest in that, as considered in Chapter 1, there is evidence of an increasing degree of humanitarianism over time in the treatment of enemies captured in war. The lot of the prisoner in ancient warfare was generally harsh, and even in later eras the standard of treatment, especially of non-officer prisoners, left much to be desired. Much progress has been made in provision for prisoners of war in the 19th and 20th centuries, even if there have been some notorious lapses. The systematic protection of prisoners of war remains a complex issue, however, and one in which much sensitivity and alertness is necessary if effective implementation is to be secured.

Combatant and Prisoner of War Status

Not all persons captured in the course of armed conflict are entitled to the status of 'prisoner of war' and the legal protection associated therewith. The basic principle is that persons who are recognised as 'combatants' under the 1949 Conventions and 1977 Additional Protocol I are entitled to be treated as prisoners of war upon capture by an adverse party in armed conflict. The basic category is defined by 1949 Geneva Convention III, article 4, as:

> Members of the armed forces of a Party to the conflicts as well as members of military or volunteer corps forming part of such armed forces.

It is not necessary for the authority upon which such a force depends to be recognised by the capturing power for its members to be entitled to prisoner of war status upon capture.[2] Such a force must be under 'responsible command', however, meaning a hierarchic chain of command answerable for the conduct of the force to the party upon which it depends; it must be subject to a system of internal discipline which, *inter alia*, enforces the laws of armed conflict; it must wear uniform or some other 'fixed distinctive sign', and it must carry arms openly.[3] In addition to members of armed forces, the following are also entitled to prisoners of war status upon capture under 1949 Geneva Convention III, article 4A:

1 members of militias and volunteer corps, including resistance movements, whether inside or beyond their own territory, and whether or not the latter is under adverse occupation; however, such bodies must satisfy the same qualificatory criteria as regular armed forces[4]
2 members of the crews of merchant ships and civil aircraft of parties in conflict who do not otherwise benefit from more favourable treatment
3 civilian support staff accompanying armed forces, including labour units, welfare staff and accredited war correspondents; to qualify for protection, such persons must be authorised to act in their stated capacity by the armed force which they accompany, and must be provided with an identity card of a form set out in Annex IV to the convention
4 members of a *levée en masse* acting in immediate response to invasion; these are the people of a non-occupied territory who rise in arms to resist invasion without having had time to organise in regular units; however, they must carry arms openly and observe the laws and customs of war.

1977 Additional Protocol I specifically provides for the incorporation into regular armed forces of paramilitary or armed law enforcement agencies, but such incorporation must be notified to other parties to the conflict.[5] Article 67 of the Protocol also extends prisoner of war status to captured members of civil defence units.

Amongst the most controversial provisions of Protocol I are those which significantly relax the qualificatory criteria for the identification of 'armed forces' whose members are entitled to prisoner of war status upon capture. These ideas were the product of certain perceived changes in patterns of armed conflict since 1949. It is certainly the case that 'guerrilla' and other less 'formal' types of warfare have come into marked prominence since 1949.

The armed conflicts in Vietnam, Afghanistan, the Lebanon and, in different ways, in former Yugoslavia and in Somalia emphasised the difficulties which may arise in this type of warfare. The opinion voiced in the 1970s, in the light of the experience of the Vietnam War, that guerrilla war would be the 'typical' pattern of any future conflicts has, unsurprisingly, been proven wrong by subsequent events. The examples of the 1982 Falklands Conflict, the 1980–88 Gulf War and the 1990–91 Gulf Conflict all serve to demonstrate the continuance of 'traditional' patterns of warfare between formally identified national forces. The treatment of captured personnel in guerrilla warfare is nevertheless an important issue in the modern development of the *jus in bello*. Of course, guerrilla warfare is not a phenomenon which first arose in the second half of the 20th century. The term itself originated in resistance to Napoleonic occupation in Spain, and there were widespread and well known resistance 'guerilla' movements in occupied territories during the Second World War. The new factor in the modern era is the development, in parallel with the political debate on the internationalisation of certain internal conflicts,[6] of a perceived need to take into account, in humanitarian provision, 'informal' combat, which would otherwise be excluded from the operation of 'Geneva' provision. The traumatic experience of the Vietnam War also had a marked effect on the drafting and concerns of Protocol I, and this factor is of crucial importance in understanding the thrust of the Protocol on many matters.

1977 Additional Protocol I provides by article 44(3) that whilst combatants should clearly distinguish themselves from civilians, to facilitate the protection of the latter, it may be that 'the nature of hostilities' will in some cases effectively preclude such distinction. In that case, members of a fighting force will none the less retain 'combatant' status and entitlement to 'prisoner of war' status upon capture, so long as they 'carry arms openly' during actual military engagements and are visible to the enemy during deployment in preparation for such engagements. Where these requirements are met, there will be no grounds for charges of 'perfidy' under the conventions or Protocol I. The scope of this relaxation is carefully limited by express provision that the accepted practice of members of the armed forces wearing uniforms is not intended to be generally compromised.[7] It is further provided that a combatant who is captured while failing to satisfy the minimum criteria set out in the Protocol will not be entitled to prisoner of war status, although such a person will benefit from 'equivalent' protections, with particular reference to the fundamental guarantees of treatment and due process in the context of offences committed prior to capture.[8]

This provision has proven highly controversial, and was, together with the provisions of Protocol I for the extension of the scope of application of 'Geneva' protection,[9] one of the principal obstacles to the ratification of the Protocol by the governments of the United

States and the United Kingdom. The effect of the provision is that 'combatants' entitled to prisoner of war status upon capture now fall into three broad categories:

1 members of regular armed forces and duly authorised supporting personnel
2 combatants who, although otherwise satisfying the qualificatory criteria, are not in 'uniform', but carry arms openly and distinguish themselves with some distinctive sign which is visible at a distance
3 combatants who otherwise satisfy the qualificatory criteria, but who are precluded by particular circumstances from wearing any distinctive sign or clothing, even though they do carry arms openly.

The third of these three categories in particular has proven controversial. It is not, as might be implied by its more extreme critics, a 'terrorists' charter'. For reasons already considered, such organisations as the IRA in Northern Ireland and ETA in the Basque territories of northern Spain could not reasonably be considered to be legitimised by the Protocol.[10] This in itself excludes their consideration under the provisions of the Protocol, but in any event such organisations would fail to meet even the relaxed qualifications for 'combatant' status because of their unwillingness to apply a 'Geneva' regime in their own activities. Clearly, too, whether a force which carries arms openly is entitled to prisoner of war status open capture has no effect on the legitimacy of the conduct of hostilities against them prior to that point. However, there is some cause for genuine concern about the relaxation of the qualificatory criteria for 'combatant' status.

One of the great problems in Vietnam, as in any 'guerrilla' conflict, was the difficulty in distinguishing civilians from fighters. It was this factor which to a large part underlay the climate of feeling which led to the My Lai massacre. This problem of distinction is one of the most difficult aspects of the changes made by Protocol I. The drafters of the Protocol sought to find a balance between the extremities of the traditional view of informally organised fighters, especially in occupied territories, as simply *francs-tireurs* standing outside the laws of armed conflict, and the opposing view of them as patriots literally 'up in arms', and entitled as such to full 'combatant' status under the 'Geneva' regime. The requirements of responsible command and internal discipline incorporating observance of the laws of armed conflict make it somewhat unreasonable to construe the relevant provisions of the Protocol as a comfort to terrorists, but the relaxation of the qualificatory criteria does blur the line of demarcation between 'combatants' and 'civilians', to the possible detriment of the latter. The requirement of carrying arms openly does afford a viable distinction on paper, but in the confusion of 'guerrilla' warfare, distinguishing accurately who is 'carrying arms openly' may well be extremely difficult, and this cannot be to the advantage of the genuine 'civilian' population. It must be stressed that persons engaged in hostile military action whether as designated 'combatants' or not, are *ex hypothesi* open to military response, the question of their status becoming significant only upon capture. However, there remains the serious potential difficulty of confusion between 'combatants', of whatever type, and civilian non-combatants in 'guerrilla' warfare – especially in the light of the much-enhanced protection for civilians provided for elsewhere in the Protocol.[11]

At this point, some doubts must be raised in relation to the relaxation of the general requirement for combatants to wear uniform or some other distinguishing mark. This admittedly applies only where such distinction is 'not possible', but it is difficult to imagine circumstances in which such 'impossibility' could objectively be held to have risen. The requirement is not necessarily for military 'uniform' as it is normally conceived, but merely for some adequate distinguishing mark. A broad, coloured armband would in many cases suffice, and it seems unlikely that this could truly be beyond the resources of a force which can secure sufficient weapons to mount meaningful hostilities. Such distinction may, of course, be militarily inconvenient to a guerrilla force, but this is not the same as 'impossibility'.

Where there is doubt about the status of a person who falls into the power of an adverse party while taking part in hostilities, he or she is treated as *prima facie* entitled to the status of prisoner of war until such time as the question of status has been determined by a competent tribunal. Where a person in the hands of an adverse party is being held other than as a prisoner of war and is brought to trial for alleged offences, the accused may claim prisoner of war status and have that claim adjudicated. The representatives of the relevant protecting power should attend any such proceedings, and report upon them to the Protecting Power, unless, exceptionally, reasons of state security dictate that the proceedings should be held *in camera*.[12] Persons who have taken part in hostilities and are not entitled to prisoner of war status and who do not benefit from more favourable treatment under 1949 Geneva Convention IV are entitled at least to the minimum guarantees set out in Protocol I,[13] unless they are 'spies', in which case, for obvious reasons, the rights of communication do not apply.[14] These provisions somewhat reduce the potential for difficulty in the relaxation of the criteria for establishing 'combatant' status under Protocol I, but it seems probable that debate on the implications and application of these relaxed provisions will continue for some time. It may very well be that ultimately a further refinement of definition will be thought necessary.

A further issue has come into prominence in the 1990s in relation to the significance of the requirement of article 4A that prisoners of war be attached to a 'Party to ... conflict'. In principle, this would seem to be rather obvious, but in practice it raises difficult questions where military personnel who are not dependent upon a state engaged in armed conflict are detained by some other party which is engaged in hostilities. When Iraqi forces invaded Kuwait at the outset of the 1990–91 Gulf Conflict, the small British military mission in the Emirate were immediately detained, but were not at that point prisoners of war because there was at that time no armed conflict between the United Kingdom and Iraq. Although they were British military personnel, the members of the mission were therefore deemed to be 'civilian' internees for this purpose, and protected under 1949 Geneva Convention IV.[15] Once Coalition military action for the relief of Kuwait had commenced and an armed conflict was in progress between Iraq and the United Kingdom, their status would properly have become that of prisoners of war.

The same issue arises in a more complex form in relation to personnel of United Nations forces engaged in peacemaking action who are detained by forces opposing them. The question here is whether the United Nations can ever be a 'Party to ... conflict' in the same sense intended by article 4A of 1949 Geneva Convention III. In undertaking peacemaking action, the United Nations acts as an international law enforcement agency, and not 'as if' it were a state which had suffered a terminal breakdown in international relations with another state with which it has parity of status. Nevertheless, it is generally accepted that the norms of the humanitarian *jus in bello* do apply in cases of UN military action, and it would be odd if a law enforcement agency was not itself required to act lawfully. This matter was clarified in an exchange of letters between the International Committee of the Red Cross and U Thant as long ago as 1962. The Secretary-General of the UN assured the ICRC that:

> UNO [the United Nations Organisation] insists on its armed forces in the field applying the principles of the 1949 Geneva Conventions as scrupulously as possible.[16]

However, this does not resolve the question of the entitlement of UN personnel to prisoner of war status in the event of detention by an opposing force. The issue is far from merely technical or academic, and arose in practice in the armed conflicts in former Yugoslavia.

In June 1995, Bosnian Serb forces making an attack near Sarajevo captured a number of soldiers serving with the UN force in former Yugoslavia, UNPROFOR. The International Committee of the Red Cross took the strict view that the detained personnel were not prisoners of war, and as the law stands, this appears to have been technically correct, even if their position was clearly analogous with that set out under article 4A(1) of 1949 Geneva Convention III. So it would seem that while detained by hostile forces, a detention arguably unlawful in itself, UN military personnel would be protected 'as if' they were civilians under 1949 Geneva Convention IV in a manner parallel with the initial situation of the British military mission in Kuwait in 1990. In any event, the attempt to use the detained UNPROFOR personnel as 'human shields' against air strikes would have violated article 23 of 1949 Geneva Convention III if they were prisoners of war, and article 83 of 1949 Geneva Convention IV if they were not.[17] The same was true of the threat by the Bosnian Government to hold members of the Ukrainian contingent of UNPROFOR as 'human shields' if more air strikes were undertaken against Bosnian Serb forces.[18] The claim by the Bosnian Government that this threat was unauthorised would not have been an effective defence in case of unlawful mistreatment of such personnel, since it would have been the duty of the government to put a stop to any such unlawful action.[19]

'Captured' UN military personnel are thus protected by current international humanitarian law, if only implicitly as deemed 'civilians', but the present state of the law in this area cannot be considered satisfactory. One possible solution is offered by the Institute of International Law's draft 1971 Zagreb Resolution on Conditions of Application of Humanitarian Rules of Armed Conflict to Hostilities in which the United Nations may be Engaged. Article 7 of the Resolution states:

> Without prejudice to the individual or collective responsibility which derives from the very fact that the party opposing the United Nations has committed aggression ... [t]he United Nations is entitled to demand compliance with these [humanitarian] rules [of armed conflict] for the benefit of its Forces ...

It will be noted that the opening caveat rules out any suggestion of legitimacy of opposition to the United Nations, while at the same time reserving the right of humanitarian *jus in bello* protection to UN military personnel. This issue is one which is likely to remain controversial.[20] It must at the same time be commented that experience in former Yugoslavia has suggested that direct UN peacemaking may increasingly be replaced by mandated or otherwise delegated action by regional organisations such as NATO. In the case of former Yugoslavia, UNPROFOR was finally replaced by the NATO-led IFOR and SFOR. These forces were not beset by the flaws of ambiguous and even conflicting mandates and under-resourcing which undermined

UNPROFOR, and were treated with vastly more respect by actual and potentially hostile forces in consequence. It is possible that the ultimate solution to this problem lies in this area of development.

Persons Not Prisoners of War but Entitled to Equivalent Protection

Beyond the categories of person entitled to prisoner of war status upon capture, there are a number of persons who, although not prisoners of war, are entitled to equivalent protection where they lack the benefit of more advantageous protection under other provisions.

The first category of such persons are designated medical and religious personnel protected under 1949 Geneva Conventions I or II. Such persons are not legally liable to 'capture' by an adverse party, but may be 'retained' for the care of prisoners of war. Even if 'retained', such persons are entitled to 'equivalent protection to that afforded to prisoners of war' under 1949 Geneva Convention III.[21]

Convention III provides that such 'retained' personnel will continue to exercise their medical or spiritual functions for the benefit of prisoners of war, preferably those dependent upon their own state, under the control of the competent authorities and in accordance with military law and professional etiquette. In addition, such personnel must be authorised to visit prisoners of war in hospitals and work units outside the camps in which they are retained, and suitable transport must be provided for the purpose of such visits. In their relations with the camp authorities, 'retained' personnel are represented by the senior medical officer amongst them. To this end, agreement must be reached by the adverse parties at the outset of hostilities regarding the correspondence of ranks between their respective military medical services. Chaplains who are 'retained' deal with their own relations with the camp authorities, which is inevitable in the light of distinctions of faith and denomination. Whilst 'retained' in a prisoner of war camp, medical and religious personnel are subject to the internal discipline of the camp, but they may not be compelled to work other than in connection with their medical or religious duties.[22]

Persons who belong to, or who have belonged to, the armed forces of a territory under occupation and who are interned by the occupying power are to be 'treated as prisoners of war'. This remains the case where such persons have attempted to rejoin forces still in combat or have ignored a summons to report for internment.[23]

Finally, persons who would be entitled to the status of or treatment as prisoners of war in the hands of an adverse party to armed conflict are similarly entitled when required to be interned by a neutral power under international law. Such persons may, of course, also be entitled to more advantageous treatment under other provisions or under particular arrangements with the neutral power concerned.[24]

Children Under the Age of 15

1977 Additional Protocol I makes special provision for the protection of children in situations of armed conflict. Parties to an armed conflict must, in particular, take 'all feasible measures' to avoid the active involvement of children under the age of 15 in hostilities, and must refrain from recruiting persons under this age into their armed forces.[25] Where children under the age of 15 do take part in hostilities and fall into the hands of an adverse party, they continue to benefit from the relevant special protective measures, 'whether or not they are prisoners of war'.[26]

War Correspondents and Other Journalists

Journalists are not the most obvious participants in or victims of armed conflict, and so are little considered by international humanitarian law. At the same time, they face the dangers common to anyone in or near a combat zone, together with certain additional risks especially associated with their professional functions, in particular the danger of accusations of espionage, which has existed from the early days of modern international humanitarian law. James Edgcomb, the correspondent for the *Manchester Examiner and Times* in the 1870 Franco-Prussian War, came within two minutes of being shot by firing squad owing to difficulties in translating his identification documents. Fortunately, he was identified and released at the last moment.[27] There have been many other problems of this type, including a threat to treat certain English journalists in Argentina at the outbreak of the 1982 Anglo-Argentine Falklands Conflict as spies, although this was never acted upon. Technological developments in the 1990s have, if anything, exacerbated this potential problem. The possibility of more or less instant communication via satellite technology means that military reporting is no longer a matter of news of yesterday's battles, but of military action as it occurs. Such information could be of value to an opposing force, and this raises issues of considerable concern. There are also other potentially serious difficulties in relation to substantive reporting, especially reportage on prisoners of war, and in the relationship between journalists and their own state authorities.

The status of journalists who fall into the hands of an adverse power in armed conflict is a matter of considerable sensitivity, and for this purpose journalists fall into two categories. War correspondents are entitled to prisoner of war status upon capture, whereas other journalists will be treated as civilian internees under 1949 Geneva Convention IV. The first significant provision in this area was made by article 13 of the Land Warfare Regulations annexed to 1907 Hague Convention IV. This states that reporters carrying a 'certificate from the military authorities of the army which they are accompanying' are entitled to prisoner of war status. This provision was repeated by article 81 of the 1929 Geneva Convention in relation to the treatment of prisoners of war. 1949 Geneva Convention III, article 4A(4) affords prisoner of war status upon capture to:

> Persons who accompany the armed forces without actually being members thereof, such as ... war correspondents ... providing that they have received authorization from the armed forces which they accompany, who shall provide them for that purpose with an identity card ...

War correspondents are treated *de facto* 'as if' they were military personnel, although they are, of course, not so. The prerequisite for this status is the granting of official authorisation for their mission. For a wide variety of reasons most journalists reporting on armed conflicts do not now seek such authorisation. An exception to this was seen in the 1982 Anglo-Argentine Falklands Conflict, probably because official authorisation was the only practical way of getting to the islands. As a general rule, therefore, the status and protection of other civilian journalists has become a matter of considerable significance.

This issue, emphasised in the 1960s and 1970s as a result of experience in the Vietnam War, led the United Nations General Assembly in 1970, by its Resolution 2673(XXV) of 9 December, to direct, ultimately, the Human Rights Commission to prepare a draft Convention for the Protection of Journalists on Dangerous Missions. In the end, this concept was fed into the drafting process which led to 1977 Additional Protocol I, and found expression in article 79 of the Protocol. It provides that:

> (1) Journalists engaged in dangerous professional missions in areas of armed conflict shall be considered as civilians ...
> (2) They shall be protected as such under the Conventions and this Protocol, provided that they take no action adversely affecting their status as civilians ...
> (3) They may obtain an identity card similar to the model in Annex II of this Protocol. This card, which shall be issued by the government of the State of which the journalist is a national or in whose territory

> he resides or in which the news medium employing him is located, shall attest to his status as a journalist.

Journalists falling within this provision are different in kind from war correspondents, and are civilian internees upon capture, rather than prisoners of war. However, they are identified as journalists, and this serves to some degree to reduce the dangers of misunderstanding and abuse which they may face.

It is important to emphasise that provisions relating both to war correspondents and to other journalists are concerned with their status as protected persons, and not with the exercise of their profession. 'Journalism' is not defined, but the ICRC Commentary on the Protocol suggests in relation to article 79 that article 2(a) of the original UN Draft Convention provides useful guidance in stating that:

> The word 'journalist' shall mean any correspondent, reporter, photographer, and their technical film, radio and television assistants who are continually engaged in any of these activities as their principal occupation.[28]

The exercise of the profession of journalism can have great benefits in the maintenance and advancement of international humanitarian law, but may also hinder implementation in some cases. The sensitive question of the law and ethics of journalism with regard to news portrayal of prisoners of war is considered below.[29] In a more general context, however, journalists readily proclaim their commitment to objective reporting and ethical analysis, and this is by no means necessarily untrue. The revelation of the appalling conditions in, *inter alia*, the Omarska, Brcko and Trnoplje internment camps in former Yugoslavia in August 1992[30] is a good example of the positive interaction of journalism and international humanitarian law. On the other hand, it must not be forgotten that media outlets of every sort have their own ideological commitments and commercial or quasi-commercial interests. In most cases they are also profit-based, or at least competitive and ratings-related businesses, and are not infrequently inclined to sensationalism. Alongside much ethical journalism, there is a great deal which is non-ethical, if not actually unethical. The statements and behaviour of journalists merit at least the same sceptical scrutiny as those made or perpetrated by others.

Persons Not Entitled to Prisoner of War Status upon Capture

Spies

Spying is not contrary to international law, and is not a ground for complaint between states. However, although spying appears to be recognised by public international law, spies when captured are not protected by international law, and are expressly excluded from the status of 'prisoner of war' by article 46(1) of 1977 Additional Protocol I. Information-gathering by military intelligence officers or scouts, for example, does not amount to espionage, and such persons will not be denied prisoner of war status merely by virtue of their involvement in such activity.

Espionage involves the gathering of information of military value in territories held by an adverse – or indeed, without its consent, any – party, 'through false pretences or deliberately in a clandestine manner'.[31] It is expressly stated that a member of the armed forces of an adverse party to conflict who gathers or seeks to gather military information in the uniform of his or her own armed forces is not a spy.[32] However, not wearing a uniform does not necessarily render an individual a spy, but the burden of proof to the contrary will then be placed upon the suspect. Peter Rowe extrapolates these principles to the comparison with the penetration of a Swedish naval base by a Soviet Whisky Class submarine in 1981 and the overflight of Soviet territory by a United States U2 aircraft which was shot down in 1960. Although both were clearly engaged in attempts to obtain sensitive military information, the submarine could not reasonably be mistaken for anything other than a naval vessel, and its officers and crew were presumably in uniform. On the other hand, the US aircraft could not be distinguished as a military aircraft except by minute inspection, and its pilot was not wearing uniform. Rowe contends that in these circumstances the submarine was not technically engaged in 'espionage', whereas the U2 plane was.[30]

A member of the armed forces of a party to conflict who attempts to gather information in territory of which he or she is a resident does not by virtue of that fact alone become a spy, although he or she will do so if he or she collects information by 'false pretences or deliberately in a clandestine manner'. However, such a person may not be treated as a spy unless he or she is captured while actually engaged in espionage.[39] A member of the armed forces of a party to armed conflict who is not a resident of territory under enemy occupation and who has actually engaged in espionage in such territory may even so not be treated as a spy if he or she is captured after he or she has rejoined the armed forces to which he or she is attached.[35]

Mercenaries

Mercenaries, in the sense of soldiers on hire to the highest bidder, played a considerable part in medieval and Renaissance warfare – indeed, their supply played a major role in the economy of medieval Switzerland, but a markedly declining role in warfare since the professionalisation of armed forces in the 17th and 18th centuries. They remain a problem, however. In some recent conflicts, for example in Angola, mercenaries in the most simple sense of 'contract killers' have played a most disturbing role, and the issue is now specifically addressed in 1977 Additional Protocol I.[36]

Whilst it may be accepted that 'mercenary' action is much to be discouraged, there are considerable problems of definition involved in devising adequate provisions to this end. Not all foreigners in the service of armed forces of other countries are 'mercenaries', nor should they be treated as such. Some serve with the approval and prior arrangement of their home governments, such as the Nepalese Gurkhas in the British Army; others serve in particular conflicts for moral or ideological reasons. Examples can be seen in the case of the US citizens who served with Allied forces before the entry of the USA into the First and Second World Wars, and of the non-Spaniards who served with the International Brigade during the Spanish Civil War.

1977 Additional Protocol I, article 47, gives an extensive definition of a 'mercenary' as any person who:

1. is specially recruited to fight in an armed conflict, not being a member of the armed forces or a party to it or a national or resident of the territory of such a party
2. actually takes a direct part in the hostilities
3. is motivated by private gain and is in fact promised 'remuneration substantially in excess' of that payable to persons of equivalent rank in the armed forces of the party on whose behalf he or she fights
4. has not been sent by a state not party to the conflict on duty as a member of its armed forces.

A very similar definition is adopted by the 1975 Convention for the Elimination of Mercenarism in Africa. Further provision was made by the 1989 United Nations Convention Against the Recruitment, Use, Financing and Training of Mercenaries. The definition adopted broadly follows that set out in 1977 Additional Protocol I, but somewhat elaborates it. Article 1 essentially repeats the Protocol I definition, but article 2 of the UN Convention adds:

> A mercenary is also any person who, in any other situation:
> (a) Is specially recruited locally or abroad for the purpose of participating in a concerted act of violence aimed at:
> (i) Overthrowing a Government or otherwise undermining the constitutional order of a State; or
> (ii) Undermining the territorial integrity of a State;
> (b) Is motivated to take part therein essentially by the desire for significant private gain ...
> (c) Is neither a national nor a resident of the State against which such an act is directed;
> (d) Has not been sent by a State on official duty and
> (e) Is not a member of the armed forces of the State on whose territory the act is undertaken.

The convention bans not only mercenary activity (article 3), but also the recruitment and training of mercenaries by individuals (article 2) and by states party to the convention (article 5). Article 10 of the convention also requires that any state in which a person who is suspected of offences under its provisions is found must undertake the necessary investigations, trial or extradition proceedings.

It is clear that the drafting of article 47 of 1977 Additional Protocol I that all the conditions set out as provisos must be met before a person can be considered a 'mercenary' within the meaning of the Protocol, in which case it would seem that only the contract killers which are its target would fall within the provision. Unfortunately, this provision does carry the possibility of confusion and abuse in its terms. Its most questionable aspect is the operational paragraph which states:

> A mercenary shall not have the right to be a combatant or a prisoner of war.[37]

Prima facie, this provision would seem to apply *ab initio*, so that a 'mercenary' would at no point have the protections of Convention III and Protocol I applicable to prisoners of war. It is true that the provisions for adjudication on cases of doubt regarding prisoners of war status[38] might mitigate the apparently alarming potential for 'errors' in the application of the provision, but this would be of severely reduced value in a case where no doubt was considered to exist. However, proceedings against mercenaries would be required to conform with the minimum standards set out in the Protocol for all judicial proceedings,[39] and, certainly, summary execution upon capture would not be acceptable.

There has been one prominent trial of mercenaries in recent years: that of the white mercenaries tried in Angola for their participation in the liberation conflict in that country in the interest of parties other than the victorious FNLA. There was some doubt over the substance of the law to be applied, and as Françoise Hampson comments:

> The trial itself seems to have been fair, procedurally speaking. Compliance with the presumption of innocence is, however, in doubt ... The trial has been criticised for breaching the principle of *nulla crimen sine lege*. ... [T]here was at that time no internationally recognized criminal offence of unlawful participation in armed conflict. There was also grave doubt as to whether it was an offence under Angolan criminal law.[40]

So far as modern international law is concerned, the question of the illegality of mercenarism has been resolved by subsequent prescription so far as any future cases may be concerned.

Following findings of guilt, severe, including capital, sentences were passed. Despite the evident 'show trial' elements of these proceedings, the findings themselves appeared to accord with the facts, and at least they set a precedent for judicial proceedings rather than more summary proceedings in such cases.

The principal concern raised by the provision of 1977 Additional Protocol I lies not so much in what is actually stated as in certain of their implications for future development. The jurisprudential dimensions of the issue have been considered above,[41] but it may reasonably be commented that 'mercenary' activities might readily be criminalised in the same manner as, those of aerial hijackers, for example, without the creation of dangerously ambiguous exceptions to the humanitarian provisions for the protection of prisoners of war. An example of the potential for mischievous use of these provisions is the suggestion made by the Argentine representative in a 1982 United Nations Security Council debate on the alleged role of mercenaries in the attempted coup in the Seychelles that a valid analogy might be drawn with the Gurkha regiments in the British Army. The British representative replied:

> ... if we are going to be serious we should have a little precision in this matter. The ... internationally agreed definition of who is a mercenary ... in Protocol I ... excludes anyone who 'is a member of the armed forces of a party to a conflict'. The Gurkhas comprise units of regular troops [who] ... form a fully integrated part of the United Kingdom forces ... [in accordance with agreements openly and honourably arrived at with the Government of Nepal].[42]

The Gurkhas could quite clearly not be considered 'mercenaries', but the suggested analogy underlines the necessity for 'precision' in interpretation demanded by the British representation at the Security Council debate if the danger of abuse of such provisions is to be minimised. There have been a number of alleged or actual incidents of mercenarism in the 1980s and 1990s, but the nature and illegality of the practice can no longer seriously be held to be in doubt.

The General Protection of Prisoners of War

Under 1949 Geneva Convention III, article 12, prisoners of war are the responsibility of the capturing power from the moment of capture, and not of the individual or military units which actually capture them, although the duties of such individuals or units are not thereby diminished. This is a most important basic point which establishes that from the beginning of captivity, a prisoner of war is entitled to rely upon the authority of the capturing party for the application of the appropriate 'Geneva' provisions without there being any possibility of breaches being passed off as individual 'excesses'. A prisoner of war is precluded by article 7 of 1949 Geneva Convention III from renouncing the rights conferred by the convention and any additional, special, agreements which may have been entered into for the benefit of prisoners of war.

The basic standard of treatment is set out in article 13 of Convention III, which states that 'prisoners of war must at all times be humanely treated'. In particular, prisoners of war must not be unlawfully killed or endangered, physically mutilated or subjected to medical or scientific experiment not justified by the medical needs of the individuals concerned.[43] Reprisals against prisoners of war are expressly prohibited by the article, and they must also be protected from violence, intimidation, insults and public curiosity.

Protection against insult and public curiosity became a matter of serious concern in the 1980s and 1990s, especially, but not only, in the 1990–91 Gulf Conflict. The point at which photographs, televisual presentation and other media presentation of prisoners of war ceases to be mere reporting of fact and becomes an unlawful abuse is not necessarily easy to determine. During the 1990–91 Gulf Conflict, captured Coalition air force personnel were shown on Iraqi television with the marks of brutal treatment, reciting – clearly involuntarily – statements of Ba'ath party propaganda.[44] This was a gross violation of article 13 of Convention III, as was the beating of captured air crew followed by parading them through stone-throwing mobs in the streets. In much lesser degree, the photographs shown on Argentine television of captured Royal Marines forced to lie down on the ground for the benefit of the television cameras at the beginning of the 1982 Anglo-Argentine Falklands Conflict must also be considered to have contravened article 13. On the other hand, photographs of masses of prisoners of war with no humiliation beyond the fact of capture may not so obviously violate the article. During the 1990–91 Gulf Conflict, however, the International Committee of the Red Cross took the strict view that even such photographs would violate article 13, and some disagreement between the ICRC and the United States in particular resulted.

At present (1997) the point is moot, but the only major case which has arisen in part upon this issue, the post-Second World War Maelzer case,[45] gives some useful indications. Maelzer was a German officer who paraded Allied prisoners of war through Rome under German escort with film and photographic coverage designed to suggest, falsely, intense popular hostility towards them. He also at one point ordered the escort to fire upon them. The media element was a relatively minor aspect of the case, but as Peter Rowe remarks:

> Suppose ... that the only evidence against the accused was the act of parading the prisoners ... [c]ould Maelzer have been convicted of exposing the prisoners of war to 'public curiosity'? It would seem necessary to consider his motive in acting in the way he did. It was clearly for propaganda purposes ... It is suggested that this is the crucial point and would have resulted in the same finding by the court [a finding of guilt].[46]

This is a persuasive view, and it may be agreed that deliberate humiliation of a prisoner of war, or a group of them, is the essence of any serious violation of what is now article 13. However, it is necessary to emphasise that it is ultimately the fact of humiliation of intimidation, the *actus reus*, rather than the motivation, the *mens rea*, which is significant. So far as mass photographs of prisoners of war taken without exacerbating factors of humiliation are concerned, the ICRC view in the 1990–91 Gulf Conflict may be argued to have been somewhat over-strict, but any published photograph which focuses upon individual, visually identifiable prisoners must seem at the very least legally questionable. This is so because the individual is thus singled out both as a prisoner of war and as an object of 'public curiosity', and also because in the case of some political regimes, such attention might well expose the prisoner to persecution after repatriation.

Prisoners of war are interned to safeguard the state security of the capturing power; they are not in any sense malefactors or persons undergoing 'punishments'. Consequently, article 14 of Geneva Convention III confirms that prisoners of war retain the full civil capacity which they enjoyed at the time of their capture, subject to the obvious exigencies of internment.[47] This refers to their civil capacity under the laws of the state upon which they depend and would include capacity for marriage by proxy where procedure is permitted by the legal system in question. They must be treated honourably, and female prisoners must be treated 'with all due regard to their sex'.[48] Honourable treatment includes non-subjection to ideological pressure. The Commentary suggests, more generally, that the protection of a prisoner's honour relates to his or her position as a captured soldier who may well feel humiliated by defeat and internment and who should be treated with consideration for his or her sensibilities, both with regard to relations with the authorities and with other prisoners. Thus prisoners should not be offered the uniforms of forces opposed to them by way of clothing unless this is unavoidable, and in such a case, appropriate modifications should be made to them. In general, prisoners of war are entitled to equality of treatment, except in so far as distinctions are dictated by rank, sex or medical need,[49] and all are entitled, while prisoners, to free maintenance and medical treatment.[50]

Prisoners of war are not bound to supply information to the capturing power; they will probably be forbidden to do so by their own laws, and may not be coerced into doing so.[51] The only information which a prisoner of war is bound to supply is that required by perhaps the best popularly known provision of international humanitarian law: name, rank and number. In precise terms, 'his first names and rank, date of birth, and army, regimental or serial number, or failing this, equivalent information'.[52] The Commentary indicates that a prisoner who claims a rank superior to that actually held may be deprived, upon detection of the deceit, not only of the privileges attached to the rank falsely claimed, but also of any privileges attached to the rank actually held. These questions must be put to the prisoners in a language which they understand. Should a prisoner prove to be incapable of answering for medical reasons, which would include psychological causes such as 'shell shock', he or she must be put in the care of the medical services, and the required information must be secured from the identity card which parties to armed conflicts must issue to all who are liable to become prisoners of war.[53] Such identity cards must state at a minimum the information which prisoners of war may be required to supply to their captors. It is of prime importance that this information should be obtained, recorded and passed on to the representative of the Protecting Power, if any, or the ICRC Delegate as the case may be, since it is only by this means that the prisoner's family may be informed of the prisoner's fate.

Prisoners of war must be allowed to retain possession of their personal property, including clothing, marks of rank, decorations, items of sentimental value, helmets and gas marks, even if some of these items are part of their military equipment. Arms, horses (not now very likely), military equipment in general and military documents, except identity cards, will be confiscated, however. For reasons of security within the camp, it may be necessary for the authorities to hold money and any items of value possessed by prisoners. Where this is done, the prisoner must be given an itemised receipt legibly signed and stating the name, rank and unit of the person issuing it. Upon release, all such property must be returned to the prisoner in the same condition in which it was handed in.[54]

Once prisoners of war have been captured, it will be necessary to transfer them from the place of capture to a permanent place of internment. The capturing authority is under an obligation to evacuate prisoners as soon as possible from the zone of combat danger to camps in safe locations. Only if their medical condition renders prisoners unfit for evacuation may they be kept in the combat zone.[55] When under evacuation, prisoners of war must be treated humanely and provided with sufficient food, water and medical care. Lists of persons being evacuated must be kept by the evacuating authority.[56] This small but important provision is designed to avoid the horrors of packed 'cattle truck' transports, which are amongst the most inhumane potential aspects of internment procedures. It may be both necessary and sensible to convey newly captured prisoners initially to transit camps for questioning and assignment to permanent places of internment. Such transit camps must themselves be 'permanent' in nature,[57] and the same protections and conditions must be maintained within them as in the case of the internment camps proper.[58] Where prisoners of war are passed through such transit camps, they should be kept there for as brief a period as possible pending their transfer to the prisoner of war camp designated for them.[59]

It may prove necessary to move prisoners of war from the camp to which they were originally assigned. Where this is done, the same requirements regarding humanity apply as during initial evacuation, and the move must be carried out in conditions at least as favourable as those provided for troops of the detaining authority. Due regard for the interests of the prisoners themselves must be exercised in transfer decisions, including ease of eventual repatriation, and precautions must be taken for their safety during transport, especially when undertaken by sea or air. The sick or wounded whose health would be put at risk by transport may not be moved unless their safety imperatively demands it. The most obvious case of imperative necessity would be the nearing of a combat zone to the camp, but in such a situation a transfer may be effected only where this may be done safely or where the prisoners would be exposed to greater danger by their retention *in situ*.[60]

Where it is decided to transfer prisoners of war, they must be notified of the decision and of the postal address of the place to which they are to be transferred in good time for them to pack their effects and inform their next of kin. Where conditions of transport require it, a baggage limit may be imposed upon each prisoner of what they can reasonably carry, and this is taken to be not more than 25 kilograms. Where any such restriction is imposed, the baggage left behind and any communal property of the prisoners must be forwarded to them in accordance with arrangements between the camp commander and the prisoners' representative. In all cases, the expenses of transfer are borne by the detaining authority.[61]

A detaining power may transfer prisoners of war to the keep of another power, but only so long as the transferee power is a party to 1949 Geneva Convention III[62] and the transferring power is satisfied that it is willing and able to apply the provisions of the convention. This was done on a considerable scale by the United Kingdom during the Second World War with the transfer of German and Italian prisoners to Canada. Once such a transfer has taken place, responsibility for the transferred prisoners rests upon the transferee authority. However, should that authority fail 'in any important respect' to apply the convention, the transferor power must, upon notification by a Protecting Power, take effective steps to secure a remedy to the situation or request the transfer back of the prisoners, which request must be met with compliance.[63]

Establishment of Prisoner of War Camps

Prisoners of war are, by definition, under restraint. The detaining power may, and obviously will, place them under an obligation to remain in their place of internment, and may enforce this through disciplinary, but not criminal, sanctions. Internments may not involve 'close confinement', however, except for permitted purposes of penal or disciplinary sanction, or for reasons of medical necessity. Under 1949 Geneva Convention III, article 21, prisoners may be released on parole or promise, but this is subject to laws of the power upon which they depend, which would in practice rule out such a procedure in almost all cases. Many systems of national law or disciplinary regulation actually place captured military personnel under a duty to escape if they are able to do so. A prisoner of war owes no allegiance to the detaining power, and is obliged to conform to its commands only in so far as this may be prescribed by the convention or other relevant international norms. No prisoner may be compelled to accept liberty on parole or promise. At the outbreak of hostilities, the parties in conflict are required to notify their adversaries of any of their laws or regulations which prohibit captured personnel from accepting liberty on parole. If a prisoner does accept liberty on this basis, however, he or she will be honour bound under the terms of the convention to scrupulously observe the terms thus accepted. For its part, the detaining power must not demand from prisoners freed on parole any service incompatible with the terms of the parole.[64]

Prisoner of war camps must be located in healthy and hygienic conditions on land, and should not, unless the interests of the prisoners so demand, be located in penitentiaries.[65] Prisoners should be detained in camp compounds with others of their own nationality, language and customs, but should not be separated from other members of the armed forces with whom they were serving at the time of their capture, unless it be with their consent. The requirement that prisoner of war camps be located on land is of long standing, and refers ultimately to the memory of the prison hulks of the Napoleonic Wars. These were usually the dismasted hulks of redundant warships, in which prisoners were confined for long periods in cramped and often insanitary conditions, even though their condition was no more perceived as 'punishment' at that time than it is at present.

During the 1982 Falklands Conflict there was no opportunity to set up prisoner of war camps, for a mixture of temporal, geographical and meteorological reasons, and prisoners were exchanged very swiftly after the conflict, and in some cases during. Argentine prisoners were for the most part repatriated by sea, and pending this, large numbers of them were held in temporary accommodation in and around Port Stanley. The ICRC made no objection to these arrangements, and, obviously, holding and early repatriation by sea was much preferable in the circumstances to setting up long-term, 'permanent', land-based camps. The nearest approach to the latter in the conflict was the transit camp set up by the British on Ascension Island.

Article 23 of 1949 Geneva Convention III forbids the internment of prisoners of war in areas where they may be exposed to fire from the combat zone or where their presence is used to shield the location concerned from attack. This practice of using both prisoners of war and civilian internees as 'human shields' was adopted by Iraq in the 1990–91 Gulf Conflict, and was the subject of international protest. Prisoners of war must be supplied with air raid shelters and similar protective facilities to the same extent as the ambient civilian population. With particular reference to the dangers of aerial attack, detaining powers must, through the medium of the Protecting Power, inform the adversary power of the location of prisoner of war camps, and should, if military circumstances permit, mark such camps with the letters PW or PG to facilitate aerial identification in daytime. Under the convention, these letters may not be used for any other purpose.[66]

Prisoners' Representative

In every prisoner of war camp there must be a prisoners' representative who will represent the interests of prisoners before the military authorities of the detaining power, the Protecting Power, the ICRC and any other relevant organisations. Such representatives must be approved by the detaining power, but in case of non-approval, the grounds for this must be notified to the Protecting Power. The representatives must in all cases share the nationality, language and customs of those whom they represent, and in camps housing prisoners of mixed nationality or culture, this may well mean that several such representatives will be necessary.[67]

It is the general duty of prisoners' representatives to watch over the physical, spiritual and intellectual well-being of the prisoners they represent. Any system of mutual assistance organised by the prisoners amongst themselves will also fall under the aegis of the prisoners' representative. The representative may not be held responsible by the detaining authority merely by virtue of his or her office for any offences which prisoners may commit.[68] To facilitate the performance of their duties, prisoners' representatives are accorded certain privileges by Convention III. They may not be required to perform work which would impede the execution of their duties, and they must be allowed the freedom of movement necessary to perform them. This includes permission to visit labour units and other locations of prisoners in their charge outside the camp. Representatives must also be allowed adequate postal and communications facilities for their contacts with the detaining authorities, the Protecting Power, ICRC Delegates and other appropriate persons and bodies. If a prisoners' representative is transferred out of the camp in which he or she holds office, he or she must be allowed adequate time in which to explain the duties to his or her successor.

A prisoners' representative may be dismissed by the detaining power, but where this is done, the reasons for the action must be communicated to the Protecting Power. It would, of course, be considered a serious impropriety for such a dismissal to occur on grounds of assiduity or effectiveness in pursuing prisoners' interests. On the other hand, if a prisoners' representative finds the duties too burdensome, he she may appoint assistants from amongst the prisoners for whom he or she is responsible.[69]

The method of appointment of prisoners' representatives depends upon the nature of the camp concerned, and in particular whether or not officer prisoners are detained there. In a camp in which officers are present, the prisoners' representative will be the most senior by rank amongst them. If the camp is exclusively an officers' camp, the representative's assistants will be chosen by the officers from amongst their number. In a camp holding both officer and non-officer prisoners, the assistants are elected by the non-officer prisoners from amongst their number. In a camp holding only non-officer prisoners, the prisoners' representative will be freely elected by the prisoners for six-month periods, with 'by-elections' in the case of vacancies occurring for whatever reason in mid-term. Retiring prisoners' representatives are eligible for re-election.[70]

Camp Command Structures

A prisoner of war camp will be under the command of a commissioned officer in the regular armed forces of the detaining power. He or she must have a copy of Convention III, ensure that the camp staff are familiar with its requirements, and will be responsible, under the direction of his or her government, for their application within the camp. All non-officer prisoners must salute and otherwise show formal signs of respect applicable to officers in their own forces to officers of the detaining power. Officer prisoners need only salute officers of the detaining power who outrank them, with the exception of the camp commandant, whom all prisoners must salute irrespective of rank. The prisoners themselves are allowed to retain insignia of rank, national markings and any decorations to which they may be entitled.

The general regulations for the camp, together with copies of 1949 Geneva Convention III and any relevant special agreements must be displayed in the camp in places visible to the prisoners, and in a language which they can understand. If a prisoner does not have access to the publicly posted information, for example by reason of medical confinement, he or she must be supplied with a copy upon request.[71]

General Conditions of Internment

Prisoners of war must in general be treated both humanely and honourably, but specifically detailed provisions are necessarily laid down for the maintenance of this simple principle. The accommodation must be of at least equivalent standard to that provided for the armed forces of the detaining power billeted in the same area, making due allowance for the habits, customs and health of the prisoners. In particular, due safeguards against fire and damp must be ensured, and there must be adequate lighting, especially between dusk and lights out. Female prisoners of war must be accommodated in separate dormitories from their male counterparts.[72]

Food which is sufficient in quantity and nutritional quality, taking account of the accustomed diet of the prisoners and of the need for extra rations occasioned by unusual labour, must be supplied in prisoner of war camps. Prisoners should also, as far as possible, be allowed to take part in the preparation of their own food, including any additional food which they may have in their possession. Collective reduction of rations as a disciplinary sanction is prohibited, and by the same token, prisoners must at all times be supplied with adequate amounts of drinking water.[73] The convention expressly provides that the 'use of tobacco shall be permitted' by prisoners of war.[74] In 1949, this was perceived as a simple benevolent measure; whether in the light of modern medical opinion, especially regarding the dangers of 'passive smoking', this provision will be thought ripe for a change in the direction at least of restriction of 'smoking' areas remains to be seen. It is quite clear that the permission of use of tobacco does not extend by analogy to the abuse of any other damaging, addictive substances.

The detaining power must supply adequate and appropriate clothing, underwear and footwear to prisoners, and may use captured enemy uniforms for this purpose, provided such garments are suitable for the climate in the area of the camp. This requirement extends to facilities for the repair of clothes, and the supply of appropriate work clothing, where required.[75]

Prisoners in a prisoner of war camp must be afforded facilities within the camp for the purchase of food, soap, tobacco and ordinary articles of daily use at price levels not in excess of the locally prevailing market rate. Profits made from such sales within the camp must be put in a special fund to be managed, with the assistance of the prisoners' representative, for the benefit of the prisoners. When a prisoner of war camp is closed down with a credit balance in such a fund, the balance must be passed to an international welfare organisation for the benefit of prisoners of war of the same nationality as those from whom it arose. Upon general repatriation, however, such a balance may be retained by the former detaining power, unless there is an express contrary agreement amongst the powers concerned in the conflict.[76]

Prisoner of war camps must be maintained in a sanitary condition for the general health and comfort of the prisoners and for the avoidance of epidemics. Adequate bathing, showering and laundry facilities, together with sufficient water and soap, must be provided for these purposes, as must an adequate number of hygienic 'conveniences', meaning lavatories.[77] Separate lavatory facilities must be provided for female prisoners, this being a specific instance of the requirement to treat women prisoners with due regard for their sex.[78]

The convention requires that due care be taken of prisoners' general health and medical requirements. A prisoner of war camp must have an adequate infirmary, including, where necessary, isolation wards for the treatment of contagious or mental illnesses. In serious cases requiring surgery or other hospital care, prisoners of war must be admitted to a suitable military or civilian medical facility, and in case of disablement or blindness, rehabilitative facilities must be provided. A certificate of medical treatment must be issued upon request, and a duplicate forwarded to the 'central prisoners of war agency', probably the ICRC Central Trading Agency. The cost of all treatment, including the supply of dentures and other appliances, is borne by the detaining power.[79] Medical inspections must be held in prisoner of war camps at least once per month, both to monitor general health and cleanliness and to detect contagious diseases such as tuberculosis, malaria and venereal disease, and to this end the most efficient available methods of diagnosis must be used.[80] Whether it will be thought necessary to add AIDS to this list remains to be seen. The detaining power may require that prisoners who have been medically trained but are not attached to their armed forces' medical service should exercise their professional skills for the benefit of prisoners of their own nationality or who are dependent upon the same power as themselves. Where this is done, the prisoners affected continue to be 'prisoners of war', but may not be required to perform any other kind of work.[81] The position of members of armed forces' medical services who are 'retained' in a prisoner of war camp has been considered above.[82]

Religious activity is protected by 1949 Geneva Convention III in a manner parallel with the provision for medical care. Prisoners have 'complete latitude' in the exercise of religion, including communal attendance at religious observances in suitable premises, subject only to the dictates of necessary camp discipline.[83] Prisoners who are ministers of religion but not formally designated chaplains or their equivalent are at liberty to minister to members of their faith, and are entitled to the same treatment as chaplains 'retained' in the camp, including exemption from other forms of work.[84]

If no chaplain or equivalent minister formally designated as religious personnel is present in the camp, a suitable lay person may, when confessionally appropriate, be appointed at the request of the prisoners to perform religious duties.[85] Such an appointment can only be made with the approval of the camp authorities, and, if necessary, that of the local authorities of the denomination concerned. Any lay person who is so appointed must exercise their functions in accordance with relevant security and disciplinary regulations within the camp.

The legal provision for the protection of religion is unequivocal, and does not in itself present much difficulty. Securing proper application of the protection may be challenging in some circumstances, however, and has become a matter for some modern concern. Difficulty is likely to arise where parties in conflict have radically opposed faith or non-faith traditions, and especially so in the context of so-called 'fundamentalism'. Allied troops stationed in the territory of a friendly state do not enjoy the protection of 1949 Geneva Convention III or 1977 Additional Protocol I, but the potential for difficulty can be seen by analogy with events in the 1990–91 Gulf Conflict. As discussed in Chapter 4, non-Islamic worship is forbidden in Saudi Arabia, and severe restrictions on worship by members of Coalition forces stationed in Saudi Arabia who were committed to faiths other than Islam were imposed during the conflict. Non-Islamic worship did take place, but very discreetly in desert camps far removed from Saudi centres of population. US military chaplains from other faiths were forbidden to wear any outward signs of their religious function, and observances for Christmas 1990 were conducted in secret without notice. The Archbishop of Canterbury's Christmas message to British troops was barred from entry to the kingdom, and it reached only a small number who were ferried by a journalist across the border into a neighbouring state in which the message could be freely received.

The sensitivity of the Saudi authorities, as guardian of the most holy places of Islam, is understandable, and perhaps especially so in the delicate diplomatic context of the 1990–91 Gulf Conflict. Be that as it may, had there been any Iraqi prisoners of war held in Saudi Arabia of a faith other than Islam, the imposition of the restrictions placed upon non-Muslim Coalition personnel would have been unequivocally illegal, whatever the sensitivities of the detaining power.

In the end, the provisions of 1949 Geneva Convention III for the protection of freedom of religion for prisoners of war is a specific expression of a general right which is by no means confined to that narrow context.[86] The final issue in this context is the meaning of 'religion'. As mentioned in Chapter 4, the *Oxford Reference Dictionary* offers the following.

> 1. belief in a superhuman controlling power, especially in a personal God or gods entitled to obedience and worship; the expression of this in worship. 2. a particular system of faith.

One might debate the specific applicability of this definition to certain forms of faith, but the general concept is clear enough. However, what of a system of ethical or ideological commitment without, or even opposed to, belief in God or some gods? Would political meetings convened by a Party Commissar or an equivalent official be covered by provisions for freedom of 'worship'? The answer to this must be 'no' if the provision is to retain any substantive meaning.

That is not to say, of course, that such meetings could therefore be repressed, assuming that they did not imperil camp discipline.

A different and important issue, arises in the present context: the right to non-religion, whether in the form of agnosticism or of atheism. The right to freedom of religion is conceived in positive terms as an entitlement to take part in the relevant form of worship; it does not *prima facie* state a positive right *not* to take part. To take a hypothetical circumstance, what would be the position of a prisoner of war from a 'fundamentalist' state who did not share the faith in question and who found him or herself compelled by his or her compatriots to take part in their worship? The answer to this lies in the general duty arising from article 13 of 1949 Geneva Convention III to protect prisoners of war from 'acts of violence or intimidation', which must be taken to include such acts perpetrated by other prisoners. An analogous situation did arise on a number of occasions during the Second World War when Nazi fanatics sought to apply severe coercion against less committed fellow prisoners of war who were therefore, for their own safety, transferred to other camps. The combined conclusion must therefore be that a prisoner of war may neither be prevented from nor compelled into participating in any given form of religious observance. Participation may be limited only by reference to objective perception of imperilment of camp discipline.

Intellectual and Recreational Pursuits

Article 38 of 1939 Geneva Convention III requires that:

> While respecting the individual preferences of every prisoner, the Detaining Power shall encourage the practice of intelligent, educational, and recreational pursuits, sports and games amongst prisoners and shall take the measures necessary to ensure the exercise thereof by providing them with adequate premises and necessary equipment.
>
> Prisoners shall have opportunities for taking physical exercise including sports and games and for being out of doors. Sufficient open spaces shall be provided for this purpose in all camps.

The categorisation of these pursuits is necessarily somewhat vague. So far as intellectual pursuits are concerned, the range of potential activity is obviously considerable, and might even extend to the pursuit of degree-level study by some form of what would now be termed distance learning. There have been cases of successful degree study by prisoners of war during internment, a process demanding great determination and adaptability to less than ideal conditions. It may be added that the requirement for provision of 'adequate premises and necessary equipment' in this context may not be taken to embrace provision of a university library! More typically, evening (or other) classes set up by the prisoners amongst themselves from whatever skills bases may be available have done much in many conflicts to alleviate the basic tedium of internment.

The various forms of sport and other exercise also play a self-evidently valuable role in maintaining the health and morale of prisoners of war, and this must be facilitated to the greatest degree possible and be compatible with the maintenance of camp discipline. The latter would obviously preclude any sport involving weapons training, such as target shooting or archery, but most other sports require as a necessary minimum no more than the availability of the requisite open space and the capacity to obtain or manufacture the basic equipment.

Work by Prisoners of War

A detaining power may make use of the labour of prisoners of war, provided that physically inappropriate demands are not made of any individual prisoner. In this there are certain distinctions of rank. Officers and 'persons of equivalent status' may not be required to work, but must, as far as possible, be found suitable work if they request it. Prisoners of non-commissioned officer rank may only be required to perform supervisory work, but if not so employed, they must, if possible, be found other suitable work upon request. Prisoners of other ranks may be required to work, taking due account of their physical capacities and health.

A specific list of the work which prisoners may be required to perform is set out in 1949 Geneva Convention III.[88] The most important restriction in this context is a ban on work of direct military relevance. Of course, in one sense all work by a prisoner of war is of military relevance as a contribution to the 'war economy', even if only through the release of a worker for military service, but a clear line of demarcation may be drawn between, for example, vegetable-growing and work in a munitions factory. A prisoner may also not be employed in unhealthy or dangerous work, including clearing minefields or similar tasks,[89] unless he or she volunteers for it. During the 1982 Falklands Conflict, it was found upon the recapture of Port Stanley by British forces that extensive minefields had been sown. Some Argentine prisoners who were specialist engineers assisted in the work of clearance, and were confirmed by the ICRC to have done so voluntarily, there being thus no breach of Convention III. However, the employment of Argentine prisoners in this work was discontinued following the explosion of an unmarked mine.[90]

No prisoner may be employed in unhealthy or humiliating labour unless he or she has volunteered for it.[91]

The working conditions of prisoners of war must accord with the safety regulations applicable to nationals of the detaining power, and must in any event be safe; suitable work training must also be given where necessary. In no case may labour of prisoners be made more arduous as a disciplinary measure.[92] The working day of a prisoner of war must not be excessive or exceed that ordained for nationals of the detaining power engaged in similar work. Prisoners must be allowed a midday rest of not less than one hour, or more if the national norm exceeds this. Working prisoners must also be allowed 24 hours' complete rest in each week, on Sunday or the other day of rest appointed within the country in which they are detained, for example on Friday in an Islamic country. Prisoners who have worked for one year must be allowed a consecutive eight-day period of rest.[93] Prisoners who are employed in external labour units must be enabled to maintain contact with the relevant prisoners' representative.[94]

Prisoners of war engaged in work must be fairly renumerated at a level fixed by the detaining authorities, subject to conventional minimums. This provision includes prisoners' representatives and those engaged in medical or spiritual work. In the case of the prisoners' representatives, payment will be made out of the profits of the canteen sales, if any. If there are none, the payment will be made directly by the detaining authority.[95]

Finances of Prisoners of War

Apart from any working pay, prisoners are entitled to monthly advances on their service pay according to a scale fixed by the detaining power. However, this is ultimately a charge on the power upon which they depend, which is to be adjusted between the detaining and the home power at the conclusion of hostilities. Such payments may be varied by special agreement or where they would grossly exceed the scale of remuneration applicable within the armed forces of the detaining power.[96]

For reasons of camp security, the detaining authority may determine the amount in ready cash which prisoners may have in their possession at any time. A formal arrangement may be made with the Protecting Power to this end.[97] Convention III sets out detailed provisions for the management of the financial accounts of prisoners of war.[98]

Relations of Prisoners of War with the Outside World

An obvious humanitarian consideration for prisoners of war is the maintenance of contact with their families. Upon capture, or not later than a week after arrival in a prisoner of war camp or transit camp, prisoners must be allowed to write to their family and to the Central Tracing Agency or other special prisoner of war agency, informing them of the fact of their capture, address and state of health. This information will be conveyed in the form of a *capture card*, as set out in Annex IV to 1949 Geneva Convention III. These cards must, upon completion, be forwarded to their destination without delay.[99] In addition to the capture card, prisoners must be allowed to send and receive letters and cards, ideally without limitation on number, but in any event no less than two letters and four cards per month. Numerical restrictions on correspondence may be imposed only at the request of the power upon which the prisoners depend, and never as a disciplinary sanction. In cases of urgent necessity for communication or of long absence of news, a prisoner must be permitted to send telegrams but these will be paid for directly by the prisoner or charged to his or her account in camp.[100] Facilities must also be provided for prisoners to prepare and to transport, through the Protecting Power or other appropriate agency, legal documents, most particularly testamentary dispositions and powers of attorney.[101]

Censorship of correspondence is permitted under Convention III, but may be done only once by each power concerned, and must not be used unreasonably to delay receipt of mail. Goods sent to prisoners may be scrutinised, but not in a manner injurious to the goods themselves.[102] Prisoners are entitled to receive individual and collective relief materials, including the well-known 'Red Cross parcels' organised by the ICRC.[103]

Complaints by Prisoners of War

Under 1949 Geneva Convention III, article 78, prisoners have the right to make requests regarding their treatment to the representative of the Protecting Power, either through the appropriate prisoners' representative or, if necessary, directly. Such complaints may not be counted against any correspondence quota which may have been imposed, nor may any such complaint be made a ground for punishment, even if it turns out to have been unfounded.

Judicial and Disciplinary Proceedings

Prisoners of war owe no allegiance to the power by which they are detained, since they have been placed in its power by circumstances which are beyond their control. They are thus not precisely in the position of a visitor to a foreign country who may reasonably be deemed to accept its laws before undertaking to go there, subject only to relevant international human rights provisions. The position of prisoners of war therefore raises interesting questions of legal obligations.[104] However, prisoners of war are stated to be subject to the 'laws, regulations and orders in force in the armed forces of the detaining power', in addition to any special disciplinary regulations made for the government of prisoner of war camps.[105] In recognition of the involuntary nature of their presence in the 'host' country, prisoners of war benefit from a general presumption of leniency in the conduct of judicial and disciplinary proceedings against them. Thus, where an offence committed by a prisoner of war could be dealt with through either judicial or disciplinary mechanisms, the latter are urged to be adopted wherever possible.[106]

Allegations made against a prisoner of breaches of camp discipline must be investigated by the camp authorities immediately. A disciplinary hearing must accord with normal procedural standards; in particular, the accused must be informed of the charge and given the opportunity to defend him or herself, including calling witnesses and the services of an interpreter, where this is necessary. A prisoner under disciplinary investigation may only be confined if a member of the armed forces of the detaining power would be so in similar circumstances, or if this is essential for the maintenance of camp order and discipline. Any such preliminary confinement must not exceed 14 days, and must comply with the general requirements imposed upon confinement of prisoners.[107] Such periods of confinement must be deducted from any custodial sentence subsequently imposed in respect of the offence concerned.[108]

The disciplinary jurisdiction of the camp commandant is without prejudice to the higher jurisdiction of the judicial authorities.[109] It is also important to stress that neither judicial nor disciplinary powers may ever be exercised by or delegated to a prisoner of war.[110]

Disciplinary penalties may in no case be 'inhuman, brutal or dangerous to ... health'. The permitted sanctions are: a fine not exceeding 50 per cent of pay due to the offender over a period not exceeding 30 days; discontinuance of any privileges granted in excess of the requirements of the convention; confinement, or, except in the case of officer offenders, fatigue duties not exceeding two hours daily.[111] Sentences of confinement may not exceed 30 days at any one time; even where the offender is liable in respect of more than one custodial sentence, a period of at least three days must elapse between service of any two periods of which one is 10 days or more in duration. Service of a sentence of disciplinary confinement may not commence more than one month after sentence.[112] Such sentences must be served in the camp, and not in an external penitentiary, and remain subject to the general requirements of Convention III regarding health, hygiene and medical treatment, including separation of accommodation according to rank and sex. Prisoners undergoing disciplinary confinements must be allowed reading and writing materials, receipt of mail and a minimum of two hours' open-air exercise daily. Parcels may be withheld from them, but must then be put in the keeping of the prisoners' representative, who must transfer any perishable items to the camp infirmary.[113]

The most obvious disciplinary offence by a prisoner of war is an attempt to escape, and this may only ever be treated as a disciplinary offence.[114] However, if a prisoner commits other offences, such as murder, in the course of an escape attempt, he or she will then become answerable in judicial proceedings.[115] It is naturally the duty of the camp authorities to restrain escape attempts, and this may include the use of weapons, but this is treated by the convention as an extreme measure, to be avoided if possible, and in all cases to be preceded by warnings in a form appropriate to the circumstances.[116] Prisoners who do attempt to escape may therefore be subjected to surveillance, but not to an extent injurious to their health or in breach of the convention.[117]

A sharp distinction is drawn in Convention III between unsuccessful escape attempts, which may be treated as disciplinary offences, and successful escapes, which, in the event of later recapture, may not. A successful escape is achieved when the prisoner rejoins his or her own armed forces or those of an ally, leaves the territory controlled by the detaining power or its allies, or joins a ship flying his or her own flag or that of an ally which may be in the territorial waters of the detaining power, but not under its control.[118]

In cases of more serious offences, prisoners are answerable in judicial proceedings. They may be tried only by a military court, unless members of the armed forces of the detaining power would be triable by a civilian court in equivalent circumstances. In any event, the court trying a prisoner of war must meet the minimum internationally accepted standards of independence and impartiality, including rights of legal representation, defence and access to documents.[119] Where the prisoner is unable to select a counsel to represent him or her, which would, of course, be difficult, the Protecting Power has the duty to do so on his or her behalf, and must be allowed a week in which to do so. Documents and charges must be presented to prisoners in a language which they understand, and a representative of the

Protecting Power must be allowed to attend the trials unless in an exceptional case, the trial is held *in camera* for reasons of security, in which case the Protecting Power must be so advised.[120]

Especially difficult problems may arise in case of offences committed by a prisoner of war before capture. Article 85 of Convention III accepts that prisoners may be prosecuted for offences committed prior to capture, but also provides that such prisoners retain the benefits of the convention even if they are convicted. There are two basic difficulties here. Where an offence was committed before capture, it is highly unlikely that all the material witnesses will be within the jurisdiction of the detaining power, and in these circumstances the possibility of conducting an adequate and fair trial of the alleged offender must be very doubtful. Secondly, the potential for such a prosecution to be misconstrued as harassment or persecution is considerable, and has dangerous implications in a 'Geneva' context, in fact if not in theory.

The question of proceedings in respect of offences alleged to have been committed prior to capture by a prisoner of war arose during the 1982 Falklands Conflict, in what has become known as the 'Astiz affair'.[121] Captain Alfredo Astiz[122] was the commander of the Argentine occupation force in South Georgia, an island associated with the Falkland Islands. When South Georgia was recaptured by the British, Captain Astiz signed the document of surrender as senior Argentine officer, and was then taken prisoner along with the men under his command. There was no suggestion that Captain Astiz has acted in contravention of the laws of armed conflict during the Falklands Campaign, but he was suspected of having played a shadowy 'secret police' role during the so-called 'dirty war' of internal repression of dissent by the Argentine military government. In particular, it was suspected by the Swedish and French governments that he had played a leading role in the 'disappearance' and presumed murder of Miss Dagmar Hagelin, a Swedish girl, and of two French nuns, Sisters Alice Doman and Renée-Léonie Duquet. The Swedish and French governments were eager to question Captain Astiz about these matters. When the prisoners captured on South Georgia were repatriated during the continuance of hostilities, Captain Astiz was kept a prisoner at the urgent request of the Swedish and French authorities, being diverted from repatriation at the transit camp on Ascension Island.

The situation was somewhat sensitive. It was clear that Astiz would not submit to interrogation, and anyway there were serious doubts about the propriety and practicality of putting him on trial in the United Kingdom or of extraditing him to Sweden or France. Although 1949 Geneva Convention III urges leniency, it contains nothing which would preclude the trial of prisoners for offences alleged to have been committed before capture, even if unrelated to the armed conflict. The only restriction on transfer of a prisoner to another power is, as noted above, its willingness and ability to abide by the Geneva Conventions, and both Sweden and France clearly satisfied this requirement. However, whilst a considerable number of prosecution witnesses, mainly in political exile from Argentina, could probably have been found for such a trial, defence witnesses, who were mainly in Argentina, would not have been able to attend in the course of the continuing armed conflict, even had they been willing to do so. In these circumstances, it must be doubted whether a fair trial could have been conducted by either the United Kingdom, Sweden or France, and this being the case, the propriety of extraditing Astiz to any of these countries must be seen as dubious.[123] In the event, Captain Astiz was brought to the United Kingdom and held at a military establishment in Chichester, where a number of questions submitted by the Swedish and French authorities were put to him by senior member of the West Sussex Constabulary, all of which he declined to answer, in accordance with his rights under the convention. There was also some suggestion at the time that British journalists held in Argentina would be treated as spies if the Astiz matter was pursued, though the British Government denied that the two issues were coupled.

Astiz was finally repatriated to Argentina on 10 June 1982. It is difficult to see what else could reasonably have been done in the circumstances. It will almost invariably be the preferable course to defer the resolution of such issues until after the conclusion of hostilities – as, for example, in the much more wider-ranging case of Rudolf Hess – even in the case of genuine 'war crimes', and in most other cases to leave the matter to the appropriate competent municipal authorities. Sweden and France might later have taken the matter up directly with Argentina, although admittedly, as matters then stood, with little hope of success. In the event, Captain Astiz was eventually tried in Argentina after the fall of the military junta for his alleged part in the 'dirty war', and was acquitted because of a statute of limitations.[124]

Although the legal and practical difficulties in the way of trying prisoners of war for offences alleged to have been committed prior to capture will always be considerable, it should be remembered that 1949 Geneva Convention III does provide by article 112 that prisoners of war against whom criminal proceedings are pending may be retained for this purpose after the conclusion of hostilities. In extreme cases, there is also the precedent of the war crimes tribunals after the Second World War in Nuremberg and Tokyo.[125]

Even here, however, there remain some outstanding questions. The Warsaw Pact states have made reservations to the convention to the effect that they will not consider themselves bound to treat as 'prisoners of war' persons convicted of war crimes in accordance with Nuremberg principles. A number of Western states have protested against these reservations, although Italy has taken the view, without express reservation, that the benefits of prisoner of war status do not extend to 'war criminals'. A similar view was taken in the case of captured USAF personnel during the Vietnam War by what was then North Vietnam, and some of these men were treated very harshly. The exclusion of alleged 'war criminals' from prisoner of war status cannot readily be accepted as concording with either the letter or the spirit of the convention, and notwithstanding the admitted difficulties, the preferable course must be the trial of war crimes and other alleged offences within the 'Geneva' provisions and also their punishment.

Death of Prisoners of War

It is inevitable that in any extended conflict, some prisoners of war will die, from natural causes or otherwise, while in captivity. It is then obviously important that clear procedures should be followed to avoid, as far as possible, potentially dangerous misunderstandings.

All cases of death or serious injury of a prisoner resulting from the action of sentries, other prisoners and persons in other categories or from unknown causes must be investigated immediately by the detaining power. If culpable responsibility is found, the persons concerned must be prosecuted. In any event, a copy of the report of the investigation accompanied by witness statements must be sent to the Protecting Power.[126] This was done in the case of the five Argentine prisoners who died and one who was seriously injured during the 1982 Falklands Conflict. No offences were found to have been committed.[127] In one of these cases, an Argentine sub-officer on the captured submarine *Santa Fe* was shot and killed by a sentry who believed, apparently erroneously, that he was engaged in an immediately act of sabotage. The subsequent investigation found that no offence had been committed, and this conclusion was communicated to the ICRC, and through them to the Argentine Government, which apparently raised no objection.[128]

In cases of natural death, a death certificate in the form set out in Annex IV of the convention, or a list certified by a responsible officer setting out the same information, must be transmitted to the appropriate international agency, and by them to the power upon which the deceased prisoner depended. Deceased prisoners must be subjected to post-mortem examination, and thereafter receive honourable obsequies in accordance with same principles as those set out under 1949 Geneva Convention I in relation to the treatment of the sick and injured on land.[129]

Termination of Captivity, and Repatriation

It is obviously desirable from a humanitarian viewpoint that prisoners of war should be repatriated as soon as possible after the end of hostilities, and in some compassionate cases, even during their continuance.

Detaining powers are required by Convention III to repatriate directly certain categories of prisoner whose condition effectively precludes their playing a further part in hostilities, once they are in a medically fit state to stand the journey involved. These are, broadly, the incurably wounded and sick, those who are unlikely to recover within one year and who have suffered severe mental or physical impairment, and those who, although recovered, have suffered severe mental or physical impairment.[130] However, no such repatriation may take place against the subject's will during the conflict.[131]

Those who are less seriously affected but would be placed at health risk by continued captivity or would benefit from medical treatment in a neutral country may be transferred to the care of a neutral power. Similar arrangements may also be made for those who have undergone long-term captivity.[132] A model agreement for direct repatriation and neutral transfer is set out in Annex I to the convention, together with appropriate procedural regulations for mixed medical commissions to oversee the implementation of such arrangements.[133] Prisoners who suffer accidental, other than self-inflicted, injury are eligible for repatriation or neutral transfer,[134] but in all cases repatriation may be delayed on grounds of the service of a disciplinary sentence of confinement.[135] The costs of repatriation or transfer to a neutral country are borne by the detaining power up to their frontier, and by the power upon which the beneficiaries depend beyond that point.[136]

No express provision is made for the direct repatriation of able-bodied prisoners of war, but this has been done in a number of cases during the continuance of conflict. During the Vietnam War, a number of captured US servicemen were released by the North Vietnamese and Vietcong between 1968 and 1972 to various self-appointed 'anti-war' groups in the USA. The motivation for these releases seems to have been more propagandist than humanitarian, as the random and arbitrary nature of the selection of the men to be released strongly suggests. The question arose in this context of the status of the 'anti-war' groups as 'neutral humanitarian institutions' within the meaning of the Geneva Conventions; on the whole, this seems a more than dubious claim in the light of their clear causal commitment.[137]

During the 1982 Falklands Conflict, an unusual number of repatriations took place during the continuance of the conflict, and here the importance of the provision of article 117 of Convention III that 'no repatriated person may be employed on active military service' becomes obvious.

The small group of marines and civilians captured by Argentine forces in the Falkland Islands and in South Georgia was repatriated to the United Kingdom almost at once. These men later returned to the Falklands, and were symbolically present in Port Stanley after its recapture: this raises clear questions under article 117.[138] It is true that article 117 is framed in the context of provision for the repatriation of the seriously wounded and sick, and that no specific provision is made for the direct repatriation of the able-bodied. However, the article itself clearly deals with repatriation, and it would seem reasonable to apply the same principle, at least by analogy, to repatriation of the able-bodied – not least because otherwise the motivation for such repatriation would be lacking. In this light, the return of the repatriated marines to Port Stanley must be seen as not necessarily unlawful according to the letter of the convention, but certainly an undesirable precedent. Well over 1,000 Argentine prisoners of war were repatriated by the British during the conflict, both with and without ICRC participation.[139] This must be regarded as desirable, although it is worth commenting that both the nature of the conflict and the difficulty in caring adequately for large numbers of prisoners in the climatic conditions of the South Atlantic created rather unusual conditions in the Falklands Conflict.

Once active hostilities have ceased, 1949 Geneva Convention III requires by article 118 that 'prisoners of war shall be repatriated without delay'. Where no other specific agreement is entered into, the costs of repatriation are divided equally between the detaining power and the power upon which the prisoners depend. If the formerly adverse powers are contiguous, each party will bear the cost of transport on its side of the frontier, and agreements will be entered into regarding the final apportionment and balancing of expenses. Such negotiations must not be allowed to impede the progress of repatriation however.[140] The procedures for repatriation are basically similar to those for the transfer of prisoners while in captivity.

It has already been commented that prisoners of war against whom criminal, including war crimes, charges are pending may now be retained to face trial,[141] but it is clear that this provision refers to specific individuals against whom charges are pending, and does not allow for general retentions on the basis that some of the prisoners may have been involved in war crimes.[142]

A final problem lies in the question of involuntary repatriation. It is generally assumed that prisoners of war wish to be repatriated as soon as possible and, consequently, Convention III makes no reference to repatriation as a specifically voluntary process. However, such reference is made in the case of repatriation of the seriously sick or injured during the continuance of armed conflict, with primary reference to the dangers of transport under such circumstances. After the conflict, some prisoners may be in danger of persecution upon return to their home countries. This may arise on various grounds, a common one being fear of ideological 'contamination', or perhaps inconsistency with propaganda for home consumption to the effect that no soldiers of the state concerned have been captured. An especially difficult case arose with the repatriation to the former Soviet Union of Russians and Ukrainians who had served with the German armed forces. Some of these people may have been war criminals, especially considering the presence of the SS element, but the majority almost certainly were not. War criminals or otherwise, they were certain to be severely punished; indeed it was probable that they would be summarily shot as traitors upon return to the USSR. The British authorities nevertheless repatriated them, and many did face firing squads. It was later claimed that this could not have been anticipated, which implies a surprising lack of knowledge of conditions in Stalin's Russia. It seems more likely, although this is pure supposition, that little thought was given to the fate of prisoners who had betrayed a wartime ally by fighting for the enemy. This may have been understandable in 1945, but in retrospect the issue clearly merited more sympathetic consideration. The Stalinist regime inflicted unspeakable oppression upon the peoples of the former Soviet Union during the 1930s, as later Soviet leaders themselves admitted. In this situation there were not a few who welcomed the Germany army as 'liberators'. Some later became fervent Nazis; many others learnt their terrible mistake in due course, when it was too late.

Today, 1949 Geneva Convention III provides by article 118 simply that 'prisoners of war shall be released and repatriated without delay after the cessation of hostilities'. This is, in general, the proper and humanitarian course of action. However, there is now a greater sensitivity to the possibility that prisoners might be in danger, upon repatriation, perhaps simply from the fact of having been captured. During the 1990–91 Gulf Conflict, the ICRC expressed the firm view that prisoners should not be repatriated against their will,[143] and Iraqi prisoners of war were given the opportunity to object to repatriation if they so desired. Peter Rowe remarks that:

> representatives of the International Committee of the Red Cross interviewed all Iraqi prisoners of war who expressed an unwillingness to

> return to Iraq and took the view that they should be considered as refugees ... [o]n April [1991] King Fahd of Saudi Arabia offered to 'take in 50,000 Iraqi refugees ...'[144]

The involvement of the ICRC is clearly essential, not least to ensure that the prisoners who do not want to return are making a voluntary decision as much as those who do. Nevertheless, the arrangements made in the Gulf Conflict seem much the best and most humanitarian approach to an issue which can pose very sensitive humanitarian, legal and political questions.

Notes

1 See Chapter 1.
2 1949 Geneva Convention III, article 4A(3).
3 1977 Additional Protocol I, article 43.
4 Under 1977 Additional Protocol I, militias are treated more directly as members of armed forces *stricto sensu*.
5 1977 Additional Protocol I, article 43(3).
6 See Chapter 3.
7 1977 Additional Protocol I, article 44(7).
8 Ibid., articles 44(4) and 45.
9 Ibid., article 1(4).
10 For discussion, see Chapter 3.
11 1977 Additional Protocol I, article 45(3).
12 1949 Geneva Convention III, article 45.
13 Ibid., article 75.
14 Ibid., article 45(3).
15 See H. McCoubrey and N.D. White, 'International Law and the Use of Force in the Gulf' (1991) X *International Relations*, p. 347, at p. 361.
16 This letter is set out in (1962) 2 *International Review of the Red Cross*, p. 16.
17 For discussion of the status of 'captured' and detained UN military personnel, see H. McCoubrey and N.D. White, *The Blue Helmets: Legal Regulation of UN Military Operations* (Dartmouth, 1996), pp. 166–9.
18 *The Times* (London), 19 July 1995.
19 See 1949 Geneva Convention III, article 12, in relation to prisoners of war, and 1949 Geneva Convention IV, article 29, in relation to 'civilians' in this context.
20 In the context of increased UN military activity, this issue is under active consideration by the United Nations in the late 1990s, although to what ultimate effect remains to be seen at the time of writing. For another view, see H. McCoubrey and N.D. White, op.cit., Chapter 10.
21 See Chapter 7.
22 1949 Geneva Convention III, article 33.
23 Ibid., article 4B(1).
24 Ibid., article 4B(2). Articles 8, 10, 15, 30(3), 58–67, 92 and 126 of the convention are excluded in this case, as in all provisions relating to Protecting Powers where diplomatic relations exist between the neutral detaining power and the power upon which the detained persons relies.
25 1977 Additional Protocol I, article 77(2). For discussion, see pp. 193–5.
26 Ibid., article 77(3).

27 A detailed account of this incident was given by A.E. Bonsor, 'War Correspondent' (1896) XVIII *Boy's Own Paper*, pp. 538–9.
28 Y. Sandoz, C. Swinarski and B. Zimmerman (eds) with J. Pictet, *Commentary on the Additional Protocols of 8 June 1977 to the Geneva Conventions of 12 August 1949* (ICRC/Martinus Nijhoff, 1987), p. 921, para. 3,260.
29 See pp. 141–3.
30 See *Guardian* (London), 7 August 1992.
31 1977 Additional Protocol I, article 46(3). See also article 29 of the Land Warfare Regulation annexed to 1907 Hague Convention IV.
32 1977 Additional Protocol I, article 46(2).
33 P. Rowe, *Defence: The Legal Implications* (Brassey's Defence Publishers, 1987), p. 161. Naturally, the question of espionage or otherwise has no impact upon the exercise of protective measures against intrusions by unauthorised naval vessels or military aircraft of a foreign power.
34 1977 Additional Protocol I, article 46(3). For judicial discussion of conduct amounting to espionage, see *Public Prosecutor* v. *Koi* [1968] 1 All ER, 417, and *Mohamed Ali* v. *Public Prosecutor* [1968] 1 All ER, 488.
35 1977 Additional Protocol I, article 46(4).
36 For an account of the development of the law relating to mercenaries, see L.C. Green, *Essays on the Modern Law of War* (Transnational Publishers, 1985), p. 175. See also F. Hampson, 'Mercenaries: Diagnosis before Prescription' (1991) XXII *Netherlands Yearbook of International Law*, p. 3, and P.W. Mourning, 'Leashing the Dogs of War: Outlawing the Recruitment and Use of Mercenaries' (1982) 22 *Virginia Journal of International Law*, p. 589.
37 1977 Additional Protocol I, article 47(1).
38 Ibid., article 45.
39 Ibid., article 75(4).
40 F. Hampson, op.cit., at p. 27.
41 See Chapter 1.
42 (1982) 53 *British Yearbook of International Law*, p. 418.
43 See also Chapter 4.
44 *Independent* (London), 22 January 1991. For a detailed account of this and other incidents, see *Thunder and Lightning: The RAF in the Gulf* (HMSO, 1991), Chapter 9.
45 XI *War Crimes Reports*, p. 53.
46 P. Rowe, 'Prisoners of War in the Gulf Area', in P. Rowe (ed.), *The Gulf War 1990–91 in International and English Law* (Sweet and Maxwell/Routledge, 1993), p. 188, at p. 194.
47 1949 Geneva Convention III, article 14.
48 Ibid.
49 1949 Geneva Convention III, article 16.
50 Ibid., article 15.
51 Ibid., article 17.
52 Ibid.
53 Under article 17, such an identity card must measure 10 cm by 6.5 cm and be issued in duplicate. A prisoner should present it upon demand but it may not be confiscated. If a prisoner does not have an identity card upon capture, the detaining power should issue one (1949 Geneva Convention III, article 18).
54 1949 Geneva Convention III, article 18.
55 Ibid., article 19.
56 Ibid., article 20.
57 'Permanent' means here 'established' rather than 'temporary'; it does not imply perpetual existence.
58 1949 Geneva Convention III, article 24.

59 Ibid., article 20.
60 Ibid., articles 46 and 47.
61 Ibid., article 48.
62 The transferee power need not be a party to 1977 Additional Protocol I.
63 1949 Geneva Convention III, article 12.
64 Ibid., article 21.
65 Ibid., article 22. If prisoners are located in unhealthy areas or a deleterious climate, they must be moved as soon as possible into more favourable conditions.
66 Ibid., article 23.
67 Ibid., article 79.
68 Ibid., article 80.
69 Ibid., article 81.
70 Ibid., article 79.
71 Ibid., articles 39–41. Equivalence of ranks between the armed forces of opposing parties must be established at the outbreak of hostilities, and the detaining power must recognise promotions of prisoners of war which are duly notified to it (1949 Geneva Convention III, article 4).
72 Ibid., article 25.
73 Ibid., article 26.
74 Ibid.
75 Ibid., article 27.
76 Ibid., article 28.
77 Ibid., article 29.
78 Ibid.
79 Ibid., article 30.
80 Ibid., article 31.
81 Ibid., article 32.
82 Ibid., article 33. As to the law in this regard relating to naval warfare, see Chapter 5.
83 Ibid., articles 34 and 35.
84 Ibid., article 36.
85 Ibid., article 37.
86 For discussion of this issue, see B. Dickson, 'The United Nations and Freedom of Religion' (1993) 44 *International and Comparative Law Quarterly*, pp. 327–57.
87 1949 Geneva Convention III, article 49. Monthly medical checks are required to take account of fitness for work by article 55 of the convention. Every care must be taken of victims of industrial injury, and provision must be made for payment of compensation in such cases (article 48).
88 1949 Geneva Convention III, article 50.
89 Ibid., article 52.
90 See S. Junod, op.cit., p. 30.
91 1949 Geneva Convention III, article 52.
92 Ibid., article 51.
93 Ibid., article 53.
94 Ibid., articles 56–7.
95 Ibid., article 62.
96 Ibid., articles 60, 61 and 67.
97 Ibid., article 58.
98 Ibid., articles 59, 63, 64–7.
99 Ibid., article 70.
100 Ibid., article 71. Models for the letter forms and cards are set out in Annex IV to the convention.
101 Ibid., article 77.

102 Ibid., article 76.
103 Ibid., articles 72–4. See also article 75 with regard to transport.
104 For an interesting discussion of this in the particular context of escape attempts, see R. Dworkin, *Taking Rights Seriously* (Duckworth, 1978), Chapter 7, at p. 189ff.
105 1949 Geneva Convention III, article 82.
106 Ibid., article 83.
107 Ibid., articles 95 and 96.
108 Ibid., article 90.
109 Ibid., article 96.
110 Ibid., articles 84 and 96.
111 Ibid., article 89.
112 Ibid., article 90.
113 Ibid., articles 97 and 98.
114 Ibid., article 92.
115 There will still be a presumption of leniency. Offences committed solely for the facilitation of escape not involving violence or self-enrichment are to be treated as disciplinary offences only (article 93).
116 1949 Geneva Convention III, article 42.
117 Ibid., article 92.
118 Ibid., article 91.
119 Ibid., article 84.
120 Ibid., article 105.
121 For discussion see M.A. Meyer, 'Liability of Prisoners of War for Offences Committed Prior to Capture: The Astiz Affair' (1983) *International and Comparative Law Quarterly*, p. 948.
122 His actual rank at the time was intermediate between those of Captain and Commander in Royal Naval equivalence.
123 It appears very unlikely that Astiz could have been extradited: see M.A. Meyer, op.cit., at pp. 970–1. It would have been very difficult indeed for the UK to establish any *prima facie* jurisdiction, since the alleged offences had been committed neither in the UK nor even against UK nationals.
124 *Independent* (London), 20 November 1987.
125 See Chapter 10.
126 1949 Geneva Convention III, article 121.
127 See S. Junod, op.cit., p. 32.
128 See A. Coll and A. Arend, *The Falklands War* (Allen & Unwin, 1985), p. 72.
129 See Chapter 4.
130 1949 Geneva Convention III, articles 109 and 110.
131 Ibid., article 109.
132 Ibid., articles 109 and 110.
133 Ibid., articles 111–13.
134 Ibid., article 114.
135 Ibid., article 115.
136 Ibid., article 116.
137 For discussion, see H.S. Levie, 'International Law Aspects of Repatriation during Hostilities: A Reply' (1973) 67 *American Journal of International Law*, p. 693. This was a response to R. Falk in (1972) 66 *American Journal of International Law*, p. 465.
138 For discussion, see P. Rowe, *Defence: The Legal Implications* (Brassey's Defence Publishers, 1987), at p. 174.
139 The details are given in S. Junod, op.cit., at p. 31.
140 1949 Geneva Convention III, article 118.
141 Ibid., article 119.

142 See H.S. Levie, 'Legal Aspects of the Continued Detention of the Pakistani Prisoners of War by India' (1973) 67 *American Journal of International Law*, p. 512.
143 See P. Rowe, 'Prisoners of War in the Gulf Area' in P. Rowe (ed.), *The Gulf War 1990–91 in International and English Law* (Routledge/Sweet and Maxwell, 1993) p. 188 at pp. 212–13.
144 Ibid., p. 188 at p. 203.

7 Protection of Civilians

The protection of civilians is a self-evident imperative in humanitarian provision to mitigate the effects of armed conflict. Such provision is found, with severe limitations, even in the medieval *jus armorum*. In the modern era, provision for the protection of civilians in the conduct of hostilities and in occupied territories was first set out in an extensive treaty in the Land Warfare Regulations annexed to 1907 Hague Convention IV, articles 25–8 and 42–56, dealing respectively with aspects of hostilities and the law of occupation.

The present (1997) provision for civilian protection is found principally in 1949 Geneva Convention IV and 1977 Additional Protocol I. The latter builds upon many important principles of customary law, as well as adding significant innovatory norms, and in general greatly supplements the rather limited provision of Convention IV. There are also measures which afford direct or indirect protection to civilians in a variety of other treaties. It would be misleading to suggest that civilian protection is fully comprehensive even now, and further provision may be thought necessary. Areas of concern include the adequacy of the protection offered to women, children, and also to the environment in circumstances of armed conflict.

Provision for the protection of civilians falls into four broad areas:

1 protection against the general effects of hostilities
2 protection in cases of hostile occupation
3 protection of people especially at risk, including, but not only, women and of children
4 protection of civilian internees.

Protection Against the General Effects of Hostilities

The general principles of protection can be reduced to two broad propositions. Firstly that:

> The civilian population and individual civilians shall enjoy general protection against dangers arising from military operations.[1]

Secondly, a provision ultimately derived from the 1868 Declaration of St Petersburg states:

> In any armed conflict, the right of the Parties to the conflict to choose methods or means of warfare is not unlimited.[2]

For this purpose, a 'civilian' is any person who is not a member of the belligerent armed forces (whether or not the authority upon which such a force depends is recognised by the adverse party) or of associated militia, incorporated paramilitary police or volunteer corps, including organised 'resistance' units, or of a *levée en masse* acting in immediate resistance to invasion. In any case of doubt, the presumption is made in favour of civilian status.[3] A 'civilian population' is simply a population composed of civilians, and it will retain its status even if there are some non-civilians within it. However, a civilian population may not be used as 'shield' for military objectives, and it will not be protected from the effects of a *legitimate* attack upon it which is made with due consideration for the fact of its presence.[4] Nor may civilians themselves take a direct part in hostilities.[5]

The most fundamental protection afforded to the civilian population is set out in 1977 Additional Protocol I, article 48.

> Parties to ... conflict shall at all times distinguish between the civilian population and combatants and between civilian objects and military objectives and accordingly shall direct their operations only against military objectives.

Specifically, civilian populations and individuals may not be made an object of attack in themselves, nor may they be put at risk by 'indiscriminate attacks'. These prescriptions are principal norms of the law relating to bombardment, and are discussed in Chapter 8.

One particular matter arising in relation to bombardment requires further comment in the present context: the prohibition of attack upon installations containing 'dangerous forces'. 1977 Additional Protocol I provides by article 56(1) that:

> Works or installations containing dangerous forces, namely dams, dykes and nuclear electrical generating stations, shall not be made the object of attack, even where these objects are military objectives, if such attacks may cause the release of dangerous forces and consequent severe losses among the civilian population. Other military objectives located at or in the vicinity of these works or installations shall not be made the object of attack if such attack may cause the

> release of dangerous forces ... and consequent severe losses among the civilian population.

However, article 56(2) states that the ban does not apply where such works or installations are used 'in regular, significant and direct support of military operations and if such attack is the only feasible way to terminate such support'. In the case of dams and dykes, this use must also be outside their 'normal function'.

This would now raise serious doubts about, for example, the RAF 'dambusters' raid during the Second World War, although the principal dams concerned – the Möhne and Sorpe dams – undoubtedly supplied power for a vital war industry. The former *Reichsminister* for Armaments, Albert Speer, commented upon this raid that:

> On May 17 1943 ... the RAF tried to strike at our whole armaments industry by destroying the hydroelectric plants of the Ruhr ... That night ... the British came close to a success which would have been greater than anything they had achieved hitherto [with much larger forces] ... But ... they divided their forces and ... destroyed the Eder Valley [but not the Sorpe] dam, although it had nothing whatsoever to do with the supply of water to the Ruhr.[6]

More recently, there have been at least two incidents involving bombing of civil nuclear power stations: an Iranian nuclear power station was bombed by Iraq during the 1980–88 Gulf War, and an Iraqi reactor was bombed by Israel. Some small Iraqi nuclear facilities were also bombed during the 1990–91 Gulf Conflict. There was no escape of radioactive material in any of these cases: in the first two instances the installations were under construction and the nuclear fuel rods were not in place, and in the latter case the attacks were conducted in such a way as to avoid breaching the containment vessels. In all of these instances the motivation appears to have been to frustrate the production of weapons-grade plutonium for possible military purposes. It must be pointed out that such a use, if established, would clearly be a 'significant ... support of military operations' within the meaning of the exception set out in article 56(2) of 197 Additional Protocol I. An attack might thus be justified in armed conflict, especially if release of radioactive materials can be avoided. The 'anticipatory' Israeli attack upon the Iraqi reactor clearly raises other questions pertaining to the *jus ad bellum*. Where escape of radioactive materials cannot be avoided, however, a strong case indeed would need to be made out.

Had the reactors bombed in the Middle East been operative, and had their containment vessels been breached, the probable consequences can be judged by reference to the disastrous civil nuclear disaster at Chernobyl in the Ukraine: there was devastating contamination in the immediate area, and nuclear fallout was spread over much of Europe and Scandinavia. It may finally be remarked that an attack precipitating 'Chernobyl'-scale fallout would manifestly be a form of 'nuclear' attack in its own right, and might be held to fall within the restrictions applicable to nuclear bombardment *stricto sensu*, which are considered in Chapter 8. As such they could well cross the 'nuclear threshold', and precipitate rather than avert the escalation of a conventional conflict into a nuclear war.

1977 Additional Protocol I provides by article 56(7) and Annex I, article 16, for the marking of installations containing dangerous forces by a group of three bright-orange discs of equal size placed on the same axis at a distance of one radius apart. The sign may be repeated at intervals, flown on flags and illuminated at night.

Finally, in terms of general protections, 'civilian objects' may not be made the object of attacks or reprisals. A 'civilian object' for this purpose is any object (a term which includes buildings) which does not by virtue of its nature, location or use make an 'effective contribution to military action' and whose neutralisation would not in the circumstances obtaining afford a 'definite military advantage'. In cases of doubt, any object normally in civilian use is presumed to be a 'civilian object' for this purpose.[7]

A number of special protections are also afforded which are defined either by the nature of the objects concerned or by locality. The first of these is defined as 'cultural objects and places of worship'. There are two problems here: the destruction of buildings, and the looting of treasures, whether material or artistic. Both of these have been commonplaces of past armed conflicts. The museums of Europe are full of objects taken in the course of armed conflict, some of them several times. A good example is the Rosetta Stone, an ancient multilingual text which played a crucial role in the deciphering of ancient Egyptian hieroglyphics, which was seized by Napoleon during his Egyptian campaign and placed in the Louvre, then surrendered to the British in the peace settlement and placed in the British Museum, where it may now be seen.

Both looting and destruction took place to an extreme degree during the Second World War. Massive incidental damage was done to cultural objects by bombing, the raids on Coventry and Dresden being examples of this, and there was also a considerable amount of deliberate spoliation. Examples may be seen in the destruction of the Royal Castle at Warsaw by German occupation forces, and the comprehensive looting and destruction of the former summer palace of the Tsars at Tsarskoe Selo (later Pushkino) during the German siege of Leningrad (St Petersburg). The former Soviet Union undertook a massive restoration project on the Catherine Palace. (In 1997 there are plans for major restoration works on the Alexander Palace, although not directly related to war damage.) Looting took place on a massive scale, primarily through forced 'sales', particularly on the part of *Reichsmarshall* Goering for his private collection, and on that of Hitler himself for a proposed museum and art gallery planned to be built at Linz.[8]

1977 Additional Protocol I provides by article 53 that objects which constitute the 'cultural or spiritual heritage of peoples' – specifically, historic monuments, places of worship and works of art – may not in themselves be made the object of hostility, used in support of military efforts or made the object of reprisals. More extensive provision is made by the 1954 Hague Convention for the Protection of Cultural Property in the Event of Armed Conflict. 1977 Additional Protocol I is expressly stated to be without prejudice to the 1954 Convention[9] which defines 'cultural property' as 'property of great importance to the cultural heritage of every people'.[10] Specifically, this includes architectural, artistic or historical monuments, archaeological sites, books, manuscripts or scientific collections, and the buildings or other 'centres' in which such objects might be maintained or stored. This would obviously include specially built air raid shelters for the safe storage of works of art.

Property and objects falling within the scope of the convention is marked by a shield carrying a royal-blue square, the angles of which form at the base the point of the shield, with a royal-blue triangle stood upon the upper point of the square so that its upper edge forms the top edge of the shield, the spaces left on either side being white triangles.[11] This emblem, repeated three times, is used to mark protected immovable cultural property, transport employed in connection with movable cultural property, and 'improvised refuges' created for the protection of cultural property. The emblem is used singly to designate cultural objects not under special protection, personnel engaged in the regulation or protection of cultural property, and on their identity cards. The emblem may not be used for any other purpose.[12] It may be displayed on flags, armbands or on the surfaces of objects, in appropriate forms. In the case of protected transport, it must be clearly visible in daylight from the air as well as from the ground.[13]

The 1954 Convention places obligations in respect of cultural objects on both the party in whose territory they lie and on adverse and occupying powers. In the former case, general precautionary measures are required as may be appropriate; in particular, cultural property may not be used for purposes likely to expose it to destruction in armed conflict, nor may the enemy direct hostile acts specifically against such property, but both these obligations are subject to the dictates of imperative military necessity.[14]

For the special protection of cultural property, a party to armed conflict is permitted to set up a 'limited number'[15] of shelters for important movable cultural objects. Such a shelter may be designated as under special protection as long as it is situated at an adequate distance from military objectives, or at least so constructed as to be more or less immune from bomb damage, and if it is not used for any military purpose.[16] It is also permissible in emergency to set up 'improvised refuges' for the protection of cultural objects threatened by unforeseen exigencies of armed conflict.[17] In the event of a violation of the conditions for the granting of specially protected status, for example, the use of a refuge for military purposes, the immunity from attack will be terminated. However, the adverse party should first, wherever possible, request cessation of the violation, and allow reasonable time for compliance.[18]

Where it is urgently necessary to transport cultural objects, the transport used may be placed under protection, and when possible, notification of such transport should be given to the adverse party. Such transports, and the objects being transported, are then immune from seizure or capture, although not from visit and search.[19]

Personnel engaged in the protection of cultural property who fall into the hands of an adverse party are requested to be permitted to continue to perform their duties wherever the cultural property with whose care they have been charged falls into the hands of that party to the conflict.[20]

Detailed provision for the execution of the 1954 Convention is set out in the annexed Regulations. This includes provision for the appointment of Commissioners-General for Cultural Property,[21] who will act in conjunction with the Protecting Power, if any, or if there is none, will themselves act in place of the Protecting Power so far as cultural property is concerned. The Commissioner-General will also make technical reports to UNESCO regarding the performance of these duties. Provision is also made for the appointment of appropriate inspectors and technical experts. The expenses of the Commissioners-General, inspectors and experts will be met by the party to whom they are accredited.[22]

Additional provision regarding 'looting' is made by 1954 Hague Protocol for the Protection of Cultural Property in the Event of Armed Conflict. A power in adverse occupation of another power's territory may not export from that territory any cultural objects which may be found within it. If, for whatever reason, it does so, it must ensure the return of the property concerned to the territory upon the cessation of hostilities, and must then pay an indemnity to anyone who has subsequently held the property in good faith.[23] Cultural property may never be comprised within 'war reparations'.[24]

Where any party to the 1954 Protocol finds that cultural property which has been improperly exported from the territory of a party to an armed conflict has been imported into its own territory, it must take control of it with a view to returning it either immediately or, at the latest, upon the request of the party from whose territory it came.[25] Parties to an armed conflict have the right to entrust items of their cultural property to a neutral power for safe keeping during the conflict. Where this is done, such property must be returned to the entrusting party at the conclusion of the conflict.[26]

It should perhaps be stressed that what applied at a governmental level will also apply at a more personal level. The individual soldier is thus as much precluded from looting or calculated destruction of cultural property as is the authority upon which he or she depends.

Zones of Special Protection

1997 Additional Protocol I makes provisions for the special protection of *non-defended localities* and *demilitarised zones*. The former are any inhabited areas so declared by a party to an armed conflict near to or actually within a combat zone which is open for occupation by an adverse party without opposition. Such a locality must have been cleared of all mobile military equipment, no hostile use may be made of fixed military installations, and no acts of hostility or acts in support of military operations must be undertaken by the authorities or population of the locality. The status of such a locality is not endangered by the presence within it of police forces for the maintenance of law and order,[27] but its status will be lost upon any breach of the basic qualifying criteria set out above.[28] The declaration of a non-defended locality is addressed to the adverse party, and must define as precisely as possible its location and extent; the territory may also be marked out by agreed visible signs. The party receiving notice of the declaration of such a zone must acknowledge receipt, and providing the qualificatory criteria are met, must then refrain from hostile attacks within the designated locality.[29] Even where a territory does not fall within the qualificatory criteria set out for non-defended localities, the parties may agree to confer non-defended status on special terms, if they so choose.[30]

The idea of non-defended localities is not a new one, although it is given institutional expression by Protocol I. It has an obvious humanitarian value where a territory is likely to be subjected to adverse occupation in any event, and where the loss and damage to civilians and civilian objects entailed in a prolonged defence would serve no real purpose. A notable example of such a move can be found in the decision to declare Paris an 'open city' in the face of advancing German forces in 1940. At this point there was no realistic chance of defending the city, and its severe damage or destruction in street fighting would have served no real purpose.

A demilitarised zone is one expressly so declared between the controlling and the adverse parties, directly or through a Protecting Power or an impartial humanitarian organisation such as the ICRC.[31] Such a zone will normally be one from which all combatants and mobile military equipment have been withdrawn, in which no hostile use is made of fixed military installations, and no hostile acts or activities linked to the military effort are undertaken by the authorities or the population in the designated area. The presence of a police force for the maintenance of law and order in the zone does not endanger the status of the designated territory. Any zone which is designated as 'demilitarised' must be marked, as far as possible, by agreed symbols which are clearly visible, especially on the perimeter and at highway boundaries.[32]

Subject to the details of the specific agreement on particular demilitarised zones, military operations may not be extended into such zones, and should the combat zone draw near to one of them, it may not be used by any party to the conflict for purposes related to the conduct of military operations, nor may a party to the conflict unilaterally revoke its status.[33] In the event of serious breaches of the status of a demilitarised zone, the other party is released from its obligations under the agreement conferring the status. No provision is made for advance warning of such a termination of status in the case of demilitarised zones.[34]

Under the provision of 1949 Geneva Convention IV, states may, either in peacetime or by arrangement with the adverse party, after hostilities have commenced, establish *hospital and safety zones* in their own territory and, if necessary, in any occupied territories. The purpose of such zones is the creation of areas removed from the effects of the armed conflict for the safety of wounded, sick and aged persons, children under the age of 15, expectant mothers and mothers of children under the age of seven. During an armed conflict, the parties to it should conclude agreements for the mutual recognition of such zones in each other's territory, and the Protecting Powers and the ICRC are invited by the convention to lend their good offices for the facilitation of such agreements.[35]

During an armed conflict, any party may propose to an adverse party, either directly or through the mediation of a neutral power or a humanitarian organisation such as the ICRC, that a neutralised zone or zones be set up in the combat area. Such a zone is intended to afford shelter to the wounded and sick, whether combatant or non-combatant, and to civilians who do not take part in the hostilities and who perform no 'military' work while in the zone. The agreement for the creation of a neutralised zone must state its location, the duration of its status and the arrangements made for supervision and provisioning.[36]

Civil Defence and Civil Defence Personnel

Civil defence personnel – those engaged in such activities as fire-fighting – are especially at risk during armed conflicts, and most especially in circumstances of the establishment of adverse occupation of territory. Such personnel tend to be in uniform, and may thus appear to be combatants, even though they are not, and may also be engaged in activities which might be mistaken as being 'military' in nature. 1977 Additional Protocol I makes extensive provision for the protection of civil defence personnel and organisations.[37] 'Civil defence' tasks are listed by article 61 of the Protocol as comprising: air raid and related precautions, first aid and religious assistance, fire-fighting, location and marking of danger areas, decontaminatory measures, provision of emergency accommodation and supplies, emergency restoration and maintenance of order in 'distressed areas', emergency repair of indispensable public utilities, emergency burial or other disposal of the dead, preservation of objects essential for survival, and complementary activities to any of these, including, but not limited to, planning and organisation.[38]

Civilian civil defence personnel and organisations, including civilian volunteers who respond to appeals to assist in civil defence tasks, are entitled to respect and protection, and to perform their tasks unhindered except in case of 'imperative military necessity'. Civil defence buildings and equipment, including civilian shelters, may not be calculatedly destroyed or diverted from their proper use except by the party to which they belong.[39] This protection extends also to members of armed forces who are permanently assigned to civil defence organisations and who do not perform any 'military' duties during the conflict. Such personnel may carry 'light individual weapons' for the purpose of self-defence and maintenance of order. The protection also extends to buildings and equipment used by such permanently assigned military units.[40]

Parties to armed conflicts are required to do their utmost to identify civil defence personnel, buildings and equipment with the international distinctive sign of civil defence: an equilateral blue triangle placed apex uppermost on an orange background.[41] This symbol may also be used for identification purposes, but parties to the Protocol are required at all times to make provision for restraint of abuses of the symbol. Appropriate agreed signals may also be used for purposes of identification and protection. Where the protection is accorded to those engaged in specific activities such as civil defence, it is obviously necessary that they should in some way be adequately identified, and it is difficult to imagine how this might be done other than by the use of a designated symbol. However, without being able to suggest any alternative approach, it seems necessary to voice concern over the multiplication of identificatory symbols, on the same grounds as those already expressed over the multiplication of alternatives to the protective red cross symbol. It may be noted that in addition to the civil defence symbol, there are symbols for the identification of installations containing dangerous forces and for the designation of 'cultural property' and the personnel and installations connected with it. Bearing in mind that all of these symbols need to be immediately recognisable and appropriately acted upon by members of armed forces in circumstances of combat, there is some cause for concern and, if possible, for a limit on further multiplication.

Civil defence personnel are also required to be issued with an identity card similar in form to that issued to protected medical and religious personnel. Such an identity card will carry the civil defence symbol.

Where a territory is under adverse occupation, civil defence personnel must not be hindered in the proper performance of their duties, and should be allowed the continued use of facilities to this end; however, they may be deprived of personal weapons for reasons of security. They may not be required to perform tasks contrary to the interests of the civilian population, nor may they be required to give priority in the performance of their duties to the nationals or the interests of the occupying power. That power may requisition civil defence buildings and equipment for other purposes, however, provided that such diversion is not harmful to the civilian population, is necessary for some other of their needs, and continues only for so long as alternative necessity exists. In no case may civilian shelters be diverted from their proper use.[42]

It is permissible for civil defence agencies from neutral countries to supply assistance in the territory of a party to armed conflict without this being considered interference in the armed conflict or a breach of neutrality. Where possible, such assistance by a neutral civil defence organisation should be notified to the adverse party in advance. Where such neutral assistance is rendered in territory under adverse occupation, the occupying power may not exclude the neutral organisation(s) unless it can make up the resulting shortfall from its own resources.[43]

The protection afforded to civil defence personnel, buildings and equipment by Protocol I will cease, after due warning from the adverse party, allowing a reasonable time limit for compliance where appropriate, if they are involved in the commission of acts harmful to the enemy outside the scope of the performance of their proper tasks. Qualification by reference to the performance of proper tasks is obviously important in this context because mitigating the effect of bombing raids by fire-fighting, for example, might be seen, in a general sense, as 'harmful to the enemy'. Certain activities are expressly stated not to be 'harmful to the enemy':

1 the conduct of civil defence work under the direction of the military authorities
2 assignment to or co-operation in civil defence tasks of some military personnel
3 carrying of light weapons by civil defence personnel for purposes of self-defence or the maintenance of order
4 the organisation of civil defence along military lines, and/or compulsory service by personnel in its organisation.[44]

General Provision for Those in Medical Need

General protective provision is made for the wounded, sick, infirm and aged, and for expectant mothers. They must be respected and protected, and in so far as military considerations permit, all parties to a conflict must do their utmost to search for them and for the dead, to assist them and others in grave danger, and generally to protect them from pillage and ill-treatment. Whenever possible, parties to armed conflict are urged to enter into appropriate local agreements for the evacuation of such people from besieged or encircled areas, and for the safe inward passage of medical and religious personnel and medical equipment. The convention gives no specific guidance regarding how this is to be achieved, but the most obvious method would be through the mediation of a neutral or impartial humanitarian agency such as the ICRC, which has taken place in a number of instances, such as in the Lebanon.

Civilian hospitals 'organised' to give care to the wounded and sick, the infirm and maternity cases' are required by the convention to be respected and protected at all times, and in no circumstances may they be made the object of attack. Their status must be certified by the power upon which they depend, and they must be indicated by the protective emblem (either a red cross or red crescent), which should, as far as militarily feasible, be made visible to enemy forces to obviate accidental attack. For the same reason, it is urged by the convention that as far as possible, such hospitals should not be sited in the vicinity of possible military objectives. Civilian hospital staff are similarly protected, and should carry an identity card stating their duties, and an armband bearing the protective symbol. The protected status of a civilian hospital will cease only if it is used, outside its humanitarian functions, for the perpetration of acts harmful to the enemy, and in that case only after a warning, allowing time for compliance in appropriate cases. The presence of sick and wounded from the armed forces, or of small arms taken from such patients, is not in this context to be construed as an act harmful to the enemy, but obviously the siting of an anti-tank gun on the roof of such a hospital would be so construed.[45]

Civilian medical transport is protected in the same fashion as civilian hospitals, and is similarly indicated by the protective emblem of a red cross or red crescent. This protection covers convoys of medical vehicles, hospital trains and specially provided hospital ships at sea. It would presumably also extend to the kind of hospital craft used on inland waters during the Franco-Prussian and First World Wars, although the convention does not expressly provide for this. Civilian medical air transport for patients, personnel and equipment, as long as it flies on routes and at times and altitudes expressly agreed between the parties to the conflict, is also protected. Flights of such aircraft over enemy-held territory are prohibited unless specially agreed. All parties to the convention, including adverse parties in conflict, must allow free passage of medical stores and religious objects intended solely for the use of civilians; this extends to essential food, clothes and 'tonics' for children under 15, expectant mothers and maternity cases. Appropriate supervision may be demanded, in particular to avoid diversion of supplies from their proper destination, ineffective control, or the derivation of military advantage from such supplies.[46]

A particular humanitarian problem resulting from the chaos of armed conflict is the dispersal of families, and in particular the effect on children. Parties to armed conflicts are required to ensure that children under the age of 15 who are orphaned or separated from their families in armed conflict are properly provided for in material, educational and religious terms. Education should, where possible, be in the hands of persons of the same culture as the children in their care. Where possible, arrangements should be made for the evacuation of such children to safe neutral territory for the duration of the conflict. Children under 12 should, as far as possible, be supplied with appropriate identity discs. Alien children may only be evacuated from the territory of a party in conflict for compelling reasons of health, medical treatment or, except in the case of occupied territories, the dictates of safety. Information about the identity of such evacuees must be recorded and sent to the ICRC Central Tracing Agency. Personal news should be enabled to be exchanged between family members, by ordinary post if possible, or if this is not possible, through a humanitarian organisation such as the ICRC. Similarly, the tracing of dispersed family members should be facilitated, notably through the efforts of the ICRC Central Tracing Agency.[47]

Protection of Persons in the Power of a Party to Armed Conflict

The scheme of protection for civilians in the power of a party to armed conflict covers all who 'at a given moment and in any manner whatsoever, find themselves in case of a conflict or occupation, in the hands of a Party to the conflict or Occupying Power of which they are not nationals'. This does not extend to nationals of a neutral or co-belligerent state which enjoys normal diplomatic relations with the state in whose power they are.[48] However, the scheme of protection does extend to persons who, before the commencement of hostilities, were considered stateless persons or refugees under relevant laws or recognised international provisions without any adverse distinction.[49] Any person who is protected under Convention IV or the relevant provisions of Protocol I and engaged in activities hostile to the security of the state, particularly espionage or sabotage, may be deprived of such rights under the convention or the Protocol as would be prejudicial to the security of the state if exercised. This would apply, for example, to rights of communication in the case of definitely suspected spies.[50] The presence of protected persons may not be used as a shield for military operations.[51]

All persons protected under 1949 Geneva Convention IV and the related provisions are entitled to humane treatment, protection from violence, insults and public curiosity, and respect for their persons, honour, family rights, religion, manners and customs. No adverse distinctions may be drawn amongst them on the bases of age, sex, health, race, religion or politics. Women in particular must be protected against attack, and especially against rape, indecent assault and enforced prostitution.[52] The treatment of protected persons is the responsibility, *ab initio*, of the party in whose power they are, irrespective of any individual responsibility which may attach to its agents.[53] This is essentially a parallel with the provision of 1949 Geneva Convention III that prisoners of war are in the hands of the capturing power, and not of individual units, from the moment of capture – the logic being similarly related to the avoidance of responsibility for breaches upon grounds of individual 'excess'.[54]

Protected persons in the power of a party to armed conflict are generally protected from harsh treatment. No moral or physical coercion may be applied to protected persons with a view to obtaining information.[55] Protected persons are also immune from all measures which would cause physical suffering or extermination. This applies to all 'measures of brutality whether applied by civilian or military agents', including murder, torture, corporal punishment, mutilation and any medical or scientific procedures not intended for the benefit of the protected person involved. So far as judicial or other penalties are concerned, a protected person may not be punished for any offence which he or she has not personally committed; thus collective punishments and all intimidations and terrorism are prohibited.[56] Protected persons may also not be made the subjects of pillage, reprisals against their persons or property, or of hostage-taking.[57]

Specific Protection of Women in Armed Conflict

The suggestion sometimes made that 'women ... are arguably the major victims of warfare'[58] seems a distinct overstatement – the many men who are killed, maimed, suffer loss of family or are displaced in armed conflict may to no less an extent be termed victims of warfare. The general protection of the wounded, sick and shipwrecked, prisoners of war and civilians – including the range of humanitarian provisions governing weapons and tactics – applies to all people, regardless of gender, who find themselves in the relevant situations. However, the provision made for women in the humanitarian laws of armed conflict can, in some respects, be argued to be both inadequate and outdated. The general problem is expressed in a number of feminist critiques of legal provision, going far beyond the *jus in bello*: that legal provision made for women treats them 'as if' they were men, without considering the realities of distinctively female experience.[59]

In one respect it can be argued that international humanitarian law avoids to a significant degree the pitfall of confusing gender equality with sameness. By considering pregnancy, as a normal but not a normative or inevitable dimension of the experience of women, international humanitarian law provision seems clearly to distinguish pregnancy from 'illness', thus avoiding the common legal error of treating a pregnant woman as if her condition was directly equivalent to that of an injured or sick man. Evidence for this may be sought in articles 14, 16–18, 20–3, 27 and 91 of 1949 Geneva Convention IV and, more especially, in article 76(2) of 1977 Additional Protocol I, all of which deal, in whole or part, with the protection and care of pregnant women.

Another very important issue arises in protecting the security of women who may be interned. Here, articles 85 and 91 of 1949 Geneva Convention IV are of special importance. The primary concern of article 85 is that interned women should be afforded accommodation separate from that of male internees. Thus article 85 provides, *inter alia*, that:

> Wherever it is necessary, as an exceptional and temporary measure, to accommodate women internees who are not members of a family unit in the same place of internment as men, the provision of separate sleeping quarters and sanitary conveniences for the use of such women shall be obligatory.

The reference to membership of family units refer back to article 82, which requires that, wherever possible, members of a family who are interned should be housed together in suitable and separate family accommodation along with other families who are also interned.

One of the most obvious aspects of the specific victimhood of women in armed conflict is vulnerability to sexual assault and rape, which may not only be criminal acts by individuals, but may form part of systematic policies directed against a given population, thus constituting, in effect, an unlawful method of warfare. Somewhat differing examples of this can be seen in the practices of enforced prostitution in the Second World War in the Far East, and in former Yugoslavia in the 1990s, which is not to suggest that these were the only conflicts in which such abuse has taken place. In the 1990s, surviving 'comfort women' who were forced to become military prostitutes by Japanese occupying forces have campaigned for apologies and compensation. In former Yugoslavia, it was revealed that military brothels had been set up in some Bosnian Serb-controlled areas in which, mainly, Bosnian Muslim women had been 'interned' and repeatedly raped in order to cause them to give birth to 'Serb' children. In December 1992, *The Times* of London reported that at least ten such brothels existed, from which Bosnian women had been released in advanced stages of pregnancy.[60] This outrage can be seen as a case of rape as a method of warfare, in that it was a systematically organised assault upon women from a given community, also intended as an attack on that community. The victims have suffered not only the horror of rape, and in many cases bearing a child who is the product of rape, but have been rejected by their own community as a result. Attempts are made to deal with the outrage of rape and other sexual assaults in article 27 of 1949 Geneva Convention IV, and article 76(1) of 1977 Additional Protocol I. Article 27 provides, *inter alia*, that:

> Women shall be especially protected against any attack on their honour, in particular against rape, enforced prostitution, or any form of indecent assault.

This provision is repeated by article 76(1) of 1977 Additional Protocol I. It may be added that in relation to non-international armed conflicts,[61] article 4(2)(e) of 1977 Additional Protocol II includes the same proscription. Common article 3 of the four 1949 Geneva Conventions does not expressly refer to rape or forced prostitution, but does prohibit 'outrages upon personal dignity, in particular humiliating and degrading treatment', which can only be taken to include these forms of abuse. The rape and forced prostitution of women in former Yugoslavia was clearly a gross contravention of international humanitarian law, at whatever level it might have been taken to apply.

Also in former Yugoslavia, the outrage of 'ethnic cleansing' – the forced expulsion of members of adverse communities by invading or occupying forces – obviously affected the whole populations involved.

However, it had a particularly immediate impact on the female population, who in many, although be no means all, cases were the people actually resident at the time of the expulsions. Again, 'ethnic cleansing' was unequivocally unlawful upon a variety of grounds. Article 49 of 1949 Geneva Convention IV provides in relation to occupied territories that:

> Individual or mass forcible transfers, as well as deportations of protected persons from occupied territory to the territory of the Occupying Power or to that of any other country, occupied or not, are prohibited, regardless of their motive.
>
> Nevertheless, the Occupying Power may undertake total or partial evacuation of a given area if the security of the population or imperative military reasons so demand.

In relation to non-international armed conflicts, such forced movements are forbidden by 1977 Additional Protocol II, article 17. Neither of these provisions refers expressly to women in distinction from men, nor is it clear why they should do so. The forced movement of populations, with the limited exception set out in article 49 of 1949 Geneva Convention IV, is forbidden, whatever the gender balance in the given population at the time in question.

Whether a further Geneva Convention or Additional Protocol is needed for the specific protection of women may be debated.[62] It can reasonably be argued, however, that the fundamental protections offered by international humanitarian law are applicable to people, whether female or male, and the introduction of gender-specific conventions might have the unintended effect of undermining the vital principle of impartiality. The grossest abuses to which women are especially, but not solely, vulnerable are already expressly forbidden by the present law, so the issue is not so much adequacy of provision as efficacy of enforcement. There remains the degree to which some of the older humanitarian provision does not properly represent female experience of and in armed conflict, particularly the widespread assumption that combatants will be male. This was overwhelmingly the case in 1949, but can by no means be assumed in the 1990s or into the 21st century. It may be doubted whether this calls for significant amendment to the present *substance* of humanitarian provision, but in future development of the law it is essential that the particular experience and concerns of women should be adequately provided for. The simplest and most effective way of doing this is to ensure the effective participation of women in the preparation and drafting of future laws.

Protection of Children in Armed Conflict

Children may be civilian victims of armed conflict through both the direct and indirect effects of hostilities. In this respect they are covered by many of the protective provisions for the civilian population in general, but they also require some specific protections. Unfortunately, during the second half of the 20th century child combatants have been an increasing and alarming phenomenon in certain types of armed conflict, especially, as Goodwin-Gill and Cohn note, in 'internal armed conflict and violent strife'.[63] This must be a matter for grave humanitarian concern. The most extensive provision for the specific protection of children in armed conflict, supplementary to the general provisions for civilian protection from which they in any event benefit, is found in articles 77 and 78 of 1977 Additional Protocol I.[64]

In addressing the serious question of child combatants in modern armed conflicts, article 77(2) provides that:

> The Parties to the conflict shall take all feasible measures in order that children who have not attained the age of fifteen years do not take a direct part in hostilities and, in particular, they shall refrain from recruiting them into their armed forces. In recruiting among those persons who have attained the age of fifteen years but have not attained the age of eighteen years, the Parties to the conflict shall endeavour to give priority to those who are oldest.

In relation to non-international armed conflicts, the recruitment of children under the age of 15 is expressly forbidden by article 4(3)(c) of 1977 Additional Protocol II.

Additional Protocol I's provisions in particular have been criticised by some commentators as being too feeble. Fifteen is certainly a young age at which to be engaged in active military service, and there is a good case to be made for a significantly older minimum entry age, as the prioritisation of the older element of the 15–18-year-old range required by article 77(2) clearly implies. As is commonly the case in the development of international humanitarian law, however, it is probably better to set a lower objective which can be achieved in practice than to set a higher and more desirable standard which will in all too many instances be ignored. Another criticism lies in the apparent laxity of the requirement merely for 'all feasible measures' to be taken. However, as Goodwin-Gill and Cohn argue:

> That which is 'feasible' is that which is capable of being done and, by definition, whatever is under the jurisdiction and control of a party is *prima facie* capable of being done. It will always be 'feasible', for example, for organized fighting forces to have a policy of non-recruitment

> of children. It may not always be feasible to ensure implementation at every level, however, particularly where forces are dispersed among a population whose younger members themselves actively seek to participate [in the conflict] ...[65]

The infeasible will, by definition, not be attained; that which is feasible is required to be attained, and it would be very unrealistic to demand more. The practical problems suggested by Goodwin-Gill and Cohn are by no means new phenomena. The well-known experience of the First World War, in which significant numbers of patriotic youths in many of the belligerent countries 'lied about their age' in order to serve in the fighting forces earlier than they should properly have done so, illustrates this. Where record-keeping is of a standard sufficient to render the necessary checks practically possible, this type of evasion can to some extent be precluded. Even then, sometimes doubtful judgements as to how old a person looks (a matter of civilian difficulty in the far removed context of alcohol and tobacco sales in many countries, for example) will have to made, and possibly be made in error.

When, as happens all too frequently, under-age combatants are involved in an armed conflict, other and no less difficult questions may arise in returning them to their appropriate civilian environment. Article 77(1) of 1977 Additional Protocol I requires that parties in conflict:

> shall provide [children] ... with the care and aid they require, whether because of their age or for any other reason.

Much will depend upon the age of the child or young person in question, of course, but it may be noted that in relation to child evacuees, article 78(2) of 1977 Additional Protocol I requires that the child's education should be continued during the period of evacuation. Granted also the requirement of article 38 of 1949 Geneva Convention III in relation to prisoners of war that, *inter alia*, educational pursuits should be made available for prisoners of war who desire it, article 77(1) of Additional Protocol I seems implicitly to demand that some educational provision should be available for any children who became prisoners of war. Education for combat-experienced children presents enormous difficulties, but it is also essential if the cycles of inter-communal hatred which often generate the sorts of conflict in which children are most likely to become involved as combatants are to be diminished and ended. An analogy may be seen in some of the efforts at inter-communal work with children in the context of the internal disturbances in Northern Ireland, which may be seen as an important contribution to any long-term fruition of positive 'peace processes'. This is not in a context of combatancy, but it may be seen as an instructive instance nevertheless.

Other protections will apply to all children in armed conflict, whether or not they have taken an active part in hostilities. Article 77(1) requires expressly that all children should be protected from indecent assault. Article 77(4) requires, to the same end, that children who are detained or interned for reasons connected with the conflict shall be housed separately from adults, unless housed together in family units, as provided for in article 75(5). The sense of this is obvious, but where a young prisoner of war has effectively grown up in the society of his or her fellow combatants, complete isolation may in itself be damaging, so long as that society is not in itself abusive.

Evacuation of children to places of relative safety in times of armed conflict has a pedigree stretching at least back to the Second World War, when children in the United Kingdom were moved into the countryside in large numbers to avoid the dangers of bombing in the great industrial cities. This may be an obvious measure, but removal overseas, and especially in occupied territories, is a matter of serious legal concern, quite apart from the practical dangers of movement of this type, as shown tragically by the torpedoing of the transport ship *City of Benares* in the Second World War. 1977 Additional Protocol I provides by article 78(1) that:

> No party to the conflict shall arrange the evacuation of children, other than its own nationals, to a foreign country except for a temporary evacuation where compelling reasons of the health or medical treatment of the children or, except in occupied territory, their safety, so require. Where the parents or legal guardians can be found, their written consent to such evacuation is required.

The article also makes detailed provision for continuation of evacuees' education and the recording of their details to facilitate return to their families. This provision in part reflects the horrors of the virtual kidnapping of children in some conflicts. A gross example can be seen in the practice of the SS in parts of Eastern Europe during the Second World War in which children deemed to look 'aryan' according to a bizarre racial pseudo-science were taken away from their families and forcibly adopted by German families to be raised in the Hitler Youth organisations. Many of these unfortunate children suffered double traumas in being uprooted at various stages not from one, but from two families, and often experienced great difficulties in being accepted back into their original communities.

Foreigners in the Power of a Party to Armed Conflict

Protected persons may leave the territory of a party to armed conflict at the outset or during the continuance of conflict, taking necessary funds with them if they so desire, unless their doing so would threaten the national interests of the state concerned. Applications to depart must be processed as swiftly as possible, and in case of refusal, the applicant must be allowed to appeal to an appropriate administrative or judicial tribunal. The Protecting Power must request reasons for such refusals, which should be supplied except where reasons of state dictate otherwise.[66]

Journalists

General *jus in bello* provision for journalists has been considered in Chapter 6, but further comment on the practice of journalism is required here. Journalists frequently complain of military 'censorship' and other restrictions when reporting upon armed conflicts, and represent such control as an intolerable impediment to the presentation of objectively truthful accounts and analysis to their readers, listeners or viewers. It is clear that proper reporting of armed conflict plays an essential role in informing society, and not least in advancing knowledge and appreciation of humanitarian principles. It is no less clear that military security is an imperative necessity in the conduct of armed conflict. The abuse of security as a means of stifling unwelcome comment is objectionable, as is any journalistic presumption that soldiers' lives are a consideration of secondary importance in relation to the commercial and/or ideological concerns of media outlets. Even without invoking such extreme positions, a delicate balance will always need to be drawn between press freedom and the necessary exigencies of genuine security concern, both in armed conflict *stricto sensu* and in other types of 'emergency' security situation.

Just how difficult this can be is evident from the analogy of reporting the internal 'troubles' in Northern Ireland. In 1988 two British soldiers were brutally murdered by IRA sympathisers during a funeral service for some IRA members. Film footage of the incident in the possession of British television media organisations, including footage of the brutal beating of the two soldiers which was shown on television news broadcasts, was demanded by the Royal Ulster Constabulary as part of their investigation, and was refused unless a court order was first obtained. The film was surrendered in the end under threat of prosecution under anti-terrorist legislation, which must be seen as the proper outcome of the affair. However, the incident was the subject of wide variety of interpretations. On the one hand, it was contended that if the media handed over the material voluntarily, they would be seen as 'police agents', and thus be placed under a level of terrorist threat which would severely compromise their ability to report adequately on the situation in Northern Ireland. On the other hand, their unco-operative attitude was seen by some as little short of outright collaboration with terrorism. The basis for both views is not difficult to see, and by the same token, both may be seen as considerably oversimplified, but the affair does illustrate by analogy the very delicate position of journalists reporting in situations of conflict.

Minimum Guarantees of Treatment Under Protocol I, Article 75

All persons who are in the power of a party to an armed conflict and who do not otherwise benefit from more favourable provisions are entitled at least to certain minimum guarantees of treatment which are set out in 1977 Additional Protocol I, article 75. These, as might be anticipated, fall into a general framework of 'human rights' and guarantees of due process. All persons are to be treated at all times humanely, without any adverse discrimination founded on race, colour, sex, language, religious, political or other belief or opinion, wealth, status or any similar criteria. Their person, honour, convictions and religion must also be respected. In particular, acts of violence and outrages to personal dignity are prohibited. These include murder, torture (physical or mental), corporal punishment, mutilation, humiliating and degrading treatment, enforced prostitution, indecent assault, hostage-taking, collective punishment, and threats of any of these.

These fundamental guarantees do not preclude either internment or the imposition of penalties through due judicial process, but either may be done only in accordance with the provisions of the article. Internment for reasons associated with the conflict should be for the minimum possible duration, certainly not longer than the duration of the circumstances which occasioned it, and the reasons for it should be explained to the internee. Throughout the period of internment, the internee will benefit at least from the minimum guarantees set out above. Women internees must be quartered separately under female supervision, except when housed in family accommodation with their own families.

Penal offences and punishment may therefore only be dealt with by an impartial and duly constituted court which observes internationally recognised procedural norms. These are stated by article 75 to include: information without delay about the details of the charge and the rights of the accused; conviction only upon grounds of individual responsibility under relevant international or municipal law applicable at the time of the alleged offence; a presumption of innocence pending proof of guilt; trial in person; non-compulsion to self-incrimination; the right to call and examine witnesses; absence of double jeopardy; public pronouncement of the judgment, and advice of rights of appeal. These procedural guarantees apply to all persons accused of crimes who do not benefit from other and more favourable provisions, including those accused of war crimes or of crimes against humanity.

Provision for Occupied Territories

The effects of armed conflict upon civilian populations take an especially problematic form in the case of territories under adverse occupation: not only must the dangers of armed conflict be contended with, but also the factor of an essentially 'hostile' administration. Within an occupied territory, the general provisions for civilian protection which are relevant apply as they would in other territories, but there are also specific additional provisions.

An initial problem is the satisfactory definition of 'occupation'. Adam Roberts quotes Michael Veuthey to the effect that 'the concept of "occupation" is judicially inoperative or disputed in practically all contemporary conflicts'.[67] Roberts himself concludes: 'the law on occupation is formally applicable to, and capable of being applied in, a wide variety of situations', arguing for flexibility of response in the light of the wide range of situations which might be found under the umbrella of 'occupation'.[68] Clearly, the 'Geneva' humanitarian provision must be capable of flexible application in any given situation, but such flexibility should always tend towards maximising humanitarianism, rather than lessening it, especially in the case of particular local arrangements. In the immediate context, the notion of 'occupation' is, like that of 'armed conflict', factual rather than technical. Thus common article 2 of the four 1949 Geneva Conventions provides for application in 'all cases of partial or total occupation of territory of a High Contracting Party, even if the said occupation meets with no armed resistance'. The factual nature of the criteria defining a military occupation is also made clear by the provision of article 42 of the Hague Land Warfare Regulations annexed to 1907 Hague Convention IV:

> Territory is considered occupied when it is actually placed under the authority of a hostile army. The occupation extends only to the territory where such authority has been established and can be exercised.

This is extended by article 1 of Protocol I to include all cases of 'alien occupation'. This extension, like much else in 1977 Protocol I, contains a marked element of well-meaning, but necessarily desirable, ambiguity. The general position is clear enough, however, in that 'occupation' for this purpose involves the uninvited imposition of administrative control over a territory attached to some other state, usually but not absolutely necessarily by means of military force in the course of armed conflict.

An occupying power must not under any circumstances abrogate the benefits of applicable 'Geneva' protections as a result of occupation administration, whether or not such changes in administration are agreed between the local authorities and the occupying power.[69] Once occupation is established, individual or mass forcible transfers or deportations are prohibited, apart from the evacuations dictated by imperative military necessity, and these should be of minimum distance and duration as far as possible in the prevailing circumstances. Any such transfers must take place in circumstances of adequate accommodation, hygiene, health, safety and nutrition. In no circumstances may evacuated areas be repopulated by nationals transferred from the home territories of the occupying power.[70] Proper care must also be taken of children in occupied territories, including the facilitation of 'the proper working of all institutions devoted to care and education of children'. In particular, the identification of children must be maintained, and proper provision must be made for orphans who cannot be cared for by close relatives. The personal status of children may in no circumstances be altered, nor may they be enlisted in organisations subordinate to the occupying authority, such as paramilitary or 'political' youth groups.[71]

Within an occupied territory, the occupying power has general responsibility for hygiene and public health, with the co-operation of the local authorities, and it must also guarantee the food and medical supplies of the population. The latter may not be requisitioned by the occupying authority if this would injure the civilian population of the territory, and in any event, fair compensation must be paid if such requisitioning does take place. The occupying authority must permit and facilitate the supply of relief aid if the population is, in whole or in part, inadequately supplied, whether such aid is supplied by other states or by impartial humanitarian organisations such as the ICRC.[72] In practice, this can prove problematic, especially when it is not clear exactly who is the controlling authority within a given territory. This was the case in relief operations in connection with the Palestinian refugee camps in the Lebanon, and in the conflicts, 'internal' or otherwise, in the Sudan, Eritrea, Tigray and former Yugoslavia. This is an area where it must be conceded that technical legal provision must at times yield to the practical exigencies of a given situation, and in which the humanitarian diplomacy of the ICRC inevitably plays a central role.

An occupying power may under no circumstances compel protected persons to serve in its armed or auxiliary services or to take any other part in military operations. They may volunteer to do so, although they would no doubt then be guilty of treason under the municipal law of their national state – as in the case of the Ukrainian volunteers in the German army during the Second World War, but the occupying power may not utilise either propaganda or any other form of pressure to secure such enlistment. The occupying power may compel persons over the age of 18 to perform work which is necessary for the needs of the occupying forces, public utilities or the feeding and other needs of the civilian population of the occupied territory, but it is forbidden to induce unemployment in order to encourage volunteering for work desired by the occupying authority. Workers, whether voluntary or otherwise, must be fairly remunerated, and must benefit from at least the same health and safety provisions as those applicable in the home territory of the occupying power. It would not be permissible to argue that working conditions in the home territory of the occupying power are customarily thoroughly dangerous.

In all circumstances, workers in occupied territories retain the right to make applications to representatives of Protecting Powers about their treatment or conditions.[73]

An occupying power may not destroy real or personal property in the occupied territory, whether it is in personal, collective or state ownership. This protection is complete, subject only to absolute military necessity.[74] The difference between 'absolute' military necessity in this context and 'imperative' military necessity in others is unclear, but, assuming there is one, it is minimal, and both terms clearly require the most strongly overriding exigencies of conflict to become operative.

Widespread destruction and seizure of civilian property and facilities was a marked feature of the brutal 1990–91 Iraqi occupation of Kuwait. There was some individual looting, especially in the later stages of the occupation, as some of the property abandoned on the Iraqi line of retreat indicated.[75] Much more serious, however, was the official and systematic depredation of Kuwaiti assets. This included the removal of very significant quantities of commercial goods and possibly also of technical and even medical equipment, although reports of this latter made at the time were vastly exaggerated.[76] Although of much less humanitarian significance, it must also be remarked that large-scale cultural looting took place, notably of the internationally significant collection of Islamic antiquities in the Dar al-Athar al-Islamiyyah Museum,[77] as well as the outright destruction of the National Museum of Kuwait towards the end of the occupation.[78]

An occupying power is, as the repository of force in the territory, responsible for the maintenance of law and order during the continuance of occupation. The penal laws of an occupied territory remain in force, subject to such changes as the occupying power may make in the interests of its own security or for the better application of Convention III or Protocol I. Administration of justice should ideally remain in the hands of the established officials in an occupied territory who were in place prior to the commencement of occupation. However, if judges or other public officials in the territory refuse to perform their duties for reasons of conscience, no coercion may be applied to them, nor may they be punished for this.[79] This may place local judges and officials in a somewhat delicate position, since they may on the one hand wish to avoid the stigma, and possible penalties, of appearing to 'collaborate', whilst on the other hand they may feel that their continued administration is likely to be more 'sympathetic' than any likely alternative set up by the occupying power. Ultimately, such decisions can only be made in the light of applicable municipal law and the dictates of individual conscience, although participation in breaches of Convention IV or in war crimes in general could not be justified.

Be that as it may, an occupying power may, up to a point, promulgate provisions necessary for it to fulfil its obligations under Convention IV and Protocol I to maintain orderly government and to ensure its own security. Such legislation may not be retrospective in effect, and may not be brought into effect until it has been published to the population of the territory in their own language.[80] This raises in an acute form the same issues of legal obligation which arise in the context of the duty owed to the detaining authority by prisoners of war. The population of an occupied territory has not chosen or acquiesced in the authority of the occupying power; such 'authority' as it may have derives solely from an act of force by way of military occupation, and may in that sense be understood more as a matter of 'power' than of 'authority'.[81] At the same time, day-to-day administration of justice, including marriages, civil claims and contracts, must continue in the territory, and in the end this can only be done by, or at least with the consent of, the occupying power, since it is *de facto* exercising administrative control. Simply to regard its acts as void would therefore be wholly impractical, so the real question is not so much the existence as the extent of the authority of the occupying power.

It is clear that an occupying power may not generally introduce its own laws into an occupied territory, which would amount to annexation, but equally, such a power does have some degree of legislative competence within the territory. The basic test is one of necessity. Article 43 of the 1907 Rules on Land Warfare annexed to Hague Convention IV of that year provides that an occupying power should, so far as possible, 'restore, and ensure ... public order and safety, while respecting, unless absolutely prevented, the laws in force in the country'. The same idea is found in 1949 Geneva Convention IV, which provides that the penal laws of an occupied territory will remain in force, subject to repeal or suspension where they are a threat to the application of the convention. However, the occupying power is stated to have legislative competence in matters concerned with the fulfilment of its obligations under the convention, the maintenance of orderly government, and the security of itself, its personnel, equipment and establishments.[82] The position is well expressed by Peter Rowe in the comment that: '[the occupying power] becomes administrator rather than sovereign ... the occupier's law-making powers could be exercised only [as] ... a matter of necessity ... and not merely where the occupier considered it expedient ...[83]

Granted the limited legislative competence of an occupying power, there still remains the issue of the quality of the obligation owed by the population of the territory. There was formerly a complex structure of legal doctrine surrounding such concepts as 'war treason' and 'war rebellion" in occupied territories, but these do not sit easily with the form of modern 'Geneva' law. Major Richard S. Baxter argues convincingly that such ideas have now become obsolete, and that in the light of the 1949 Geneva Conventions the question of obligation in belligerent occupancy may be reduced to three broad propositions:

1 subject to certain general and specific limitations, a belligerent occupant may both prohibit and penalise, but international law does not in itself prohibit the commission by inhabitants of an occupied territory of acts hostile to the belligerent occupant
2 an occupying power has a range of legislative competence to prohibit acts which may reasonably be considered to imperil the security of either itself or its personnel, or to hinder the implementation of Convention IV
3 an individual who commits acts hostile to an occupying power may not be penalised after he or she has succeeded in joining or rejoining his or her own national armed forces.[84]

This seems a very reasonable approach, in that it recognises both the legislative competence of necessity embodied in Convention IV and the qualified nature of the duty to obey on the part of the population. The latter is not expressly stated in the convention, but is strongly implied in the presumption of leniency set out in the provisions on sentencing. Thus it is stated that in sentencing, due regard should be had to the fact that 'the accused is not a national of the Occupying Power',[85] and, more strongly, that 'the accused is not a national of the Occupying Power, [and] he is not bound to it by any duty of allegiance'.[86] All of this supports the basic proposition of a legislative competence of necessity which imposes only a qualified duty to obey, even though disobedience may, subject to 'Geneva' provision, be penalised.

Again, the 1990–91 Iraqi occupation of Kuwait was marked by widespread violation of these requirements: the substitution of Iraqi law and the emplacement of Iraqi officials as part of the policy of 'Iraqisation' of Kuwait as the claimed '19th Province' of Iraq went far beyond any 'necessary' legislative or administrative capacity, and was, indeed, an overt policy of annexation.

Within an occupied territory, the administration of justice must accord with internationally recognised norms; in particular, norms of due process must be respected. Accused persons must be informed of the charges brought against them in writing, in a language comprehensible to them, and the Protecting Power must also be informed of the commencement of any proceedings which might result in a custodial sentence of two or more years, or a capital sentence. If evidence of compliance with these requirements is not produced at the commencement of the trial, it may not proceed. The trial itself, and in the case of a finding of guilt, the sentencing process, may only be conducted by a duly established court after a 'regular' trial.[87] Protected persons may not be proceeded against in respect of offences committed before the commencement of the occupation, or during an interruption of it, unless the offences concerned were breaches of the laws and customs of war. Even nationals of the occupying power who took refuge in the territory before occupation may not be deported therefrom or proceeded against, other than in respect of matters arising after the outbreak of hostilities or which, according to the law of the state originally in control of the territory, would have justified extradition in peacetime.[88] Accused persons have rights to defence, interpretation and appeal similar to those provided for in respect of judicial proceedings affecting prisoners of war. They may also object to the interpreter assigned to them, and ask for his or her replacement. Representatives of the Protecting Power have the right to attend the trial of a protected person, unless the trial is held *in camera* for reasons connected with the security of the occupying power, on much the same terms as those applicable in cases of trials of prisoners of war.[89] In general, all judicial proceedings must also comply with the minimum procedural guarantees set out in Protocol I.[90] The law applicable is that obtaining at the time of the commission of the offence, and carries a proportionate penalty.[91]

Protected persons who are convicted and sentenced to custodial penalties must serve their sentences within the occupied territory, and any period of detention before and during trial must be deducted from the time to be served.[92] No more than a sentence of imprisonment may be imposed upon a protected person for any offence intended solely to harm the occupying power without attempts upon the life or limbs of members of the occupation personnel or serious damage to the property of the occupation authorities, and even such sentences may be commuted to internment by a competent tribunal.[93] Conditions of imprisonment must at least equal those obtaining in the national state of the occupied territory, and in particular, prisoners are entitled to adequate medical and spiritual ministrations, monthly relief parcels, if sent, and visits by representatives of the Protecting Power and of the ICRC. Women must be accommodated separately and supervised by women, and due regard must be had to the proper treatment of minors.[94] On termination of occupation, all convicted protected persons, including those serving custodial sentences, must be handed over to the authorities administering the liberated territory, together with all relevant records.[95]

Sentences of death may be imposed upon a convicted protected person only in accordance with the pre-existing laws of the occupied territory, or in the case of legislation promulgated by the occupying power, in cases of espionage, sabotage against military installations of the occupying power or of international offences causing the death of one or more persons, and then only if such offences carried capital penalties under the pre-existing law of the occupied territory. A capital sentence may only be pronounced if the attention of the court has been expressly drawn to the fact that the protected person owes no allegiance to the occupying power, and may not in any case be pronounced upon a protected person who was aged less than 18 at the time of the commission of the offence.[96] Any person condemned to death must be afforded the right of petition for pardon or reprieve. In any event, no capital penalty may be carried out less than six months from receipt by the Protecting Power of notification of final judgment or denial of pardon or reprieve, except in individual circumstances of 'grave emergency involving an organized threat to the security of the Occupying Power or its forces'.

Even in the case of expedited implementation of a capital sentence, the Protecting Power must be notified of the reduced timescale, and be given reasonable time and opportunity to make representations about the sentence and its proposed implementation.[97] Detaining powers are required to 'endeavour to avoid' pronouncing the death penalty upon pregnant women or upon women with dependent children. Even if such a penalty is formally pronounced it may not actually be carried out upon such a woman or upon any person who had not attained the age of 18 at the time the offence was committed.[98]

In no case may an occupying power impose sentences prohibited as 'brutal'. These include torture, corporal punishment, mutilation and medical or scientific procedures unrelated to the medical needs of the subject.[99]

As an example of the type of regime these provisions are designed to avert, the treatment of the Kuwaiti people during the 1990–91 Iraqi occupation will serve all too starkly. Any sign of resistance or disaffection was met with brutal suppression. A description of the appalling and sometimes fatal torture of suspects was given at a press conference organised by the British House of Commons All-Party Conference on Human Rights on 19 February 1991.[100] A British bank worker told this press conference that he had seen Iraqi soldiers shoot a man, his son and three grandchildren in front of the mother and grandmother because US passports had been found in a house search. Robert Fiske reported at second hand in the *Independent* newspaper the soaking of dissidents in petrol and burning them to death.[101] Such treatment would violate international norms in any situation, and most certainly does so in circumstances of military occupation.

Conditions of Civilian Internment

Enemy civilians in the territory of a state party to an armed conflict, and protected persons in a territory under adverse occupation, may be subjected to internment. In the former case, this may be done only if it is 'absolutely necessary' on security grounds, or if an enemy alien requests internment, for example for reasons of his or her own safety from a hostile population, through representatives of the Protecting Power.[102] In the latter case, internment is permissible only for 'imperative reasons of security'.[103]

Internment is in no case or sense a penal measure, but simply a restriction imposed on grounds of security. It exactly parallels the detention of prisoners of war, and the provisions in respect of its implementation are virtually identical.[104] However, granted that civilian internees are not, as civilians, accustomed to military discipline, their conditions of internment are in some particular respects more relaxed. Wherever possible, internees from the same family are to be accommodated together, with facilities for a 'proper family life', separate from other internees. Internees whose children are left without parental care as a consequence of internment may request that they be interned with them.[105] Unlike non-officer prisoners of war, civilian internees may not be required to work. They may, however, volunteer to do so, provided that the work concerned is not 'degrading or humiliating', but they may then, after a working period of six weeks, give eight days' notice of cessation of work at any time. However, the detaining authority may require interned medical personnel to provide professional services for fellow internees, or that internees generally perform administrative duties or protective tasks, such as precautions against the effects of bombardment within the camp, so long as no individual is held by medical opinion to be unfit for the performance of the duties to which he or she has been assigned.[106] Provision is made for the facilitation to the greatest possible extent of continued management by internees of their property and for their conduct of litigation.[107] All internees must be allowed to receive visitors, most particularly near relations, as frequently and regularly as possible, although this may be impossible in the case of enemy aliens interned by a party to armed conflict outside their home territory. The internees themselves must be allowed, wherever possible, to visit their homes in urgent cases, particularly in cases of death or serious illness of relatives.[108]

Internees must be released by the detaining power as soon as the reasons for the internment have ceased to apply. Parties to armed conflicts must also seek to make agreements for release, repatriation or accommodation in neutral countries, especially in the case of children, pregnant women, mothers with children who are young or infant, wounded or sick persons, and long-term internees.[109] Upon the close of hostilities, internees must be released as soon as possible, and returned to their last place of residence or repatriated. To facilitate this, committees may be set up to search for displaced and dispersed internees. The ICRC Central Tracing Agency has an obvious role in this. Internees subject to penal proceedings which are not merely disciplinary, or who have already received penal custodial sentences, may be retained until the conclusion of such proceedings, or the completion of sentence.[110] The cost of returning released internees to their last place of residence, or if seized in transit, of their completing their journey or returning to their point of departure, are borne by the detaining power. However, where the detaining power bans an alien internee from further residence in its territory, it must bear the expenses of repatriation; but if the internee voluntarily elects for repatriation, the detaining power is liable only for the costs of transport to the frontier.[111]

As in the case of prisoners of war,[112] the presence of civilian internees may not be used as a shield for military installations and other targets. Article 28 of 1949 Geneva Convention IV provides that:

> The presence of a protected person may not be used to render certain points or areas immune from military operations.

In the early part of the 1990–91 Gulf Conflict, civilian internees in Iraq were located in militarily sensitive areas with a view to deterring attack, in clear violation of this provision. Such gross violations are fortunately relatively rare, and it must be borne in mind that no absolute immunity from all the effects of armed conflict can be achieved in practice. The requirement is rather that there should be no calculated exposure to risk as a means to a military end, nor should internees be located, by design or otherwise, in places adjacent to manifest potential military targets.

Notes

1 1977 Additional Protocol I, article 51(1).
2 Ibid., article 35(1).
3 Ibid., article 50(1). The exclusions are made by reference to those entitled to prisoner of war status upon capture.
4 Ibid., articles 50(3) and 51(7).
5 Ibid., article 48.
6 A. Speer, *Inside the Third Reich* (Sphere Books, 1971; 1st published MacMillan, New York, 1970), pp. 384–5.
7 1977 Additional Protocol I, article 52(3).
8 See C. de Jaeger, *The Linz File: Hitler's Plunder of Europe's Art* (Webb and Bower, 1981).
9 1977 Additional Protocol, article 53.
10 Article 1.
11 In heraldic terms, a shield pointed below, per saltire blue and white: 1954 Convention, article 16(1).
12 1954 Convention, article 17.
13 Regulations for the Execution of the 1954 Convention, article 20.
14 1954 Convention, article 4.
15 The 1954 Convention does not specify figures.
16 1954 Convention, article 8. If such a refuge is located near to a potential military objective, it may be agreed in advance that the installation concerned will not be put to military use.
17 Regulations for the Execution of the 1954 Convention, article 11.
18 1954 Convention, article 11.
19 Ibid., articles 12–14.
20 Ibid., article 15.
21 Regulations, articles 4–5.
22 Ibid., article 10.
23 1954 Protocol, articles 1, 3 and 4.
24 Ibid., article 4.
25 Ibid., article 2.
26 Ibid., article 5.
27 1977 Additional Protocol I, article 54(2)(3).
28 Ibid., article 59(7).
29 Ibid., article 59(1)(4)(6).
30 Ibid., article 59(5).
31 Ibid., article 60(2).
32 Ibid., 60(3)(4)(5).

33 Ibid., article 60(1)(6).
34 Ibid., article 60(7).
35 1949 Geneva Convention IV, article 14. A model agreement on hospital and safety zones is set out in Annex I to the convention.
36 Ibid., article 15.
37 Articles 61–7. For detailed discussion of civil defence, see B. Jacovljevic, *New International Status of Civil Defence* (Martinus Nijhoff, 1982); see also A. Roberts, 'Civil Defence and International Law', in M.A. Meyer (ed.) *Armed Conflict and the New Lane* (British Institute of International and Comparative Law, 1984), pp. 193ff.
38 1977 Additional Protocol I, article 61.
39 Ibid., article 62.
40 Ibid., article 67.
41 Ibid., article 66. A model of the signs can be found in Annex I to the Protocol, article 15.
42 1977 Additional Protocol I, article 63.
43 Ibid., article 64.
44 Ibid., article 65.
45 1949 Geneva Convention IV, articles 16–20.
46 Ibid., articles 21–3.
47 Ibid., articles 24–6; 1977 Additional Protocol I, articles 77–8.
48 1949 Geneva Convention IV, article 4.
49 1977 Additional Protocol I, article 73.
50 1949 Geneva Convention IV, article 5.
51 Ibid., article 28.
52 Ibid., article 27.
53 Ibid., article 29.
54 See p. 148, above.
55 1949 Geneva Convention IV, article 31.
56 Ibid., articles 32 and 33.
57 Ibid., articles 33 and 34.
58 J. Gardam, 'Women and the Law of Armed Conflict: Why the Silence?' (1997) 46 *International and Comparative Law Quarterly*, p. 55, at p. 89, citing Boutros Boutros-Ghali in a forum on 'Dignity for Women in War' held in Sydney in April 1995.
59 See, for example, J. Conaghan and L. Chudleigh, 'Women in Confinement: Can Labour Law Deliver the Goods', in P. Fitzpatrick and A. Hunt (eds), *Critical Legal Studies* (Blackwell, 1987), pp. 133–47.
60 *The Times* (London), 17 December 1992. See also A. Kovalovska, 'Rape of Muslim Women in Wartime Bosnia' (1997) 3 *ILSA Journal of International and Comparative Law*, pp. 931–45.
61 See Chapter 9.
62 For discussion of this, see J. Gardam, op.cit.
63 G. Goodwin-Gill and I. Cohn, *Child Soldiers: The Role of Children in Armed Conflicts* (Clarendon/Oxford, 1994), p. 23.
64 For discussion of the development of international humanitarian law in this area, see H. Mann, 'International Law and the Child Soldier' (1987) 36 *International and Comparative Law Quarterly*, pp. 32–57.
65 G. Goodwin-Gill and I. Cohn, op.cit., at p. 63.
66 1949 Geneva Convention IV, article 35. Provision for the repatriation of foreigners who are allowed to leave is set out by article 36.
67 A. Roberts, 'What is Military Occupation?' (1984) 55 *British Yearbook of International Law*, p. 249, citing Veuthey in *Droit Humanitaire* (2nd edn) (1983), at p. 355.

68 Ibid., at pp. 304–5.
69 1949 Geneva Convention IV, article 47.
70 Ibid., article 49.
71 Ibid., article 50.
72 Ibid., articles 55, 56 and 61.
73 Ibid., articles 51 and 52.
64 Ibid., article 53.
75 *Independent* (London), 18 February 1991.
76 See I. Freedman and E. Karsh, *The Gulf War 1990–91* (Faber & Faber, 1993), pp. 217–19.
77 Ibid., 17 September 1990.
78 Ibid., 19 February 1991.
79 1949 Geneva Convention IV, articles 54 and 64.
80 Ibid., articles 64 and 65.
81 See H.L.A. Hart, *The Concept of Law*, (2nd edn), with Postscript ed. by P.A. Bulloch and J. Raz (Clarendon/Oxford, 1994; 1st published without Postscript, 1961); cf. R. Dworkin, *Taking Rights Seriously* (Duckworth, 1977).
82 1949 Geneva Convention IV, article 64.
83 P. Rowe, *Defence: The Legal Implications* (Brassey's Defence Publishers, 1987), p. 184.
84 R.S. Baxter, 'The Duty of Obedience to a Belligerent Occupant' (1950) 27 *British Yearbook of International Law*, p. 235, at p. 266.
85 1949 Geneva Convention IV, article 67.
86 Ibid., article 68.
87 Ibid., article 71.
88 Ibid., article 70.
89 Ibid., articles 72–4.
90 1977 Additional Protocol I, article 75.
91 1949 Geneva Conventional IV, article 67.
92 Ibid., articles 76 and 69.
93 Ibid., article 68.
94 Ibid., article 76.
95 Ibid., article 77.
96 Ibid., article 68.
97 Ibid., article 77.
98 1977 Additional Protocol I, articles 76 and 77.
99 1949 Geneva Convention IV, article 32.
100 *Independent* (London), 20 February 1991.
101 Ibid., 28 February 1991.
102 1949 Geneva Convention IV, article 42.
103 Ibid., article 78.
104 As to prisoners of war, see Chapter 6; as to civilian internees, see 1949 Geneva Convention IV, articles 79–85.
105 1949 Geneva Convention IV, article 82.
106 Ibid., article 95.
107 Ibid., articles 114 and 115.
108 Ibid., article 116.
109 Ibid., article 132.
110 Ibid., articles 133–4.
111 Ibid., article 135.
112 See p. 153, above.

8 Methods and Means of Warfare

The 'Hague' division of international humanitarian law is concerned with the regulation of methods and means of warfare, meaning on the one hand lawful and unlawful tactics, and, on the other, the law relating to weapons types and usage. Traditionally, a division was made between this provision and 'Geneva' law, concerned with the humanitarian protection of victims of armed conflict. In fact, there is a very considerable degree of overlap between the two, especially in relation to matters such as bombardment and targeting, and even where the distinction might logically be maintained, the motivating imperative behind 'Hague' law is as much one of humanitarian restraint in the conduct of armed conflict as is the case for 'Geneva' law. For this reason, accepted modern usage is to treat the 'Hague' and 'Geneva' limbs of the *jus in bello* as equally part of international humanitarian law. The logic of this joint categorisation is evident in the relevant treaties and their development, as considered in Chapter 1. Thus humanitarian provision for prisoners of war emerged in the Land Warfare Regulations annexed to 1907 Hague Convention IV – in fact as well as name very much a 'Hague' provision – whilst 1977 Protocol I Additional to the 1949 Geneva Conventions, for example, contains extensive and significant provision for methods and means of warfare. For the present purpose, it is convenient to draw a broad distinction between the regulation of methods of warfare and that of the means of waging it, although even this distinction is by no means absolute or without exceptions.

Before proceeding to consideration of the substance of this area of the humanitarian *jus in bello*, a preliminary point of principle needs to be addressed. The protection of the victims of armed conflict, who, by definition, either are or have been rendered *hors de combat*, cannot be said to impede the proper pursuit of legitimate military objectives. The setting of restrictions on the methods and means of warfare might be, and has on occasion been, argued to do precisely this. The argument has a superficial persuasiveness, but is in fact false. The fundamental purpose of the 'Hague' division of the *jus in bello* is clearly set out in the Preamble to one of its oldest functional treaty provisions, the 1868 Declaration of St Petersburg. The 1868 Declaration is an arms control provision banning the use of small-calibre anti-personnel explosive projectiles,[1] but its Preamble underlines principles of much more general application. In particular, it states that:

> the only legitimate object which States should endeavour to accomplish during war is to weaken the military forces of the enemy ... for this purpose it is sufficient to disable the greatest possible number of men ... this object would be exceeded by the employment of arms which uselessly aggravate the suffering of disabled men, or render their death inevitable ... the employment of such arms would, therefore, be contrary to the laws of humanity.

This principle, known as the 'doctrine of unnecessary suffering', is fundamental to the law of arms control in particular, and to the *jus in bello* in general. It is restated, for example by the provision of article 22 of the Land Warfare Regulations annexed to 1907 Hague Convention IV, that:

> The right of belligerents to adopt means of injuring the enemy is not unlimited ...

This is reinforced by article 23:

> In addition to the prohibitions provided by special Conventions, it is especially forbidden ...
> (e) To employ arms, projectiles, or material calculated to cause unnecessary suffering ...

The same principle is affirmed by 1977 Additional Protocol I, article 35, which states as a 'basic rule' that:

> (1) In any armed conflict, the right of the Parties to the conflict to choose methods or means of warfare is not unlimited.
> (2) It is prohibited to employ weapons, projectiles and material and methods of warfare of a nature to cause superfluous injury and unnecessary suffering.

The 'principle of unnecessary suffering', as applied to weapons types and usage, and implicitly to battlefield tactics, does not serve to impede any legitimate military objective, and there is no historic or contemporary evidence that inflictions beyond the 'St Petersburg' level in any way enhance military efficacy. Indeed, the more ruthless an enemy is perceived to be, the more desperate the resistance will become, and the more difficult it will become to bring the conflict to a close and re-establish peaceful relations.

It will also be observed, in relation to arms control in particular, that in the case of many specific restrictions, the express 'principle of unnecessary suffering' is also associated with an implicit principle, which might fairly be termed a 'principle of excessive cruelty', that the attainment of objectives by certain means not only causes militarily 'unnecessary suffering', but is by its nature inherently 'excessively cruel'. The interface between the explicit and implicit principles can be seen in the further development of bans on 'conventional' weapons in the 1990s, in which the campaign to ban landmines was founded straightforwardly upon the infliction of 'unnecessary suffering' (as elaborated into rules regarding indiscriminacy), whereas the banning of blinding laser weapons was very distinctly based upon the implicit 'principle of excessive cruelty'. Again, the aim is not to impede the attainment of legitimate military objectives, but, rather, to place some limits on the barbarity of the range of means which are available, bearing in mind that the most barbarous are not necessarily the most efficacious.

Restrictions on Methods of Warfare

This sector of substantive 'Hague' law is concerned with tactical conduct: the conduct of military operations, including such matters as deception and the distinction between legitimate ruses of war and unlawful perfidy, forbidden practices such as orders of 'no quarter', and practices of bombardment, including in particular bans on indiscriminate bombardment. Many of these rules and principles are applicable in all sectors of warfare, on land, at sea and in the air, but in some cases the distinctive nature of the medium concerned will inevitably demand distinctive treatment.

Deceiving the Enemy: Ruses and Perfidy

To deceive the enemy about one's intentions is a fairly obvious and in itself unobjectionable practice in both strategic and tactical planning.[2] On the grander, strategic, level, the best-known example of deception is perhaps the Allied endeavour at the end of the Second World War to deceive the German military command as to the intended location of the D-Day landings. As Sir Winston Churchill remarked:

> The enemy were bound to know that a great invasion was being prepared; we had to conceal the place and time of attack and make

> him think we were landing somewhere else and at a different moment. Our major deception was to pretend that we were coming across the Straits of Dover. ... The final result was admirable. The German High Command firmly believed the evidence we put at their disposal [and were] ... convinced that the Pas de Calais was our objective.[3]

Such deception is, of course, unexceptionable. Tactical deception is a more complex and troublesome issue, defined by the distinction between 'ruses', which are lawful, and 'perfidy', which is not.

The distinction is referred to in the Land Warfare Regulations annexed to 1907 Hague Convention IV, which by article 23(b) forbids killing or wounding enemy individuals 'treacherously', that is perfidiously, and expressly permits ruses of war under article 24. A much fuller definition is now given by article 37 of 1977 Additional Protocol I. Article 37(1) bans perfidy in the following terms:

> It is prohibited to kill, injure or capture an adversary by resort to perfidy. Acts inviting the confidence of an adversary to lead him to believe that he is entitled to, or is obliged to accord, protection under the rules of international law applicable in armed conflict, with intent to betray that confidence, shall constitute perfidy.

The paragraph goes on to offer as examples of perfidy: feigning desire to negotiate under a flag of truce, feigning incapacity or sickness, feigning civilian or other non-combatant status, or feigning protected status through misuse of United Nations emblems or those of neutral or other non-involved states.

Some cases of apparent perfidy are very simple, but others are much less so. In the course of the 1990–91 Gulf Conflict, a British officer observed a white flag displayed by an enemy unit (a white flag being a sign of desire to negotiate, not necessarily – as is commonly thought – to surrender), came out into the open to communicate with them, and was immediately shot dead by another enemy unit nearby which was not showing a white flag. Had he been killed by the unit showing the white flag, or by the other unit in collusion with them, the act would unequivocally have been one of perfidy in inviting his confidence in an established sign of desire to negotiate. Since the shot was fired by another unit which was not in collusion with that showing the white flag, there was no perfidy, merely a brave but unwise response on the officer's part, who would have been better advised to remain under cover and to have required the enemy representative to come to him or to communicate by more distant means.

Abuse of the white flag would be an example of abuse of emblems which have a recognised protective function. To mount an attack from vehicles marked with the red cross or red crescent emblems would clearly be not only perfidy, but a particularly gross example thereof. Such allegations have been made in various conflicts, although not usually on very good grounds.[4] Sadly, a number of fictional books and films have also been made depicting such abuse as rather clever, and in the case of at least one film this led to a requirement of a public apology before each showing of the film in France, but sadly not in the United Kingdom.[5]

A further issue arises in the context of wearing enemy uniform while engaged in hostile action. The classic instance of this occurred during the Battle of the Bulge towards the end of the Second World War. A number of German units commanded by Otto Skorzeny, a notable figure who, amongst other covert operations, had succeeded in rescuing the Italian dictator Mussolini after he had been overthrown and interned in a *coup d'étât* in Italy,[6] went behind Allied lines wearing US uniforms in vehicles carrying US markings and carried out acts of sabotage. The group immediately with Skorzeny were not detected by Allied sabotage. The group immediately with Skorzeny were not detected by Allied forces, and did not come into direct hostile contact with them. Skorzeny himself was later captured and charged with a war crime as a result of this operation, but was acquitted. In relation to this, Peter Rowe remarks:

> Skorzeny's acquittal suggests that the particular use he made of the enemy's uniform was not 'improper'. Had he used any weapon while so disguised, there would hardly have been any doubt as to his guilt.[7]

In fact, 18 other members of Skorzeny's group were captured while wearing US uniforms, and summarily shot by American firing squads.[8] Whether they were considered to have been acting perfidiously or engaging in espionage, these executions were illegal at the time under the 1929 Geneva Prisoners of War Convention, articles 61, 62, 63 and 66, in the absence of any form of trial and due process, and would most certainly be unlawful now.[9] Today, article 39(2) of 1977 Additional Protocol I provides that:

> It is prohibited to make use of the flags or military emblems, insignia or uniforms of adverse Parties while engaging in attacks or in order to shield, favour, protect or impede military operations.

Clearly, this provision would delegitimise any operation such as Skorzeny's,[10] although it would certainly not render the participants liable to summary execution. Whether this is an extension of the traditional concept of perfidy might be debatable, but in the light of article 23(b) of the 1907 Hague Land Warfare Regulations, although possibly not of article 37 of 1977 Additional Protocol I, the level of covert action suggested by Peter Rowe[11] may reasonably be considered perfidious, even within the meaning of the customary *jus in bello*.

In contrast with unlawful acts of perfidy, there are legitimate ruses of war, permitted by article 24 of the 1907 Hague Land Warfare Regulations. Again, 1977 Additional Protocol I affords a useful clarificatory definition by article 37(2), which provides that:

> Ruses of war are not prohibited. Such ruses are acts which are intended to mislead an adversary or to induce him to act recklessly but which infringe no rule of international law applicable in armed conflict and which are not perfidious because they do not invite the confidence of an adversary with respect to protection under the law. The following are examples of such ruses: the use of camouflage, decoys, mock operations and misinformation.

The distinction is this: a ruse is a deception which does not rely on an implication of international legal protection, whilst perfidy relies precisely upon such a (false) implication. Examples of ruses of warfare are not hard to find. A number of instances from naval warfare will serve to illustrate the point. In the early years of the First World War, before the completion of the defences at Scapa Flow, the Royal Navy sought to deceive German intelligence as to fleet dispositions by disguising 14 elderly merchant ships with false wooden superstructures and other fittings so as to resemble, in silhouette at a distance, selected major naval units. As an example, the aged Canadian-Pacific liner *Ruthenia* (ex-*Lake Champlain*) was disguised as the battleship *King George V*, and deployed in order to misinform the enemy as the warship's location.[12] A similar endeavour on a much smaller scale was also undertaken in the Second World War. This was clearly a legitimate ruse of war by way of misdirection and misinformation.

The same may be said of the well-known incident following the Battle of the River Plate in 1939, when the UK disseminated false information suggesting that a very large and powerful naval force was gathering off the Plate in order to discourage KM *Graf Spee* from sailing while the British cruiser force off the river mouth regrouped. Ultimately, the *Graf Spee* sailed, but was scuttled by its crew in the estuary. For ruses of war in the course of battle, a good example may be seen in the First World War action of the German commerce-raiding cruiser SMS *Emden* at Penang. The *Emdem* was a three-funnelled cruiser, but on approaching Penang a false fourth funnel was erected, and smoke was led into it so that, to a casual observer at a distance, the ship appeared generally to resemble a British 'Town' class cruiser, despite a considerable disparity in size. Under guise of this deception, the *Emden* entered Georgetown Harbour at Penang on 28 October 1914 and destroyed various merchant ships along with the small Russian cruiser *Zhemtchug* and the French destroyer *Mousquet*.[13] The imperial German naval ensign was flown throughout the approach, and the action of altering a ship's silhouette is by no means the same thing as wearing enemy uniform, so this again was a case of legitimate deception amounting to a ruse of war, rather than perfidy.

The reference to camouflage in article 37(2) seems a little curious, since this is surely concealment rather than deception *stricto sensu*. The two concepts may be conceded to have in common the factor of confusing the enemy, but are hardly to be considered identical practices in reality. It does confirm the lawfulness of camouflage, however, if anyone had been disposed to doubt it.

Orders of 'No Quarter'

An order of 'no quarter' means essentially an order that there should be no survivors on the opposing side in a military action. There is no legal debate upon the point: such orders are unequivocally unlawful. They are expressly banned by the Land Warfare Regulations annexed to 1907 Hague Convention IV, article 23(d), and by 1977 Additional Protocol I, article 40, which provides, at rather greater length than the 1907 Regulations, that:

> It is prohibited to order that there shall be no survivors, to threaten an adversary therewith or to conduct hostilities on this basis.

Such an order would anyway violate a number of other *jus in bello* provisions, for example in relation to the humanitarian treatment of prisoners of war. Very few orders of this type have been issued in modern warfare, although an example may be seen in the notorious 'Commando Order' issued by Hitler on 18 October 1942. This order, which was to be secret and on no account to fall into Allied hands, stated:

> From now on all enemies on so-called commando missions in Europe or Africa challenged by German troops, even if they are in uniform, whether armed or unarmed, in battle or in flight, are to be slaughtered to the last man.[14]

The order was denounced as illegal by the International Military Tribunal at Nuremberg in 1945. The 'Commissar Order' of March 1941, which was similar in tone and effect, applied to Soviet Commissars during the Nazi invasion of the Soviet Union, and was also condemned by the International Military Tribunal at Nuremberg.

The Law of Bombardment

Bombardment is, self-evidently, a central aspect of the conduct of hostilities, and is subject to a number of constraints by international humanitarian law, all of which relate ultimately to the basic 'principle of unnecessary suffering'[15] in so far as they are designed largely to limit target selection and to proscribe indiscriminate attacks. The basic principle is that bombardment must be directed to legitimate military objectives, and must not be indiscriminate in effect. The clearest statement of this is found in 1977 Additional Protocol I, articles 48, 51, 52 and 57. Article 48 provides that:

> In order to ensure respect for and protection of the civilian population and civilian objects, the Parties to the conflict shall at all times distinguish between the civilian population and combatants and between civilian objects and military objectives and accordingly shall direct their operations only against military objectives.

Article 52(2)(3) then provides in elaboration of this basic principle that:

> (2) Attacks shall be limited strictly to military objectives. In so far as objects are concerned, military objectives are limited to those objects which by their nature, location, purpose or use make an effective contribution to military action and whose total or partial destruction, capture or neutralization in the circumstances ruling at the time, offers a definite military advantage.
> (3) In case of doubt whether an object is normally dedicated to civilian purposes, such as a place of worship, a house or other dwelling or a school is being used to make an effective contribution to military action, it shall be presumed not to be so used.

Moving beyond the question of deliberate targeting, article 51(4)(5) addresses the issue of indiscriminate bombardment in which civilians, and other protected people and places, may not actually be targets, but are within the field of a general bombardment which is aimed without adequate precautions in targeting. Article 51(4) provides that:

> Indiscriminate attacks are prohibited. Indiscriminate attacks are: (a) those which are not directed at a specific military object; (b) those which employ a method or means of combat which cannot be directed at a specific military objective; or (c) those which employ a method or means of combat the effects of which cannot be limited as required by this Protocol; and consequently, in each case, are of a nature to strike military objectives and civilians or civilian objects without distinction.

Article 51(5) cites as an example of indiscriminate attacks what is generally known as 'area bombardment',[16] in which a number of military objectives found in an area of civilian population are treated as one target, and the whole area is bombarded without reference to the civilian presence and locations. Article 51(5)(b) adds more generally any attack which may be expected to cause incidental civilian injury or loss 'which would be excessive in relation to the concrete and direct military advantage anticipated'. Article 57 requires that all possible precautions be taken in attack to ensure that the targets are indeed civilian rather than military, and that the methods and means of attack chosen are such as to facilitate the infliction of minimum damage upon the civilians and civilian objects.

These were not new principles in 1977, although they were then stated in more detail than had previously been the case. The basic principles so far as land warfare is concerned were also found in the Land Warfare Regulations annexed to 1907 Hague Convention IV, in particular in articles 25, 26 and 27. Of these, article 25 bans attacks upon 'undefended' towns, villages, dwellings or buildings. In the context of modern air warfare, this might apply at the lower end of the scale, but for a town or city to be 'undefended' by anti-aircraft artillery may seen rather unlikely. The Japanese courts did, however, refer to article 25 in connection with the nuclear bombardment of Hiroshima and Nagasaki in 1945 in the Shimoda case,[17] although on this specific point the 'undefended' quality of the two cities may be doubted.

Article 26 is perhaps rather outdated, and refers more to the conditions of the late 19th century than to anything which would normally arise at present. It requires that the officer in command must warn the enemy authorities, if that is possible, before commencing a bombardment, 'except in cases of assault'. Today, most, if not all, bombardments will be in the course of an assault, and advance warning would merely serve to invite air attack upon the artillery positions.

Article 27 of the 1907 Land Warfare Regulations is highly significant and worth quoting in full. It provides that:

> In sieges and bombardments all necessary steps must be taken to spare, as far as possible, buildings dedicated to religion, art, science, or charitable purposes, historic monuments, hospitals, and places where the sick and wounded are collected, provided they are not being used at the time for military purposes.
>
> It is the duty of the besieged to indicate the presence of such buildings or places by distinctive and visible signs, which shall be notified to the enemy beforehand.

The basic principle of limitation of legitimate bombardment to military objectives is clearly implicit here, even if most of the specific substance of the provision has been included in and superseded by later treaty provision.

It is also interesting to note that the 1923 Hague Draft Rules of Aerial Warfare, which were never adopted as a legal instrument but were nevertheless considered an accurate summary of the law then existing, also made provision for bombardment which accords closely with the present position. Article 24 of the Draft Rules provided, *inter alia*, that:

> (1) Aerial bombardment is legitimate only when directed at a military objective, that is to say, an object of which the destruction or injury would constitute a distinct military advantage to the belligerent.
> (2) Such bombardment is legitimate only when directed exclusively at the following objectives: military forces; military works; military establishments or depots; factories constituting important and well-known centres engaged in the manufacture of arms, ammunition or distinctively military supplies; lines of communication or transportation used for military purposes.

Paragraphs (3) and (4) forbid indiscriminate bombardment, but allow bombardment of towns and cities where the military concentration is sufficient to justify this, with due precautions for the civilian population.[18] Article 24(1) expressly forbids terror bombardment of the civilian population, which was ultimately the bombing policy of both Axis and the Allies in the later stages of the Second World War. The general rules governing bombardment are supplemented by a variety of specific restrictions on targeting of protected installations, including those protected by 1949 Geneva Conventions I and II,[19] and by other 'Geneva' provisions, as well as by the 1954 Hague Convention and Protocol for the Protection of Cultural Property in the Event of Armed Conflict, for example.[20]

The legal rules governing bombardment are thus relatively simple, but their practical interpretation and application in the real exigencies of armed conflict pose some difficulty. In the first place, careful distinctions need to be drawn between calculated attacks on civilians, indiscriminate attacks, and the infliction of 'collateral' injury and damage in the course of lawful attacks. Modern warfare has raised many problems with respect to discrimination in bombardment. Both Axis and Allied bombing policy in the Second World War involved indiscriminate bombardment; this was almost certainly unlawful at the time and would clearly be so now. It has been suggested that some mistaken bombing of civilians areas occurred initially, and finally, on 4 September 1940, in a speech at the *Sportpalast* in Berlin, Hitler stated: 'we will raze their [British] cities to the ground'.[21] In the latter part of the war in Europe, both Axis and Allied bombing were clearly unlawful then, and would certainly be so now, and it was partly for this reason that the question of bombing did not feature in the Nuremberg indictments. The unlawfulness of terror bombardment of civilians is, as stated above, unequivocal; so is a policy of 'area bombardment', although attempts were made to justify this practice, for example by J.M. Spaight.[22] The ultimate perils of this approach are clearly stated by Hans Blix in his comment that:

> The danger [lies in] … the vagueness of the [concept] … of 'concentration' … and the departure from the principle that only military objectives may be attacked. … [A]rea bombardment on big cities during the Second World War would seem to demonstrate amply how the elasticity of the doctrine allowed it to turn into … terror bombing of civilians.[23]

The direct linkage between 'area' and 'terror' bombardment may be doubted, but it is clear that area bombardment is unlawfully indiscriminate, almost certainly under customary law, and expressly so under article 51(2)(a) of 1977 Additional Protocol I.[24]

There have been other examples of indiscriminate bombardment in modern armed conflict, not least in the course of the armed conflicts in former Yugoslavia in the 1990s. Amongst all too many examples, the shelling of the marketplace in Sarajevo on 5 February 1994, leading to many civilian deaths, may be cited as an especially notorious one. Again, the unlawfulness of this action was unequivocal.[25]

A more complex question emerges from the use and effects of modern automated and rapid-reaction weapons systems. This issue came into prominence in both the 1980–88 Gulf War and the 1990–91 Gulf Conflict. During the 1980–88 Gulf War between Iran and Iraq, USS *Vincennes*, while engaged in convoy protection duties and under attack by Iranian Revolutionary Guard units, fired upon and shot down an approaching Iranian aircraft in the belief that it was a hostile military plane, and then discovered that it was in fact Iran Air Flight 655, a civilian airliner.[26] Essentially, the *Vincennes* had automated weapons which fired automatically unless the instruction was manually countermanded – in this case the classical procedure of a decision to fire is replaced by one involving a decision not to fire, and the commanding officer was faced with a situation in which he had to make a split-second decision either not to fire, or to let the firing proceed. If he decided not to fire and the aircraft was a hostile military plane, his ship might well have been destroyed; on the other hand, if he allowed firing to proceed he might destroy a civilian airliner – which, tragically, he did. In later investigations, serious criticism was made of the particular procedures in place on board USS *Vincennes*, but the general dilemma is nevertheless genuine, and one which requires consideration. It must be emphasised that whether the requisite decision is to fire or not to fire, the governing legal norms are the same, and technology cannot be held to override such very basic rules and principles.

Another incident which raises serious issues of technology in bombardment may be found in the bombing of the Amirayah bunker in Baghdad during the 1990–91 Gulf Conflict. With regard to this incident, Christopher Greenwood remarks cogently that:

> Coalition statements ... suggest that the United States Air Force commanders who decided to attack the bunker were convinced that it was a military command and control centre and did not suspect that there were civilians present. Acting on that basis, they then took all the precautions which were required ... to minimize the risk to civilians. ... The attack did not raise difficult questions about the applicable law, but rather factual questions about whether the requirements of that law were complied with ...[27]

It seems that intelligence received indicated use of the bunker as a military headquarters, but by the time of the attack such use, if any, had ceased, and the bunker was in use as a civilian air raid shelter. In short, the standard of precautions in attack demanded by article 57, and implicitly required by earlier law, were *prima facie* complied with, but not with adequate effect, and some 400 civilians were killed in the attack. The claim that the civilians in the bunker were the families of senior Iraqi military personnel which was later advanced was utterly irrelevant – being married or related to a soldier (of however exalted a rank) does not make a civilian a legitimate target! The bombing of the Amirayah bunker was a tragic accident rather than a war crime, but it serves to illustrate the necessity for accurate and *recent* intelligence reports in the processes of target-selection. The provisions in relation to 'doubt' as to target identity in article 52(3) of 1977 Additional Protocol I should also be borne in mind.

The final substantial issue in relation to general targeting arises in the context of 'collateral damage'. States are enjoined to do their utmost to separate military and civilian areas by article 58 of 1977 Additional Protocol I, but in practice many military targets will be near to, or even in, centres of civilian population, especially in the case of military industries, some of which may have been converted from civilian plant for a period of war emergency. Given the inevitable existence of 'mixed' targets, the supremely difficult decision demanded by article 51(5)(b) of 1977 Additional Protocol I is whether the potential injury to civilians 'would be excessive in relation to the concrete and direct military advantage to be anticipated'. Many examples of this may be cited, especially in relation to urban military industrial plant and major communications links, both of which may clearly be military objectives of major significance, and both of which are commonly to be found in civilian urban areas. An example from the 1990–91 Gulf Conflict is the bombing of a bridge on a vital road link in the town of Fallouja, in the course of which there was also significant collateral damage in the surrounding civilian area.[28]

Some level of collateral damage may be unavoidable, but its elimination when at all possible, and its minimisation in all circumstances, including considering the actual necessity for the attack in the prevailing circumstances, remain fundamental imperatives which cannot be overridden by arguments of so-called 'realism'.

Particular Issues in Naval Warfare

The legal constraints on naval warfare are in many respects precisely parallel with those applicable to land and air warfare, and are considered elsewhere in this chapter and in Chapter 5. However, two particular matters require further consideration here: the question of submarine warfare, and the issue of maritime exclusion zones.

The question of the application of duties of search and rescue to submarines has been considered above.[29] However, there remains the somewhat related issue of sinking without warning, which also derives from the basic vulnerability of submarines on the surface. This first arose as a major issue during the First World War, when Germany declared that, with effect from 19 February 1915, the waters around the British Isles would be considered a 'war zone', in which enemy merchant ships would be sunk without consideration for passengers and crew (that is, without warning), and neutral shipping would be placed at risk. An early and famous victim of this policy was the Cunard record-breaker *Lusitania*, sunk on 7 May 1915 off the Old Head of Kinsale in Ireland by U-20. This practice, widely condemned as an example of 'frightfulness' at the time, reflected to some extent the Allied use of Q-ships: small ships giving the outward appearance of merchant vessels, but crewed by naval personnel and carrying a concealed heavy armament for their size. If a U-boat surfaced to order the crew off and sink the ship by gunfire, it would itself be destroyed by the Q-ship's armament. The idea of using warships with a 'merchant' silhouette was not new: the French cruiser *Châteaurenault* of 1898 had been given a profile which might, at long distance, suggest a 'four-funnelled liner unknown'. Later, the British 'Flower' class sloops, which served in both the First and Second World Wars, had a vaguely 'mercantile' profile, although they were unequivocally warships. The later development of the convoy system in both world wars in any event rendered attack without warning virtually inevitable. This was evidenced at the Nuremberg War Crimes Trial when Captain Kranzbuehler, the highly skilled and effective defence counsel for Grand Admiral Dönitz, secured an answer to an interrogatory upon Allied naval law and practice from Admiral Chester W. Nimitz. On this, Ann and John Tusa comment that:

> [Admiral Nimitz's] views on the recent applications of naval law had to be seen as authoritative. ... [His] answers to the interrogatory were concise and unwavering: The United States had designated theatres of operations and within them they had attacked without warning ... Nimitz argued and had acted in these matters exactly the same way as Doenitz claimed to have done.[30]

The charges of unrestricted submarine warfare were not pursued against Dönitz, and this must be concluded to have defined the law upon this point. In modern submarine warfare, this may indeed be represented as the only logical conclusion, but it must again be emphasised that this in no way signifies a justification for further attack upon the crew and other personnel of sunken ships.[31]

Exclusion zones follow on directly from the discussion above, and arose in their sharpest form in the context of the 1982 Anglo-Argentine Falklands Conflict. The Exclusion Zone around the Falkland Islands was declared by the United Kingdom on 9 April 1992, with a 200-mile radius around the islands in which Argentine naval vessels and auxiliaries would unequivocally be liable to attack. On 28 April this first provision was extended by the announcement of a Total Exclusion Zone covering the same area, but in which:

> Any ships and any aircraft, whether military or civil, ... found within this zone without due authority from the Ministry of Defence in London will be regarded as operating in support of the illegal occupation [of the Falklands Islands] and will therefore be regarded as hostile and will be liable to be attacked by British forces.[32]

The right to attack Argentine forces engaged in the occupation of the islands was self-evident under both the *jus ad bellum* and the *jus in bello*, but the declared zone did not create any additional rights; it merely served notice of intention to exercise those rights. In the 20th century, belligerents have tended to claim some right of control over shipping, including neutral merchant shipping, in war zones, and in this case the United Kingdom in any event claimed territorial jurisdiction over the islands and their adjacent waters. This would not have admitted a policy of general assault upon neutral merchant shipping, and nothing of the sort took place. The controversy over the Exclusion Zone arose over the question of whether, by declaring the zone, the United Kingdom had actually *limited* its rights of action, especially with regard to the sinking of the cruiser *General Belgrano* when it was outside and sailing away from the designated area. Some have argued that the sinking was, on this basis, unlawful.

Whatever view may be taken of the political dimension of the sinking, it is difficult to see how this view can be maintained in the context of the *jus in bello*. The *General Belgrano* was a major enemy surface warship, and even as a somewhat outdated 'big-gun' cruiser of Second World War vintage (the former USS *Phoenix*, which was one of the few US warships in Pearl Harbor to escape unscathed on the day of the Japanese attack), it could still have inflicted serious damage on the British task force sailing to the Falklands had encounter occurred between them. In short, a statement that action *will* take place in a certain area does not mean that all other belligerent rights are abandoned. For example, what if the task force had been attacked outside the declared zone? Would the existence of the zone have precluded counter-action? The suggestion would be bizarre. As to the fact that the *General Belgrano* was sailing away from the declared zone, ships can readily change course, quite apart from the fact that the *General Belgrano* was not at sea for peaceful purposes, and represented a continuing threat to British forces in an armed conflict situation.

After the end of the 1982 Falklands Conflict, the Total Exclusion Zone was replaced with a Protection Zone, rescinded in 1991, from which Argentine shipping was ordered off, although a disabled Argentine yacht was admitted to Port Stanley for emergency repairs as an obvious humanitarian exception. Other post-1982 maritime zones around the Falkland Islands, related to fishing and other economic resources, inevitably also proved problematic,[33] but in the present context this serves merely to illustrate the difficulties in resuming normalcy after an armed conflict.

During the 1980–88 Gulf War, Iraq declared an Exclusion Zone around the Iranian oil terminal at Kharg Island, in which shipping was to be attacked without warning – the primary targets being oil tankers, with a view to damaging the Iranian oil economy. Iran itself maintained a defensive Exclusion Zone around its port on the Gulf, but also launched general attacks on oil tankers proceeding to Iraqi oil terminals. Both Iraqi and Iranian attacks exceeded normally legitimate exercises of control over neutral shipping in a war zone, and were almost certainly illegal. A number of states, including the UK and USA, arranged convoys for the protection of shipping, and the presence of these warships in the war zones in itself created problems, illustrated by the *Vincennes* incident[34] and the Iraqi shelling of USS *Starke*. Ross Leckow remarks that:

> The use of war zones can be justified ... only ... where the dictates of 'reasonableness' are respected. ... [In] the war between Iran and Iraq little respect ... for this principle of restraint [was displayed]. It is

> because of this ... that attacks on neutral vessels by both sides must be condemned as violations of international law.[35]

In the final analysis, it must reasonably be concluded that whilst states clearly can declare specific intentions through the declaration of 'exclusion' and other zones, they cannot in so doing exempt themselves from the application of *jus in bello* norms or in any way create new belligerent rights.

There remains the question of mine warfare at sea. This is currently much less controversial than mine warfare on land,[36] but nevertheless raises important issues of principle. As for landmines, the primary problem is one of indiscrimination, and this arose as an issue early in the 20th century with the experience of the 1904–5 Russo-Japanese War. Several important warships were sunk by mines in the course of the war; including the Russian battleship *Petropavlovsk* and the Japanese battleships *Hatsuse* and *Yashima*. The loss of the *Petropavlovsk* may even have had a significant effect on the outcome of the war, since Admiral Makarov, who was drowned in the sinking of his flagship, was undoubtedly one of the Russian Imperial Navy's more talented officers.

Such sinkings were legitimate acts of war, but a large number of neutral merchant ships also fell victim to mines, including randomly drifting unanchored mines. As a result, 1907 Hague Convention VIII Relative to the Laying of Automatic Submarine Contact Mines was concluded. The convention provides by article 1 that unanchored submarine contact mines are forbidden unless they are so constructed as to become harmless after a maximum of one hour. Article 3 requires that in laying anchored mines, all care should be taken for 'peaceful shipping', and in particular that the minefield should either remain under surveillance, or if this is not done, the relevant government should be informed of the location of the field 'as soon as military exigencies permit'.

These measures are not a perfect protection, as the sinking of the hospital ship HMHS *Britannic* demonstrated in 1916,[37] but they have gone far to eliminate many of the problems which are particularly associated with the (mis)use of landmines. Despite this, technology has moved on since 1907, and some concern has been voiced over the application of the convention to remote-controlled naval mines, which can, of course, be used 'discriminately' without notification of location, whilst accepting that the 1907 Convention still retains a very large measure of relevance.[38]

Environmental Protection

The question of damage to the environment in armed conflict has been a prominent issue in the *jus in bello* over the last quarter of the 20th century. The issue arose in connection with the use of certain defoliants and potential, although not actual, environmental modification techniques in the Vietnam War. This led to the inclusion of significant protective provision in 1977 Additional Protocol I. Subsequently, the burning of the Kuwaiti oil field and the release of a large oil slick into the Gulf in the 1990–91 Gulf Conflict renewed concern, and has led to debate regarding the possible need for a new convention or Protocol dealing further with this issue.

Warfare has always tended to inflict at least some local environmental damage, and has sometimes done so on a large scale, as the shell-cratered landscape of the First World War western front showed. Once the conflict was over, however, such damage was, with considerable effort, repaired. Beyond such 'incidental' damage, the use of environmental damage as a method of warfare in its own right is also of antique provenance, as in the Roman practice of contaminating enemy fields with salt by sea flooding. The dividing line between 'collateral' environmental damage and environmental damage as a method of warfare is not always simply drawn. The Vietnam experience is a case in point. The problem here was the need to expose enemy supply lines in jungle territory, and the desire to protect roads in friendly territory from sniper fire. In pursuit of these aims, US forces used defoliants such as Agents Blue and Orange, which did severe environmental damage, and at least in the case of the former, proved to have carcinogenic effects in human beings who came into contact with them. They also used so-called 'Rome plows' to tear up roadside vegetation with a view to eliminating sniper cover, and this too had lasting deleterious effects. The arguments in these cases is essentially one of the level of acceptability of 'collateral' damage, and the effect of arguments of 'military necessity'.[39] The nature of the fundamental dilemma is clearly set out by L.F.E. Goldie in the comment that:

> given the choice of saving the lives of combatants or of saving even important environmental assets, one should, even with possible difficulty, choose the former.[40]

Nevertheless, there is not necessarily a simple choice between protecting human life and protecting the environment. Human beings live and die in their environment, and damage to the environment may well also be very damaging to people. The difficulties of separating the issues are graphically illustrated by the carcinogenic effects of Agent Blue.

Different issues arose in the 1990–91 Gulf Conflict. The deliberate burning of oil installations in Kuwait commenced on 22 January 1991, and by the end of the Iraqi occupation the majority of the Kuwaiti oil fields were on fire. The actual context of the burning is somewhat unclear. A small proportion of the fires may have been the collateral effects of bombardment. The calculated fire-raising may have been partly an aspect of economic warfare with a view to denying the oil wells to the returning Kuwaitis, and partly part of a 'scorched earth' policy in retreat. In either case, the phenomenon was hardly new: Adam Roberts cites the burning of the Romanian oil fields in the First World War as an example.[41] Scorched earth tactics in occupied territories are forbidden by 1949 Geneva Convention IV, article 53, which provides that:

> Any destruction by the Occupying Power of real or personnel property ... is prohibited, except where such destruction is rendered absolutely necessary by military operations.

Such destruction is, indeed, defined by article 147 of the convention as a 'grave breach' when extensive and wanton. Article 54(2) of 1977 Additional Protocol I, protecting objects indispensable to the survival of the civilian population, is similar in implication. No military necessity justified the burning of the oil fields, and this must be seen at least as a 'scorched earth' action. The smoke from the burning oil field also caused major environmental damage, although not, fortunately, on the cataclysmic scale at one time predicted. Nevertheless, the consequences included a heavy smog which caused a significant increase in respiratory disease in the region,[42] which may have been a 'collateral' effect, but was clearly a very serious one.[43]

The spillage into the Gulf of several million gallons of crude oil from Kuwaiti storage facilities between 25 and 28 January 1991, at which point the outlets were closed by bombing, led to serious environmental consequences. The feared impact on Saudi Arabian and other Gulf desalination plants was averted, but the natural environment of the Gulf suffered very severely, on a scale greater than that of the largest of civilian oil tanker disasters. Again, the motives are not clearly established, and were no doubt various, possibly a combination of economic warfare with an element of intended environmental attack on the desalination plants.

These experiences, from Vietnam onwards, have generated a number of provisions and heated argument in relation to protection of the environment in armed conflict. The most important modern treaty provisions are articles 35(3) and 55 of 1977 Additional Protocol I. The former provides that:

> It is prohibited to employ methods or means of warfare which are intended, or may be expected, to cause widespread, long-term and severe damage to the natural environment.

Article 55 then requires that:

> (1) Care shall be taken in warfare to protect the natural environment against widespread, long-term and severe damage. This protection includes a prohibition of the use of methods or means of warfare which are intended or may be expected to cause such damage to the natural environment and thereby to prejudice the health or survival of the population.
> (2) Attacks against the natural environment by way of reprisals are prohibited.

These provisions are parallel in nature, each emphasising a ban on the infliction of 'widespread, long-term and severe' damage to the environment. The distinction between them is that article 35(3) is concerned exclusively with the 'environment', whereas article 55 emphasises prejudice to 'the health or survival of the population'. Had these provisions been directly applicable to the 1990–91 Gulf Conflict, the burning of the oil fields would have fallen primarily under article 55, whereas the release of the oil slick into the Gulf would have fallen foul of both article 35(3) and article 55.

A range of other provisions, mainly in the area of civilian protection, also imply environmental protection, although they are not necessarily phrased in that way. This is true of certain of the constraints on weapons types and uses, including those relating to chemical and bacteriological weapons.[44] By the same token, environmental provisions can have major implications for weapons types and use, this being perhaps notably the case for nuclear weapons.[45]

A rather different environmental concern is reflected in the 1977 UN Convention on the Prohibition of Military or any Other Hostile Use of Environmental Modification Techniques (ENMOD). ENMOD, article 2, proscribes:

> any technique for changing – through the deliberate manipulation of natural processes – the dynamics, composition or structure of the Earth, including its biota, lithosphere, hydrosphere and atmosphere, or of outer space.

This convention arose from fears about the possibilities of weather-manipulation through attempts at 'cloud seeding' during the Vietnam War. There is much doubt about the practical likelihood of the fulfilment of these fears. Cloud seeding has not proven particularly effective. Alteration of the atmosphere may be within human capacities, in the shape of possible global warming through release of 'greenhouse' gases, although this could hardly be done on a timescale and in a defined area such as would be useful for hostile military purposes. Major geological events, such as a large-scale earthquake or volcanic eruption, would indeed be militarily relevant. Mount Vesuvius, near Naples, erupted in 1944, and the clouds of ash caused a major hazard to Allied airfields in the vicinity.[46] This was not, of course, militarily induced, but if such events could be artificially generated, the consequences could be devastating. In practice, the concern must be seen as exaggerated. A new volcano or fault line could not be created by any present, or presently likely, technology. It might be possible to bring forward an eruption or earthquake which was about to happen anyway by heavy bombing, but this would depend upon the natural presence of an active volcano or earthquake, and one which was in any event about to erupt or move. Volcanoes and fault lines are rarely situated to suit military convenience, and cataclysmic events associated with them are even less so. The ENMOD proscription may be a useful legal safeguard, but its concerns are by no means the most urgent in the context of environmental protection in armed conflict.

The question of the efficacy of provision for the protection of the environment has been raised in particular response to the events of 1990–91 Gulf Conflict.[47] The Gulf Conflict, at the very least, demonstrated inadequate observation of the existing provisions for environmental protection in armed conflict. A case for a new Environmental Protection Convention might certainly be made out in the light of this. The wisdom and utility of such a move may, however, be doubted. The danger of instant recourse to new treaty provision in the face of international difficulty lies in an apparent reality of activity which serves only to conceal an actual absence of achievement. The substantial difficulties which arose in the 1990–91 Gulf Conflict are in fact covered to some extent by provisions of 1949 Geneva Convention IV, and very substantially by provisions of 1977 Additional Protocol I, so it may be suggested that the broad spectrum of problems of environmental damage in armed conflict is covered in existing provision. The issue is therefore not so much one of devising new law, but rather one of enforcing and making effective the provision which has already been made. In relation to the 1990–91 Gulf Conflict. Adam Roberts remarks that:

> Some of the immediate post-war discussion was centred on proposals for a new international treaty. A possible 'fifth Geneva Convention', to address directly the issue of environmental damage in war, was discussed. However, the weight of opinion ... favoured ... more modest steps, including, fuller ratification, exposition, implementation and development of existing law.[48]

This seems to be the most effective way forward for the development of environmental protection in armed conflict at the present time.

Arms Control

Arms control is a wide-ranging area of law which to some extent straddles the boundary between the *jus ad bellum* and the *jus in bello*. The discouragement of 'arms races', such as the pre-1914 Dreadnought battleship 'race' and the Cold War nuclear armaments competition, may place a role in the aversion of conflict – assuming that the discouragement is effective and equitable. The same may be said, subject to the same caveat, of discouragement from or bans on stockpiling of certain weapons. Such provisions are evidently *jus ad bellum* restrictions. There are also a wide range of restrictions on both weapons types and uses which clearly fall within the *jus in bello*. Both require consideration, and are not very usefully set into absolutely distinct categories, since they overlap in both concept and application at many points.

Small-calibre Explosive Projectiles

In 1863, the Imperial Russian Army developed an explosive shell originally intended for use against armoured ammunition transports. In 1867, a much smaller-calibre version of this weapon was developed which would explode on contact with the human body, causing devastating injury vastly in excess of that inflicted by a normal bullet. The government of Tsar Alexander II realised that it had on its hands a practically inhumane weapon, which could no doubt be produced in vast quantities by any of the more industrialised potential enemies of the Russian Empire, including Britain, France and Germany, and called an international conference at St Petersburg with a view to banning such weapons.

The result was the 1868 Declaration of St Petersburg, which bans:

> the employment by ... military and naval troops of any projectile of a weight below 400 grammes, which is either explosive or charged with fulminating or inflammable substances.

The latter reference to bullets charged with 'fulminating or inflammable substances' goes beyond what the Imperial Government had originally had in mind, but was clearly a logical extension of the concern felt in relation to small-calibre explosive projectiles in anti-personnel use. The declaration preserved the legitimacy of use of large-calibre explosive shells against large or armoured targets. The proscription found in the 1868 Declaration of St Petersburg has been one of the more successful arms control measures, and few if any significant violations have been recorded in the many wars of the later 19th and 20th centuries. It may be added that, as remarked above, the general 'principle of unnecessary suffering' set out in the Preamble to the declaration has played an important role, not only in the subsequent development of the law of arms control, but also to some degree in the general development of international humanitarian law.[49]

Expanding (Dumdum) Bullets

Dumdum bullets (named after the Dum Dum Arsenal near Calcutta where they were first manufactured in the 19th century) are bullets in which the hard casing is pierced or partly removed, causing them to flatten out on impact. This causes much more severe injury than would be the case for an ordinary fully cased bullet. These bullets were originally designed for big game hunting (which is not to imply that they were acceptable in that role) but were also rapidly adopted for military use by the British Army. The effect of a dumdum bullet would clearly be similar in practice to that of an explosive bullet, although not precisely the same in mechanism. On this basis, many states represented at the 1899 Hague Peace Conference took the view that such bullets fell within the proscription set out by the 1868 Declaration of St Petersburg in relation to small-calibre explosive projectiles. Britain resisted this conclusion on the basis of arguments which were in part manifestly racist in tone and intention, and in part self-contradictory.[50] These arguments were inevitably abandoned, and 1899 Hague Declaration 3 Concerning Expanding Bullets was duly concluded, The declaration provides that:

> The contracting Parties agree to abstain from the use of bullets which expand or flatten easily in the human body, such as bullets with a hard envelope which does not entirely cover the core or is pierced with incisions.

The ban is clearly stated, and it must be emphasised that it is not limited to bullets which are *manufactured* in this fashion, but also includes bullets which have been *adapted*, for example by cutting incisions in the hard casings of ordinary bullets, whether on an organised basis or as an act of delinquency by individual soldiers. This proscription is, like the 1868 Declaration of St Petersburg, accepted as a part of the customary *jus in bello*, and has similarly proven to be very effective. There have been allegations of sporadic violation in armed conflicts which have occurred since 1899, but there has been no evidence of widespread disregard of this universally accepted ban.

The 1980 UN Convention on Conventional Weapons

1977 Additional Protocol I was originally intended to include certain restrictions upon conventional weapons,[51] but agreement was not reached on these in time, so the matter was taken up, pursuant to a UN General Assembly Resolution in 1977, by a UN Conference on Conventional Weapons in 1979. After much debate, the 1980 UN Convention on Prohibitions or Restrictions on the use of Certain Conventional Weapons Which May be Deemed to be Excessively Injurious or to have Indiscriminate Effects was agreed upon. The convention itself is largely a preamble and provision for implementation, dissemination[52] and review. The substantive provision was contained in the first place in three Protocols governing, respectively, fragmentation weapons where the fragments are non-detectable, mines or booby-trap weapons and incendiary weapons.

Weapons injuring by undetectable fragments Protocol I is extremely simple:

> It is prohibited to use any weapon the primary effect of which is to injure by fragments which in the human body escape detection by X-rays.

The primary concern here is with plastic mines, which embed fragments in the victim's body which cannot normally be discerned through X-ray investigation, and can therefore only be found by invasive exploratory surgery, which may well exacerbate the effects of the original injury. Medical techniques have advanced since the drafting of the Protocol, and advanced medical technologies do now exist which can detect such plastic fragments without surgical investigation, but the availability of such equipment in battlefield medical facilities may reasonably be thought unlikely, so the proscription set out in the Protocol has lost none of its practical importance.

Mines, booby-traps and other devices Protocol II restricts the use of landmines, booby-traps and analogous devices. The question of landmines has moved on since the Protocol was drafted, and in 1996 the Review Conference of the 1980 UN Convention significantly amended the Protocol further to restrict the use of landmines. This move was associated with a vigorous campaign for the total abandonment of mines conducted by the ICRC and national Red Cross and Red Crescent societies, and associated in the United Kingdom with the late Diana, Princess of Wales. The amendments did not achieve this objective in full, and at the time of writing (1997) the campaign for a total ban continues. The amended article 2 of the Protocol offers, *inter alia*, the following definitions:

> (1) 'Mine' means a munition placed under, on or near the ground or other surface area and designed to be exploded by the presence, proximity or contact of a person or vehicle.
> (2) 'Remotely-delivered mine' means a mine not directly emplaced but delivered by artillery, missile, rocket, mortar, or similar means, or dropped from an aircraft. ... [This does not include] mines delivered from a land-based system from less than 500 metres ...
> (3) 'Anti-personnel mine' means a mine primarily designed to be exploded by the presence, proximity or contract of a person and that will incapacitate, injure or kill one or more persons.

The definition of a booby-trap, which is essentially a weapon disguised as an innocent object which explodes when picked up or touched, is repeated in its original form in the new article 2(4) as:

> any device or material which is designed, constructed or adapted to kill or injure and which functions unexpectedly when a person disturbs or approaches an apparently harmless object or performs an apparently safe act.

The use of booby-traps, aside from the general ban on perfidy,[53] is restricted by article 7 of the amended Protocol. In particular, by article 7(1) they may not be attached to or associated with:

> (a) internationally recognized protective emblems, signs or signals;
> (b) sick, wounded or dead persons;
> (c) burial or cremation sites or graves;
> (d) medical facilities, medical equipment, medical supplies or medial transportation;
> (e) children's toys, or other portable objects or products specially designed for the feeding, health, hygiene, clothing or education of children;
> (f) food or drink;
> (g) kitchen utensils or appliances except in military establishments, military locations or military supply depots;
> (h) objects clearly of a religious nature;
> (i) historic monuments, works of art or places of worship which constitute the cultural or spiritual heritage of peoples; or
> (j) animals or their carcasses.

The purpose of these restrictions, like the ban in article 7(2) on booby-traps in the form of apparently harmless portable objects designed to explode, is to avert the use of such devices, by calculation or misadventure, to attack civilians.

The Protocol also covers other manually placed injurious devices which are operated by remote control or a time-lapse mechanism by reference to the new article 2(5), which also repeats the original definition. The focus of Protocol II, in both its original and amended form, is partly upon civilian protection, in view of the inherently indiscriminate nature of such devices, and partly with the question of perfidy, particularly in relation to booby-trap devices. Article 3 of the amended Protocol makes provision for general restrictions on the use of the weapons concerned, stating in particular that:

> (3) It is prohibited in all circumstances to use any mine, booby-trap or other device which is designed or of a nature to cause superfluous injury or unnecessary suffering. ...
> (4) Weapons to which this Article applies shall strictly comply with the standards and limitations specified in the Technical Annex ...
> (5) It is prohibited to use mines, booby-traps or other devices specifically designed to detonate the munition by the presence of commonly available mine detectors ...
> (6) It is prohibited to use a self-deactivating mine equipped with an anti-handling device ... capable of functioning after the mine has ceased to be capable of functioning.
> (7) It is prohibited in all circumstances to direct weapons to which this Article applies, either in offence, defence or by way of reprisals, against the civilian population as such or against civilians or civilian objects.
> (8) The indiscriminate use of weapons to which this Article applies is prohibited ...
> (10) All feasible precautions shall be taken to protect civilians from the effects of weapons to which this Article applies. ...

The basic purpose of these provisions is to limit the use of landmines to their original and legitimate purpose: to block approach to a military objective by declared and marked minefields which will not have indiscriminate effects and which can be deactivated and cleared at the earliest feasible time. The root objection to landmines lies not in the nature of the weapons themselves, but in their common and highly dangerous misuse. The result is widespread injury to civilians who wander into unmarked minefields, and a perpetuation of this long after hostilities have terminated because of extreme difficulty in clearing unmarked and unrecorded minefields. The tragic toll of civilian death and injury from unrecorded minefields has been seen to an appalling extent in Afghanistan in the 1990s. Even in a conflict such as the 1982 Anglo-Argentine Falklands Conflict, unmarked minefields sown in the last stages of the conflict around Port Stanley remained a problem a decade later, because although the areas were fenced off, precise location and clearance of the mines proved exceedingly difficult.

Detailed specifications for the avoidance of these problems are set out in the Technical Annex to the amended Protocol. This requires that mines, other than remotely delivered mines, must be accurately recorded in location, along (with a view to effective clearance) with complete information about the type, number and mode of emplacement.[54] Remotely delivered mines must be located approximately, and the area within which they have fallen must be marked on the ground as soon as possible.[55] Mines must be marked in English or the relevant national language or languages, with the country of origin, month and year of production and serial or lot number.[56]

In order to avert the long-term effects of mines, Technical Annex article 2 requires that anti-personnel mines be rendered readily detectable to mine detection equipment. Article 3 requires, to the same end, that all remotely delivered anti-personnel mines should have self-destruct mechanisms which would cause a minimum of 90 per cent of such mines to self-destruct within 30 days of emplacement. Finally, article 4 of the Technical Annex set out an international sign for the marking of minefields, in the form of a triangle not smaller than 28 centimetres by 20 centimetres, or a sign not less than 15 centimetres square which is red or orange in colour with a yellow reflecting border. The sign is also required to contain the word 'mines' in Arabic, Chinese, English, French, Russian or Spanish, and also in the languages prevalent in the area concerned, unless, presumably, it is already included in this list.

Article 10 of the Protocol, significantly, requires by paragraph 1 that:

> Without delay after the cessation of active hostilities, all minefields, mined areas, mines, booby-traps and other devices shall be cleared, removed [or] destroyed ...

Given the differences in technical capacities of states, article 11 requires technological co-operation and assistance between states in the processes of mine clearance.

The historic problem with the law governing landmines has been the great difficulty in ensuring compliance, and the disastrous humanitarian consequences which have flowed from this. There was considerable disappointment that the decision of the Review Conference in amending the Protocol fell far short of an outright ban on landmines.[57] It may be suggested that if the amended Protocol is observed and maintained in practice, it will go far towards addressing the major concerns about the indiscriminacy of later 20th-century landmine usage and the long-term difficulties of clearance. This remains to be seen at the time of writing (late 1997), but if observance is not secured, the case for an outright ban will become unanswerable. A vigorous international campaign for a world-wide ban on landmines in the later 1990s continues, led by the International Committee of the Red Cross.[58]

Incendiary weapons Protocol III to the convention defines incendiary weapons by article 1(1) as:

> any ... which is primarily designed to set fire to objects or to cause injury to person through the action of flame, heat, or a combination thereof, produced by a chemical reaction of a substance delivered on the target.

Fire weapons are almost as old as organised warfare, and examples may be cited of medieval 'Greek fire' (almost certainly a primitive form of napalm), and later the fire ships used in 1588 against the Spanish Armada during the attempted invasion of England in the reign of Elizabeth I. Many weapons, including conventional explosive shells and bombs, are also very likely to cause fires on impact and explosion. However, article 1(1)(b)(ii) of Protocol III is careful to exclude:

> Munitions designed to combine penetration, blast or fragmentation effects with an additional incendiary effect, such as armour-piercing projectiles, fragmentation shells, explosive bombs and similar combined effects munitions in which the incendiary effect is not specifically designed to cause burn injury to persons, but to be used against military objectives, such as armoured vehicles, aircraft and installations or facilities.

Article 1(1)(b)(i) excludes weapons with 'incidental' potential incendiary effects, such as tracer bullets. There is a direct comparison to be made here with the 1868 Declaration of St Petersburg, which, it will be recalled, was concerned to exclude anti-personnel use of a weapon type which had originally been developed, quite legitimately, as a means of attack on armoured vehicles (in the 1860s, this meant armoured trains).

Article 2 of the Protocol forbids the use of incendiary weapons so defined against the civilian population as such, or against military targets in a concentrated area of civilian occupation when the weapon is air-delivered, and even when delivered by other means unless the target is sufficiently far removed from the civilian area to allow effective measures to minimise civilian loss. Forests and other plant cover cannot be made the subject of incendiary attack unless they are being used to conceal military objectives or have otherwise by their use become military objectives.

Protocol III is largely aimed to avert the horror of the firestorms which resulted from some of the episodes of very heavy mixed incendiary and conventional bombing in the later stages of the Second World War. The best-known, but by no means only, example was the Hamburg firestorm of 28 July 1943,[59] but an earlier example was seen in the vast fires created by the incendiary bombing of London on 10 May 1941.[60]

The Review Conference and the addition of Protocol IV on Blinding Laser Weapons Article 8 of the 1980 UN Convention on Conventional Weapons provides for Review Conferences to consider additions or amendments to existing Protocols or the addition of new Protocols. Starting in 1995, a Review Conference considered a range of possible further Protocols, including one presented by Switzerland to ban the use of small-calibre weapons which at ranges of 25 metres would transfer 25 joules or more of energy per centimetre for the first 15 centimetres of entry to the human body.[61] Ultimately, however, debate centred on landmines and laser weapons. The most difficult debate concerned landmines, and concluded with agreement on 3 May 1996 to the amendments to Protocol II to the convention referred to above. This was a useful step, although it fell far short of what the ICRC had hoped for.[62]

A more sweeping success was obtained with the adoption of Protocol IV to the convention, dealing with blinding laser weapons. Laser weapons have something in common with the 'death rays' which were a staple of the wilder dimensions of military speculation before the Second World War. They are silent, sudden and effectively undetectable before they strike. They also have the potential, if they strike the eyes of an adversary, to cause permanent blindness. It is this fact which has, in effect, classified them as a weapon causing 'unnecessary suffering' contrary to the spirit enshrined in the 1868 Declaration of St Petersburg. The Protocol is extremely simple, comprising only four articles. Article 1 provides that:

> It is prohibited to employ laser weapons specifically designed, as their sole combat function or as one of their combat functions, to cause permanent blindness to unenhanced vision, that is to the naked eye or to the eye with corrective eyesight devices. The High Contracting Parties shall not transfer such weapons to any State or non-State entity.

Article 3 excludes laser systems which may blind as an incidental or collateral effect of legitimate military use – for example, this would include modern laser-guided weapons systems. Where such systems are employed, however, states are required by article 3 to take 'all feasible precautions', including suitable training of operating personnel, to avoid the infliction of permanent blindness. 'Permanent blindness' is defined precisely as:

> irreversible and uncorrectable loss of vision which is seriously disabling with no prospect of recovery. Serious disability is equivalent to visual acuity of less than 20/200 Snellen measured using both eyes.

It will be noted that emphasis in Protocol IV is on *deliberate* infliction of permanent blindness as a calculated objective of a weapon system. 'Collateral' infliction of such injury is not outlawed, although every endeavour to avoid it is urged. (It is worth noting here the irony that in their potential military use laser weapons are feared as inflictors of blindness, whilst in medical use they have been the means of saving sight in many cases.[63])

Poison Weapons

Such weapons have been banned from ancient times, and they were proscribed in ancient Greek and Roman practice. The ban is found in its modern form in article 23 of the Land Warfare Regulations annexed to the 1907 Hague Convention IV which provides that 'it is especially forbidden ... to employ poison or poisoned weapons'. This was anciently conceived in terms of poisoned-edge weapons, such as poison arrowheads, but it has been raised as an issue in relation to much more modern weapons. However, this ban did not include the proscription of gas weapons such as were used in the First World War, which were very clearly for the most part poison weapons, nor has it proven very relevant to nuclear weapons, which are, perhaps, rather more dubiously 'poisonous' in the terms intended here.

The end result is that most of the modern armaments which might generally be thought to fall within the area of 'poison weapons' have been the subject of new provision. This illustrates the difficulty in expanding the scope of a ban into areas which might seem at the very least closely analogous, which was also encountered in relation to extending the ban on small-calibre explosive projectiles to dum-dum bullets in the late 19th century.[64] Nevertheless, the traditional ban on poison weapons retains some value in modern warfare, and would certainly cover any deliberate attempt to contaminate sources of drinking water, for example, although this would also be unlawful from a variety of other points of view, including basic provisions for the protection of civilians.[65]

Chemical and Biological Weapons

Chemical and biological warfare is rightly considered one of the more terrible dimensions of warfare in the 20th century, but it was not an innovation of that century. Choking smokes were used in ancient warfare to drive defenders out of confined spaces, and in the medieval period bodies of plague victims were catapulted into besieged towns to spread plague amongst the population. In the 19th century, Thomas Cochrane, Lord Dundonald, who served victoriously in the Greek, Chile-Peruvian and Brazilian navies as well as the Royal Navy, suggested the military use of sulphur fumes, and a commission was set up to study the plan, but the idea was rejected in the Crimean War of 1855.

Gas warfare was expressly banned by 1899 Hague Declaration 2, which proscribed the use of projectiles solely devised for the diffusion of asphyxiating gases. Despite this, gas weapons were widely used in the First World War. The first chemical gas attack in the war was launched by German units against French Colonial troops near Ypres on 22 April 1915, and thereafter gas was used by both the Central and Allied powers, with mass casualties until the end of the war in 1918. A number of chemical agents were used, lethal as well as irritant or lachrymatory (tear-inducing), including chlorine, phosgene and dichlorethyl sulphide (mustard gas). In February 1918, the International Committee of the Red Cross denounced this 'criminal' means of warfare, without mentioning a specific state, observing the usual, non-confrontational ICRC discreet diplomatic pressure for observance of law.[66] After the war, the 1919 Treaty of Versailles, article 171, reaffirmed the unlawfulness of chemical gas warfare, as did the 1922 Treaty of Washington. Finally, the 1925 Geneva Protocol for the Prohibition of the Use in War of Asphyxiating, Poisonous or Other Gases and of Bacteriological Methods of Warfare (the 1925 Geneva Gas Protocol) was concluded. The Protocol provides that:

> Whereas the use in war of asphyxiating, poisonous or other gases, and of all analogous liquids materials or devices, has been justly condemned by the general opinion of the civilised world; and Whereas the prohibition of such use has been declared in Treaties; [the High Contracting Parties declare that they] … accept this prohibition [and] agree to extend this prohibition to the use of bacteriological methods of warfare …

This prohibition, in marked contrast with its predecessor of 1899, has been one of the most successful arms control provisions. There have been some violations, the known instances being by Italy in the invasion of Ethiopia in 1935–36, by Japan in the invasion of Manchuria and China from 1937 onwards, and by Iraq during the 1980–88 Gulf War. Iraq's transgression led to a protest from the International Committee of the Red Cross, in similar terms to that issued in 1918,[67] and more explicit condemnation was issued by the United Nations Security Council on 21 March 1986. A number of other possible instances have been reported, with some initial scientific backing.[68] The claims that 'yellow rain' was a product of Soviet chemical warfare agents in Afghanistan, Cambodia (then Kampuchea) and Laos made in 1981 by the USA were not supported by scientific evidence.[69] However, gas was used in non-international conflict against the Kurdish minority population in northern Iraq in the late 1980s, for example in an attack on the town of Halabjah in March 1988.[70] These violations were for the most part characterised by the absence of equivalent technological capacity on the part of the victims, and a belief that the action could be concealed from the rest of the world.[71] The case of the 1980–88 Iran–Iraq Gulf War was different, and here the Iraqi motivation seems to have been to break a massive infantry stalemate along an extended front, much as was attempted in the First World War, and with equal lack of success.

The absence of gas warfare in the Second World War in Europe merits mention. Both the Third Reich and the Allies had large stocks of chemical warfare materials, including agents like tabun. Hitler, who had been mildly gassed as a Corporal in a Bavarian infantry regiment in the First World War,[72] withheld gas use on the western front because he was well aware that it was unreliable weapon which could be redirected back against his own forces by a mere change of wind direction, and also from fear of likely retaliation in kind by the Allies. He did, apparently, consider the use of gas against Russian forces on the eastern front, and in a broadcast on 10 May 1942, the British Prime Minister, Winston Churchill, stated:

> We shall treat the unprovoked use of poison gas against our Russian ally exactly as if it were used against ourselves, and ... carry [out] gas warfare ... [on] Germany.[73]

Britain itself considered a chemical response in the days of imminent Axis invasion in 1940, but rejected the idea on ethical, political and practical grounds.[74] Biological weapons have seen even less use, although experiments into the feasibility of anthrax toxin weapons were certainly carried out in the 1930s, and it is possible, although very far from certain, that biological weapons may actually have been used in the Sino-Janapese War just prior to the Second World War in the Far East.[75] More recently, it has been argued that 'Gulf War Syndrome' – ill health and debility suffered by a significant number of Coalition military personnel after the 1990–91 Gulf Conflict – may have resulted from such weapons, but the case for this must at the time of writing (1997) be considered at best unproven in the light of the information which has been made public.

Despite the very considerable success of the 1925 Geneva Gas Protocol, it is subject to two considerable limitations. In the first place the Protocol was ratified by many states subject to a reservation permitting second or responsive, but not first, use of the proscribed weapons and, in consequence, this must be regarded as the general law which has emerged from it. Secondly, the Protocol is entirely a proscription on *use*, and no reference is made to manufacture or stockpiling. In order to address these issues in relation to biological weapons, the 1972 UN Convention on Prohibition of the Development, Production and Stockpiling of Bacteriological, Biological and Toxin Weapons and Their Destruction was concluded.

As its title suggests, the convention prohibits the manufacture and stockpiling of agents of this type for hostile purposes. The key point here is that of 'hostile' purposes. Many biological toxins, etc., have perfectly legitimate uses, for example in medical prophylaxis and research, so the judgement of what is 'hostile' is largely contextual and quantitative. The retention of a small quantity of anthrax toxin, for example, could be viewed as medically or scientifically legitimate, but holding large quantities of it cannot be seen as other than 'hostile' and illegitimate. The 1972 Convention also prohibits transfer of biological toxin agents, etc., between states as part of any planned hostile activity, and makes provision for mandatory assistance to any state which is a victim of biological attack.

There are obvious difficulties of monitoring and judgement here, and these arise in even more acute form in the context of chemical agents. Amongst the difficulties are the fact that many chemical agents have large-scale legitimate uses – chlorine, for example, is a commonplace industrial chemical – and judgements about when a holding is legitimate or illegitimate are thus rendered much more difficult than is the case for biological toxins. For this reason, twenty years elapsed before an equivalent convention dealing with these weapons and agents was agreed. The 1992 UN Convention on the Prohibition of the Development, Production and Stockpiling of Chemical Weapons follows the pattern of the 1972 Biological Weapons Convention, and provides by article I(1) that:

> Each State Party to this Convention undertakes never under any circumstances:
> (a) To develop, produce, otherwise acquire, stockpile or retain chemical weapons, or transfer, directly or indirectly, chemical weapons to anyone;
> (b) To use chemical weapons;

(c) To engage in any military preparedness to use chemical weapons;
(d) To assist, encourage or induce, in any way, anyone to engage in any activity prohibited to a State Party under this Convention.

To avoid weakening the convention's effect, reservations are forbidden by article XXII. The main problems are again those of monitoring and enforcement. With this in view, the 1992 Convention sets out detailed provision in articles VIII and IX for the International Organization for the Prohibition of Chemical Weapons (IOPCW). Under Article IX(8)–(25), provision is made for the conduct of on-site challenge inspections at the request of any state party to the convention, with only 72 hours' notice, to check on alleged non-compliance. This sounds impressive, but the experience of UN weapons inspectors in Iraq after the 1990–91 Gulf Conflict must give rise to some moderation of expectations.

In cases of violations, article XII of the convention sets out three basic levels of response. These range from restrictions on a state's rights under the convention pending restoration of compliance, through peaceful 'collective measures' by the other states party to the convention, to reference, in especially grave cases, to the UN Security Council. In the latter event, measures of force would be within the range of options, notionally pursuant to article 43 of the UN Charter, but in current circumstances practically under article 39.

Nuclear Weapons

From time to time, an ultimate 'horror weapon' is produced which creates, or is perceived to create, a crisis for political and military ethics and for legal regulation. In the Middle Ages, horror was expressed over the crossbow and 'Greek fire' (an early form of napalm). The pre-eminent horror weapon of the second half of the 20th century has undoubtedly been nuclear armaments. Early civil and medical experimentation with radioactive substances was conducted with considerable ignorance of their dangers, with the result that many, if not most, of the early workers in this field died from cancers induced by handling these materials.

The military use of nuclear technology developed during the Second World War, which in its closing phases became the first, and so far only, nuclear war, and it is to be hoped that the experience will not be repeated. In subsequent debate, the myth has become generally accepted that it was only the Allies, and specifically the USA, who were engaged in military nuclear developments, but this is not true. The Third Reich was actively engaged in military nuclear research, although this was somewhat impeded by paucity of materials, Hitler's ethnic prejudices, and possibly by internal sabotage. It is nevertheless highly likely that the 'secret weapon' on which Hitler based so many hopes as the Reich lurched towards defeat may not have been the V1 and V2 'flying bombs', but a form of nuclear bomb. It seems that the Nazis were working towards a bomb which would release a cloud of radioactive materials by means of a conventional explosion, and whilst this would have been much less devastating than the fission weapons dropped on Hiroshima and Nagasaki, it would still have had a profoundly injurious effect.[76] Japan was also engaged in military nuclear research, but abandoned it early on, on the grounds that lack of resources meant that no useful weapon was likely to be produced by the anticipated end of the war.[77]

Since 1945 there has been intense debate on the legal status of the possession and use of nuclear weapons. The argument sometimes advanced that such weapons are in some sense *sui generis*, and therefore outwith the general law of arms control, has always seemed both curious and illogical. Nuclear weapons are *weapons*, and, although they do raise specific questions of considerable difficulty, the general legal principles of 'unnecessary suffering' and the ban upon indiscriminacy must clearly apply as much to them as to a conventional explosive projectile. The question is rather *how* such principles apply, and with what effect.

The lawfulness of the nuclear bombing of Hiroshima and Nagasaki was considered by the Tokyo District Court in *Ryuichi Shimoda et al.* v. *The State*.[78] The plaintiffs in this case sought to establish that the nuclear bombings had been unlawful, and that the Japanese Government, which had abandoned all and any potential claims against the USA arising from the Second World War under the peace treaty, was therefore liable to compensate them from their losses suffered as a result of the bombing. The action failed because of the plaintiffs' lack of *locus standi* in public international law, but the court found, in effect *obiter dicta*, that the bombings of Hiroshima and Nagasaki had been unlawful as they were 'indiscriminate' attacks on 'undefended' towns, and also because they tended to inflict 'unnecessary suffering'. The reference to 'undefended' towns, taken from the Land Warfare Regulations annexed to 1907 Hague Convention IV, article 25, appears to have been both rather anachronistic and strictly inaccurate. The 1907 reference was really to towns under siege which declared non-resistance, whereas Hiroshima and Nagasaki were, like any modern cities in time of war, defended by anti-aircraft artillery, and were also the location of major military industries and military facilities. In other words, a properly directed conventional bombardment would have been entirely lawful in 1945, or indeed under the terms of the present *jus in bello*.

The more important arguments, which are still central to the military nuclear issue, were those of 'indiscriminacy' and 'unnecessary suffering'. The bombs dropped on the two Japanese cities were very 'dirty' in terms of the resulting nuclear fallout, so they can only be considered to have been indiscriminate in their effects. The long-term suffering that they inflicted, notably but not only their carcinogenic effects, makes out a strong case that they may also have fallen foul of the basic St Petersburg prohibition on the infliction of 'unnecessary suffering'. The counter-case commonly made out – that the bombings averted a sanguinary conventional campaign fought through the islands of Japan, in an ultimate continuation of the savage fighting through the Pacific 'island-hopping' campaign, which would have caused vastly greater numbers of casualties – has some strength, certainly in the light of the limited technical knowledge of the time. However, it may still be wondered why some warning demonstration could not have been staged far from population centres, if the aim was indeed to underline to the Japanese Government the fact that continuation of the war would be pointless. With the benefit of hindsight, the primitive, 'dirty' bombs used at Hiroshima and Nagasaki must be considered to contravene basic principles of the *jus in bello*.

It follows from what has been said above that, at the minimum, many *uses* of nuclear weapons must be considered unlawful. The larger question is whether nuclear weapons are unlawful *per se*, and if not, when, if ever, they might lawfully be used.

Arguments have been advanced since the Shimoda case, based on the general St Petersburg 'principle of unnecessary suffering', that their use would be unequivocally unlawful.[79] Others have argued on the basis of more specific prohibitions, as did Schwarzenberger in contending that radiation effects might be brought within the ancient customary proscription of poison weapons.[80] In the 1996 Advisory Opinion of the International Court of Justice (see below), this idea was rejected on the basis that the 'prime or exclusive' use of nuclear weapons is not to 'poison or asphyxiate', which leaves open the question of the nature of the effects of radiation upon human beings. One of the reasons for the adoption of this view seems to have been that nuclear weapons are to a significant degree intended in their immediate effect as 'blast' weapons. There is a strict logic to this view, but as Eric David suggests:

> [This] is tantamount to stating that if one merely adds explosives to a chemical weapon it is no longer chemical, or even that if one combines legal effects with the illegal effects of a weapon it is no longer illegal.[81]

Nevertheless, the law of arms control is supremely an area in which ambiguity and arguments by analogy cannot safely be relied upon, as the instance of dumdum bullets showed in 1899.[82] It may reasonably be contended that an argument founded on indiscriminacy, which would apply to most uses of nuclear weapons, is more strongly based.

The United Nations General Assembly condemned the use of nuclear weapons as contrary to the ban on indiscriminate attacks and to the principles of the UN Charter in its Resolution 1653 (XVI) of 1961 on the Prohibition of Use of Nuclear Weapons for War Purposes, which was further supported by UN General Assembly Resolution 1936 of 1961. UN General Assembly Resolutions are not in themselves a source of public international law,[83] although they can indicate the trend of international consensus, and thereby the crystallisation of developing law and practice, being to that extent possibly a form of 'soft law'. To suggest, as some have, that in this context a UN General Assembly Resolutions are *ex hypothesi* law-constitutive 'state practice' grossly exaggerates their significance.[84] In the case of Resolution 1936 of 1961, 55 states supported it, 20 opposed it and 26 abstained, and whilst this was a clear majority in favour, it was hardly an overwhelming consensus.

The question of nuclear weapons finally received formal international legal consideration in 1996, when the International Court of Justice issued its Advisory Opinion on the Threat or Use of Nuclear Weapons.[85] The court had received two requests for an advisory opinion on the matter, one from the World Health Organization, which was held to fall outside the competence of the organisation, and one from the UN General Assembly which led to the ultimate substantive opinion.[86] The opinion of the court disappointed many expectations, and has been treated with derision by some commentators. The question put to the court posed many difficulties, because it was, and is, an intensely 'political' issue – as the fury of some of the reaction to the court's opinion suggests – and it is also a matter in which the law is by no means as clear as advocates of all the possible views tend to suggest.

The court's opinion included many positive and useful elements. In the first place, it disposed once and for all of the extraordinary idea that nuclear weapons somehow fall outwith the laws of armed conflict, and made it clear that the relevant rules and principles of that law apply to nuclear weapons as much as to any others. It remarked that:

> [The] threat or use of nuclear weapons should ... be compatible with the requirements of the international law applicable in armed conflict, particularly those of ... international humanitarian law ...[87]

The court considered the spectrum of legal objections to nuclear weapons and their actual or potential use, including both the *jus ad bellum* and *jus in bello* dimensions of the potentially applicable law. So far as the *jus ad bellum* is concerned, the central issues were inevitably the interpretation of articles 2(4) and 51 of the UN Charter. The former essentially bans aggressive threat or use of force in the conduct of international relations; the latter permits use of armed force in the exercise of the 'inherent' right of individual or collective self-defence if 'an armed attack occurs'. The court's conclusion on this was the now notorious *non liquet*, stating, in essence, that the law is not clear.[88] The court therefore stated that it could not:

> conclude definitely whether the threat or use of nuclear weapons would be lawful or unlawful in the extreme circumstance of self-defence, in which the very survival of a State would be at stake.[89]

This *non liquet* has been much scorned on the basis that a court which is asked a question must necessarily supply an answer. In contentious litigation this is undoubtedly the case, and in the case of the International Court of Justice, article 38 of its Statute provides that the function of the court 'is to *decide* such disputes as are submitted to it'. In contrast, article 65 of the Statute provides that, 'The Court *may* give an advisory opinion on any legal question ...' (emphases added). An 'opinion' that the law is unclear is quite a different matter from a refusal to reach a judgment in a contentious case arising from particular facts. It may be suggested that in this case opinion was reserved unless and until such a case may arise, which it must devoutly be hoped it will not.

In the area of the *jus in bello*, the various arguments which sought to bring nuclear weapons within the scope of specific proscriptions, such as that on poison weapons, failed, largely for the reasons set out above. This left the essential arguments of indiscriminacy and disproportionality of response. It would be very difficult to counter the proposition that nuclear weapons would in the vast majority of cases fall foul of either or both of these proscriptions. It is often contended that in terms of target discrimination, 'surgical strike' battlefield weapons would be very different from the large and 'dirty' bombs dropped on Japan in 1945, for example, but this would depend on where and in what circumstances they were used, and even then the question of proportionality – including, implicitly, 'unnecessary suffering' – would remain as a hurdle to be surmounted.

The ultimate conclusion of the court, by seven votes to seven, with the casting vote of the President, was that:

> the threat or use of nuclear weapons would generally be contrary to the rules of international law applicable in armed conflict, and in particular the principles and rules of humanitarian law.

> However, in ... the current state of international law ... the Court cannot conclude definitively whether the threat or use of nuclear weapons would be lawful or unlawful in the extreme circumstance of self-defence, in which the very survival of a State would be at stake.[90]

This opinion has angered many who campaigned for a definitive ban, but it must be pointed out that the court does not have the power to create such a ban if none exists in the present law. What the court has in practice done, as even its critics admit, is to present its advice in such a way that under existing principles of both the *jus in bello* and the *jus ad bellum*, it is difficult to imagine many, or in reality even any likely, circumstances in which the *use* of nuclear weapons would be lawful. Professor Greenwood has commented that:

> the Court was right to find that international law does not at present contain a specific prohibition of the use of nuclear weapons. Any use of a nuclear weapon would be subject to the ordinary principles of the law on the use of force and of international humanitarian law. Those principles do not permit an abstract determination that, irrespective of what circumstances might exist at any time in the future, no use of any sort of nuclear weapon could ever be compatible with them.[91]

The court may be argued to have stated the legal position correctly as it found it, and indeed, to have done much to disperse some of the more obfuscatory arguments, on both sides, which have beset this question since 1945. Further development in this area is a matter for political debate and, perhaps, ultimately new treaty provision.

In addition to the general law, notice must be taken of regional nuclear bans. The 1967 Treaty of Tlatelolco and the 1985 Treaty of Rarotonga respectively impose bans on nuclear armaments in South America and the South Pacific area, and similar bans have been proposed in Scandinavia and the Balkans. Such regional bans do not in themselves create general law, although they do represent evidence for regional state practices, and may indicate a trend of general opinion.

In the 1990s, the focus of nuclear debate in the post-Cold War era is at least as much on the dangers of proliferation as anything else. The tendency for 'lost' weapons, skills and technology to find their way into dangerously unstable parts of the world, where even such assurance as the 'mutual assured destruction' strategies of Cold War deterrence may have afforded cannot be assumed, represents a different, and no less serious, danger to the perilous balance which the Cold War itself represented. In this, as in many other such issues, the fundamental problem may be that once a technology has been devised or invented, it is practically impossible to 'disinvent' it, and so, as ever, the price of safety may be said to be eternal vigilance – not least in maintaining the legal safeguards which do exist.

Notes

1 See pp. 231–2.
2 It may very broadly be said that strategy involves planning and setting the objectives for a military campaign, whereas tactics involve the planning and implementation of conduct in specific encounters with the enemy in the course of such a campaign.
3 W.S. Churchill, *The Second World War* (Penguin, 1989; 1st published by Cassell, 1959), pp. 777–8.
4 See p. 123.
5 See p. 105.
6 See Denis Mack Smith, *Mussolini* (Paladin, 1883; 1st published by Weidenfeld and Nicolson, 1981), pp. 349–50.
7 P. Rowe, *Defence: The Legal Implication* (Brassey's Defence Publishers, 1987), p. 113.
8 See M. Gilbert, *Second World War* (Phoenix, 1995; 1st published by Weidenfield and Nicolson, 1989), p. 622.
9 See pp. 164–7.
10 For general discussion of special forces operations in this context, see P. Rowe, 'The Use of Special Forces and the Laws of War: Wearing the Uniform of the Enemy or Civilian Clothes and of Spying and Assassination' (1994) XXXIII *Revue de Droit Militaire et de Droit de la Guerre*, pp. 209–34.
11 See above.
12 For an interesting discussion of this, see D. Williams, *Liners in Battledress* (Conway Maritime Press, 1989), pp. 46–8; see also J.H. Isherwood, *Steamers of the Past* (Journal of Commerce and Shipping Telegraph, 1966), p. 61.
13 For an account of this action, see F. Forstmeier, *SMS Emdem* (Warship Profile 25, Profile Publications, 1972), pp. 11–14.
14 W.L. Shirer, *The Rise and Fall of the Third Reich* (Pan, 1964; 1st published in the UK by Secker & Warburg, 1960), p. 1,137, citing *Nazi Conspiracy and Aggression* (Nuremberg Documents) Vol. III, pp. 416–17.
15 See p. 19.
16 This term, which is not used by the Protocol, derives from air warfare.
17 See p. 244.
18 Article 24(4).
19 See Chapters 4 and 5.
21 W.L. Shirer, op.cit., p. 933; see general discussion in ibid., pp. 927–36.
22 See J.M. Spaight, *Air Power and War Rights* (Longman Green, 1947), p. 271.
23 H. Blix, 'Area Bombardment: Rules and Reasons' (1978) 59 *British Yearbook of International Law*, p. 31, at p. 57.
24 See pp. 218–23.
25 As to the application of international humanitarian law to the armed conflict(s) in former Yugoslavia, see p. 255.
26 For discussion, see Agora, 'The Downing of Iran Air Flights 655' (1989) 63 *American Journal of International Law*, p. 318.
27 C. Greenwood, 'Customary International Law and the First Geneva Protocol of 1977 in the Gulf Conflict', in P. Rowe (ed.), *The Gulf War 1990–91 in International and English Law* (Sweet & Maxwell/Routledge, 1993), p. 63, at p. 85, citing US

Department of Defense, *Conduct of the Persian Gulf Conflict: An Interim Report to Congress* (July 1991), p. 4.
28 *Independent* (London), 18 February 1991.
29 See pp. 115–6.
30 A. and J. Tusa, *The Nuremberg Trial* (BBC Books, 1995; 1st published by Macmillan London, 1983), p. 360.
31 See pp. 116–7.
32 (1982) 53 *British Yearbook of International Law*, p. 542.
33 See C.R. Symmons, 'The Maritime Zones around the Falkland Islands' (1988) 37 *International and Comparative Law Quarterly*, pp. 283–324.
34 See p. 103.
35 R. Leckow, 'The Iran–Iraq Conflict in the Gulf: The Law of War Zones' (1988) 37 *International and Comparative Law Quarterly*, pp. 629–44.
36 See p. 233.
37 See p. 122.
38 See A.G.Y. Thorpe, 'Mine Warfare at Sea – Some Legal Aspects of the Future' 18 *Ocean Development and International Law*, p. 272.
39 For general discussion of this, see Chapter 10.
40 L.F.E. Goldie, in Trooboff and Goldie (eds), *Law and Responsibility in Warfare: The Vietnam Experience* (University of North Carolina Press, 1975), p. 93.
41 A. Roberts, 'Failures in Protection the Environment in the 1990–91 Gulf War', in P. Rowe (ed.), *The Gulf War 1990–91 in International and English Law* (Routledge/Sweet & Maxwell, 1993), p. 111, at p. 114.
42 *Independent* (London), 2 March 1991.
43 For discussion, see B. Bakan, 'Climate Response to Smoke from the Burning of Oil Wells in Kuwait' (1991) 351 *Nature*, pp. 367–71.
44 See pp. 240–3.
45 See p. 243.
46 See P. Francis, *Volcanoes* (Penguin, 1976), pp. 113–14.
47 See, for example, K. Hulme, 'Armed Conflict, Wanton Ecological Devastation and Scorched Earth Policies: How the 1990–91 Gulf Conflict Revealed the Inadequacies of the Current Laws to Ensure Effective Protection and Inadequacies of the Current Laws to Ensure Effective Protection and Preservation of the Environment' (1997) 2 *Journal of Armed Conflict Law*, p. 45–81.
48 A. Roberts, 'Failures in Protecting the Environment in the 1990–91 Gulf War', in P. Rowe (ed.), *The Gulf War 1990–91 in International and English Law* (Sweet & Maxwell/Routledge, 1993), p. 111, at p. 144.
49 See p. 19.
50 For discussion, see G. Best, *Humanity in Warfare* (Methuen, 1983; 1st published by Weidenfeld and Nicolson, 1980), p. 162.
51 As to the meaning of this phrase, see p. 244.
52 This is provided for in article 6 in the same terms as the equivalent provision in the four 1949 Geneva Conventions.
53 See p. 213.
54 Technical Annex, Article 1(a).
55 Ibid., article 1(b).
56 Ibid., article 1(d).
56 See P. Herby, 'Third Session of the Review Conference of States Party to the 1980 UN Convention on Certain Conventional Weapons' (1996) 36 *International Review of the Red Cross*, pp. 361–8
58 See below.
59 See M. Gilbert, op.cit., pp. 447–8.
60 See W.S. Churchill, op.cit., pp. 391–2.

61 See E. Prokosch, 'The Swiss Draft Protocol on Small-calibre Weapon Systems' (1995) 35 *International Review of the Red Cross*, pp. 411–25.
62 See P. Herby, 'Third Session of the Review Conference ...' (1996) 36 *International Review of the Red Cross*, pp. 361–8.
63 Not least in cases of retinal haemorrhage which may be associated with diabetes melitus.
64 See p. 232.
65 See Chapter 7.
66 *Appeal to the Belligerents*, 6 February 1918; see Stockholm International Peace Research Institute, *The Problem of Chemical and Biological Weapons* (Almqvist and Wiksell, Stockholm, 6 vols, 1971–75), Vol. VI, p. 44.
67 ICRC Press Release No. 1567, 23 March 1988.
68 They include Afghanistan, Cambodia and Angola. Dr Aubin Heyndrickz is reported after study of these conflicts to have considered that Cuban forces in Angola may have used gas against Unita forces in Angola. See report in *Daily Telegraph* (London), 10 August 1988.
69 See J. Goldblat, 'The Biological Weapons Convention: An Overview' (1997) 37 *International Review of the Red Cross*, pp. 251–65, at p. 263.
70 *Guardian* (London), 24 March 1988.
71 For discussion, see H. McCoubrey, 'The Regulation of Chemical and Biological Weapons', in H. Fox and M.A. Meyer (eds), *Armed Conflict and the New Law, Vol. II: Effecting Compliance* (British Institute of International and Comparative Law, 1993), pp. 123–39 at p. 134–6.
72 See A. Speer, *Inside the Third Reich* (Sphere, 1971; 1st published by Macmillan, 1970), pp. 552–3.
73 Cited by E.M. Spiers, *Chemical Warfare* (Macmillan, 1985), p. 73.
74 See ibid.
75 See V. Adams, *Chemical Warfare, Chemical Disarmament* (Macmillan, 1989), p. 11, citing Atthur H. Westing, 'The Threat of Biological Warfare' (1985) 35 *Bioscience*, No. 10, p. 627.
76 For discussion of the Third Reich's military nuclear research, see G. Brooks, *Hitler's Nuclear Weapons* (Leo Cooper, 1992).
77 See ibid., pp. 190–2.
78 (1964) *Japanese Annual of International Law*, p. 212; see also L. Friedman, *The Law of War: A Documentary History* (Random House, 1972), Vol. II, p. 1,688; see also R.A. Falk, 'The Shimoda Case: A Legal Appraisal of the Atomic Attacks upon Hiroshima and Nagasaki' (1965) 59 *American Journal of International Law*, p. 759.
79 See N. Grief, 'The Legality of Nuclear Weapons', in I. Pogany (ed.), *Nuclear Weapons and International Law* (Avebury, 1987), p. 25.
80 See G. Schwarzenberger, *The Legality of Nuclear Weapons* (London, 1958), especially at p. 28.
81 E. David, 'The Opinion of the International Court of Justice on the Legality of the Use of Nuclear Weapons' (1997) 37 *International Review of the Red Cross*, pp. 21–34, at p. 26.
82 See above.
83 See article 38 of the Statute of the International Court of Justice.
84 See Advisory Opinion of the International Court of Justice, *Legality of the Threat or Use of Nuclear Weapons*, 8 July 1996.
85 International Court of Justice Communiqué 96/23, 8 July 1996.
86 For discussion, see D. Kritsiotis, 'The Fate of Nuclear Weapons after the 1996 Advisory Opinions of the World Court' (1996) 1 *Journal of Armed Conflict Law*, pp. 95–119, at pp. 95–102.
87 International Court of Justice Advisory Opinion, para. 105(2)D.

88 For discussion, see T.L.H. McCorack, 'A *Non Liquet* on Nuclear Weapons: The ICJ Avoids the Application of General Principles of International Humanitarian Law' (1997) 37 *International Review of the Red Cross*, pp. 76–91.
89 International Court of Justice Advisory Opinion, para. 105(2)E.
90 Ibid.
91 C. Greenwood, 'The Advisory Opinion on Nuclear Weapons and the Contribution of the International Court to International Humanitarian Law' (1997) 37 *International Review of the Red Cross*, pp. 65–75 at p. 75.

9 Humanitarian Provision in Non-international Armed Conflicts

Civil wars are amongst the most bitterly fought of all armed conflicts, primarily because the adherents of the opposing side, whether military or civilian, tend to be seen as either traitors or oppressors, rather than as citizens of a hostile state doing their own duty. As a result, humanitarianism is even less regarded in such conflicts than in international armed conflicts. By the same token, both the substance and the application of humanitarian norms in non-international armed conflicts present significantly greater difficulties.

An initial difficulty is the definition of a non-international armed conflict. A bank robbery involving a confrontation between armed robbers and the police is obviously in one sense a 'non-international armed conflict', but is hardly one attracting the governance of the *jus in bello*. At the other extreme, a non-international armed conflict on the grand scale may well take on many of the attributes of a quasi-international conflict.

Common article 3 of the four 1949 Geneva Conventions, which sets out a minimum humanitarian provision for non-international armed conflicts, is stated to apply to armed conflicts:

> not of an international character occurring in the territory of one of the High Contracting Parties.

This is somewhat open-ended definition, which the ICRC Commentary on the 1949 Conventions interprets at least as requiring a 'genuine armed conflict' on a level greater than mere banditry. The potential ambiguities are significantly clarified by the much more extensive definition afforded by 1977 Protocol II Additional to the 1949 Geneva Conventions, article 1(1), which defines the 'material field of application' of the Protocol as:

> all armed conflicts ... not covered by Article 1 of [1977 Additional Protocol I] ... relating to ... International Armed Conflicts ... which take place in the territory of a High Contracting Party between its armed forces and dissident armed forces or other organized armed groups which, under responsible command, exercise such control over a part of its territory as to enable them to carry out sustained and concerted military operations and to implement [Protocol II].

This avoids many of the natural doubts which arise over the application of international humanitarian law to violent internal confrontations, and in particular fears over the potential or apparent legitimisation of terrorism.[1] The dissident armed forces must be under 'responsible command', meaning that they must have a hierarchical chain of command responsibility under some ultimate directing authority. They must also exercise quasi-governmental control of territory within the state concerned which enables them to carry out 'sustained and concerted military operations'. The Protocol does not precisely define this phrase, but the ICRC Commentary on 1977 Additional Protocol II refers to:

> continuity and persistence ... [in] military operations conceived and planned by organized armed groups.[2]

Sporadic terrorist activity is thus placed outwith the Protocol. Article 1(2) of 1977 Additional Protocol II expressly excludes:

> situations of internal disturbances and tensions, such as riots, isolated and sporadic acts of violence and other acts of a similar nature ...

Finally, and most significantly, the dissident forces must be both willing and able to implement the provisions of the Protocol themselves. Further complications arise where a *prima facie* non-international armed conflict may be 'internationalised' under the provision for self-determinatory armed struggles 'against colonial domination and alien occupation and against racist regimes' made by 1977 Additional Protocol I, article 1(4), but these are rare.

These definitions are probably the best that can be achieved, but there remain dangerous ambiguities, and perhaps understandably, states have been extremely reluctant to accept that either common article 3 or 1977 Additional Protocol II might be applicable to internal conflicts within their territory. The obvious need is for some external system of objective assessment, but this hardly seems to be a practical possibility. The International Committee of the Red Cross is for good reasons unwilling to assume this role, and it is unlikely that any bodies having *locus standi* to raise such an issue before the International Court of Justice would wish to become involved. The answer no doubt lies in an accepted canon of juristic interpretation, but how such a canon might be developed in practice is far from clear. However, the ICRC Commentary on common article 3 to the 1949 Geneva Conventions does make the important point that much of the article, and indeed much of 1977 Additional Protocol II, is essentially an affirmation of basic human rights provision which might be taken to be applicable in any event.

It is also essential to note that a proviso to common article 3 of the 1949 Geneva Conventions makes clear that its provision does not carry any implication as to the legal status of the parties in conflict. This point is repeated in greater detail by article 3 of 1977 Additional Protocol II, which states that the Protocol may not be invoked to compromise the sovereignty of a state affected by internal armed conflict or to impugn the right of such a state to maintain or re-establish law and order within its territory or to defend its national unity and integrity.

The difficulties of definition were painfully illustrated by the armed conflicts in former Yugoslavia during the 1990s. In so far as the conflicts involved hostilities between successor states of the former Federal Republic of Yugoslavia, they must clearly be considered to have been 'international' in character, but in so far as they involved hostilities between the Bosnian Government and dissident forces within Bosnia-Herzegovina, the warfare must, notwithstanding external encouragement and support, be taken to have been 'non-international' in character. As a legal issue, this question was largely avoided as a result of a meeting held in November 1991 under the auspices of the International Committee of the Red Cross, at which the parties in conflict agreed that the preponderance of *jus in bello* norms applicable in international conflicts should be applied.[3] These undertakings were, sadly, devoid of value for practical humanitarian purposes, but they did play an important part in shaping the later jurisdiction of the International Criminal Tribunal for Former Yugoslavia.[4] A further somewhat 'academic' question may be raised as to whether 1977 Additional Protocol I (or indeed Protocol II) was applicable in the conflicts. The former Federal Republic of Yugoslavia ratified both 1977 Additional Protocols on 11 June 1979, subject to a reservation which became meaningless on the fragmentation of the Federal Republic. Whether a successor state inherits those of its predecessor's international obligations which are not founded on customary norms may be doubted, although Serbia-Montenegro (which considers itself the surviving Federal Republic of Yugoslavia) must be considered to have remained bound by former Yugoslav obligations. In practice, this hardly mattered, since the gross violations of humanitarian norms which occurred transgressed even the most minimal provisions which were unequivocally applicable.

Other difficulties have been illustrated by others of the all too many non-international armed conflicts of the later 20th century, including those in Afghanistan, Nicaragua and the Sudan. The disastrous conflict in Afghanistan displayed some of the characteristics of a mixed'-status armed conflict, although in less complex circumstances than those later obtaining in former Yugoslavia. The core conflict was between the former communist government in Kabul and the various *mujaheddin* groups, some of which were also in conflict *inter se*. However, there was also large-scale intervention by the former Soviet Union in support of the Kabul government, in a move which, in view of the level of commitment, death toll and political consequences, can reasonably be considered to have been 'Russia's Vietnam'. The USSR represented itself as having been invited to assist the Kabul government, and it is possible that on this basis the conflict may, formally at least, be considered to have remained non-international in character, and the ICRC treated the conflict as such. It must further be said that the general level of humanitarian observance in the conflict was abysmal, although ICRC Delegates operating from Pakistan did successfully achieve some isolated acts of humanitarian protection in very difficult circumstances.

The armed conflict in Nicaragua raised important questions because of the indirect involvement of the United States of America. In the *Military and Paramilitary Activities in and against Nicaragua (Nicaragua* v. *United States) (Merits)* case,[5] the International Court of Justice determined, *inter alia*, that in respect of the conflict within Nicaragua, the hostilities were non-international between the government and the dissident Contras, but that the action of the USA attracted the regulation applicable to international armed conflicts.[6] However, the court added that the *minimum* standards were very much the same in each case. Rosemary Abi-Saab has commented upon this case that:

> In this Judgment the Court [affirms] ... that the fundamental general principles of humanitarian law (common article 3 in the opinion of the Court) belong to the body of general international law; in other words, they apply in all circumstances. ... This approach is not based on the legal classification of armed conflicts ... the 'fundamental principles' ... apply regardless of the situation, [varying] ... only in their measure of specificity.[7]

This is an important point, but one which must be treated with some caution. It is clearly true to say that common article 3 of the 1949 Geneva Conventions represents the bare minimum of humanitarian provision in armed conflict – indeed, that is its very nature. However, it is not true to say that the provision for non-international and international armed conflicts is substantially the same, with some supplements for the former. The opposite is the case. The provision for non-international armed conflicts is a much reduced, minimal form of that applicable to international armed conflicts, with an express injunction in common article 3 of the 1949 Geneva Conventions, that as much of the full regime should be adopted as circumstances permit. In other words, the full humanitarian regime is the presumptive norm, and the reduced provision is in essence, an accepted 'exception'.

The situation in Somalia raised different and highly complex issues. By 1993, national government in Somalia had for practical purposes collapsed, and the country was engulfed in conflict between armed factions ranging from potential contenders for sovereignty over all or part of the territory to groups which were unequivocally engaged in mere banditry, the distinctions between these groups being by no means unequivocal. The humanitarian law applicable was to some degree ambiguous, because both common article 3 of the 1949 Geneva Conventions and 1977 Additional Protocol II suppose conflict between government and dissident forces, rather than a simple degeneration into military anarchy in the absence of government. It is interesting to note that the ICRC Commentary remarks that:

> In its draft the ICRC had provided that the Protocol would be applicable in the case of several factions confronting each other without involvement of the government's armed forces, for example, if the established government had disappeared or was too weak to intervene. Such a situation, it appeared to the [Diplomatic] Conference, was merely a theoretical textbook example and the provision was dropped ... Thus unfortunately the definition does not cover such cases and only common article 3 will apply to them.[8]

This was precisely the situation which arose in Somalia in the early 1990s, and as the Commentary remarks, common article 3 must be considered the maximum provision which could have been applicable, although even this was not applied in practice. The matter was further complicated in terms of questions of legal applicability with the development of the US Operation Restore Hope and, later, the introduction of the UN force UNOSOM.[9]

These difficulties and ambiguities are perhaps inevitable, but it must be admitted that they can constitute a serious obstacle to humanitarian implementation in practice.

The Question of Terrorism

As has been suggested above, both common article 3 of the 1949 Geneva Conventions and article 1 of 1977 Additional Protocol I are carefully drafted to avoid the inclusion of terrorist violence within the category of non-international armed conflict for the purposes of the application of their provision. The question of terrorism and its definition is nevertheless a serious issue in the context of non-international armed conflict.

There have been many attempts to define terrorism, from the 1937 draft League of Nations Convention for the Prevention and Punishment of Terrorism, which followed the assassination of King Alexander of Yugoslavia in Marseilles, onwards. The 1937 draft convention failed, and was ratified by only one country. No attempts since have achieved universal, or even widespread, acceptance. This is primarily because whilst certain key elements such as indiscriminacy, randomness and collective terrorisation might be agreed, there are too many 'grey areas' and political sympathies to permit an unequivocally accepted general definition. Thus in October 1997 the USA published a definitive list of organisations which it then considered to be terrorist in nature, not including the IRA. This organisation has conducted a long terrorist campaign in the United Kingdom whilst attracting considerable political sympathy, and private financial support, in the USA. The US decision was based on a 'ceasefire' which had been announced as part of the Northern Ireland peace process, but nevertheless serves to illustrate the difficulties of definition which will inevitably be encountered in any attempt to produce a definitive description or list of terrorist organisations. On this issue, E. Chadwick remarks that:

> Acts of international terrorism are not generally viewed as crossing thresholds of intensity sufficient to trigger [international humanitarian law]. The operation of state-centric anti-terrorist codifications, continues to be plagued by political considerations. ... Nonetheless, where appropriate, terrorist acts can be prosecuted as illicit forms of warfare.[10]

In the context of the humanitarian *jus in bello*, the question of positive definition may be less important than might *prima facie* be thought to be the case.

The most pernicious aspects of what is generally taken to be 'terrorist' activity are in any event implicitly placed outside the scope of legitimate combatancy in the course of armed conflict, in particular by the parameters set by article 4A of 1949 Geneva Convention III and articles 43(1) and 44(3) of 1977 Additional Protocol I. However, this does not mean that those who are suspected of terrorism in the course of armed conflict, including non-international armed conflict, are therefore deprived of all rights under international humanitarian law. Torsten Stein usefully remarks that:

> Terrorist acts are attacks on the most fundamental human rights, but the neglect terrorists show for human rights is irrelevant for the question, how much human rights terrorists deserve themselves. ... Terrorists may not 'deserve' respect for their human rights in the proper sense of the word, but ... democratic States ... have to maintain the credibility of the rule of law and of human rights every day and under all circumstances ...[11]

This is a reasonable statement. If a suspected terrorist is found wounded, then he or she will be as much entitled to treatment under 'Geneva' provision as anyone else. In determining the fact and consequences of his or her terrorist activity, the suspect will also be entitled to due process and the right to advance a defence. That is not to say that once terrorist activity has thus been determined, appropriate punishment cannot be inflicted, but, again, this must be individual, and not in the form of collective penalties or reprisals.

Basic Humanitarian Provisions

International humanitarian provision for non-international armed conflicts is essentially a minimum human rights prescription. The primary emphasis of common article 3 to the 1940 Geneva Conventions is basic humane treatment and minimum procedural guarantees. The article requires that:

> Persons taking no active part in the hostilities, including members of armed forces who have laid down their arms and those placed *hors de combat* by sickness, wounds, detention, or any other cause, shall in all circumstances be treated humanely, without any adverse distinction founded on race, colour, religion or faith, sex, birth or wealth, or any other similar criteria.

The article then expressly forbids murder, mutilation, torture or other 'cruel treatment' and other outrages upon personal dignity, and finally, the passing of sentences and carrying out of executions other than by a duly constituted court observing internationally recognised norms of due process.

1977 Additional Protocol II substantially restates and expands upon these principles, but also usefully sets out certain 'fundamental guarantees in article 4. Article 4(1) provides that:

> All person who do not take a direct part or who have ceased to take part in hostilities, whether or not their liberty has been restricted, are entitled to respect for their person, honour and convictions and religious practices. They shall in all circumstances be treated humanely, without adverse distinction. It is prohibited to order that there shall be no survivors.

In the context of the cultural and religious dimensions of a number of conflicts in the 1990s, including those in former Yugoslavia, the provision in the Additional Protocol with regard to 'convictions and religious practices' is of considerable interest and potential value. Article 4(2) then adds a list of specific bans, without prejudice to the generality of article 4(1). These comprise violence, murder, torture and corporal punishment; collective punishment; hostage-taking; terrorism;[12] humiliating and degrading treatment, including rape, enforced prostitution[13] and indecent assault; slavery; pillage; and threats to commit any of these.

Article 4(3) makes particular provision for the protection of children which closely parallels that afforded in circumstances of international armed conflict.[14] In particular, children under the age of 15 may not be recruited into armed forces or otherwise participate in hostilities. Sadly, this has been a common feature of non-international armed conflicts in the second half of the 20th century. In the internecine conflicts in the Lebanon, for example, very young children were frequently found participating in hostilities, and this was by no means a phenomenon unique to that area of conflict. The problems of treatment of such children are the same as those found in international conflicts. Returning a child with substantial combat experience, and the trauma associated therewith, to 'normal' education presents self-evident difficulties which are perhaps not amenable to legal solution, but are none the less real.

Where, as is again common, families have become dispersed and separated, article 4(3)(a) of Protocol II requires that all feasible steps be taken to facilitate their reunion. This is very important for adults, but has an especially vital significance for children and infant family members.

The Wounded, Sick and Shipwrecked

This most basic element of humanitarian provision in warfare is covered briefly by common article 3 of the 1949 Geneva Conventions, which provide that:

> (1) Persons taking no active part in hostilities, including ... those placed *hors de combat* by sickness, [or] wounds ... shall in all cases be treated humanely ... .
> (2) The wounded and sick shall be collected and cared for ...

This sparse but important provision is considerably expanded by articles 7–11 of 1977 Additional Protocol II. Article 7(2) in particular closely parallels the basic provision made for care of the wounded and sick in international armed conflicts in providing that:

> In all circumstances they [the wounded and sick] shall be treated humanely and shall receive to the fullest extent practicable and with the least possible delay, the medical care and attention required by their condition. There shall be no distinction among them founded on any grounds other than medical ones.

This does not necessarily add to the requirements set out by common article 3 to the 1949 Geneva Conventions; indeed the additional provision is clearly implicit in that made earlier. The Protocol does usefully make the direction express in an area in which ambiguity may be supremely dangerous, however. The emphasis on the prohibition of non-medical discrimination is of special value in a context of non-international conflict beset with arguments regarding legitimacy of combatancy.

A necessary prerequisite for the effective treatment of the wounded and sick is their retrieval and conveyance to an appropriate medical facility. Article 8 of 1977 Additional Protocol II requires that 'all possible measures' be taken 'without delay' for search and rescue, and also for the protection of the wounded and sick against 'pillage and ill-treatment'. This again is closely parallel with the provision made for international armed conflicts.[15] The questions of what is practically possible arise in non-international as in international armed conflicts, and are subject to the same definitions and parameters of consideration.[16] In particular, it must be stressed that recognising what is impossible in a given situation should never be permitted to degenerate into wilful and avoidable neglect. The question of wilful neglect is not directly addressed by 1977 Additional Protocol II, but the provision of article 7(2) quoted above would seem at least to imply a requirement similar to that set for international armed conflicts by 1949 Geneva Convention I in providing that:

> [the wounded and sick] shall not wilfully be left without medical assistance and care, nor shall conditions exposing them to contagion or infection be created.

The appalling conditions found in internment camps such as Omarska and Brcko during the 'mixed' armed conflict(s) in former Yugoslavia[17] very clearly fell foul, *inter alia*, of this requirement.

Protection of Medical Personnel

It is an important strand of 'Geneva' protection for the wounded and sick that medical personnel with responsibility for their care should not themselves be made an object of attack or be penalised for their professional endeavours in caring for their patients. That is perhaps a matter of special importance in non-international armed conflicts, where medical personnel engaged in treating wounded from an opposing faction may be at special risk of charges of treachery or treason. The point is made clear by 1977 Additional Protocol II, article 10(1), which provides that:

> Under no circumstances shall any person be punished for having carried out medical activities compatible with medical ethics, regardless of the person benefiting therefrom.

One of the more difficult questions of law and ethics arising in this context is that of information received from their patients by medical personnel. Such information might be offered voluntarily or involuntarily, for example while in a confused state or under anaesthetic, and could be politically sensitive or indeed personally damaging to the patient. Article 10 endeavours to deal with this delicate issue in providing that:

> (3) The professional obligations of person engaged in medical activities regarding information which they may acquire concerning the wounded and sick under their care shall, subject to national law, be respected.
> (4) Subject to national law, no person engaged in medical activities may be penalized in any way for refusing or failing to give information concerning the wounded and sick who are, or have been, under his care.

The caveat with regard to 'national law' is a potentially large exception with, presumably, as large a range of possible provision as in the case of information given to a priest in confession. However, it may at least be taken that a doctor or nurse could not be required to apply improper pressure in order to acquire information from a patient, since this must be assumed to contravene generally acceptable medical ethics.

Medical Units and Transport

1977 Additional Protocol II requires by article 11(1) that medical units, meaning hospitals, medical field stations and similar units:

> shall be respected and protected at all times and shall not be the object of attack.

As in the case of international armed conflicts, protection will only cease in the event of units being used 'to commit hostile acts, outside their humanitarian function'. Warning must first be given, allowing, 'whenever appropriate', a reasonable period before the protection is withdrawn. If a military unit is actually being fired upon from a hospital or ambulance, little or no warning period could reasonably be expected. On the other hand, it must be noted that attacks on hospitals in a number of instances in siege actions in the armed conflicts in former Yugoslavia, as in the attack on Dubrovnik, appear to have been 'indiscriminate' if not indeed deliberate bombardments, with no evidence of hostile action from the medical units concerned.[18] 'Collateral' damage in the course of militarily justifiable action may be unavoidable, but this must be minimised, and can certainly not be pleaded in an effort to cloak outright assault upon a protected establishment or vehicle.

A more difficult question arose in the course of action by the United Nations force in Somalia, UNOSOM, in September 1993, when response with automatic weapons was made to shots fired from the Benadir Hospital in Mogadishu. Three US servicemen were wounded while searching for weapons stocks at a militia stronghold adjacent to the hospital. The UN spokesperson, Major Stockwell, was reported to have said that the hospital became a target after the assailants had taken up position on the roof and started firing upon the UNOSOM personel.[19] The involvement of UN forces raises additional legal complications, but Major Stockwell's statement accurately reflected the general legal position in such circumstances. Again any 'collateral' damage to the hospital should be minimised to the greatest degree feasible, and deliberate attacks upon patients and medical staff who refrain from hostile action would be manifestly unlawful.

Captured Members of Opposing Forces

As has been suggested above, one of the most sensitive issues in the law relating to non-international armed conflicts is the question of the combatancy of dissident forces. Governments are extremely reluctant to concede that armed dissident factions within their territory have any legitimacy, and for that reason both common article 2 to the 1949 Geneva Conventions and 1977 Additional Protocol II, article 3(1), are very careful to emphasise that the application of the relevant 'Geneva' provision in no way impinges upon the legal status of the parties in conflict. For this reason there is no provision for 'prisoner of war' status in non-international armed conflicts, since the parties are *ex hypothesi* in a condition of allegiance which does not (yet) involve forces of different states. Captured dissident, or indeed former government, troops may later face trial for treason or similar offences,[20] although article 6(5) of 1977 Additional Protocol II does specify that:

> At the end of hostilities, the authorities in power shall endeavour to grant the broadest possible amnesty to persons who have participated in the armed conflict ...

The fact that 'prisoner of war' status is not provided for in common article 3 to the 1949 Geneva Conventions or by 1977 Additional Protocol II does not mean that it cannot be conceded. It will be recalled that the provision for non-international armed conflicts is a *minimum* prescription, and that states are enjoined to implement as much of the humanitarian provision for *international* armed conflicts as possible.[21]

In some large-scale non-international armed conflicts which are effectively secessionary in nature, 'prisoners of war' status has in effect been accorded *de facto*. One example stems from the course of the Algerian War of Independence, in which the willingness of the FLN (the National Liberation Front) to treat captured French military personnel in effect as 'prisoners of war' and to admit ICRC inspection of the camps in which they were held went far towards establishing their claim to be a provisional government and to establishing the status of captured FLN fighters. It may also be noted that during the secessionist war in Eritrea, the Eritrean forces created 'prisoner of war' camps.

A further possible complication arises where foreign personnel become involved in a non-international armed conflict. If such persons are acting in the course of their duties as members of the armed forces of a foreign power – such as the German 'Condor Legion' in the Spanish Civil War in the 1930s – this may raise questions about the 'non-international' status of the conflict, but it may remain so if the foreign power is simply spending assistance to an ally.[22] In such a case, captured members of the foreign forces will be entitled to at least the same standard of treatment as that accorded to nationals of the state affected by the conflict, and this should accord with at least the minimums set out by the applicable provisions of international humanitarian law. The same is essentially true of foreign civilians volunteering for service in such a conflict, such as the International Brigade volunteers in the Spanish Civil War. Such persons may be at risk of being categorised as mercenaries,[23] although if they are ideologically motivated volunteers receiving no greater remuneration than the forces alongside whom they are fighting, they will not be open to this charge.

Conditions of Internment or Detention

Persons interned or detained in the course of a non-international armed conflict are entitled to at least a minimum level of protection in terms of their conditions of detention. Article 3 common to the 1949 Geneva Conventions does not make express provision for conditions of internment or detention, but does expressly forbid a variety of malpractices, including cruel treatment, torture and humiliating treatment, which would apply as much in that context as any other. Article 5 of 1977 Additional Protocol II makes extensive provision for 'persons whose liberty has been restricted'. 1977 Additional Protocol II, article 5, makes more extensive provision for conditions of internment. In particular, it requires that the treatment of the wounded and sick conform to the standards set out by the Protocol,[24] that food and water be provided to the same extent as for the local civilian population, that individual and collective relief supplies be admitted, that internees be permitted to practise their religion (if any), and that internees, 'if required to work', shall have the same working conditions and safeguards as the 'local civilian population'. In relation to the last stipulation,[25] it may be noted that internees may be 'required to work', but in the same conditions as local 'civilian' employees. What, then, if those 'normal, conditions amount to near slavery, with few if any safety provisions? The ICRC Commentary does not refer directly to this question, remarking only that:

> persons deprived of their liberty must have the benefit of working conditions and safeguards similar to those enjoyed by the local civilian population. Thus it is prohibited to force detainees to carry out unhealthy, humiliating or dangerous work, bearing in mind the conditions in which the local population works.

Reference may be made to the general law of human rights in this respect, but this has been of little if any avail in respect of general working conditions in many parts of the world, and would hardly be so in the case of internees in a non-international armed conflict. The safeguards offered in non-international armed conflict are implicitly similar to those offered in international armed conflicts, so comparison may be made with article 51 of 1949 Geneva Convention III and article 95 of 1949 Geneva Convention IV. As for these provisions, the presumption must be made that certain humanitarian minimums are expected, but these are not precisely defined.

A further series of requirements are set by article 5(2) of 1977 Additional Protocol II which are to be met by the detaining authorities 'within the limits of their capabilities'. Except where families are accommodated together, women should be detained in separate headquarters from men, and should be under the supervision of women. This is of special importance in view of the threats of sexual harassment and attack posed to women, particularly, but not only, in non-international armed conflicts, as the experience of forced prostitution in the 'mixed' conflicts in former Yugoslavia in the 1990s demonstrated.[26] Internees and detainees should be permitted to send and receive letters and cards, but the numbers of these may be restricted by the detaining authorities. Places of internment or detention should not be located in dangerous proximity to a combat zone, and the detainees or internees should be evacuated, if this is possible, under adequate conditions of safety if the combat zone should move threateningly close to a camp.[27] Due care must be taken of the medical needs of internees and detainees; in particular, they should receive regular medical examination, and their physical and mental health should not be put at risk by any unjustified procedure which falls outside normal medical practice in the case of patients whose liberty is not restricted.[28] This means, *inter alia*, that protected persons may not under any circumstances be subjected to medical experimentation.

Protection of the Civilian Population

Civilians are at risk in all armed conflicts, and especially in non-international armed conflicts. This again flows from the particular embitterment of such conflicts, and the tendency to regard the civilian population sympathetic to the opposing side as in some sense 'traitors' or 'outcasts' in a way not common in international armed conflicts. The protection afforded to civilians by 1977 Additional Protocol II is somewhat similar, if less in extent, to that afforded in international armed conflicts, especially by the relevant provisions of

1977 Additional Protocol I. The basic principles are set out by article 13 of 1977 Additional Protocol II, which provides that:

> (1) The civilian population and individual civilians shall enjoy general protection against the dangers arising from military operations. To give effect to this protection, the following rules shall be observed in all circumstances.
> (2) The civilian population as such, as well as individual civilians, shall not be the object of attack. Acts or threats of violence the primary purpose of which is to spread terror among the civilian population are prohibited.
> (3) Civilians shall enjoy the protection afforded by this Part, unless and for such time as they take a direct part in hostilities.

Article 14 then forbids starvation of civilians as a methods of warfare, including destruction of objects indispensable to the survival of the civilian population, such as foodstuffs and agricultural areas dedicated to their production. Article 15 then forbids attacks upon installations containing 'dangerous forces' – meaning dams, dykes, and nuclear power stations – where such attack would release such forces and inflict severe civilian losses. This provision parallels article 56 of 1977 Additional Protocol I applicable to international armed conflicts.[29]

The forced movement of civilians, except on grounds of their own security or 'imperative military reasons', is forbidden by article 17i of 1977 Additional Protocol II. This would apply to the practice of so-called 'ethnic cleansing' widely practised by the parties in conflict in former Yugoslavia in the 1990s.[30] Such forced movement on racial, cultural or religious grounds may be expected especially in certain types of non-international armed conflicts, as, for example, in former Yugoslavia and to a degree in Rwanda, and may especially be the case in any secessionary conflict. However, it must not be forgotten that such events may also occur on a massive scale in international armed conflicts and in situations of genocide. Both the Nazi Holocaust, some of the Soviet persecutions and the atrocities of the Khmer Rouge in Cambodia (then Kampuchea) were characterised in their first stages by precisely such forced population movements.

Finally, article 16 of 1977 Additional Protocol II forbids military use of and acts of hostility directed against:

> historic monuments, works of art or places of worship which constitute the cultural or spiritual heritage of peoples …

Such damage was again a significant feature of the conflicts in former Yugoslavia. Article 16 is stated to be without prejudice to the 1954 Hague Convention for the Protection of Cultural Property in the Event of Armed Conflict.[31] Article 19 of the 1954 Hague Convention requires that, at the minimum, the provisions of the convention regarding respect for 'cultural property' should be applied in non-international armed conflicts. Under article 1(a), such property includes 'monuments of architecture, art or history, whether religious or secular'. Article 4(1) of the convention states that 'respect' means neither using such 'monuments' for purposes likely to expose them to damage in armed conflict, nor attacking them, but if a 'monument' were itself being used for offensive military purposes, that protection would cease until the illicit use was terminated, although resulting damage should still be kept to whatever minimum is possible.

Refugees in Non-international Armed Conflicts

Non-international armed conflicts in the late 20th century have involved large population movements as people have fled both from the hostilities themselves and from fear of an advancing adverse party. In some cases they have been unlawfully expelled from their home territory by such parties. The harrowing scenes in the armed conflicts in former Yugoslavia and in Rwanda in the 1990s may be cited as examples of this.

The first problem is one definition. The basic definition of a 'refugee' offered by the 1951 UN Convention Relating to the Status of Refugees, article 1(A)(2), as amended by the 1967 Protocol Relating to the Status of Refugees, article 1(2),[32] requires that the claimant shall be outside the country of his or her nationality, and unable to return thereto by reason of well-founded fear of persecution for reasons of race, religion, nationality, group membership or political opinion. This definition is not very helpful in the context of non-international armed conflicts, especially where a person may fear returning to their home territory even while such territory, nominally, remains within their country of nationality, albeit under adverse control. The difficult legal questions which may arise were illustrated in the English case of *R.* v. *Secretary of State for the Home Department, ex parte Sivakumaran*.[33] The case concerned the protracted crisis in Sri Lanka, and in the course of judgment, Lord Keith of Kinkel made reference to the question of refugee status in non-international armed conflicts. He stated:

> for a considerable period of time Sri Lanka, or at least certain parts of that country, have been in a serious state of civil disorder, amounting at times to civil war. The authorities have taken steps to suppress the disorders and ... [t]hose steps, together with the activities of the subversives, have naturally resulted in painful and distressing experi-

> ences for many persons ... . The [British] Secretary of State has ... expressed the view that army activities aimed at discovering and dealing with Tamil extremists do not constitute evidence of persecution of Tamils as such.[34]

Whatever view was taken of the particular situation in Sri Lanka, this opinion seems to support the general proposition that non-international armed conflict may generate, but not in itself guarantee, claims to refugee status. It may be suggested that the present condition of international law relating to refugees is in this respect less than adequate. Whether there is the requisite political will to change the law may be debated, but the rather negative response which refugee issues seem to encounter must raise some doubt. However, it must be added that many of the inflictions from which those claiming refugee status flee in non-international armed conflicts constitute serious violations of applicable norms of either or both the *jus in bello* and the general law of human rights, and must be addressed in those contexts.

Protection of Religious Freedom

Where non-international armed conflict involves religious divisions, the bitterness already inherent in such a conflict may be vastly inflamed, with the temptation to characterise an opposing party as not only in some sense 'traitors' or 'oppressors', but also potentially as 'enemies of God', or at least received religion. The armed conflicts in former Yugoslavia in the 1990s were characterised, at least in part, by tripartite religious divisions between Serbian Orthodox and Roman Catholic Christian traditions and Islam. It would be an exaggeration to say that these divisions of faith were the *cause* of the conflicts, which arose rather from a complex collision of political, historical and cultural as well as religious factors, but the religious divisions played a part, not least in 'labelling' the opposed communities. As a result, serious damage was done to a number of historic churches and mosques, often deliberately as attacks upon visible symbols of their faith communities. The outrage of so-called 'ethnic cleansing' in former Yugoslavia was also characterised to some extent by inter-faith conflict.

An even clearer case of inter-faith conflict was shown in the Sudan. Sudan comprises a politically dominant Islamic north, which looks culturally to the Middle East, and a largely Christian south, which looks culturally to sub-Saharan Africa. The conflict in the Sudan had complex origins, but was very much embittered by the religious distinction between north and south and the determination of the northern-based government to impose *Shari'at* Law upon the largely unwilling non-Islamic southern population. The combined effects of embittered civil strife and severe famine produced what Patrick Brogan has called:

> one of the greatest disasters of modern times, a holocaust in the … heart of Africa which the outside world is powerless to stop.[35]

Sadly, great military disasters can never be considered definitive, and the tragedy of the conflicts in Rwanda and Burundi in the 1990s must now be considered to have a claim to that disgraceful eminence. Religious division may also have played a small part in the attack on the minority Shiite Marsh Arab population in southern Iraq in the 1980s and 1990s, although this was almost certainly a minor factor in comparison with political imperatives. On the level of internal disturbances, the conflict between Roman Catholic and Protestant Christian traditions has had a profoundly negative effect in the long 'troubles' in Northern Ireland.

Under the heading of 'fundamental guarantees', article 4(1) of 1977 Additional Protocol II provides, *inter alia*, that:

> All persons who do not take a direct part or who have ceased to take part in hostilities, whether or not their liberty has been restricted, are entitled to respect for their … convictions and religious practices.

This clearly forbids religious repression; it would also, expressly by the inclusion of the word 'convictions', forbid the imposition of any religious practice upon agnostics or atheists. 'Religious personnel' (a neutral term adopted by the 1977 Additional Protocols which avoids faith- or denomination-specific implications) are protected, along with medical personnel, by article 9(1) of the 1977 Additional Protocol II. It requires that they are to be respected and protected and to be afforded any available help in performing their duties. They may not be compelled to act in any way incompatible with their humanitarian functions. This protection is vital, since 'religious personnel' are, to an even greater extent than buildings, dedicated to worship, symbolic of the public representation of their faith tradition.

Attacks upon, *inter alia*, 'places of worship which constitute the cultural or spiritual heritage of peoples' are forbidden by 1977 Additional Protocol II, article 16, as noted above. This is a slightly curious provision, since not all places of worship are necessarily to be considered part of a people's 'cultural heritage', but they are presumably, by definition, part of their 'spiritual heritage'. It must therefore be presumed that attacks upon places of worship, whatever their cultural and architectural merit or lack thereof, are forbidden. The 1954

Hague Convention for the Protection of Cultural Property in the Event of Armed Conflict applies to religious buildings as to other 'monuments' in the manner considered above. Again, if a place of worship were itself to be used for aggressive purposes, the protection afforded would be suspended for the duration of such an illicit usage.

Methods and Means of Warfare

The development of 'Hague' law dealing with methods and means of warfare, in non-international armed conflict is more restricted than that of 'Geneva' law. This is partly because in the formative years of the modern *jus in bello* – roughly from the mid-19th century to the First World War[36] – it was not generally considered that the right of governments to suppress rebellion or other armed insurrection within their territory was subject to legal, as compared with ethical, restraint. This view remained largely the international consensus until the Second World War. The recognition of the horrors perpetrated by 20th-century totalitarian regimes in the 1930s and afterwards gave rise to modern human rights law, and in its train brought in such limited 'Hague' elements as now exist in the *jus in bello* applicable to non-international armed conflicts.

Some of the basic constraints to which military actions are subjected in this context have been considered above under the heading 'Protection of the Civilian Population'. As remarked in that context, civilians are required by article 13 not to be the object of attack nor the object of operations the purpose of which is to spread terror amongst them. Bans on attacks upon installations containing dangerous forces, denying civilians the means necessary for their survival, attacks upon a people's cultural heritage and forced movement of civilians in cases other than objective 'necessity' have also been considered above.

More difficult questions arise in the specific context of controls on use of weapons. This has become a real issue in non-international armed conflicts, for example in the case of chemical attacks launched by Iraqi forces against the northern Kurdish population of Iraq in the 1980s. International outrage was occasioned by the chemical attack on the town of Hallabjah in March 1988.[37] Patrick Brogan states that Western reports indicate a minimum of 100 dead, whilst Iran claimed that some 2,000 people had been killed.[38] A number of other chemical attacks on the Kurdish population have also been reported, with varying tolls of death and injury. There can be no doubt that attacks such as these are illegal, if only on the basis of their indiscriminacy. Common article 3 of the 1949 Geneva Conventions, it will be recalled, requires that 'persons taking no active part in the hostilities ... shall in all circumstances be treated humanely ...'. This would clearly preclude chemical attacks upon a centre of civilian population such as Hallabjah.

As to the use of such weapons in general, in particular against opposing hostile forces, the legal provision in relation to non-international armed conflicts is somewhat ambiguous. The 1925 Geneva Gas Protocol is phrased clearly in terms of *international* armed conflicts. The 1992 UN Chemical Weapons Convention,[39] however, provides more broadly, by article I(1)(b), that:

> Each State Party to this Convention undertakes never under any circumstances: ...
> (b) To use chemical weapons.

This ban on use 'under any circumstances' at least implicitly extends to non-international armed conflicts. The same may be said of the 1972 UN Convention on Biological and Toxin Weapons.

The use of nuclear weapons in a non-international armed conflict might be considered unthinkable, but the question must be addressed. The International Court of Justice in its *Advisory Opinion upon the Threat or Use of Nuclear Weapons*[40] concluded that the threat or use of such weapons would generally contravene international humanitarian legal norms, except, possibly, in very extreme circumstances of self-defence where the very existence of the state was at stake. The *Advisory Opinion* is framed in terms of international armed conflict, but in the present context the question of a secessionary conflict must obviously arise. It may be doubted that the court had such a case in mind in phrasing the 'extreme defensive' exception to its general proposition, so it must be concluded that the same arguments of indiscriminacy and excess advanced in relation to the question of use of other 'unconventional' weapons must also apply to nuclear weapons.

In view of the paucity of general 'Hague' provision for non-international armed conflicts, it may generally be concluded that aside from the specific restrictions referred to above, general protection must be sought in the overarching principles of common article 3 to the 1949 Geneva Conventions, and article 13 of 1977 Additional Protocol II, which shade in many respects into general norms of the law of human rights.

The Role of International Organisations

The national Red Cross or Red Crescent society in a country in which a non-international armed conflict breaks out is evidently placed in a position of considerable difficulty. However, as the 10th International Red Cross Conference in 1921 declared by Resolution XIV(ii):

> In every country in which civil war breaks out, it is the National Red Cross Society of the country which, in the first place, is responsible for dealing ... with the relief needs of the victims ...[41]

The basic principles of impartiality and humanity continue to apply, but in practice, access to give assistance in areas controlled by the opposing side may be difficult, if not impossible. 1977 Additional Protocol II provides by article 18(1) that:

> Relief societies located in the territory of the High Contracting Party, such as Red Cross ... organizations, may offer their services for the performance of their traditional functions in relation to the victims of the armed conflict.

The ICRC Commentary on Protocol II makes the point that in a non-international armed conflict, the central national Red Cross organisation may be prevented from acting effectively, and thus the term 'organisations' is used in order to emphasise that divisions of a national society may act, including those which find themselves in territory under dissident control.[42] This is a valuable provision, but in some cases the national organisation, including its local units, may be wholly or partially incapacitated.

In such cases, the International Committee of the Red Cross is faced with immensely sensitive political questions. Can it, while remaining visibly neutral, offer impartial humanitarian assistance without appearing to express an opinion on the potential or actual disintegration of the state in question? Common article 3 of the 1949 Geneva Conventions tries to deal with this problem by providing that an impartial humanitarian body such as the ICRC 'may offer its services to the Parties to the conflict'. As Marion Harroff-Tavel remarks, this provision of common article 3:

> Does not oblige States to accept the ICRC's offer of services. However, they have a duty at least to examine it in good faith and to reply. They may not consider an offer of services as interference in their internal affairs.[43]

Once such an offer has been accepted, the ICRC may perform a number of humanitarian services. It may seek to get food and medical relief supplies through to beleaguered elements of the population, which is a basic humanitarian activity, but one which, as experience in former Yugoslavia in the 1990s showed all too clearly, may be both difficult and dangerous to perform. It will, through its Delegates, seek to gain access to internment camps to monitor conditions there. This too may be very difficult, as experience in Afghanistan and former Yugoslavia demonstrated.[44]

Finally, and vitally, the ICRC will seek to trace the often very large numbers of missing persons in such situations. More generally, the ICRC will try to disseminate knowledge and to secure observation of international humanitarian legal norms.

Where there is a serious refugee problem in a non-international armed conflict, the United Nations High Commissioner for Refugees will work to secure their safe resettlement. In ways less directly related to the conflict as such, bodies such as Amnesty International may seek to address some of the political effects. Finally, the diversity of other humanitarian relief agencies, including Médecins sans Frontières, Oxfam and Christian Aid, may in their diverse ways afford valuable aid and assistance.

The United Nations may also play a role in humanitarian relief, in addition to that played by some of its specific agencies such as the UN High Commissioner for Refugees. The UN Charter includes amongst the organisation's purposes, by article 1(3), achievement of 'international co-operation in solving international problems of [a] ... humanitarian character'. In practice, UN forces have been involved in securing passage of humanitarian relief supplies to threatened populations in a number of non-international armed conflicts, including to the Kurdish people in northern Iraq and to besieged enclaves in former Yugoslavia. In the latter case, UNPROFOR faced difficulties of conflicting mandates which required it to serve simultaneously as an agency for both enforcement and neutral humanitarian relief.[45] It remains to be seen whether the organisation of UN forces can be resolved in a manner capable of accommodating satisfactorily such a wide, and to a degree incompatible, range of functions in any future cases of such necessity.

Criminal Proceedings in Relation to Non-international Armed Conflicts

The question of international response to war crimes committed in non-international armed conflicts, as in the International Criminal Tribunal for Rwanda, is considered below.[46] However, serious questions also arise in the context of municipal proceedings in or after non-international armed conflicts.[47] A range of criminal charges may arise before national criminal jurisdictions in such situations, ranging from criminal violations, which are the stuff of commonplace, day-to-day jurisdiction, to matters of treason and 'war crimes'. It is with these latter two categories that this discussion is primarily concerned. Article 6 of 1977 Additional Protocol II sets out certain requisites of due process in criminal trials arising from a non-international armed conflict. In particular, article 6(2) requires that:

> No sentence shall be passed and no penalty shall be executed on a person found guilty of an offence except pursuant to a conviction pronounced by a court offering essential guarantees of independent and impartiality.

Specific requirements are then spelt out by article 6(2)(a)–(f), and these include communication of charges and affording of means of defence, bans on findings of collective guilt, the principle of *nullem crimen sine lege* and a ban on retrospective criminalisation, a presumption of innocence until guilt has been proven, the right of a defendant to be present at the trial, and a ban on compulsion to self-incrimination. Article 6(5) also calls for the 'broadest possible amnesty' to be granted at the end of hostilities.

Nevertheless, the Protocol in no way denies the right of the lawful authority to try those who have set up armed opposition to it – an activity which almost any state would tend to categorise as criminal, if not treasonable. The great question is what, in a context of non-international armed conflicts, is a lawful authority. In practice, this tends to be whatever authority has emerged victorious in the territory, or part thereof, in question. The reference of Protocol II is to criminal proceedings, and whilst offences such as treason clearly have a 'political' element in their motivation, it may be suggested that this should not extend to merely having sympathised with a losing and/or subversive party. The call for amnesty goes further, and suggests that merely *fighting* on an adverse side should not lead to punishment in such circumstances, although this may not include higher command functions and other more specific offences such as terrorism or war crimes *stricto sensu*. Trials have taken place in conflicts at the end of the 20th century, including the trials of two Serbian fighters, Boris Herak and Sretko Damjanovic, captured by Bosnian forces in former Yugoslavia. They were each charged with massacre of civilians and rape of interned women. They were convicted on 30 March 1993, and condemned to death, subject to appeal against sentence.[48] The problem with such trials is evidently that not only must justice be done, it must be seen unequivocally to be done, and in the context of armed conflict this may not readily be accepted. In general, it may be said here, as for international armed conflicts, that the best time for trials is after the end of hostilities, rather than during them. It may also be said that where possible, international proceedings are to be preferred, although this may not be an option in most cases, even if a permanent International Criminal Court is established.

Notes

1 For a discussion of terrorism, see pp. 258–9.
2 Y. Sandoz, C. Swinarski and B. Zimmermann (eds) with J. Pictet, *Commentary on the Additional Protocols of 8 June 1977 to the Geneva Convention of 12 August 1949* (ICRC/Martinus Nijhoff, 1987), p. 1,353, para. 4,469.
3 *International Committee of the Red Cross Bulletin: Yugoslavia* (ICRC, 1992).
4 See Statute of the International Criminal Tribunal for former Yugoslavia, articles 2 and 3.
5 ICJ Reps 1986, p. 14.
6 For discussion, see T. Meron, *Human Rights in Internal Strife: Their International Protection* (Grotius, 1987), p. 48.
7 R. Abi-Saab, 'Humanitarian Law and Internal Conflicts: The Evolution of Legal Concerns', in J.M. Delissen and G.J. Tanja (eds), *Humanitarian Law of Armed Conflict, Challenges Ahead: Essays in Honour of Frits Kalshoven* (Martinus Nijhoff, 1991), p. 209 at p. 223.
8 Y. Sandoz, C. Swinarski and B. Zimmermann (eds) with J. Pictet, op.cit., p. 1,351, para. 4,461.
9 As to this, see H. McCoubrey and N.D. White, *The Blue Helmets: Legal Regulation of United Nations Military Operations* (Dartmouth, 1996), Chapter 8, *passim*.
10 E. Chadwick, *Self-determination, Terrorism and the International Humanitarian Law of Armed Conflict* (Martinus Nijhoff, 1996), p. 128.
11 T. Stein, 'How Much Humanity do Terrorists Deserve?', in J.M. Delissen and G.J. Tanja (eds), *Humanitarian Law of Armed Conflict, Challenges Ahead: Essays in Honour of Frits Kalshoven* (Martinus Nijhoff, 1991), p. 567, at p. 581.
12 As to this, see above.
13 See pp. 191–2.
14 See pp. 193–5.
15 See 1949 Geneva Convention I, article 15, and 1949 Geneva Convention II, article 18.
16 See pp. 91–2.
17 See p. 72.
18 For discussion, see H. McCoubrey, 'The Armed Conflict in Bosnia and Proposed War Crimes Trial' (1993) XI *International Relations*, p. 411, at p. 420–1.
19 *Daily Telegraph* (London), 14 September 1993.
20 See p. 72.
21 See common article 3 to the 1949 Geneva Conventions.
22 In the case of the Spanish Civil War, the Condor Legion was aiding the fascist dissident forces, and the International Brigade were foreign civilian volunteers aiding the government forces.
23 For discussion of mercenaries, see pp. 145–8.
24 In particular, that they conform to the requirements of article 7.
25 Article 5(1)(e).
26 See above, p. 191.
27 Article 5(2)(c).
28 Article 5(2)(d)(e).
29 See p. 179.
30 See p. 8.
31 See p. 181.
32 See p. 53.
33 [1988] All ER, p. 193.
34 Ibid., at p. 198
35 P. Brogan, *World Conflicts* (2nd edn) (Bloomsbury, 1992), pp. 115–16.

36 For discussion, see Chapter 1.
37 *Guardian* (London), 24 March 1988
38 P. Brogan, op.cit., p. 327
39 For general discussion, see pp. 240–42.
40 ICJ Communiqué 96/23, 8 July 1996; see pp. 246–9 above.
41 The full text will be found in *International Red Cross Handbook* (12th edn) (ICRC, 1983) at p. 641.
42 Y. Sandoz, C. Swinarski and B. Zimmermann (eds) with J. Pictet, op.cit., p. 1,477, para. 4,873
43 M. Harroff-Tavel, 'Action Taken by the International Committee of the Red Cross in Situations of Internal Violence' (1993) 33 *International Review of the Red Cross*, p. 195, at p. 202.
44 See pp. 47–8.
45 For discussion, see H. McCoubrey and N.D. White, *International Organizations and Civil Wars* (Dartmouth, 1995), pp. 143–5.
46 See Chapter 10.
47 For further discussion, see H. McCoubrey and N.D. White, op.cit., Chapter 11.
48 *Daily Telegraph* (London), 31 March 1993.

10 Questions of Obligation and Enforcement

Enforcement – specifically processes of criminal enforcement – tends to be emphasised in external observation of the operation of law and legal systems. It is certainly the case that 'war crimes' are much the most prominent aspects of the laws of armed conflict as far as the general public are concerned, but it can be argued that this is a seriously misplaced emphasis. In countries of common law tradition, it derives in part from the influence exercised by a somewhat debased tradition of analytical positivist jurisprudence deriving from the early 19th-century work of Jeremy Bentham, filtered through that of John Austin. The conventional understanding of their concept of law as the command of a sovereign backed by a sanction, which is a considerable oversimplification of their actual argument,[1] implies a centrality of penal sanctions which is, from a broader perspective, unsustainable.

In the context of the humanitarian *jus in bello*, it may readily be seen that the primary function of the law is not to punish war criminals, but to protect victims of armed conflicts by preventing war crimes from being committed. Before any question of war crimes trials or other enforcement action can arise, failure in that primary endeavour must be presupposed. In this sense, 'enforcement' must be seen as very much a secondary office of the laws of armed conflict. In particular, in terms of the maintenance and implementation of the law, the imperatives of effective dissemination and training considered in Chapter 3 must be seen as more important. Nevertheless, where serious violations of this or any other law occur in practice, questions of penal enforcement are important, both in terms of deterrence and the maintenance of norms which may otherwise be placed at risk of degenerating into practical if not theoretical desuetude.

In the case of international humanitarian law, both the rather limited number of international proceedings in relation to violations at

Nuremberg and Tokyo in 1945 and in the 1990s before the Criminal Tribunals for former Yugoslavia and Rwanda, and the rather larger numbers of municipal court martial proceedings must be considered. At the same time, whilst international humanitarian law is not intended to be subject to any exceptions, the practical exigencies of its operation preclude any such simple absolutism. A preliminary consideration of the question of derogations and exceptions is therefore necessary.

The Question of Reciprocity

The 1949 Geneva Conventions and the 1977 Additional Protocol are multilateral treaties, and therefore, like all other treaties, subject to the principle of reciprocity which derives ultimately from the norm that *pacta sunt servanda* ('agreements are to be observed') recited in article 26 of the 1969 Vienna Convention on the Law of Treaties. This would suggest that the conventions and Protocol I[2] will apply only between states which are mutually bound by their provisions, except to the extent that such norms have attained the status of customary international law and are *ex hypothesi* binding upon all states. That this is indeed the case appears to be confirmed by common article 2 of the four 1949 Geneva Conventions, which is unequivocally phrased in terms of reciprocity of obligation. However, it must be remembered that the overwhelming proportion of the 1949 Geneva Conventions' provision has achieved customary status, and it can be argued that at least some of the provisions of 1977 Additional Protocol I also have that status.[3] The same can be said of such 'Hague' law provisions as the 1868 Declaration of St Petersburg, the 1899 and 1907 Hague Declarations and Conventions, and the 1925 Geneva Gas Protocol. All of these are therefore binding upon all states, irrespective of their treaty relations. In relation to non-customary humanitarian norms, there then arises the question of whether a serious breach of the norms set out by the conventions or the Protocol by a party in conflict could be treated by other parties as a repudiation of treaty obligations capable of acceptance by them, thus liberating them from obligation to observe the treaties in relation to the party in material breach by reference to article 60(2)(b) of the Vienna Convention on the Law of Treaties. The answer to this must be 'no'.

International humanitarian law is closely related to, albeit distinct from, the general law of human rights, and this generates a powerful argument that the obligations created by it are essentially unilateral and non-reciprocal in nature. Common article 1 of the four 1949 Geneva Conventions provides that:

> The High Contracting Parties undertake to respect and to ensure respect for the present Convention *in all circumstances* [emphasis added]

Jean Pictet comments on this article that:

> [The Convention] is not an engagement concluded on a basis of reciprocity, binding each party to the content only in so far as the other party observes its obligations. It is rather a series of unilateral engagements solemnly contracted before the world as represented by the other Contracting Parties.[4]

This argument of general non-reciprocity relates ultimately back to the Martens clause, named after the Russian statesman Frederic de Martens, who was legal adviser to the Imperial Russian Government at the 1899 and 1907 Hague Peace Conferences. The Martens clause was adopted by the Peace Conferences, and reads as follows:

> ... the High Contracting Parties deem it expedient to declare that in cases not included in the Regulations adopted by them, the inhabitants and the belligerents remain under the protection and the rules of the principles of the law of nations as they result from the usages established amongst civilized peoples, from the laws of humanity and the dictates of public conscience.

Although found only in a Preamble, and therefore in a sense only advisory, the Martens clause does confer a very particular status upon at least some fundamental provisions of international humanitarian law.[5] This was accepted by the war crimes tribunals sitting in Germany after the Second World War in response to the argument *nulla crimen sine lege* ('no crime without [prior] law') raised by the defence.[6] In conclusion, it is difficult to resist the view advanced by Ingrid Detter de Lupis:

> There ... appear to be several layers of rules pertaining to ... war ... some of which are subjected to ordinary requirements of reciprocity and others, of a rather more fundamental type, which are exempt from denunciation and which do not seem to be the subject of reciprocity.

At least three levels of obligation can be suggested to arise in connecting with international humanitarian legal norms:

1 those rules and principles which form part of customary international law or *jus cogens*, and are therefore binding upon all states irrespective of reciprocity; this would apply to the bulk of, *inter alia*, the 1949 Geneva Conventions and much of established 'Hague' provision

2 those fundamental principles which otherwise fall within the scope of the Martens clause and are also not subject to a requirement of reciprocity
3 other provisions which are either innovatory and not yet established as customary (as for parts of 1977 Additional Protocol I) or non-customary and not fundamental in nature will remain subject to the principle of reciprocity.

There remains to be considered the technical but significant distinction between the categories of customary international law and *jus cogens* in this context. The nature of customary law is sufficiently explained by article 38(1)(b) of the Statute of the International Court of Justice, which describes it as: 'international custom, as evidence of a general practice accepted [by states] as law'. The wide or near universal acceptance of a treaty provision may clearly confer customary status upon its substance, as for the bulk of the 1949 Geneva Conventions. *Jus cogens* overlaps with but goes beyond this concept. It embodies 'peremptory norms of international law', which are defined by article 53 of the 1969 Vienna Convention on the Law of Treaties as those which are:

> accepted and recognized by the international community as a whole as a norm from which no derogation is permitted and which can be modified only by a subsequent norm of general international law having the same character.

A case may be made out that at least the fundamental humanitarian principles of the *jus in bello* have the quality of *jus cogens*.

Reservations

A state may agree to be bound by a treaty subject to reservations, as long as the treaty itself does not prohibit this. Such departure from the contractual notion of a *consensus ad idem* is of special importance in the context of broad, multilateral treaties such as the 1949 Geneva Conventions, in which some concessions to the circumstances in which particular states find themselves must reasonably be made if wide compliance is to be secured. A reservation is defined by article 2 of the 1969 Vienna Convention on Treaties as:

> a unilateral statement ... made by a state, when signing, ratifying ... or acceding to a treaty, whereby it purports to exclude or to modify the legal effects of certain provisions of the treaty in their application to that state.

This is formally distinct from 'memoranda of understanding' and the like, although the borderline may be less clear in practice. The permissible extent of reservations and their impact upon other states party to a treaty are obviously important issues. In the Reservations to the Genocide Convention case,[8] the International Court of Justice held that a state may become party to a treaty subject to a reservation, even if other parties object to this, as long as the reservation is not so fundamental in nature as to be 'incompatible with the object and purpose of the Convention'.

There is no prohibition on reservations in the 1949 Geneva Conventions or the 1977 Additional Protocols, or indeed most other *jus in bello* treaties, including 1907 Hague Convention IV and the 1925 Geneva Gas Protocol. Indeed, a significant number of states have entered reservations to the 1949 Geneva Conventions. For example, both the UK and USA reserved the right to impose capital punishment under article 68(1) of Convention IV, whether or not the death penalty had been applicable under the original criminal law of an occupied territory.[9] However, the United Kingdom withdrew this reservation on 15 December 1971.[10] In the light of the decision in the Reservations to the Genocide Convention case, clearly no reservation could exempt a state from fundamental humanitarian treaty norms and, *ex hypothesi,* have an effect upon norms of the international humanitarian laws of armed conflict which have attained the status of customary law or *jus cogens*. In the case of other norms, a reservation may have one of three possible effects:

1 If a reservation is accepted by other states party to the treaty, it will come into effect as between the reserving state and other states, subject to the reservation.
2 Where a state party objects to the reservation, the part affected by the reservation will not come into force between the reserving and objecting states, but treaty relations between them will be otherwise unaffected unless the objecting state stipulates otherwise.
3 If the objecting state does so stipulate, the treaty will not enter into force between the reserving and objecting states, but relations with other states party to the treaty will not be affected.

The Effect of Denunciation

Provision is made in both the 1949 Geneva Conventions and the 1977 Additional Protocols for denunciation by states party to them.[11] The provisions of the four 1949 Geneva Convention in this respect are in common form, and are drafted primarily with a view to the obviation of abuse through instant denunciations in the course of an armed conflict.

Denunciation is achieved by notifying the depository for the conventions, the Swiss Federal Council, which will transmit the notification to the governments of other states party. The denunciation will not take effect until after the expiry of one year after the notification. If notification is made during an armed conflict in which the notifying state is involved and which continues for more than one year after the notification, the denunciation will not take effect until after the conclusion of peace and the repatriation of all persons protected by the convention(s) concerned. The denunciation clauses in the 1977 Additional Protocols are in similar form.

Obviously, a denunciation can only affect those obligations which arise solely through the operation of the treaty; those arising from customary laws or *jus cogens* could not be avoided in this way. For this reason, the potential effect of denunciations on the substantive application of international humanitarian norms would be very slight. The denunciation clauses of the four 1949 Geneva Conventions expressly affirm this by stating that a denunciation:

> shall in no way impair the obligations which the Parties to ... conflict shall remain bound to fulfil by virtue of the law of nations, as they result from the usages established among civilized peoples, from the laws of humanity and the dictates of public conscience.

In practice, there have been no denunciations of the 1949 Geneva Conventions. It was rumoured during the 1980–88 Gulf War that Iran might denounce the conventions as 'unIslamic', but this was not done; indeed most modern Muslim scholars hold that the humanitarian *jus in bello* by no means conflicts with *Shari'at* norms.[12] The official Iranian view is made manifest by the fact that in the later course of the 1980–88 Gulf War, Iran made a number of serious complaints about Iraqi violations of the *jus in bello*.

Investigation of Infractions

The investigation of serious breaches of the international humanitarian laws of armed conflict poses potentially serious difficulties. The duty of investigation, like the duties of dissemination, training and maintenance, falls in the first place upon the state whose personnel may be responsible.[13] This does happen on occasion, a well-known example being the case of *United States* v. *First Lieutenant William L. Calley*,[14] arising from the My Lai massacre in the Vietnam War, and more recently, following UN intervention in Somalia, *Re: Brown and*

Fisher et al.[15] Where appropriate national investigation is not forthcoming, one or another form of international investigation may be necessary.

In the case of the preparation for the trials which followed the Second World War, a large *ad hoc* bureaucracy was set up to process the vast amounts of paperwork which needed to be sifted, together with a large prosecutorial staff to develop the individual indictments and cases, but this was a rather different order of activity from that now under consideration.

The bodies which, in a given situation, might be involved in investigatory (fact-finding) activities in relation to breaches of the laws of armed conflict include the parties themselves, non-governmental organisations, UN forces and *ad hoc* commissions of one sort or another. In former Yugoslavia, a number of such bodies functioned as an UN-appointed Commission of Experts and a Special Rapporteur to the UN Commissioner on Human Rights.[16] In principle, it may be imagined that there would be no impediment to any of these bodies reporting evidence of violations of the laws of armed conflict which might come, or be brought, to their attention, but this is by no means necessarily the case. In the case of humanitarian relief agencies, and especially the International Committees of the Red Cross, the need for impartiality and maintenance of access to victims of armed conflict effectively precludes public accusatory action, in contrast with discreet diplomatic pressure for compliance. The ICRC never issues public denunciations, but will sometimes denounce given practices in non-party-specific terms, leaving the world to draw its own conclusions. One example may be seen in the denunciation by the ICRC on 6 February 1918 of gas attacks in the First World War,[17] and another in the general public condemnation by the ICRC of conditions in the internment camps in former Yugoslavia on 14 August 1992.[18] An adversarial investigatory role would severely impede the performance of the basic humanitarian functions of the ICRC, however; to an equal, and possibly even greater, extent, so would the appearance of ICRC personnel as prosecution witnesses in any trials – an event which might well bar all ICRC access to prisoners of war in the country concerned in that or any future armed conflict. This point has been expressed elsewhere, in the narrower context of evidence relating to unlawful armed proliferation:

> Their effectiveness [in humanitarian action] depends to a significant degree on observance of the basic principles of Impartiality and Neutrality in relations with the parties engaged in conflict. That might obviously be put in danger if they came to be regarded as playing an adversarial role. For this reason, requiring evidence from such humanitarian aid agencies or individual staff could be counter-productive.[19]

The same may be said of the staff the United Nations High Commissioner for Refugees, for example.

United Nations forces face related but somewhat different problems. A force like UNPROFOR in former Yugoslavia or UNOSOM in Somalia relies for the scope of its action upon its mandate. Sadly, such mandates are frequently not only unclear, but self-contradictory, a particular problem for UNPROFOR, which was at times supposed to undertake both humanitarian relief missions and enforcement action simultaneously. Again, the investigation of actual or alleged war crimes and the arrest of suspects are clearly adversarial activities which may be incompatible with other imperatives. In practice, not only UNPROFOR but the later NATO-led IFOR and SFOR were much criticised for not seeking more actively to locate and arrest war crimes suspects. Some significant action was taken, for example the arrest of one suspect and the death of another resisting arrest in June 1997 by British special forces serving with SFOR,[20] but this was in a situation significantly changed from that which had gone before.

There also arises the question of civilian police forces. So far as national police units are concerned, this is simply a part of municipal enforcement such as is considered below.[21] More interesting in the present context is the position of UNCIVPOL, the United Nations civilian police serving in association with a United Nations force. These are trained police officers with the necessary investigatory skills base, but they too are limited by the force mandate, and in former Yugoslavia this very severely curtailed their potential usefulness for this purpose.

Ultimately, the duty of investigation will in most cases – other than the very rare, if not unique, circumstances obtaining after the Second World War – rest upon a 'network' of agencies. This is clearly indicated by the phrasing of article 18 of the Statute of the International Criminal Tribunal for former Yugoslavia, which provides that:

> (1) The Prosecutor shall initiate investigations ex officio or on the basis of information obtained from any source, particularly from Governments, United Nations organs, intergovernmental and non-governmental organizations. The Prosecutor shall access the information received or obtained and decide whether there is sufficient basis to proceed.
> (2) The Prosecutor shall have the power to question suspects, victims and Witnesses, to collect evidence and to conduct on-site investigations. In carrying out these tasks, the Prosecutor may, as appropriate, seek assistance of the State authorities concerned.

So far as general provision of international humanitarian law is concerned, article 52 of 1949 Geneva Convention I provides, *inter alia*, that:

> At the request of a Party to the conflict, an enquiry shall be instituted, in a manner to be decided between the interested Parties, concerning any alleged violation of the Convention.
>
> If agreement has not been reached concerning the procedure for the enquiry, the Parties should agree on the choice of an umpire who will decide upon the procedure to be followed.

This, it must be admitted, is not a very strongly phrased provision, nor one that is likely to overcome the very considerable obstacles in the way of such procedures in the heated exigencies of actual armed conflict. Much more detailed provision is now made by article 90 of 1977 Additional Protocol I. This provides for the creation of an International Fact-finding Commission of 15 members[22] with competence to:

> (i) enquire into any facts alleged to be a grave breach as defined in the [1949] Conventions or and this Protocol or other serious violation of the Conventions or of this Protocol;
> (ii) facilitate through its good offices, the restoration of an attitude of respect for the Convention and this Protocol.[23]

In other cases – those not involving 'grave breaches' of the 1949 Geneva Conventions of 1977 Additional Protocol I – the commission may institute inquiries only at the request of a party to the conflict and with the consent of other parties involved.[24] It may reasonably be imagined that in many such cases the requisite consents would not be forthcoming, but the provision with respect to 'grave breaches' may be of very considerable potential value. The consideration of the possibility of establishing a permanent International Criminal Court in the light of the experiences of the conflicts in the 1990s in former Yugoslavia and Rwanda may again focus attention on this issue, and a fact-finding commission may well form part of that structure, should one be established successfully.[25]

War Crimes: The Historic International Response to Abuses

The history of the international or quasi-international criminal jurisprudence of armed conflict is largely confined to the second half of the 20th century. The specific examples of importance are the proceedings before the International Military Tribunals at Nuremberg and Tokyo in 1945, together with associated lesser tribunals, and those in the 1990s before the International Criminal Tribunals for Former Yugoslavia and Rwanda. Historic instances prior to this are not entirely lacking, however, nor are they devoid of significance.

Such medieval examples as are recorded are few in number, and for the most part of doubtful implication. The summary executions which followed the battles of South Foreland in 1217 and Sluys in 1340 may be cited as examples.[26] More substantial claims may be made for the response of Western canon law to some early military outrages. The Western world was so shocked by the savagery displayed by the victorious Burgundians at the Battle of Soissons in 923 and by the Normans at the Battle of Hastings in 1066 and the subsequent 'harrying of the north', which would today have been termed genocidal, that the Church issued decrees imposing varying levels of penance on the members of the armies concerned.[27] However, the most significant early example is the 1474 Hagenbach case.[28] The case arose from the Burgundian occupation of the town of Breisach, during which an atrocious regime was imposed under the authority of the occupation Governor, Peter von Hagenbach. After the recapture of the town and its return to the legitimate sovereignty of the Archduke of Austria, von Hagenbach was put on trial before a court which may fairly be seen as the first international war crimes tribunal. It was technically convened within the authority of the Holy Roman Empire, subject to the status of Switzerland at the time, but the 'Empire' could only loosely be considered a single entity in the late 15th century.[29] The crimes with which Hagenbach was charged would today have fallen primarily within the category of violations of human rights, but since they occurred in the course of a military occupation, they would also have been violations of the *jus in bello*. The trial was in some respects thoroughly 'medieval' – for example, in its emphasis on violations of Hagenbach's oath of chivalric knighthood – but it also included a strikingly 'modern' consideration of a plea of 'superior orders'. Ultimately, Hagenbach was convicted and beheaded.

Interesting as the Hagenbach case is, little followed in the development of an international criminal jurisprudence of armed conflict – despite an undoubted juristic element in the discourse of the Congress of Vienna which terminated the Napoleonic Wars – until the early 20th century and the end of the First World War in 1918. There can be no doubt that very serious violations of the laws of armed conflict were perpetrated in the First World War, although to a lesser extent than propaganda suggested, and to a much lesser extent than was to occur in the Second World War. At the end of the war, the victorious Allies proposed to set up an international, or more accurately inter-Allied, tribunal to try a considerable number of personnel from the Central Powers. The Commission on the Responsibility of the Authors of the War and on the Enforcement of Penalties prepared a list of 896 alleged 'war criminals', headed by ex-Kaiser Wilhelm II. The scheme was flawed in a number of fundamental respects. The spirit of the proposal was thoroughly vindictive, and the guilt of the accused was virtually presupposed; the avowed aim of the British

Prime Minister, Lloyd George, to 'hang the Kaiser' indicates the mood. In the end – and it may be said, fortunately – this scheme came to nothing. This was in large part because Germany was unwilling to surrender the large number of defendants in its territory for trial. The ex-Kaiser himself was by this time in exile in the neutral Netherlands, which, properly, refused to hand over him. (It is worth noting that at the time of the Nazi invasion of the Netherlands, the British Government let it be known that Wilhelm II would be granted asylum in the United Kingdom if he so desired. The ex-Kaiser, who loathed Nazism, was, not surprisingly, unwilling to avail himself of his former enemy's offer, and died on 4 June 1941 at Doorn in the Netherlands.[30]) The Allies did carry out a few rather pointless trials *in absentia*, including that of the last commander of the Richthofen air corps, Hermann Goering, who was to achieve much greater notoriety in the Second World War. Of much greater significance were the trials conducted, at Allied insistence, in Germany, including the two cases arising from hospital ship sinkings, the *Dover Castle* case[31] and the *Llandovery Castle* case,[32] which remain important in the modern *jus in bello*.

The Second World War and the Modern Era

The modern era in international legal response to war crimes, as well as crimes against peace and crimes against humanity, may be considered to have commenced with the end of the Second World War. The crisis disclosed at the end of the war was unprecedented in scale, if not in type. The Third Reich was a state erected on contempt for law, whether domestic or international, and which substituted for it a 'leadership principle', the *Führerprinzip*, in which whatever the leadership willed was 'law'. The gross violations of both the *jus ad bellum* and the *jus in bello* perpetrated by the Nazi state between 1939 and 1945 raised in a new and more pointed form the question of international response to gross violations of the laws of armed conflict. The policies of the extreme nationalist clique which dominated the Japanese Government during the war years, starting much earlier in the Far East with the outbreak of the Sino-Japanese War in 1931, raised very similar questions, although the legal contexts of the trial which followed was somewhat different. In both cases, the complete collapse of the wartime governments with military defeat, and the *de facto* assumption of governing authority by the Allied powers, rendered international trials practically possible and arguably necessary.

In Germany, the International Military Tribunal (IMT) at Nuremberg was established by the USA, UK, USSR and France under the 1945 London Agreement, acting as occupying powers in transition to a new and legitimate German regime.[33] In Japan, the International Military Tribunal (Far East) (IMT(FE)) was established by General MacArthur as Allied Supreme Commander in the Far East, under powers delegated from the Allied governments of the USA, UK, USSR and China.[34] There was a significant distinction for the structure at Nuremberg, in so far as the *Reich* government had been treated as a defunct criminal regime, whereas the Imperial Japanese Government was treated as a legitimate and continuing authority which had temporarily fallen into criminal hands.

The proceedings before the IMT and IMT(FE) in 1945 were of profound significance in the development of the criminal jurisprudence of armed conflict in several regards. In particular, the trials laid the foundations for the modern categorisation of 'war crimes', and their influence can clearly be seen in the Statutes of the International Criminal Tribunals for former Yugoslavia and Rwanda drafted in the 1990s. They also established clearly the jurisprudential basis of the criminal liability of individuals for violations of the international laws of armed conflict. Finally, the IMT and IMT(FE), together with the various lesser tribunals established by the Allied powers to try lower-level war crimes defendants,[35] made a large, and varyingly helpful, contribution to such issues as 'defences' or pleas of superior orders and military necessity.

The trials which followed the Second World War have, together with many other aspects of that conflict, become subject to 'revisionist' historical analysis, with a tendency to dismiss them as 'victor's justice' and mere acts of 'revenge'. The proceedings were not beyond criticism: some of the sentencing was bizarre, for example the contrasting sentences passed on Speer (20 years' imprisonment) and Sauckel (death). As Ann and John Tusa comment:

> The most striking example of what might be seen as an illogical decisions was in the case of Albert Speer. The American judge's aides argued forcibly that Speer had demanded slave labour for German industry and had been fully aware of the squalid and brutal conditions in which it had been employed. Sauckel was to hand for securing those slaves, why not Speer who ordered and allocated them?[36]

The frequently voiced suspicion that Speer (the astute professional architect) benefited compared to Sauckel (the street thug) from irrelevant issues of 'image and presentation' seems difficult to rebut. Whether both should have been hanged or both been imprisoned is another question, but the inequality of treatment is striking. It is also possible to criticise the things that the tribunals did *not* do. Not all war crimes were committed by the Axis powers, and in this context the question of the Katyn Forest massacre must be raised. At Nuremberg, this mass murder of Polish officers was conveniently blamed on the SS, although it is now well established, and the evidence in 1945 strongly suggested, that it was in fact a Soviet crime.

Nevertheless, the IMT and IMT(FE) conducted trials which were, on the whole, concordant with the best principles of due process, certainly infinitely better than anything which had been on offer in the Third Reich – the contrast between Nuremberg and the Nazi political courts such as the *Sondergerichthof* could hardly have been more striking. The case against those defendants who were convicted was overwhelming, and the attempts of modern revisionists to rehabilitate them must be viewed in the light of the horrors which the evidence so plainly demonstrated. The single most valuable legacy of the criminal proceedings at the end of the Second World War was perhaps to establish once and for all that those who create and run a criminal state cannot be assured that the facade which they have erected will necessarily permanently shield them from the consequences of their actions.

The Nuremberg and Tokyo trials made an important contribution to the international criminal jurisprudence of armed conflict, but it was not the precursor to any systematic *international* response to violations of the laws of armed conflict. The next developments did not occur for another half century, until the 1990s. There were proposals for an international tribunal following the 1990–91 Gulf Conflict, but this came to nothing, not least because of the unavailability of potential defendants. The events of the armed conflicts in former Yugoslavia and the genocidal conflict in Rwanda finally led to the establishment of further *ad hoc* International Criminal Tribunals. The Tribunal for Former Yugoslavia was established by UN Security Council Resolutions 808 and 827 of 1993 for the prosecution of those responsible for 'serious violations of international humanitarian law' in former Yugoslavia after 1991. The International Criminal Tribunal for Rwanda was set up in the same way, and its Statute essentially followed the model of that of the Tribunal for Former Yugoslavia. The Tribunal for Former Yugoslavia faced certain problems deriving from the nature of the conflicts in that region: a conflict within Bosnia-Herzegovina between the government and the Bosnian Serb dissidents based at Pale, but also involving other forces from outside Bosnia-Herzegovina, including those emanating from Croatia. As a result, the conflict combined 'international' and 'non-international' levels of confrontation, and therefore, in principle, involved the applications of differing levels of international humanitarian law. In practice, the so-called 'networks of agreements' between the parties brokered by the International Committee of the Red Cross in November 1991 established that the parties to the conflicts would be bound by the principles of the four 1949 Geneva Conventions and the broad principles of the general international laws of armed conflict.[37] This position is reflected in the jurisdictional provisions of articles 2, 3 and 5 of the Statute of the International Criminal Tribunal for Former Yugoslavia. The undertakings given by the parties to the conflicts proved of little, if any, value in the actual conduct of hostilities, but they did establish the criteria by which their subsequent liabilities were to be judged. Both the Tribunals for Former Yugoslavia and Rwanda experienced considerable difficulty in bringing defendants before them. Some were captured, either being handed over by authorities in the states concerned or in third states, or in some cases being detained by peacekeeping or enforcement forces – as in the case of one defendant arrested and another killed resisting arrest by British Special Forces attached to SFOR in former Yugoslavia in July 1997. Indicted political and military leaders remained elusive, however, and in many cases enjoyed the shelter of sympathetic governments or factions. Significant cases have been conducted, not least the Tadic case before the Tribunal for Former Yugoslavia. Dusko Tadic, a Bosnian Serb who had been handed over to the tribunal by Germany, was tied and convicted on charges of very serious offences committed in the internment camp at Omarska. The case was also interesting for the challenges mounted by Tadic to the legality of the tribunal, its primacy over municipal tribunals, and its specific jurisdiction over the matters with which he was charged. On the central question of the legitimacy of its constitution, the Appeals Chamber of the tribunal held that it was both established by a lawful process within United Nations competence, specifically as a 'measure' under Chapter VII of the UN Charter, and included within its constitution those guarantees of due process which are the criteria of identification for a court properly so called in international law. The decision was hardly surprising, but the robust determination of the Appeals Chamber must be seen as a reasonable interpretation of the available rules and principles, and a useful affirmation of both international legal competence and the procedural parameters within which it must operate.[38] At the time of writing (1997), these two tribunals must be considered a step forward in the processes of international enforcement, and have also sparked further consideration of the possibility of a permanent International Criminal Tribunal.[39] Much may come from this, although serious questions must also be raised about the procedural obstacles which may be encountered, and the need from the beginning to ensure the pragmatic credibility of any such tribunal. Judge Guillaume remarks wisely that:

> In this connection, as well as for the *ad hoc* tribunals already established, one inevitably has mixed feelings: on the one hand, any progress in the punishment of international crimes is praiseworthy; but, on the

> other hand, the obstacles to this are formidable, and it would be a mistake for governments to create international criminal courts limiting their scope for action in such a way that failure would be inevitable and that the idea would suffer from lack of success.[40]

These institutional developments are highly significant in themselves, but their contribution to the clarification of criminal liabilities may be considered much their most important contribution to the development of a criminal jurisprudence of armed conflict.

What are War Crimes?

In principle, a war crime might be taken to be any serious breach of the international laws of armed conflict. However, so simple a definition could not be considered adequate since a distinction must clearly be drawn between serious breaches meriting criminalisation and mere technical defaults. Article 6(b) of the Charter of the International Military Tribunal at Nuremberg defines war crimes very simply as:

> violations of the laws or customs of war. Such violations shall include, but not be limited to, murder, ill-treatment, or deportation to slave labor or for any other purpose of civilian population of or in occupied territory, murder or ill-treatment of prisoners of war or persons on the seas, killing of hostages, plunder of public or private property, wanton destruction of cities, towns, or villages, or devastation not justified by military necessity.

This was obviously a broad summary, which was adequate for the purposes of a tribunal considering the liabilities of the military and political leadership of a criminal regime. Useful further definition was afforded by the definition of 'grave breaches' of the four 1949 Geneva Conventions, although these were naturally limited to breaches of those conventions.

However, the most recent and effective definition of war crimes is offered by articles 2 and 3 of the 1993 Statute of the International Criminal Tribunal for Former Yugoslavia. Article 2 is founded upon grave breaches of the 1949 Geneva Conventions which it defines as:

> the following acts against persons or property protected under the provisions of the relevant Geneva Convention: (a) wilful killing; (b) torture or inhuman treatment including biological experiments; (c) wilfully causing great suffering or serious injury to body or health; (d) extensive destruction and appropriation of property, not justified by military necessity and carried out unlawfully and wantonly; (e) com-

> pelling a prisoner of war or a civilian to serve in the armed forces of a hostile power; (f) wilfully depriving a prisoner of war or a civilian of the rights of fair and regular trial; (g) unlawful deportation or transfer or unlawful confinement of a civilian; (h) taking civilians as hostages.

This sets out the basic elements of 1949 Geneva Convention I, article 49, 1949 Geneva Convention II, article 50; 1949 Geneva Convention III, article 129, and 1949 Geneva Convention IV, article 146, dealing, respectively, with 'grave breaches' of those conventions. Article 3 goes on to list the basic elements of serious violations of the 'Hague' dimension of international humanitarian law. This it defines, somewhat anachronistically, as violations of the 'laws or customs of war', and states that:

> Such violations shall include but not be limited to: (a) employment of poisonous weapons or other weapons calculated to cause unnecessary suffering; (b) wanton destruction of cities, towns or villages, or devastation not justified by military necessity; (c) attack or bombardment, by whatever means, or undefended towns, villages, dwellings or buildings; (d) seizure of, destruction or wilful damage done to institutions dedicated to religion, charity and education, the arts and sciences, historic monuments and works of art and science; (e) plunder of public or private property.

This formulation includes important elements from the 1868 Declaration of St Petersburg and the Land Warfare Regulations annexed to 1907 Hague Convention IV, notably articles 23(a)(e), 25, 27 and 47.

These are much more detailed formulations than those offered by the IMT Charter, but are still, naturally, devised by reference to the matters arising before the particular *ad hoc* tribunal for which they were drafted. There are still some notable, and in some cases rather curious, omissions. These include omission of any reference to abuse of the red cross, red crescent or other protective emblems, which is forbidden by article 23(f) of the Land Warfare Regulations annexed to 1907 Hague Convention IV as well as article 44 of 1949 Geneva Convention I and articles 44 and 45 of 1949 Geneva Convention II. Admittedly, such abuse is not defined by the 1949 Geneva Conventions as a 'grave breach',[41] but the Statute's formulation is by no means limited to such breaches.

The Statute of the Tribunal for Former Yugoslavia also does not take account of the further 'grave' breaches defined by 1977 Additional Protocol I, although their relevance to the conflict before the tribunal may be doubted, even though the former Federal Republic of Yugoslavia had ratified both 1977 Additional Protocols. Articles 11 and 85 of 1977 Additional Protocol I are of special interest. Article 11(4) provides, in the context of medical care of protected persons, that:

> Any wilful act or omission which seriously endangers the physical or mental health or integrity of any person who is in the power of a Party other than the one on which he depends ... shall be in grave breach of this Protocol.

Article 85(3) defines as grave breaches of the Protocol:

> (a) making the civilian population or individual civilians the object of attack; (b) launching an indiscriminate attack ... in the knowledge that such attack will cause excessive loss of life, injury to civilians or damage to civilian objects ... (c) launching an attack against works or dangerous forces in the knowledge that such attack will cause excessive loss of life, injury to civilians or damage to civilian objects ... (d) making non-defended localities and demilitarized zones the object of attack; (e) making a person the object of attack in the knowledge that he is *hors de combat*; (f) the perfidious use ... of the distinctive emblem of the red cross, red crescent ... or other protective signs recognized by the [1949] Conventions or this Protocol.

Article 85(4) then adds five further actions constituting 'grave breaches' when they are 'committed wilfully and in violation of the Conventions or the Protocol':

> (a) the transfer by the Occupying Power of parts of its own civilian population into the territory it occupies, or the deportation or transfer of all or parts of the population of the occupied territory within or outside this territory ... (b) unjustifiable delay in repatriation of prisoners of war or civilians; (c) practices of *apartheid* and other inhuman and degrading practices involving outrages upon personal dignity, based on racial discrimination; (d) making ... the cultural or spiritual heritage of peoples ... to which special protection has been given by special arrangement ... the object of attack, causing as a result extensive destruction thereof, when there is no evidence of ... [relevant] violation by the adverse Party ... and when such [heritage locations] ... are not located in the immediate proximity of military objectives; (e) depriving a person protected by the [1949] Conventions or referred to in paragraph 2 of this Article of the rights of fair and regular trial.

Some elements of these listings do no more than reaffirm what is already either express or implicit in the 1949 Geneva Conventions or other provisions. This can be argued to be the case for article 11(4). Some parts of article 85(3)(4) essentially strengthen or re-emphasise existing provision – for example, article 85(3))(a)(b)(e)(f). There are also some new provisions and emphases, especially in article 85(4). It may be noted, however, that article 85(4) is an effective definition of that practice offensively misnamed 'ethnic cleansing' in the conflicts in former Yugoslavia, although such action is in any case in violation of article 48 of 1949 Geneva Convention IV.[42]

Compilations of war crimes for the immediate purposes of *ad hoc* tribunals are, by reason of their inevitable focus upon the particular situation in question, unlikely to be wholly comprehensive. However, the combination of article 6(b) of the Charter of the International Military Tribunal at Nuremberg with articles 2 and 3 of the Statute of the International Criminal Tribunal for Former Yugoslavia together with the additional, and to some extent, innovatory provision made by articles 11 and 85 of 1977 Additional Protocol I may be taken as an effective listing of those serious violations of the humanitarian *jus in bello* which can usefully be categorised as 'war crimes'. The emphasis is, again, upon the quality of *serious violations,* and in so far as a criterion of identification is required for this purpose, this may suffice. It has been remarked elsewhere that:

> The real criterion of identification, which is implicit in all the major listings [of 'war crimes'] ... is perhaps the gravity of the *actus reus* in question and its consequences. If municipal criminal lawyers are disconcerted by such open-endedness ... it can be pointed out that the practical discretion is far from unknown in their own practice and discipline and that public international law may by its nature be more 'open textured' than most municipal law but is not so in its fundamental principles.[43]

If not a 'definition', therefore, these formulations may in combination be accepted at least as a working description of the category of war crimes as serious violations of the international laws of armed conflict. At the same time, it must be borne in mind that the list is not closed, and as some of the formulations state, there must always be entered the caveat that the violations concerned 'include but are not limited to' those expressly set out. This is not an attempt to avoid the principle of *nulla crimen sine lege* – clearly, a violation must refer to some established treaty or customary *jus in bello* norm – it is rather a denial of the claim that any of the formulations set out can be considered as definitive codifications.

The Question of Personal Liability

International humanitarian law is part of public international law, and therefore in principle a law which is concerned with the rights, duties and liabilities of states in their relations *inter se,* and not with those of individuals as such. How, then, can an individual be held liable in an international tribunal for offences against a system of law in which he or she lacks legal personality? This was inevitably a question raised at Nuremberg in 1945.

It must first be emphasised that the primary duty for the maintenance of norms of international humanitarian law and its enforcement against personnel who violate it rests upon states through their systems of criminal law and military discipline.[44] The question of international jurisdiction arises only at the point where a state cannot or will not undertake municipal enforcement, or where the circumstances otherwise dictate that this is the only viable way of proceeding. In such a case, as classically with the Nuremberg trials in 1945, the most useful analysis of the arising of personal liability is supplied by W.V. O'Brien in his remark that the visitation of international criminal responsibility upon individuals 'pierced the corporate veil of the State'.[45] As is the case for a company, the state is a group activity which is conveniently placed in a unified legal 'bracket', but its actions are nevertheless, in reality, those of individuals acting on its behalf and in its nature. Most states, like most companies, will most of the time act within the framework of legal norms by and within which their 'corporate' legal personality is defined. However, where a state or a company comes under the direction of leaders who are wholly contemptuous of the legal order within which they supposedly operate, the 'corporate' legal person may become no more than a facade for the concealment of criminal conspiracy. Where this happens in most systems of municipal company law, the courts will be able to 'pierce the veil' of incorporation, set aside the separate legal personality of the company, and hold those who are managing it liable for the malfeasances which they have caused the company to perpetrate. This was precisely the position which the International Military Tribunal at Nuremberg adopted in relation to the political and military leaders of the Third Reich. In judgment, the tribunal remarked on this point that:

> Individuals have international duties that transcend ... national obligations or obedience ... He who violates the laws of war cannot obtain immunity while acting in pursuance of the authority of the state if the state in authorizing action moves outside its competence under international law.[46]

In essence, this is a doctrine of international *ultra vires*, in which an individual undertaking unlawful action on behalf of a state cannot shelter behind the legal facade of the state if the state itself lacks the legal capacity to authorise such action. It must, of course, be added that at the Nuremberg trials the defendants were the very people who had made and directed the criminal Third Reich regime, and it could hardly be open to them to shelter behind the very thing which they had made in order to evade liability for its – meaning their – actions. It has been suggested in criticism of the Nuremberg decisions that this introduction of personal international criminal liability was an innovation, and to that degree an improper imposition of a liability not previously existing.[47] In fact, the Nuremberg Tribunal did what had certainly previously been contemplated, for example in relation to the planned trials aborted after the First World War, and such a doctrine of 'veil piercing', however rarely applied, may be argued to be implicit in any legal structure involving 'artificial' legal personality such as that attributed to a state.

A subsidiary, but important, question arises in the distinct but related issue of 'superior orders'. To what extent, if any, can an individual plead obedience to superior orders as a defence when charged with the commission of a 'war crime'? This is an issue of some complexity which requires discussion in its own right.

Superior Orders

Any system of military discipline necessarily rests upon the presumption of obedience to superior orders. However, where an order is unlawful *per se* or leads necessarily to unlawful consequences, the extent to which they may avail a subordinate accused of perpetrating a war crime become questionable. The position conventionally stated at present is that a plea of *respondeat superior* ('superior orders') can never be a defence, but may be a plea in mitigation. This was the position stated by article 8 of the Charter of the International Military Tribunal at Nuremberg, and it is repeated by article 7(4) of the Statute of the International Criminal Tribunal for former Yugoslavia, which provides that:

> The fact that an accused person acted pursuant to an order of a Government or of a superior shall not relieve him of criminal responsibility, but may be considered in mitigation of punishment if the International Tribunal determines that justice so requires.

In this respect, the legacy of Nuremberg is not necessarily to be considered helpful, and the conventional position thus stated can be argued in some respects to be questionable. As it was stated by article 8 of the IMT Charter, the Nuremberg doctrine of superior orders represented a *prima facie* departure from established law on the subject which might be characterised as having been informed by an 'ought to know' doctrine. The scope of this pre-1945 doctrine may readily be shown through a brief review of the case law.

An early English example can be found in *R.* v. *Thomas* (1816).[48] Thomas was a marine serving on board HMS *Achilles*, and had been ordered to keep all boats away from the ship other than those which had been authorised to approach by an officer. One boat approached repeatedly, intending to offer goods for sale to the ships's personnel, and after warning it off on several occasions, Thomas fired upon it, killing one of the occupants. At his trial, which appears to have been before a civilian court, Thomas was convicted of murder, but subject to a strong recommendation from the jury that he be pardoned. This was not strictly a case of an unlawful superior order – the order was as such quite lawful but, as it turned out, dangerously ambiguous and thus open to misinterpretation by Thomas. Nevertheless, the apparent sense of the jury that Thomas had sought lawfully, if under tragic mistake, to perform his duty pointed the way to later legal development.

The most important British case occurred nearly a century later, during the second Boer War, with *R.* v. *Smith* (1990).[49] Smith was a private soldier who was sent as a member of a patrol to arrest men at Jackalsfontein believed to be about to join the enemy. As the patrol approached, a rider was seen hastening in the direction of the enemy forces, presumably to seek armed assistance. One man having been arrested, the commanding officer, Captain Cox, requisitioned a horse to take the prisoner back to Naauwpoort, and ordered one of the farm labourers, Dolley, to fetch a saddle for the horse. Dolley refused to move, and on Captain Cox's orders, Smith shot him. He was tried for murder before a special tribunal set up under the Indemnity and Special Tribunals Act 1900, and was acquitted on a plea of superior orders. In judgment, Justice Solomon stated:

> if a soldier honestly believes he is doing his duty in obeying the commands of his superior, and if the orders are not so manifestly illegal that he must or ought to have known that they are unlawful, the private soldier would be protected by the orders of his superior officer.[50]

This may be taken as the classic common law statement of the 'ought to know' doctrine. It is supported by decisions in the USA, including *Riggs* v. *State* (1866) and *Commonwealth ex rel. Wadsworth* v. *Shortall* (1903). [51] The clearest exposition of the practical implications of this approach can be found in the contrast between three cases, all involving sinkings by submarines: the *Dover Castle* case, the *Llandovery Castle* case and the *Peleus* case, all of which have been referred to above.[52] The first two cases involved hospital ship sinkings in the First World War. In the *Dover Castle* case,[53] the British hospital ship HMHS *Dover Castle* was sunk on 26 May 1917 in the Tyrrhenian Sea by UC-67 under the command of *Kapitanleutnant* Karl Neumann. Neumann had acted under orders issued by the German Admiralty which stated, falsely, that Allied hospital ships were being used as troop carriers, and ordered attack upon them unless exempted by specific orders from the naval authorities. Neumann was not in a position to verify the accuracy or otherwise of the Admiralty's assertion, and therefore obeyed the order. At his trial before the Second Criminal Senate in Germany after the war, he was acquitted essentially upon a plea of *respondeat superior*. In judgment, the court stated:

> According to paragraph 47 of the [Imperial German] Military Penal Code No. 2, a subordinate who acts in conformity with orders is ... liable to punishment as an accomplice, when he knows that his superiors have ordered him to do acts which involve a civil or military crime or misdemeanor. ... The accused. ... sank the *Dover Castle* in obedience to a service order of his highest superiors, an order which he considered to be [lawful and] binding. He cannot, therefore, be punished for his conduct.[54]

The contrasting circumstances of the *Llandovery Castle* case[56] have been reviewed above.[56] It will be recalled that the British hospital ship *Llandovery Castle* was sunk in the Atlantic on 27 June 1917 by U-86 under the command of *Kapitanleutnant* Patzig, and that after the sinking the U-boat surfaced and perpetrated a massacre of the survivors, possibly in an effort to eliminate all witnesses to an unlawful attack. Patzig disappeared after the war, and was never brought to trial, but two of his subordinates were tried before the Second Criminal Senate and convicted for their parts in the massacre. Their plea of superior orders was rejected, and the court remarked in judgment that:

> It is certainly to be urged in favour of the military subordinates, that they are under no obligation to question the order of their superior officer, and they can count upon its legality. But no such confidence can be held to exist, if such an order is universally known to everybody, including the accused, to be without any doubt whatever against the law. This happens only in rare and exceptional cases. But this case was precisely one of them, for ... it was perfectly clear to the accused that killing defenceless people in the lifeboats could be nothing else but a breach of the law.[57]

The distinction between the two cases should be obvious, in that Neumann obeyed an order which credibly appeared to be lawful, even though it was not, whereas Dithmar and Boldt in the *Llandovery Castle* case obeyed without protest an order which was, on any assessment, blatantly unlawful. In sentencing them, however, the court allowed a small consideration of the orders as a mitigating factor. The reasoning adopted in the *Llandovery Castle* case was closely followed after the Second World War in the *Peleus* case,[58] which has also been considered above.[59] In that case too, a massacre of survivors was perpetrated, and whilst the commanding officer, *Kapitanleutnant* Eck, refused to plead 'superior orders', the plea did not avail his subordinates on precisely the same grounds which had led to its rejection in the *Llandovery Castle* case. It is worth noting that this adoption of the 'ought to know' doctrine by the British Military Tribunal which tried the *Peleus* case in Hamburg took place *after* the promulgation of the more restrictive 'Nuremberg' doctrine in the IMT Charter, even though it occurred in the context of a rejection of *respondeat superior* as a defence.

The question then arises of whether the 'Nuremberg' doctrine effectively superseded the earlier 'ought to know' doctrine after 1945, as the drafting of article 7(4) of the Statute of the International Criminal Tribunal for Former Yugoslavia seems to suggest. That it did so is certainly the conventional view, and may be seen plainly in the contrast between the 1944 and 1956 editions of the British *Manual of Military Law*. The 1944 edition stated:

> If the command were obviously illegal, the inferior would be justified in questioning, or even in refusing to execute it ... But so long as orders ... are not obviously [illegal] ... the duty of the soldier is to obey and (if he thinks fit) to make a formal complaint afterwards.[60]

In contrast, the post-Nuremberg, 1956 edition of the manual stated:

> The better view appears to be ... that an order ... whether manifestly illegal or not, can never of itself excuse the recipient if he carries out the order, although it may give rise to a defence on other grounds ...[61]

The reference here to 'other grounds' is interesting, but not precisely explained. The difference between the 1944 and 1956 statements does nevertheless represent a clear and rather dramatic change of view. Whether that apparent shift in the law was entirely what it has been taken to be may be questioned, however.

It must first be asked whether a new doctrine was actually intended in 1945. The defendants before both the International Military Tribunal at Nuremberg and the International Military Tribunal (Far East) at Tokyo were the senior political and military leaders respectively of Germany and Japan, and the crimes with which they were charged were of such gravity that no sustainable interpretation of the classic 'ought to know' doctrine could have afforded them a defence of 'superior orders'. It may be surmised that the reason that the restrictive statement was put into the Charter of the Nuremberg Tribunal was the 'leadership principle' upon which the Third Reich operated. Under this structure, each level of the hierarchy was strictly directed by the level above, culminating in Hitler, who directed the whole. It was clear that with Hitler conveniently dead, the defendants might be minded to plead 'superior orders' and 'act of state' as a means of seeking to evade their responsibility for what was done. In its original context, therefore, the Nuremberg restriction upon superior orders as a defence would seem entirely appropriate. However, when this restriction is expanded into a wider sphere and taken to have superseded the earlier doctrine, its effects may become highly questionable.

Is it seriously to be argued that a private soldier, or even a junior officer, who is given an apparently lawful order which he or she obeys, only to find that the order was in fact not lawful, has no defence but only a plea in mitigation? It may be argued that such a plea could mean an absolute remission of sentence, but the subordinate would still leave the tribunal branded a 'war criminal'. The matter has not, at the time of writing (1997), arisen before the International Criminal Tribunal for Former Yugoslavia, but it is again interesting to note that in the *Peleus* case, decided contemporaneously with the Nuremberg Trials, the older 'ought to know' standard was applied. It may be argued that even in the light of article 8 of the IMT Charter at Nuremberg and its repetition by article 7(4) of the Statute of the International Criminal Tribunal for Former Yugoslavia, the criterion for non-availability of 'superior orders' as a defence may still be an order which is *manifestly illegal*. Interestingly in this context, it has been argued by J. Blackett that:

> the law can recognise the military dilemma and grant the subordinate a defence in criminal proceedings in all cases, where he acted in obedience to superior orders except those where the actions required of him were objectively manifestly illegal. In those cases the subordinate's training and background should be taken into account at least to mitigate his sentence ...[62]

This must seem a very reasonable view. In most armed forces, a manifestly unlawful order can be questioned, and if the order is not manifestly unlawful, it seems unreasonable to demand that it should be questioned. If this were to be required, one would be put in mind of the protest made by Sir Charles Napier in 1869, quoted wryly by Peter Rowe, that:

> If such is the law, the Army must become a deliberative body, and ought to be composed of attorneys ...[63]

Such a conclusion would be an absurdity, and as has been suggested elsewhere, it may still reasonably be contended that:

> notwithstanding the restrictive 'Nuremberg' doctrine, an 'ought to know' doctrine such as that affirmed in the *Peleus case* ... appears still to have much to commend it. The context of this is usefully set out by [the requirements for dissemination and training in the four 1949 Geneva Conventions] ... In this context the necessities of discipline, the practical exigencies of military service and the formal norms of both the *jus in bello* and municipal military law may be maintained without conflict.[64]

According to this view, it may be suggested that 'superior orders' can never constitute a defence where it is, or ought to be, clear to the subordinate that the action being undertaken is illegal. In such a case, the orders could act only, at most, as a mitigating factor. This appears to have been the case so far as the nature of the violations considered by the IMT at Nuremberg, the IMT(FE) at Tokyo and the International Criminal Tribunals for Former Yugoslavia and Rwanda were concerned. So far as more ambiguous cases may be concerned, where the illegality was not patent upon the face of the order, a case may still be made out for the earlier 'ought to know' doctrine. This is not to suggest a 'defence' of ignorance of the law, but rather one of ignorance of factual circumstances, where that circumstance has been misrepresented by a higher authority. It is unlikely that this type of situation would arise before an *ad hoc* tribunal, or even before a permanent International Criminal Tribunal, should one be established,[65] but in the event that it did, it must also be remembered that the argument is not over the existence of culpability, but rather over its placement. Where a subordinate is deceived and thus led to undertake unknowingly an unlawful act under orders, the culpability is that of the superior authority responsible for the order.

Military Necessity

Military necessity, both in a narrower sense and in the broader sense of *kriegsrason*, is a controversial doctrine in the laws of armed conflict, not least because it is seen as having the potential to subvert the very purposes of legal regulation in armed conflict. In the sense that 'necessity knows no law', that would indeed be the case, and it must be stressed that no such concept exists in the modern *jus in bello*. In a much more narrowly defined scope, however, there not only is but indeed must be a concept of 'necessity' in the application of the law. The laws of armed conflict need to be applied in circumstances of extreme difficulty, so some flexibility in operation must be admitted if the law is to remain practically viable. A starting point may be found in the position advanced by Jean Pictet:

> there is an implicit clause in any law to the effect that no one is obliged to do what is impossible. ... [W]hen we speak of what is 'impossible' we must refer only to genuine material impossibility. ... [W]hen a party is violating the Conventions, it is up to that party to prove that it is impossible to do otherwise ... [and] the violation must cease immediately, as soon as the situation has improved, even slightly.[66]

This must manifestly be the case so far as core humanitarian norms are concerned, and indeed in the case of the most fundamental norms it is difficult, if not impossible, to imagine cases in which their application would in this sense become 'impossible'. For example in this sense, it could never become 'impossible' not to torture prisoners of war. It may be said that core humanitarian norms are, in a Dworkinian sense, so 'weighted' as always to 'trump' counter-argument.[67]

Nevertheless, international humanitarian law treaties themselves refer to 'military necessity', and always in some sense as an exception to a *prima facie* applicable norm. Pictet suggests that such references are simply acknowledgements of refusals of 'unconditional commitment' by the states which negotiate the treaties.[68] In at least some instances, this is indeed the case, but the fact remains that the provisions are there, and in this regard the helpful observation is made by Morris Greenspan that:

> the rules of war make allowance within their framework for military necessity, which cannot transcend the rules themselves. ... [M]ilitary necessity was ... taken into account when the rules were framed, and the individual rules themselves indicate to what extent [if any] they may be modified under the stress of military necessity.[69]

This is a view which has much to commend it. It notes in the first place that the doctrine of military necessity operates *within* the *jus in bello*, and is therefore strictly limited by it, in contrast with a form of 'exception' which might act wholly outwith the law, effectively suspending its operation. It also implicitly, by the inclusion of the caveat 'if any', notes that, as is suggested above, some core norms are inherently incapable of modification by reference to 'necessity'.

Therefore, it is clearly necessary to examine just what may constitute 'military necessity'. There has been a certain amount of judicial and quasi-judicial consideration of this question. Early cases commonly concerned damage to property in the course of military action where no reasonable alternative action existed, as in the Hardman claim[70] between the UK and the USA following US action in Cuba in the 1898–99 Spanish–American War, and the Russian Indemnity case[71] between the Russian and Ottoman Empires in 1912. The question of military necessity was considered at a more fundamental level in the trials which followed the Second World War, however. The Charter of the International Military Tribunal at Nuremberg included in the category of 'war crimes':

> Wanton destruction of cities, towns or villages or devastation not justified by military necessity.[72]

The question was most closely examined, not by the IMT itself, but by a United States Military Tribunal in the High Command case.[73] The wholesale destruction of property by retreating German forces was sought to be justified on grounds of 'military necessity', but an examination of the orders under which this action had been carried out soon undermined this claim. In particular, a teletype dated 22 December 1944 from Army Group South to the 11th Army required, for the performance of a *Führer* Order, that:

> Any terrain which the enemy compels us to leave ... must be made useless ... Every town and village must be burned down without consideration for the inhabitants ... Should destruction not be possible, undestroyed towns and villages must be destroyed subsequently by the airforce ...[74]

The tribunal found that this was not a matter of 'necessity', but an unlawful 'scorched earth' policy in occupied territory, and stated that 'necessity' in the present sense is essentially a defensive concept in circumstances where no reasonable alternative exists, in essence referring back to the established earlier jurisprudence.

The dividing line between 'infraction' and 'necessity' may be illustrated crudely by reference to the massacre in the *Peleus* case[75] and the abandonment of rescue attempts after the *Bismarck* sinking.[76] In the first case, the massacre was not only unequivocally a violation of basic norms, but actually placed the U-boat at needless additional risk while it was perpetrated. In the second instance, the reasonable anticipation of U-boat attack on HMS *Dorsetshire* and HMS *Maori* gave them no reasonable alternative but to depart form the scene, and indeed this has become an accepted fact of warfare at sea.

So far as treaty provision is concerned, the requirement of rescue of he wounded, sick and/or shipwrecked again offers a good starting point. It will be recalled that article 15 of 1949 Geneva Convention I provides that:

> At all times, and particularly after an engagement, Parties to the conflict shall, without delay, take all possible measures to search for and collect the wounded and sick ...

Virtually identical provision is made for warfare at sea by 1949 Geneva Convention II, article 18. The reference to 'all possible measures' is essentially a concession to the exigencies of necessity. There may, as in the sinking of the *Bismarck*, arise circumstances where rescue is either not a realistic possibility or must be abandoned in the interests of the safety of the ship attempting rescue work. This is not a derogation of the basic humanitarian duty of rescue, it is rather a recognition of practical impossibility in some cases, much in the spirit of the 'material impossibility' conceded by Jean Pictet.[77] A more difficult situation arises in relation to the rules governing bombardment. One example is the phrasing of the ban on 'indiscriminate' attacks, which are defined by article 51(5)(b) of 1977 Additional Protocol I as any:

> which may be expected to cause incidental loss of civilian life, injury to civilians, damage to civilian objects, or a combination thereof, which would be excessive in relation to the concrete and direct military advantages anticipated.

The reference to 'necessity' is again implicit rather than explicit, and in this case a very difficult objective assessment is demanded. Where a military objective is located close to civilian centres of population, a balance must be drawn between the anticipated military advantage and the potential harm to civilians, and this can never be done to everyone's satisfaction. However, the calculation must clearly be made in the light of the best information available and in good faith, also bearing in mind that a state should to the greatest possible extent distance military objectives from the civilian population, and most certainly not use the latter as 'human shields'.[78] Very similar considerations arise in relation to article 62(1) of 1977 Additional Protocol I, which provides that:

> Civilian civil defence organisations and their personnel ... shall be entitled to perform their civil defence tasks except in cases of imperative military necessity.

This also involves difficult calculation of military advantage and potential civilian injury, in so far as urgent military activity may effectively preclude civil defence action. The ICRC Commentary on the Protocol remarks that:

> 'imperative military necessity' ... is not explained here, but what it amounts to is that such [civil defence] tasks may only be forbidden or curtailed where the authorities are placed before the alternative of either changing major operational plans or doing without civil defence personnel. ... In such cases the choice must be based on the principles laid down particularly in Articles 51 (*Protection of the civilian population*) and 57 (*Precautions in attack*).[79]

The nature of 'military necessity' may therefore seem somewhat imprecise, but this may be inevitable. It has been remarked elsewhere that:

> Neither adjudicatory determinations nor treaty provision precisely define what amounts to 'necessity' for the purpose of the doctrine of military necessity ... This in fact is hardly surprising. ... All that can clearly be said is that 'necessity' connotes an immediate and overwhelming circumstance in military action, which renders strict compliance, upon rational analysis, impractical rather than [in all cases] 'impossible'. Impractical is a term here carefully chosen, it is by no means intended to imply the concession to tactical and strategic convenience which is implicit in the maxim *kriegsrason geht vor kreigsmanier*.[80]

It must also be remarked that, as Jean Pictet suggests, there is added to the more formal doctrines of military necessity a fact of 'impossibility', and it may be suggested, one of practicality of application. In the latter regard, it may be noted that, as remarked above,[81] at the end of the 1982 Anglo-Argentine Falklands Conflict, the large numbers of captured Argentine military personnel were held on board troopships for early repatriation, an arrangement admitted to be better than confinement in emergency land accommodation in sub-Antarctic conditions, notwithstanding the normal requirement that prisoners of war should be accommodated on land. It must, in conclusion, be emphasised that whatever effect the doctrine of military necessity may have in a given situation, it can never displace the core norms of humanitarian treatment of the victims of armed conflict.

Belligerent Reprisals

If military necessity represents a degree of exception in the accepted application of the humanitarian *jus in bello*, belligerent reprisals involve action which is unequivocally unlawful. They are unlawful acts in warfare undertaken in response to unlawful acts previously perpetrated by the adverse party. They are to this extent a 'self-help' remedy, of which Greenspan remarks:

> Reprisals are illegitimate acts of warfare, not for the purpose of indicating abandonment of the laws of war, but, on the contrary, to force compliance to those laws.[82]

One argument in this context requires careful analysis. Critics of the *jus in bello* constantly urge that such law confers a great advantage on the ruthless by 'tying one hand behind the back' of law-abiding states. This is a myth. The humanitarian *jus in bello* imposes little or no restriction on the effective pursuit of legitimate military objectives, and the evidence of the 20th century by no means suggests that the most ruthless power must always emerge victorious. So far as essential humanitarian norms are concerned, reprisals are severely restricted, since to open the victims of armed conflict to such action would fundamentally subvert the purposes of the law. Reprisals against the respectively protected categories of people are therefore expressly forbidden by 1949 Geneva Convention I, article 46; 1949 Geneva Convention II, article 47; 1949 Geneva Convention III, article 13; and 1949 Geneva Convention IV, article 33. Reprisal attacks on civilians or the civilian population in general are forbidden by 1977 Additional Protocol I, article 51(6) as are reprisal attacks on cultural objects and places of worship by article 53(c) of the Additional Protocol. This latter practice was not uncommon in the armed conflicts in former Yugoslavia, where attacks on historic mosques and churches, as well as on other historic monuments, were undertaken in an effort to damage the morale of civilian populations.

Beyond these restrictions, however, the possibilities of reprisals remains to some degree open. Frits Kalshoven argues that belligerent reprisals have a declining role in modern warfare because, in part, of the increasingly destructive potential of modern military technologies, but also accepts that they may have a valid role in emphasising that wilful violation of the laws of war may bring a strong, but staged and proportionate, response. He concludes:

> In this light, the subsistence to this day ... of the remnant of belligerent reprisals, not as a reasonably credible sanction of the laws of war, but as a signal in the military–political power relations between belligerents, is once again a symptom of the imperfect state of affairs in international society.[83]

This would seem an indisputable view, especially when the dangers of escalating mutual 'reprisals' are borne in mind, as Schwarzenberger remarks.[84] The best view is perhaps that such responses to gross illegality may be inevitable, but are nevertheless not to be encouraged. They are increasingly restricted, especially so far as key humanitarian norms are concerned, and it is to be hoped that in time, modes of response which do not involve the perpetration of proportionate illegalities will entirely supplant them.

Municipal Enforcement

The foregoing discussion of international enforcement action has been predicated upon an assumption of the prior failure of municipal measures of enforcement, but it must be remembered that the primary duty of enforcing the *jus in bello* rests not upon international institutions, but upon states. The discussion above of the earlier case jurisprudence regarding war crimes is necessarily phrased in terms of municipal decisions,[85] as are some of the later significant cases, such as *US* v. *First Lieutenant William L. Calley*[86] and *Re: Brown and Fisher et al.*[87] These two cases merit examination, both for their substance and to emphasise the fact that national courts martial in relation to violations of the laws of armed conflict arise under the provisions of national military law, so are not necessarily formally labelled as 'war crimes' trials, and are therefore somewhat underestimated in some accounts of the subject.

Calley was tried by court martial in the USA in 1971 on charges under article 11 of the US Uniform Code of Military Justice arising from the massacre of civilians at My Lai during the Vietnam War by a unit under his command. The village was suspected of being a centre of Vietcong activity, and Calley, acting under somewhat ambiguous orders, led his force into it and ordered the shooting of a substantial element of the population, including young children. The background lay in the difficulty in distinguishing combatants from non-combatants in the guerrilla warfare in Vietnam, but this could not justify Calley's conduct in making no attempt at such distinction. The attitudes and training that made a My Lai possible were investigated as part of the court martial, and improvements were made. Calley's conduct was unequivocally condemned, and he originally received a proportionate sentence, although this was later vastly reduced. President Nixon later pointed out that no Vietcong members were tried by their own side for violations of the laws of armed conflict, but whilst this is true, two wrongs cannot be held to make a right, and the principle affirmed by the Calley trial is a valuable one.

A number of trials followed the atrocious 1990–91 Iraqi occupation of Kuwait. However, these had a number of highly controversial elements, especially in the treatment of Palestinian workers in Kuwait, who, partly because of the PLO backing for Iraq, were routinely suspected of collaboration with the occupiers. The harshness of interpretation and sentence in some of these cases caused great unease, and it may be noted that the same problems have arisen after many other occupations, even though the very great suffering of the Kuwaiti people under a cruel occupation regime could not do other than inspire international sympathy.

The trial of Brown, Fisher and others arose from the UNOSOM action in Somalia leading to the trial by court martial in Canada of members of the Canadian armed forces on charges including murder and torture. The trials were straightforward so far as the substantive issues were concerned, and represented a simple municipal upholding of international humanitarian rules and principles, but the cases also raised an important point in relation to the particular complexities of law enforcement in the context of national contingents serving with UN forces.[88] It was argued on behalf of the defendants, *inter alia*, that article 24(1) of the Canadian Charter of Rights and Freedoms required that they be offered elections between trial by court martial or by a civil court in so far as it states that persons subject to the Code of Service Discipline who perform an act overseas such that, if perpetrated in Canada, it would lead to trial by court martial 'may be tried and punished by a civil court'. Justice Cunningham in the Ontario Court (General Division) held that this was not a provision for choice of jurisdiction, but a provision for exceptional circumstances in which no other appropriate jurisdiction was available. The trials therefore proceeded by court martial. Trials arising from Somalia have also occurred in Belgium.

Also in a context of UN service, there arose the rather bizarre case of *Jennings* v. *Markley*.[89] A US soldier was charged with assault with intent to commit bodily harm and murder during service with UN forces in the Korean War, and was convicted before a US court martial. He then argued before a US District Court that the court martial had no jurisdiction over him because, as a member of a UN force, he could be tried only by the UN Military Staff Committee, the International Court of Justice or a US civil court. This was a rather desperate argument, given that the UN Military Staff Committee, established under article 47 of the UN Charter, is not a court at all, and the International Court of Justice is a Court of civil jurisdiction only. Not surprisingly, the US District Court held that US military personnel are and remain subject to US military jurisdiction when serving with UN forces.

Municipal enforcement, along with national dissemination and military education, is a vital element in the maintenance of international humanitarian law. This will remain the case when, or if, a permanent International Criminal Tribunal is established. The obligations created by international humanitarian law are imposed on *states*, and other institutions, beneficial as their effects may well be, should in no way be permitted to dilute or lessen those obligations.

Notes

1 For discussion, see H. McCoubrey, *The Obligation to Obey in Legal Theory* (Dartmouth, 1997), Chapter 2; see also H. McCoubrey and N.D. White, *Textbook on Jurisprudence* (2nd edn) (Blackstone, 1996), pp. 12–24.

2 1977 Additional Protocol II must be considered in a different light for obvious reasons, since it deals with what are *prima facie* the 'internal' affairs of a state in much the same way as general human rights treaties.
3 See C. Greenwood, 'Customary Law Status of the 1977 Additional Protocols', in A.J.M. Delissen and G.J. Tanja (eds), *Humanitarian Law of Armed Conflict, Challenges Ahead: Essays in Honour of Frits Kalshoven* (Martinus Nijhoff, 1991), pp. 93–114.
4 J. Pictet, *Development and Principles of International Humanitarian Law* (Martinus Nijhoff, 1985), p. 90.
5 See Shiseki Miyazaki, 'The Martens Clause and International Law', in C. Swinarski (ed.), *Studies and Essays in Honour of Jean Pictet* (Martinus Nijhoff, 1984), p. 433.
6 See in particular the Von Leeb case reported in *Trials of War Criminals* (US Government Printing Office, 1850).
7 I. Detter de Lupis, *The Law of War* (Cambridge University Press, 1987), p. 352.
8 (1951) *International Court of Justice Reports*, p. 15.
9 See A. Roberts and R. Guelff, *Documents on the Laws of War* (2nd edn) (Oxford University Press, 1989), p. 336.
10 Ibid.
11 See 1949 Geneva Convention I, article 63; Convention II, article 68; Convention III, article 158; 1977 Additional Protocol I, article 99, and 1977 Additional Protocol II, article 25.
12 For discussion, see Chapter 1.
13 For discussion see pp. 66–73.
14 See L. Friedman, *The Laws of War: A Documentary History* (Random House, 2 vols, 1972), Vol. II, p. 1,703.
15 1143 DLR (1994), p. 611.
16 An interesting table of such bodies involved in investigations in former Yugoslavia is set out by F.J. Hampson in 'War-crimes Fact-finding in former-Yugoslavia' (1994) 1 *International Law and Armed Conflict Commentary*, p. 28, at p. 35.
17 *Appeal to the Belligerents*, 6 February 1918; see Stockholm International Peace Research Institute, *The Problems of Chemical and Biological Weapons* (Almqvist and Wiksell, 6 vols, 1971–75), Vol. VI, p. 44; see also V. Adams, *Chemicals Warfare, Chemical Disarmament* (Macmillan, 1989), p. 46.
18 *The Times* (London), 14 August 1992.
19 F. Hampson and H. McCoubrey, 'Evidence in Cases Involving Arms Proliferation Issues', in J. Dahlitz (ed.), *Arms Control and Disarmament Law, Vol. III: Future Legal Restraints on Arms Proliferation* (United Nations, 1996), p. 273, at p. 292. For further discussion, see M.A. Meyer, 'Public Advocacy: Why the Red Cross and Red Crescent Should Look Before it Leaps' (1996) 36 *International Review of the Red Cross*, pp. 614–26.
20 See *Sunday Telegraph* (London), 13 July 1997.
21 See pp. 309–10.
22 Article 90(1)(a).
23 Article 90(2)(c).
24 Article 90(2)(d).
25 For discussion, see p. 292.
26 See J. Mordal, trans. L. Ortzen, *25 Centuries of Sea Warfare* (Abbey Library/ Souvenir Press, 1970; 1st published as *25 Siècles de Guerre sur Mer* by Editions Robert Laffont, 1959), pp. 38 and 45.
27 See G.I.A.D. Draper 'Penitential Discipline and Public Wars in the Middle Ages' (1961) 31 *International Review of the Red Cross*, p. 1.

28 See G. Schwarzenberger, *International Law, Vol. II: Armed Conflict* (Stevens, 1968), pp. 462–6; see also R.K. Worzel, *The Nuremberg Trials in International Law* (Stevens, 1962), pp. 19–21.
29 For discussions, see Schwarzenberger, op.cit., at pp. 463–4.
30 See M. Balfour, *The Kaiser and his Times* (Penguin, 1975), p. 240.
31 See p. 126.
32 See pp. 127 and 300.
33 For discussion of the Nuremberg Trials, see A. and J. Tusa, *The Nuremberg Trial* (Macmillan , 1983; BBC World Books edn, 1995); see also A. Neave, *Nuremberg* (Hodder & Stoughton, 1978). The proceedings of the IMT can be found reported in *The Trial of German Major War Criminals* (HMSO, 1946). A very idiosyncratic Soviet view can be found in B. Polevoi, trans. J. Butler and D. Bradbury, *The Final Reckoning*, trans. J. Butler and D. Bradbury (Progress Publishers, 1978)
34 For discussion of the Tokyo trials, see A.C. Brackman, *The Other Nuremberg* (Collins, 1989); see also C. Hosoya, N. Ando, Y. Onuma and B. Minear (eds), *The Tokyo War Crimes Trial* (Kodansha International, 1986).
35 For discussion of the British Military Tribunals established for this purpose, see A.P.V. Rogers, 'War Crimes Trials under the Royal Warrant: British Practice 1945–49' (1990) 39 *International and Comparative Law Quarterly*, p. 780–800.
36 A. and J. Tusa, op.cit., p. 460.
37 See *International Committee of the Red Cross Bulletin: Yugoslavia* (ICRC, 1992).
38 For discussion, see C. Warbrick and P. Rowe, 'The International Criminal Tribunal for Yugoslavia: The Decision of the Appeals Chamber on the Interlocutory Appeal on Jurisdiction in the *Tadic* Case' (1996) 45 *International and Comparative Law Quarterly*, pp. 691–701.
39 See below.
40 G. Guillaume, 'The Future of International Judicial Institutions' (1995) 44 *International and Comparative Law Quarterly*, pp. 848–62, at p. 858.
41 It is made so by 1977 Additional Protocol I, article 85(3)(f): see below.
42 See H. McCoubrey, 'The Armed Conflict in Bosnia and Proposed War Crimes Trials' (1993) XI *International Relations*, p. 411, at pp. 424–5.
43 H. McCoubrey, 'The Concept and Treatment of War Crimes' (1996) I *Journal of Armed Conflict Law*, p. 121, at p. 131. The reference to 'open texture' is made with citation of H.L.A. Hart, *The Concept of Law* (2nd edn), with Postscript ed. by P.A. Bulloch and J. Raz (Oxford/Clarendon, 1994), Ch.X.
44 See below.
45 W.V. O'Brien, 'The Nuremberg Precedent and the Gulf War' (1991) 31 *Virginia Journal of International Law*, p. 391, at p. 393.
46 'International Military Tribunal: Judgment and Sentences' (1947) 41 *American Journal of International Law*, p. 221.
47 For discussion, see W.V. O'Brien, op.cit., at pp. 392–7.
48 (1816) 4 M&S, p. 41.
49 (1900) 17 SCR, p. 561.
50 Ibid.
51 A useful discussion of this case law will be found in L.C. Green, *Superior Orders in National and International Law* (A.W. Sijthoff, 1976), pp. 122ff.
52 See pp. 117 and 126–7.
53 (1922) 16 *American Journal of International Law*, p. 704.
54 Ibid., at pp. 707–8.
55 (1922) 16 *American Journal of International Law*, p. 709.
56 See p. 127.
57 (1922) 16 *American Journal of International Law*, at p. 722.

58 *Law Reports of Trials of War Criminals* (HMSO, 1947), Vol. I, p. 1; a more extensive account can be found in *War Crimes Trials* (William Hocky, 1948), Vol. I.
59 See pp. 117–18.
60 (1944) *Manual of Military Law*, para. 13.
61 (1956) *Manual of Military Law*, para. 24.
62 J. Blackett, 'Superior Orders – The Military Dilemma' (February 1994), *Royal United Services Institute Journal*, at p. 12, at p. 17.
63 Quoted by P. Rowe, from Clode, *The Military Forces of the Crown, Their Administration and Government* (1869), in *Defence: The Legal Implications* (Brassey's Defence Publishers, 1987), title verso page.
64 H. McCoubrey, *The Obligation to Obey in Legal Theory* (Dartmouth, 1997), p. 174.
65 See below.
66 J. Pictet, *Development and Principles of International Humanitarian Law* (Martinus Nijhoff, 1985), p. 88.
67 The reference is to the general argument in R. Dworkin, *Taking Rights Seriously* (Duckworth, 1977).
68 J. Pictet, op.cit., p. 88.
69 M. Greenspan, *The Modern Law of Land Warfare* (University of California Press, 1959), p. 314.
70 6 *UN Reports of International Arbitral Awards*, p. 25. For discussion, see G. Schwarzenberger, op.cit., pp. 131–2.
71 See ibid., p. 132.
72 Article 6.
73 *Trials of War Criminals* (USGPO, 1950), Vol. XI, p. 310.
74 Ibid., referring to Teletype, Army Group South 1a No.2298/41.
75 See p. 117–18.
76 See p. 115.
77 See pp. 303–4.
78 Such an abuse of the civilian population is expressly forbidden by 1977 Additional Protocol I, article 51(7).
79 Y. Sandoz, C. Swinarski and B. Zimmermann (eds) with J. Pictet, *Commentary on the Additional Protocols of 8 June 1977 to the Geneva Conventions of 12 August 1949* (ICRC/Martinus Nijhoff, 1987), p. 740, para. 2,445.
80 H. McCoubrey, 'The Nature of the Modern Doctrine of Military Necessity' (1991) XXX *Revue de Droit Militaire et de Droit de la Guerre*, p. 215, at p. 237.
81 See Chapter 6.
82 M. Greenspan, op.cit., at pp. 407–8.
83 F. Kalshoven, *Belligerent Reprisals* (A.W. Sijthoff, 1971), p. 377.
84 G. Schwarzenberger, op.cit., p. 106.
85 See pp. 298–9.
86 See L. Friedman, op.cit., p. 1,703.
87 113 DLR (1994), p. 102.
88 For discussion, see H. McCoubrey and N.D. White, *The Blue Helmets: Legal Regulation of United Nations Military Operations* (Dartmouth, 1996), Chapter 9.
89 (1961) 186 Federal Supplement, p. 611.

Select Bibliography

Books

Abi-Saab, R., El Kouhene, M. and Rivi, Z. (eds), *Modern Wars: The Humanitarian Challenge* (Zed Books, 1986).

Adams, V., *Chemical Warfare, Chemical Disarmament* (Macmillan, 1989).

Addington, L.H., *The Patterns of War Since the 18th Century* (Croom Helm, 1984).

Ali, S.S., Subedi, S. and McCoubrey, H., *Ideas of 'Just War' in World Faiths* (University of Hull Press, 1997).

Best, G., *Humanity in Warfare* (Methuen, 1983; 1st published by Weidenfeld and Nicolson, 1980).

Boissier, P., *History of the International Committee of the Red Cross, Vol. I: From Solferino to Tsushima* (Henry Dunant Institute, 1985).

Bowyer, T., *Blind Eye to Murder* (André Deutsch, 1981).

Brackman, A.C., *The Other Nuremberg* (Collins, 1989).

Brogan, P., *World Conflicts* (2nd edn) (Bloomsbury, 1992).

Cassese, A., *Human Rights in a Changing World* (Polity Press / Blackwell, 1990).

Castren, F., *The Present Law of War and Neutrality* (Summalaisen Tiedeakatemian Taimituksia Annales Academiae Scientiasrum Fenniciae, Helsinki, 1954)

Chadwick, E., *Self-determination, Terrorism and International Humanitarian Laws of Armed Conflict* (Martinus Nijhoff, 1996).

Clark, G., *'Doc': 100 Year History of the Sick Berth Branch* (HMSO, 1984).

Contamine, P., trans. M. Jones, *War in the Middle Ages* (Blackwell, 1984; originally published as *La Guerre au Moyen Age* by Presses Universitaires de France, 1980).

Dahlitz, J., (ed.), *Arms Control and Disarmament Law, Vol. III: Future Legal Restraints on Arms Proliferation* (United Nations, 1996).

De Jaeger, C., *The Linz File: Hitler's Plunder of Europe's Art* (Webb and Bower, 1981).

Delissen, A.J.M. and Tanja, G.J. (eds), *Humanitarian Law of Armed Conflict, Challenges Ahead: Essays in Honour of Frits Kalshoven* (Martinus Nijhoff, 1981)

Detter de Lupis, I., *The Law of Wars* (Cambridge, 1987).
Draper, G.I.A.D., *The Red Cross Conventions* (Stevens, 1958).
Fleck, D. (ed.), *The Handbook of Humanitarian Law in Armed Conflict* (Oxford, 1995).
Fox, H. and Meyer, M.A. (eds), *Armed Conflict and the New Law, Vol. II: Effecting Compliance* (British Institute of International and Comparative Law, 1993).
Friedman, L., *The Laws of War: A Documentary History* (2 vols) (Random House, 1972).
Gilbert, M., *Second World War* (Phoenix, 1995; 1st published by Weidenfeld and Nicolson, 1989).
Goodwin-Gill, G. and Cohn, I., *Child Soldiers: The Role of Children in Armed Conflicts* (Clarendon/Oxford, 1994).
Green, L.C., *Superior Orders in National and International Law* (A.W. Sijthoff, 1976).
Green, L.C., *Essays on the Modern Law of War* (Transnational Publishers, 1985).
Green, L.C., *The Contemporary Law of Armed Conflict* (Manchester University Press, 1993).
Greenspan, M., *The Modern Law of Land Warfare* (University of California Press, 1959).
Harris, D.J., *Cases and Materials on International Law* (4th edn), (Sweet and Maxwell, 1991).
Harris, R., *Gotcha! The Media, the Government and the Falklands Crisis* (Faber and Faber, 1983).
Haug, H., *Humanity for All: The International Red Cross and Red Crescent Movement* (Henry Dunant Institute/Paul Haupt Publishers, 1993).
HMSO, *The Trial of German Major War Criminals* (HMSO, 1946)
HMSO, *Thunder and Lightning: The RAF in the Gulf* (HMSO, 1991).
Hosoya, C., Ando, N., Onuma, Y. and Minear, B. (eds), *The Tokyo War Crimes Trial* (Kodansha International, 1986).
ICRC, *International Red Cross Handbook* (12th edn) (ICRC/Federation of Red Cross and Red Crescent Societies, 1983).
Jacovljevic, B., *New International Status of Civil Defence* (Martiinus Nijhoff, 1982)
Junod, M., *Warrior Without Weapons* (ICRC, 1984).
Junod, S., *Protection of the Victims of Armed Conflict, Falkland Malvinas Islands* (2nd edn) (ICRC, 1985).
Kalshoven, F., *Belligerent Reprisals* (A.W. Sijthoff, 1971).
Kalshoven, F., *Constraints on the Waging of War* (2nd edn) (ICRC, 1991).
McCoubrey, H., *The Obligation to Obey in Legal Theory* (Dartmouth, 1997).
McCoubrey, H. and White, N.D., *International Law and Armed Conflict* (Dartmouth, 1992).

McCoubrey, H. and White, N.D., *International Organizations and Civil Wars* (Dartmouth, 1995).
McCoubrey, H. and White, N.D., *The Blue Helmets: Legal Regulation of United Nations Military Operations* (Dartmouth, 1996).
McNair, Lord and Watts, A.D., *The Legal Effects of War* (Cambridge University Press, 1966).
Mason, J.K. and McCall-Smith, R.A., *Law and Medical Ethics* (4th edn) (Butterworths, 1994).
Meron, T., *Human Rights in Internal Strife: Their International Protection* (Grotius, 1987).
Meron, T., *Henry's War and Shakespeare's Laws* (Clarendon/Oxford, 1993).
Moore, W., *Gas Attack: Chemical Warfare 1915–1918 and Afterwards* (Leo Cooper/Heinemann, 1987).
Muhammad Hamidullah, *The Muslim Conduct of State* (Sh. Muhammad Ashraf, 1981).
Neave, A., *Nuremberg* (Hodder & Stoughton, 1978).
Oliver, K., *Chaplain at War* (Angel Press, 1986).
Pictet, J., *The Geneva Conventions of 12 August 1949: Commentary* (ICRC, 1952–60).
Pictet, J., *Development and Principles of International Humanitarian Law* (Martinus Nijhoff, 1985).
Polevoi, B., trans. J. Butler and D. Bradbury, *The Final Reckoning* (Progress Publishers, 1978).
Roberts, A., and Guelff, R., *Documents on the Laws of Wars* (2nd edn) (Oxford, 1989).
Rogers, A.P.V., *Law on the Battlefield* (Manchester University Press, 1996).
Rowe, P. (ed.), *The Gulf War 1990–91 in International and English Law* (Routledge/Sweet & Maxwell, 1993).
Sandoz, Y., Swinarski, C. and Zimmermann, B. (eds) with Pictet, J., *Commentary on the Additional Protocols of 8 June 1977 to the Geneva Conventions of 12 August 1949* (ICRC/Martinus Nijhoff, 1987).
Schwarzenberger, G., *International Law, Vol. II: Armed Conflict* (Stevens, 1968).
Shirer, W.L., *The Rise and Fall of the Third Reich* (Pan, 1964; 1st published in the UK by Secker & Warburg, 1960).
Stockholm International Peace Research Institute, *The Problem of Chemical and Biological Weapons* (6 vols) (Almqvist and Wiksell, 1971–75).
Swinarski, C. (ed.), *Studies and Essays in Honour of Jean Pictet* (Martinus Nijhoff, 1984).
Tusa, A. and Tusa, J., *The Nuremberg Trial* (BBC World Books, 1995, 1st published by Macmillan, 1983).
Walzer, M., *Just and Unjust Wars* (2nd edn) (Basic Books/HarperCollins, 1992).

White, N.D., *Keeping the Peace: The United Nations and the Maintenance of International Peace and Security* (Manchester University Press, 1993).
Worzel, R.K., *The Nuremberg Trials in International Law* (Stevens, 1962).

Articles

Agora, M., 'The Downing of Iran Air Flight 655' (1989) 83 *American Journal of International Law*, p. 318.
Baxter, R.S., 'The Duty of Obedience to a Belligerent Occupant' (1950) 27 *British Yearbook of International Law*, p. 235.
Berman, P., 'The ICRC's Advisory Service on International Humanitarian Law: The Challenge of National Implementation' (1996) 36 *International Review of the Red Cross*, p. 338.
Blackett, J., 'Superior Orders – The Military Dilemma' (February 1994) *Royal United Services Institute Journal*, p. 12.
Blishchenko, I.P., 'Humanitarian Norms and Human Rights', in Abi-Saab, R., El Kouhene, M. and Rivi, Z. (eds), *Modern Wars: The Humanitarian Challenge* (Zed Books, 1986).
Bugnion, F., 'From the End of the Second World War to the Dawn of the Third Millennium – The Activities of the International Committee of the Red Cross during the Cold War and its Aftermath: 1945–1995' (1995) 35 *International Committee of the Red Cross*, p. 192.
Dickson, B., 'The United Nations and Freedom of Religion' (1993) 44 *International and Comparative Law Quarterly*, p. 327.
Doswald-Beck, L., 'New Protocol on Blinding Laser Weapons' (1996) 36 *International Review of the Red Cross*, p. 272.
Draper, G.I.A.D., 'Penitential Discipline and Public Wars in the Middle Ages' (1961) 31 *International Review of the Red Cross*, p. 1.
Draper, G.I.A.D., 'The Origins of the Just War Tradition' (1964) 46 *New Blackfriars*, 82.
Draper, G.I.A.D., 'The Implementation of the Geneva Conventions of 1949 and the Additional Protocols of 1977', in *Recueil des Cours* (Hague Academy of International Law, 1979).
Draper, G.I.A.D., ed. M.A. Meyer, 'The Contribution of the Emperor Asoka Maurya to the Development of the Humanitarian Idea in Warfare' (1995) 35 *International Review of the Red Cross*, p. 192.
Falk, R.A., 'The Shimoda Case: A Legal Appraisal of the Atomic Attack upon Hisroshima and Nagasaki' (1965) 59 *American Journal of International Law*, p. 759.
Friedman, L., *The Laws of War: A Documentary History* (2 vols) (Random House, 1972).
Gardam, J., 'Women and the Laws of Armed Conflict: Why the Silence?' (1997) 46 *International and Comparative Law Quarterly*, p. 55.

Greenwood, C., 'Customary Law Status of the 1977 Additional Protocols', in Delissen, A.J.M. and Tanja, G.J (eds), *Humanitarian Law of Armed Conflict, Challenges Ahead: Essays in Honour of Frits Kalshoven* (Martinus Nijhoff, 1991), p. 93.

Greenwood, C., 'Scope of Application of Humanitarian Law', in Fleck, D. (ed.), *The Handbook of Humanitarian Law in Armed Conflict* (Oxford, 1995).

Greig, D.W., 'Self-defence and the Security Council: What Does Article 51 Require?' (1991) 40 *International and Comparative Law Quarterly*, p. 336.

Guillaume, G., 'The Future of International Judicial Institutions' (1995) 44 *International and Comparative Law Quarterly*, p. 848.

Gutteridge, J., 'The Geneva Conventions of 1949' (1965) 26 *British Yearbook of International Law*, p. 298.

Hampson, F., 'Belligerent Reprisals and the 1977 Protocols to the Geneva Conventions of 1949' (1988) 37 *International and Comparative Law Quarterly*, p. 818.

Hampson, F., 'Conscience in Conflict: The Doctor's Dilemma' (1989) XXVII *The Canadian Yearbook International Law*, p. 203.

Hampson, F., 'Mercenaries: Diagnosis before Prescription' (1991) XXII *Netherlands Yearbook of International Law*, p. 3.

Hampson, F., 'War-crimes Fact-finding in former-Yugoslavia' (1994) 1 *International Law and Armed Conflict Commentary*, p. 28.

Hampson, F. and McCoubrey, H., 'Evidence in Cases Involving Arms Proliferation Issues', in Dahlitz, J. (eds), *Arms Control and Disarmament Law, Vol. III: Future Legal Restraints on Arms Proliferation* (United Nations, 1996), p. 273.

Harroff-Tavel, M., 'Action Taken by the International Committee of the Red Cross in Situations of Internal Violence' (1993) 33 *International Review of the Red Cross*, p. 195.

Kritsiotis, D., 'The Fate of Nuclear Weapons after the 1996 Advisory Opinions of the World Court' (1996) 1 *Journal of Armed Conflict Law*, p. 95.

Lauterpacht, H., 'The Revision of the Law of War' (1952) 29 *British Yearbook of International Law*, p. 381.

Lavoyer, J., 'Refugees and Internally Displaced Persons: International Humanitarian Law and the Role of the ICRC' (1995) 35 *International Review of the Red Cross*, p. 162.

Levie, H.S., 'International Aspects of Repatriation during Hostilities: A Reply' (1973) 67 *American Journal of International Law*, p. 693.

Lissitzyn, O.J., 'The Shooting Down of Korean Airlines Flight 007 by the USSR and the Furtherance of Air Safety for Passengers' (1983) 33 *International and Comparative Law Quarterly*, p. 712.

McCoubrey, H., 'The Nature of the Modern Doctrine of Military

Necessity' (1991) XXX *Revue de Droit Militaire et de Droit de la Guerre*, p. 215.
McCoubrey, H., 'The Armed Conflict in Bosnia and Proposed War Crimes Trials' (1993) XI *International Relations*, p. 411.
McCoubrey, H., 'Before Geneva Law: A British Surgeon in the Crimean War' (1995) 35 *International Review of the Red Cross*, p. 69.
McCoubrey, H., 'Medical Ethics, Negligence and the Battlefield' (1995) XXXIV *Revue de Droit Militaire et de Droit de la Guerre*, p. 103.
McCoubrey, H., 'The Concept and Treatment of War Crimes' (1996) 1 *Journal of Armed Conflict*, p. 121.
McCoubrey, H. and White, N.D., 'International Law and the Use of Force in the Gulf' (1991) X *International Relations*, p. 347.
Mann, H., 'International Law and the Child Soldier' (1987) *International and Comparative Law Quarterly*, p. 32.
Meyer, H., 'Liability of Prisoners of War for Offences Committed Prior to Capture: The Astiz Affair' (1983) *International and Comparative Law Quarterly*, p. 948.
Meyer, M.A., 'Public Advocacy: Why the Red Cross and Red Crescent Should Look Before it Leaps' (1996) 36 *International Review of the Red Cross*, p. 614.
Miyazaki, S., 'The Martens Clause and International Law', in Swinarski, C. (ed.), *Studies and Essays in Honour of Jean Pictet* (Martinus Nijhoff, 1984), p. 433.
Modoux, A., 'International Humanitarian Law and the Journalists' Mission' (1983) 33 *International Review of the Red Cross*, p. 19.
Morgenstein, F., 'Validity of Acts of the Belligerent Occupant' (1951) 28 *British Yearbook of International Law*, p. 291.
Mossop, J.C., 'Hospital Ships in the Second World War' (1947) 24 *British Yearbook of International Law*, p. 398.
Mourning, P.W., 'Leashing the Dogs of War: Outlawing the Recruitment and Use of Mercenaries' (1982) 22 *Virginia Journal of International Law*, p. 589.
O'Brien, W.V., 'The Nuremberg Precedent and the Gulf War' (1991) 31 *Virginia Journal of International Law*, p. 391.
Ogren, K., 'Humanitarian Law in the *Articles of War* Decreed in 1621 by King Gustavus II Adolphus of Sweden' (1996) 36 *International Review of the Red Cross*, p. 438.
Pierce-Higgins, A., 'Hospital Ships and the Carriage of Passengers and Crews of Destroyed Prizes' [1910] CIV *Law Quarterly Review*, p. 408.
Pierce-Higgins, A., 'The Carriage of Sick and Wounded Soldiers by Hospital Ships' (1921–22) 2 *British Yearbook of International Law*, p. 177.
Rao, R.J., 'When Does War Begin?' (1972) 12 *Indian Journal of International Law*, p. 368.

Roberts, A., 'Civil Defence and International Law', in Meyer, M.A. (ed.), *Armed Conflict and the New Law* (British Institute of International and Comparative Law, 1984), p. 193.

Roberts, A. and Guelff, R., *Documents on the Laws of War* (2nd edn), (Oxford, 1989).

Rostow, W., 'Until What? Enforcement or Collective Self-defence' (1991) 85 *American Journal of International Law*, p. 506.

Schwarzenberger, G., *International Law, Vol. II: Armed Conflict* (Stevens, 1968).

Stein, T., 'How Much Humanity do Terrorists Deserve?', in Delissen, A.J.M. and Tanja, G.J. (eds), *Humanitarian Law of Armed Conflict, Challenges Ahead: Essays in Honour of Frits Kalshoven* (Martinus Nijhoff, 1991).

Thorpe, A.G.Y., 'Mine Warfare at Sea – Some Legal Aspects of the Future' 18 *Ocean Development and International Law*, p. 272.

von Clausewitz, C., *On War* (1832), ed. and trans. M. Howard and P. Paret (Princeton University Press, 1976).

Warbrick, C. and Rowe, P., 'The International Criminal Tribunal for Yugoslavia: The Decision of the Appeals Chamber on the Interlocutory Appeal on Jurisdiction in the *Tadic* Case' (1996) 45 *International and Comparative Law Quarterly*, p. 691.

Zhu Li-Sun, 'Traditional Asian Approaches to the Protection of Victims of Armed Conflict – The Chinese View' (1985) 9 *Australian Yearbook of International Law*, p. 143.

Index

For Product Safety Concerns and Information please contact our EU representative GPSR@taylorandfrancis.com
Taylor & Francis Verlag GmbH, Kaufingerstraße 24, 80331 München, Germany

www.ingramcontent.com/pod-product-compliance
Ingram Content Group UK Ltd.
Pitfield, Milton Keynes, MK11 3LW, UK
UKHW020019200926
475702UK00014B/1966
9780367194659